In search of the new working class

Automation and social integration within the capitalist enterprise

DUNCAN GALLIE

Lecturer in Sociology, University of Essex

CAMBRIDGE UNIVERSITY PRESS

CAMBRIDGE

LONDON · NEW YORK · MELBOURNE

Published by the Syndics of the Cambridge University Press
The Pitt Building, Trumpington Street, Cambridge CB2 1RP
Bentley House, 200 Euston Road, London NW1 2DB
32 East 57th Street, New York, NY 10022, USA
296 Beaconsfield Parade, Middle Park, Melbourne 3206, Australia

First published 1978

Printed in Great Britain at the
University Press, Cambridge

Library of Congress Cataloguing in Publication Data

Gallie, Duncan.
In search of the new working class.

(Cambridge studies in sociology: 9)
Bibliography: p. 342
Includes index.
1. Automation — Social aspects. 2. Labour and labouring classes. 3. Industrial
sociology. 4. Industrial relations. I. Title.
HD6331.G253   301.5'5   77-80834
ISBN 0 521 21771 7 hard covers
ISBN 0 521 29275 1 paperback

Cambridge studies in sociology 9

IN SEARCH OF THE NEW WORKING CLASS

This series is published under the auspices of the Committee of Management of the Department of Applied Economics, University of Cambridge

EDITORS

R. M. Blackburn, Senior Research Officer, Department of Applied Economics, Cambridge University

John H. Goldthorpe, Official Fellow of Nuffield College, Oxford University

ADVISORY COMMITTEE

J. A. Banks, Professor of Sociology, Leicester University

A. Giddens, University Lecturer in Sociology and Fellow and Director of Studies in Social Sciences, King's College, Cambridge University

J. C. Mitchell, Official Fellow of Nuffield College, Oxford University

K. Prandy, Senior Research Officer in Applied Economics and Fellow and Director of Studies in Social Sciences, Fitzwilliam College, Cambridge University

Cambridge studies in sociology

Cambridge papers in sociology

Contents

Preface

A substantial part of this book involves a critique of the work of Serge Mallet and Robert Blauner, in which their views about the implications of developments in the labour process for social consciousness are scrutinized and most frequently rejected. The cumulative effect of such critical attack may be to draw a rather dark picture of the authors and of the type of theoretical speculation in which they were engaged. As a corrective, I should perhaps make it clear that I have a considerable admiration for the work of both men. They raised central questions about the dynamics of social structure, and they put forward clear and powerfully argued theories that have enriched discussion in several countries for over a decade. It is true that the very audacity and explicitness of the theories they constructed rendered them peculiarly vulnerable to demolition. But without people who are willing to take such risks, we would not get very far. Sociology needs stimulating hypotheses as much as it needs careful empirical work, and possibly the job of the theory constructor is the harder one. Although this book is concerned to argue that the theories of both authors are irredeemably flawed, I would like it at the same time to be a tribute to the thought-provoking quality of their work.

The research is based on an international oil company — BP. It was not financed by the company, and the company made no attempt to influence the details or the direction of the research. I would like to underline this, and to thank those concerned for their discretion — for the independence of the research was an essential factor in the willingness of the different parties to co-operate. Equally, I owe a very great debt to all those who actively assisted the research by interrupting busy and sometimes quite hectic lives to answer my questions and to provide me with the information that I needed. When the help of so many people was crucial, any short list is necessarily somewhat arbitrary, but I would like especially to thank: John Callingham, Vic Nelson, 'Dock' Dockwray, Fred Elsdon, Peter

McCowan, Fred Speirs, Dave Probert, Mel Keenan, Alain Revoy, M. Ethevenin, M. Laugier, M. Vanlerberghe, M. Keller, Jean Gavino, Damien Bonhomme, Bernard Fraissigne, Guy Bollengier, Jean Flahaut, and the four Refinery Managers. Without the active help and interest of these people the project could never have been successfully completed. I doubt if any of them will approve fully of the final text, but that is as it should be.

My original ideas for the project were tried out on Basil Bernstein and Donald MacRae, and both gave me that initial encouragement without which I would never have gone ahead. Alfred Willener forewarned me about how difficult it would all be, and provided a host of useful tips for coping with France. Comments by Mick Mann, David Lockwood, Howard Newby, José Maravall and Bob Blackburn have left their mark on the final manuscript. Most especially, throughout the study, I benefited from the advice, criticism, and encouragement of John Goldthorpe. My thanks to them all.

One difficulty with this type of research is quite simply to secure enough time to get properly immersed in the organizations one is studying. I am very grateful to the Warden and Fellows of Nuffield College, Oxford, for a two-year research fellowship in which I was able to carry out the bulk of the work. The Social Science Research Council generously provided two research assistants, Jennifer Glastonbury and Jenny Allan, to help with part of the interviewing and coding. Jennifer Glastonbury, in addition, put in a great deal of her free time and prepared much of the statistical material used in chapter 3. Kleri Smith and Phil Holden struggled valiantly with their respective computers, and Francoise Jurdant and Jean Smith had the fun of typing, retyping, and typing again successive drafts of statistics-laden manuscript. Liz Lloyd Jones checked the proofs and gave useful advice on presentation. I am grateful, too, to the staff of the Cambridge University Press for the trouble they took with the final text.

My most treasured research assistant was Martine. She was translator, card-wrapper, interviewer, wife, archivist and coder; and she kept the candle alight in the fog of Dunkirk.

Duncan Gallie

To Martine

Abbreviations

CE	Comité d'Etablissement
CCE	Le Comité Central d'Entreprise
CGT	Confédération Générale du Travail
CFDT	Confédération Française Démocratique du Travail
FO (CGT–FO)	Force Ouvrière
T&GWU	Transport and General Workers Union
SCIP	Syndicat National des Cadres, Agents de Maîtrise, Techniciens et Assimilés de l'Industrie du Pétrole
CFTC	Confédération Française des Travailleurs Chrétiens
L'UCSIP	Union des Chambres Syndicales de l'industrie du Pétrole
CGC	Confédération Générale des Cadres

Part one

Theories in conflict

I

Automation and social integration within the capitalist enterprise˙

For many social analysts of the 1960s, the prolonged post-war economic expansion appeared to have shattered definitively the credibility of the orthodox Marxist account of the evolution of capitalist society. In particular, it reinforced long standing doubts about the validity of Marx's theory of the development of the class structure, and his conception of the working class as the dynamic force behind social change. Capitalism now seemed capable of overcoming catastrophic economic crisis; the standard of living of manual workers was rising rather than falling; the reserve army of the unemployed was ceasing to grow; and there were few signs of mounting worker radicalism. In such a context, it is not altogether surprising that a number of writers in France, Britain, Germany and the United States set out, at roughly the same period in time, to re-examine the factors that affected the attitudes of workers to the institutional structure of capitalist society, and to try to re-assess the likely role that the working class would come to play in the social conflicts of the closing decades of the twentieth century.

Of the new interpretations that now emerged, the view that came perhaps to have the greatest popular currency, was that the degree of social integration of the working class depended primarily on its degree of economic security and prosperity. The capitalist order had achieved stability because it had shown itself able to deliver the goods. No longer hovering on the brink of economic ruin where revolt had few costs, important sectors of the working class had increasingly come to share in the material prosperity that had hitherto been the reserve of a relatively small elite. As they came to possesss a greater stake in the prevailing economic order, and as the more overt differentials in consumption patterns between social classes began to diminish, the more affluent workers had come to assimilate the social values and perspectives of the middle class. The future lay in a progressive integration of the working class within the institutional framework of existing capitalist society.

3

This interpretation of the evolution of the class structure has been examined in the *Affluent Worker* studies.[1] On the basis of evidence collected from high income manual workers, the authors concluded that the basic assumption that the more affluent workers were assimilating middle class social norms and life styles was erroneous, and that the theory therefore collapsed both at the descriptive and at the explanatory levels. The basic pattern of the class structure in Western societies, it seemed, was not being altered in any fundamental way by a simple rise in the level of economic prosperity.

A second set of theories, however, emerged in the early 1960s that offered a radically different explanation of developments in the working class. Its most outstanding proponents were Robert Blauner in the United States and Serge Mallet in France.[2] The authors who shared this perspective placed a common emphasis on the nature of the evolution of production technology as a critical determinant of working class consciousness. In contrast to writers who had focused on the effects of changes in workers' standard of living and consumption patterns, they followed Marx's central assumption that it is in work that man establishes his self-identity and has the possibility of self-realization through creativity, and that it is hence his experience of work that moulds his wider attitudes to the society in which he lives.

However, in highlighting the importance of the technology of work, these writers were not simply returning to Marx's first principles, and reworking his theory in the light of them. They were equally influenced by the rapidly growing body of research within industrial|sociology that suggested that technology had major implications for the nature of the work task, for relations between workers, for the pattern of interaction between supervisors and the work force, and for the wider organizational structure within which work took place.[3] Technology, then, appeared to mould many of the factors that were crucial to the experience of work, and it could be argued from this that particular phases in the evolution of technology were likely to be associated with specific patterns of tension between employers and employed, and with the probability that workers would develop a specific consciousness of their position in society.

For these authors the crucial determinant of the degree of social integration of industrial workers lies in the nature of the development of the technological infrastructure of society. And, in contemporary Western societies, the single most important source of technological change is the spread of automation. Automation, it is argued, transforms both the experience of work, and the position of the worker in the firm. In so doing, it fundamentally changes the attitude of workers to the existing structure of the capitalist enterprise.

Its immediate effect is to produce a further fragmentation of the working class, and to lead to the emergence of a new stratum of workers with their own specific aspirations, and their own distinctive attitudes to management and to the capitalist systems within which it operates. This, in turn, produces a pattern of industrial relations in firms in the advanced sector that contrasts sharply with the prevalent pattern in industry, and leads to a highly problematic relationship between this new stratum of workers and the wider union movement which essentially embodies the attitudes and aspirations of the more traditional sectors of the working class.

However, in the longer term, the implications of automation are held to be even more radical. For, given the very much higher levels of productivity and profit that appear to be associated with automation, the long-term perspective is for a shift in the technological basis of industry towards an increasingly extensive use of automated production. This means that the characteristics of the workers who are at present employed in the highly automated sector may, in time, become the predominant characteristics of the working class as a whole. The inauguration of the era of automation may, then, herald a major transformation in the pattern of class relationships within Western societies.

Clearly, if these theorists are correct, what they have to say is of substantial importance both for those who are involved practically in the problems and conflicts of contemporary industrial society, and for those who are concerned with developing our theoretical understanding of the dynamics of systems of social stratification. The issues raised by these authors will provide the primary focus of this study. Our central questions are: What influence, if any, will a major shift in the technological basis of industry in Western societies have on the degree of social integration of the work force within the enterprise? What will be its effect on the pattern of management/worker relations? And, finally, what will be its implications for the strength and policies of the trade union movement?

The transformation of industrial technology

The essential backcloth to the debate about automation lies in the frequent connections that have been made between the development of mass-production industry, and the pattern of class conflict that characterized Western societies in the first half of the twentieth century.[4]

By the 1880s a major shift in the industrial infrastructure of Western societies had begun to take place. The growth of a mass market, capital concentration, and the development of electricity as a major new source of energy, combined to stimulate a transformation in the nature of production technology and the inauguration of the phase of mass production industry. The dominant trend was now towards an increasing division of labour within the factory, as management, following Taylorean principles, broke down the work task into simply repetitive acts in an attempt to minimize the possibility of error and to secure an easy supply of labour by reducing dependence on traditional scarce skills. For the worker, this meant a crisis of dequalification, subordination to the rhythms and needs of the machine, and subjection to the monotony and meaninglessness of a fragmented, narrow, and endlessly repetitive work task. In its most extreme form, this technology found expression in the assembly lines characteristic of the major car firms.

At the same time the introduction of mass-production technology transformed the organizational system of the enterprise. Initiative in the design and organization of work was now transferred from the worker himself to the management offices, and specialization in the production process involved a major expansion of managerial services to handle the co-ordination and control of the work flow. In the new giant factories the informality of the craft workshop gave way to the impersonality and formalization of a vast bureaucratic apparatus.

These changes in the work task and the organizational system of the enterprise, it is argued, were crucial in determining the primary objectives of the work force. The fight to retain autonomy in work was given up in face of the evident supremacy of the system of management organization, and concern within the organization was now limited to an effort to prevent the intensification of work by devising ways of controlling the pace of output. But this was essentially defensive, and the central objectives of the workers now switched from the sphere of production to the sphere of consumption. In a situation in which there could no longer be any hope of regaining significant control over the work task, or of creating a work life that could be a source of satisfaction, workers now concentrated on action for economic ends — an objective that had the additional advantage of providing a common basis on which workers throughout an industry could be mobilized.

For this was the phase of production technology, it is suggested, that influenced the growth of the labour movement after the First World War. At one level, the concentration of large numbers of workers at a single place of work made possible easier organization and a major expansion in union membership. But, at another, it seriously weakened the power position of the work force within the individual factory. Specialization of the work task, with its conco-mitants of a sharp reduction in skill levels and an increase of the ease with which labour could be substituted, meant that management could carry through wide-scale dismissals in periods of recession in the secure knowledge that it could easily build up again the work force when market conditions improved. The power balance was radically shifted to the disadvantage of the workers. The response to this weakness in face of the individual employer was to build up large-scale national union organizations that could deploy the weight of the co-ordinated power of labour to construct a system of generally applicable minimum guarantees at industry level. The development of mass production technology was accompanied by the growth of mass union organization controlled by highly centralized bureau-cracies, and by a situation in which conflict was large scale, endemic, and primarily directed to economic ends.

This pattern, it is suggested, still dominates the character of worker action and the nature of trade unionism. But in the period following the Second World War there were signs that a second major change in the direction of the evolution of industrial technology had begun. The development of electronics had made possible the creation of a highly automated continuous-process technology. This technological revolution appeared to have quite fundamental consequences for the nature of work and the character of the business enterprise.

In the first place, automation reversed the trend towards an ever-increasing division of labour. The worker was no longer confined to one highly specialized and trivial task and he was no longer tied to the rhythm of the machine; instead he was now responsible for the overall operation of a complex unit of production. This change was accompanied by another: the essential requirement of the work was no longer muscular strength, or physical co-ordination, but rapidity of perception, attentiveness, ability to analyse problems, and to make rapid judgements. The emphasis in work had shifted from physical effort to the manipulation of symbols. This cut into the very defining criterion of traditional manual work, and blurred the hitherto clear-cut distinction between manual and non-manual labour.

Second, automation transformed the place of labour costs in

management's economic calculations. To begin with, it drastically reduced them as a proportion of the firm's total costs. From now on, the overwhelming proportion of production costs were allocated to the immensely expensive automated capital equipment. The need for manual labour had been reduced both by the elimination of manual transfer of materials from one production point to another, and by the operating savings made possible by the incorporation of self-regulating devices. At the same time as labour costs were relatively reduced, they became a much more stable component of total costs — a fixed rather than a variable cost. A major characteristic of continuous-process technology is that operating and maintenance posts must be fully manned irrespective of the level of production. It was, then, no longer a viable management policy to meet temporary recessions in market demand by laying off labour. In sharp contrast to traditional mass-production industry, the worker in the highly automated setting was guaranteed a very high level of job security and indeed employment became akin to a career.

The indications, then, were that the introduction of a highly automated production technology changed several of the variables that could be seen as fundamental in generating the particular patterns of conflict that had dominated the first half of the century.

However, despite the broad similarity between the various authors who have focused on automation in their general picture of the evolution of industry, and in their view that automation represents a rupture with the conditions associated with more traditional technologies, we find sharp divergences in their assessments of the implications of these changes for working-class consciousness. The crucial differences of interpretation lie between those, on the one hand, who believe that automation will lead to a high degree of social integration, and those, on the other, who believe that it will generate new forms of class conflict. We shall now turn to look at the theorists who have put the most interesting arguments within these two perspectives.

Automation and social integration

The theoretical position that we shall consider first is that automation leads to a sharp reduction in the level of industrial conflict, to closer relations between management and the work force, and to the social integration of workers within the existing structure of the capitalist enterprise. The clearest and most systematic version of this thesis has been put forward by Robert Blauner in *Alienation and Freedom*. We shall begin by looking at the structure of his argument, and then move on to consider an alternative version of the 'integration' thesis that can be found in the work of Joan Woodward.

Robert Blauner

Although Blauner formulated his argument around a somewhat idiosyncratically defined concept of alienation, his thesis is basically a version of the more widely held view that the development of mass-production industry produced a sharp deterioration in the conditions of manual work, and led to the emergence of a type of worker who combined a generalized hostility to the prevailing society with a primary preoccupation with militant economic action.[5] However, where Blauner's argument becomes distinctive is in his view that the crucial importance of automation lies in the fact that it eliminates many of the deepest sources of resentment about work, and, in so doing, encourages normative integration within the existing social structure of the enterprise.

In the first part of his discussion of the new technological setting, Blauner gives us a particularly detailed and vivid account of the way in which automation transforms the worker's experience of the immediate work task.

A key characteristic of continuous-process technology is that it restores the worker's sense of control over the work process. It liberates the worker from the rhythm of the machine, and allows him to set his own pace.[6] It gives him freedom to move around the plant and to plan his own work schedule. Control is also restored in the sense that the worker becomes free to use his own initiative. The jobs in a highly automated industry are very much less standardized and repetitive than in mass production industry, and this means not only that the job is more interesting, but that the operator can choose his own techniques, and experiment with different ways of doing the job.[7] According to Blauner: 'Continuous-process technology offers more scope for self-actualization than machine and assembly-line technologies. The nature of the work encourages a scientific, technical orientation and the changing character of the technology results in opportunities for learning and personal development for a considerable section of the blue-collar force' (p. 174).

A further major consequence of automation is that it restores the meaningfulness of work. In assembly-line technology — where the division of labour is pushed to its extreme — the work process becomes fragmented and the individual is unable to see the way in which his minute and highly repetitive task fits into the wider process. Automation restores meaning in two ways. In the first place, the worker is able to gain an increased understanding of the overall process because he is no longer tied to a specific work post but can move around the plant and get a picture of the complete sequence of operations.[8] Second, automation reconstructs the collective nature of work, and thus encourages the worker to think in terms of the whole rather than the part.[9]

By restoring in this way control over the work process, and re-creating the meaningfulness of work, automation, Blauner argues, goes far towards removing the major sources of resentment inherent in mass-production technology.

In the second part of his discussion Blauner focuses on the issue which is of central importance to us here — the implications of auto-mation for social integration. He in fact uses the concept of social integration in two somewhat different ways — as a feeling of 'belongingness and identification which mitigates feelings of isola-tion',[10] and as normative consensus about organizational rules. He appears to believe that these two elements are inextricably linked, but it is the second which is of primary interest to us. Blauner's statement of the problem is unexceptional:

Industrial organizations differ in the extent of normative integration, and this is important in determining the employee's sense of belonging to a cohesive work community. Industrial organizations are normatively integrated when there is consensus between the work force and management on standards of behaviour, expectations of rewards, and definitions of fair play and justice, and where there are agreed-upon 'rules of the game' which govern the relations between em-ployees and employers. The norms and practices through which workers are disciplined and laid off, assigned wage rates relative to the earnings of others, and awarded promotions are especially critical. These matters affect the worker's sense of equity with respect to the allocation of rewards and the standards of distributive justice and therefore often determine his sense of alienation from, or integration in, the industrial enterprise. (p. 25)

It is Blauner's thesis that, in contrast to mass-production techno-logy, automation is an important factor making for social integration. He writes: 'In the chemical industry . . . continuous-process techno-logy and more favourable economic conditions result in a social structure with a high degree of consensus between workers and management and an integrated industrial community in which employees experience a sense of belonging and membership' (p. 178).

The crucial question is precisely why automation should be con-ducive to consensus about the social structure of the enterprise.

Blauner, in fact, gives us two separate accounts of the sources of social integration, accounts which differ in their points of emphasis.[11] We shall assume here that they were designed to be fused, and base our account on the order of the second of them. Blauner stresses five main factors that make for social integration.

First, highly automated factories, he argues, are characterized by a finely graded status structure. This, he suggests, is largely because there is a more even balance than in other industries between skilled, semi-skilled, and unskilled work. A highly stratified system enhances integration through its effects on motivation. As Blauner puts it:

An elaborate system of superior and inferior ranks supports a normative structure because those in higher positions have presumably internalized the goals of the enterprise and more clearly express its values. The existence of achievable higher positions also serves to motivate those of lower status to accept the goals of the organization and act in accordance with its norms. (p. 148)

Second, Blauner places considerable emphasis on the size of the factory. Automation reverses the trend towards larger factories and thus helps to break down the 'anonymity and impersonality' of the types of factory in the traditional mass-production sector.[12] Blauner is a little imprecise about quite how far he feels this trend has gone. At one point he talks about the 'small size of the plants in the industry'[13] whereas in a later section he restricts himself to stating that the plants are *relatively* smaller than those in the automobile industry.[14] In a footnote he explains that 40% of chemical workers and 53% of oil workers are employed in establishments with more than 1000 employees, compared to 82% of automobile workers. Clearly, a factory of 1000 or more is not exactly an intimate affair, and the fact that over half of his refinery workers are employed in factories of this size suggests that it is the argument about relative size, rather than actual 'smallness', that is best supported by the data he presents.

Third, and rather more important to Blauner's argument, the basic work unit is the small team. The worker apparently becomes integrated into the Company partly through the attachment and loyalty that he develops to his immediate work group.[15] Here Blauner makes explicit reference to the ideas of Elton Mayo about the importance of work teams within the factory as a means of overcoming the anomic tendencies of industrialized society.[16]

But the importance of the work team in Blauner's argument goes further than this. In the highly automated setting, the team takes over from management many of the duties of supervising the quality

of work. Freed of the need to maintain detailed control, management's role becomes primarily one of advice; the traditional one-way
flow of command is replaced by an informal process of consultation.
Indeed, given the operator's expertise, it is often management that
will be concerned to consult him. Automation, then, replaces a
system of repressive supervision by a new form of relationship based
on mutual consultation.[17] By so doing, it removes a major source of
friction that existed in the traditional factory, and leads to closer
personal relations between management and the work force.

Fourth, the transformation in the character of work in a highly
automated plant not only removes the repetitiveness, the passiveness,
and the meaninglessness of traditional factory work, but it also blurs
the dividing line between manual and non-manual work. It thereby
reduces the feeling that the factory is fundamentally dichotomous
in structure, and encourages the sense of being part of a unified
community.[18]

Finally, Blauner underlines the importance of the economic conditions associated with advanced automation. These firms both tend
to be highly prosperous and to have a cost structure that makes
possible a fundamentally new conception of management. Greater
efficiency and higher profits depend more on the development of the
technology than on an increased exploitation of the work force.
Management can, then, afford to adopt a more human approach, in
which it takes account of the workers' own needs. It moves over
from a 'commodity' to a 'welfare' conception of employment in
which it ensures the work force high pay and a wide range of fringe
benefits, together with a high level of job security.[19]

Blauner believes that the combination of these various factors
leads to a transformation in the personality of the worker. He
develops a middle-class perspective and comes to identify with the
company he works for. One major implication of this is that he is
likely to show little interest in trade unions. The important role of
trade unions in the automobile industry is attributable to the deep
cleavage that exists between management and the work force in the
traditional mass-production setting.[20] In the highly automated
setting, however, where the main sources of grievance generated by
the work task have been eliminated, where workers are paid high
wages and guaranteed job security, and where a whole series of
factors are powerfully conducive to closer relations between management and the work force, the unions are largely irrelevant. The
majority of workers do not join unions, and, if they do, they tend

to join 'company' unions, established and supported by the employer.[21] In summary, 'the social personality of the chemical worker tends towards that of the new middle class, the white-collar employee in bureaucratic industry . . . Generally luke-warm to unions and loyal to his employer, the blue-collar employee in the continuous-process industries may be a worker "organization-man" in the making.'[22]

Joan Woodward

Woodward's work is interesting because her research, although carried out quite independently, comes to overall conclusions remarkable close to those of Blauner — while offering some rather different explanations. Like Blauner, she believes that the automated setting leads to a high degree of social integration. On the basis of her investigation of the relationship between technology and organizational structure, involving a mixture of extensive and intensive studies of firms with different types of technology, Woodward reported :
' . . . the technology of process industry and the situational demands associated with it establish conditions particularly conducive to the development of harmonious and contributive social relationships'.[23]

Again, referring to process industry, she speaks of the 'building up of strong loyalties and close associations at every level between superior and subordinate. Personal relationships develop which blur the edges of role relationships and make both conflict and innovation easier to deal with.'[24]

In explaining why this should be the case, some of Woodward's arguments are identical to Blauner's. For instance, like Blauner, she points out that in the capital-intensive industries employers can be particularly generous in their spending on employee welfare and services, and that the fact that people work in small primary groups leads to closer contacts between supervisors and workers. But, in addition, she offers us several new suggestions of why management/worker relations should be particularly harmonious in the continuous-process setting. One of her principal general conclusions was that, if technologies are ranked on a scale of complexity, organizational structure is most determined by technology at the two extremes of the scale — in unit and small batch production factories on the one hand, and in continuous-process plant on the other.[25]

However, the nature of this determination was significantly different in the two cases. Whereas in the simplest forms of production the organization was necessarily subservient to the needs of technical

co-ordination, in process production technical co-ordination is incorporated in the machinery itself, and the organization is subservient
to the social needs of the people working in it.[26] Relatively unhampered by technical constraints, organization in highly automated
plant can, then, be designed in a way that minimizes friction. Thus:
' . . . in the technically advanced firm organization serves primarily
social ends, its function being to define roles and relationships within
a social system. This means that the organization planner can concentrate on establishing the network of relationships which is best
for people.'[27]

An important sign of this fundamental change introduced by
process technology lay in the new nature of the role of the chief
executive. His primary preoccupations were no longer technical
matters, but issues of organization, industrial relations, and public
relations.[28] The personal involvement of the chief executive in
industrial relations had several important effects. 'It demonstrated
to outsiders, particularly to trade union officials, that the company
valued its reputation for good industrial relations. Internally, it set
a pattern of involvement for line supervision in industrial relations
problems.'[29]

Another reason why process production makes for much better
management/worker relations, and a much higher degree of organizational consensus, is that it produces a clearly defined primary task
that gives a clear point of reference for the workers' understanding
of their own role in the organization. Given the fact that most of the
key operations for transforming the raw material are built into the
technology itself, both management and men have one primary aim
— to keep the plant running as near to full capacity as possible.[30]
The workers, then, have a clear and unambiguous job task, they
understand the purpose of what they are doing, and this, according
to Woodward, leads to a high level of identification with the objectives of the firm. As Woodward explains, in process firms:

identification of the primary task did not depend upon management's definition.
The work broke down in such a way that the relevance of a job to the achievement of the overall objective was obvious to the person doing it. They identified
through experience; little conscious effort was required. [In contrast] in batch and
intermittent production, work seldom breaks down in such a way as to enable
those doing the various jobs to assimilate the aims and values of the firm
through experience. (p. 173)

It is noticeable that, by an altogether different route, Woodward
has come strikingly close in developing this argument to Blauner's

discussion of the way in which advanced automation restores the meaningfulness of work. However, she has jumped a stage further and suggests that a clearer sense of the meaning of one's task within the overall pattern is itself a factor leading to identification with the firm's objectives.

The final, and most interesting, element of Woodward's explanation — and the one that was most central to her later work — concerned the impact of technology on the control system within the factory. By 'control system' she was thinking above all of the mechanisms by which the outcome of activities in a factory are monitored, and the necessary corrective action is ensured.[31] Developing the ideas of Blau, she argued that control systems vary in their propensity for creating friction between management and the work force, and that a critical factor determining the type of control system in a factory was its technology.[32] She goes so far as to suggest that: 'the control system may be the underlying variable linking organizational behaviour with technology'.[33]

In her elaboration of the concept of control system she distinguishes two main dimensions: the extent to which it is unified or fragmented, and the degree of impersonality of the system. Her theory is that the more the control system is fragmented, and the more that it is personalized, the more likely it is that there will be friction between management and the work force. In continuous-process industries, she argues, the structure of the control system maximizes the possibility of harmony.

In the first place the system is highly unified. In large batch and mass production firms the workers are often subjected to contradictory managerial pressures, for instance to the demand to maximize simultaneously both quantity and quality, and this type of uncoordinated system of control can but be a major source of friction and resentment. In highly automated plant, the exact balance between different objectives has to be decided at the point of the initial design of the units. Secondly, the control system is highly impersonal — indeed it is built into the machinery itself, and thus constitutes a system of mechanical control. The managerial hierarchy is thus spared its police function, and is placed in a position in which it is able to establish much closer and more human relations with the work force.

Again, by a very different route, Woodward came to a conclusion very close to that of Blauner — namely that automation eliminates the need for a repressive form of supervision, and makes for easier and closer personal relations between management and the work force.

Blauner and Woodward come to strikingly similar conclusions about
the implications of automation for social integration within the
capitalist enterprise, although the explanations they give differ in
important ways. Moreover, the initial plausibility of their overall
thesis is reinforced by the fact their studies were carried out quite
independently of each other, and were based on research findings in
two separate societies.

Automation and the emergence of new forms of class conflict

In sharp contrast to these theories of integration, we find a second
perspective in which it is argued that automation leads not to a new
era of harmony between management and workers within the prevailing capitalist system, but to the development of new forms of class
conflict that will threaten fundamentally the stability of the existing
structure of the capitalist enterprise. The boldest, most coherently
argued, and most controversial version of this thesis has been advanced by Serge Mallet in *La Nouvelle Classe Ouvrière*. We shall examine
first then the theoretical structure of Mallet's argument, and then
turn to look at a rather different version of the thesis, that can be
found in Pierre Naville's work.

Serge Mallet

Mallet's work was designed as a polemic against the existing state of
the official Marxist theory of the French Communist Party in the
early 1960s.[34] A mythical belief in the homogeneity of the working
class, he argued, had led the PCF ideologues to neglect the fundamental evolution of the work situation. They had held religiously to
the substance of Marx's argument, but had ignored his method. A
renewal of Marx's theory was needed which would take into account
the effect of the evolution of the technology of work on the nature
of the relations of production.

For Mallet, the most significant point about the work situation
that had come to characterize the traditional mass-production sectors
of industry was that it led to the abandonment of any real attempt
by the workers to bring about a structural transformation of the
capitalist system. Capitalism had heeded Marx's warning, reversed the
trend towards pauperization, and turned the worker's concern from

the sphere of production to the sphere of consumption.[35] The fragmentation of the work process involved in the increasing division of labour had made this possible by destroying the worker's self-identity as a producer. This shattered the main motivational drive that had nourished anarcho-syndicalism — namely, that those who produce should control the means of production. Worker economism had in turn affected the strategy of the unions, which had become primarily concerned with '*la lutte pour le beefsteak*' and had relegated to a utopian future the problem of the overthrow of capitalist power.[36]

The decisive turning point, in Mallet's view, had come with the development of electronics. This had inaugurated a third industrial revolution — transforming the technology of work, and in consequence the social relations of work. Alongside the traditional industrial sectors of mining, metallurgy, food, building, cement, and still the greater part of steel, had emerged a new dynamic sector which either employed an automated production technology or was concerned to develop it. It includes the chemical and oil industries, the aeronautical and aerospatial industries, electronics and electromechanics, and part of the car industry.

Despite its heterogeneity, this new sector gives to all those who work in it — operators, maintenance workers, and technicians — a common set of attitudes and a common type of behaviour: 'nothing fundamentally differentiates the least qualified stratum of workers in the "advanced" industries from the more qualified — if not the bitterness of their revolt'.[37] It is the workers in this new sector, who, according to Mallet, are the new revolutionary element of the working class.

For Mallet the fundamental change brought about by advanced automation was the *objective* integration of the work force within the enterprise. By objective integration he appears to mean that a relationship of mutual indispensability develops between a specific work force and a specific enterprise conceived as a productive unit. From the point of view of the enterprise, this objective integration is expressed in the fact that the cost of labour has become a fixed cost, and in the fact that the type of labour required is one that possesses a detailed knowledge and experience of the particular complex of machinery. This demands heavy investment in in-plant training, and involves types of skill that are difficult to find readily on the labour market. It is therefore in the interests of the efficient running of the enterprise to maintain a highly stable work force.[38]

From the point of view of the work force, this objective integration is to be found in three principal factors: the character of the salary system, the nature of the worker's skill, and the high level of job security.

With automation, Mallet argues, individually measurable work disappears. It follows that each worker's salary is determined primarily by the overall economic situation of the enterprise, and by its economic strategy, and not by the individual's own work. Integration, in the sense of identification with the enterprise and its overall performance, becomes then a necessary corollary of the desire to further one's own interests.

The second factor takes us back to the nature of skill in the automated plant. Automation places a premium on skilled work — but skilled work of a very different kind. The new emphasis is on attentiveness, and the ability to take responsibility for machinery that is both extremely expensive and highly dangerous.[39] It is a skill that can only be learned through experience with a specific complex of machinery and, in contrast to that of traditional skilled work, it is specific to a particular enterprise.[40] The same factor that makes management attach such importance to the stability of the work force simultaneously acts as a major disincentive for the worker to leave. Once outside the firm, placed on the normal labour market, he would find himself reduced to the level of a semi-skilled worker.

Thirdly, this combination of labour as a fixed cost in management's economic calculations and the specificity of the types of skill required to the particular enterprise, guarantees the work force a very high level of security of employment. The work force thus comes to view employment in the firm as a permanent career, and it sees its future as intimately tied up with the fate of the enterprise.[41]

Up to this point there is a certain similarity with the arguments deployed by Blauner. Like Blauner, Mallet has underlined the crucial importance both of the transformation of the nature of skill and of the high level of job security. Where the two authors diverge is in their assessment of the implications of these factors. Whereas Blauner claims that they lead to *social* integration — that is to say allegiance to the existing social structure of the enterprise — Mallet has argued that they lead to *objective* integration — that is to say the mutual indispensability of the specific work force and the specific production unit. For Mallet, objective integration is a completely distinct concept from social integration and, indeed, the main thrust of his argument is precisely that objective integration leads to a new form of revolutionary consciousness that aims at the overthrow of the existing pattern of social relations in the enterprise. What is distinctive about the workers in the advanced sector is not that they come to identify with managerial goals, but that their aspirations will shift from quantitative to qualitative demands, and that their primary objective will be the objective of control. Of the aims of this 'new working class', he writes: 'It's action tends to contest fundamentally, not only capitalism, but every type of technocratic formula for directing the economy. It is the hierarchical structure of industry which is put into question at each partial demand for control' (p. 43).

The work force in the advanced sector will become the spearhead of the working class movement, formulating and fighting for a radically new conception of society.[42] Mallet develops a number of arguments to explain why this will be the case. In the first place, he argues that the satisfaction of the basic consumption needs of workers will lead them to pose other more fundamental problems. He believes that consumption values are largely artificially induced, and that there is an inherent tendency for the individual to seek a reunification of his personality through self-realization in work.[43] In the traditional sectors of industry the character of the technology makes this impossible to realize. However, the development of advanced automation places the worker in a position in which he can grasp the nature of his own alienation.

The main reason for this is that he is placed at the heart of the most advanced and the most complex forms of capitalism, and this enables him to see more clearly the contradictions inherent in the system: 'Only the strata of the active population which are integrated into the most advanced processes of technical civilization are in a position to formulate its forms of alienation and envisage superior types of development' (p. 24). And again: 'Precisely because it is placed in the centre of the most complex mechanisms of organizational capitalism, the new working class is brought to realize more quickly than in other sectors the contradictions inherent in this system' (pp. 42–3).

This argument is clearly a redeployment of Marx's thesis of the increasing contradiction between the ever more collective character of the forces of production and the inefficient and anachronistic system of social relations based on private ownership.

Besides this general thesis, Mallet stresses two further factors as being important in enhancing aspirations for control. First, the worker's security of employment gives him the opportunity of developing a substantial knowledge about the firm and its activities. Second, the decentralization of responsibility, which is an inevitable concomitant of the firm's dependence on the worker's use of his initiative, both gives the work force a much greater capacity to coerce management, and, more important, gives it a consciousness of its collective power. As the strain increases between the short sighted and irrational policies of a profit-hungry capitalist management and the long term interests of a work force objectively integrated into the enterprise, the workers — conscious of their strength and knowledge — centre their efforts on the overthrow of the existing structure of managerial power, and the achievement of effective control over decision making within the firm.[44]

These profound changes in the attitudes and aspirations of the work force have major implications, Mallet argues, for the trade union movement. In the first place, the trade unions will find new life: the workers in the advanced sector are far more likely to become union-ized and active in union affairs.[45] The development of the advanced sector undermines the bureaucratic forms of trade unionism that are prevalent in the wider society and that owe their existence to the nature of the working class in the conditions of earlier mass produc-tion technology. The unions will revert to the decentralized pattern of organization typical of the era of anarcho-syndicalism in the period before the First World War.[46] Moreover, advanced technology favours a new form of union action based less on the traditional strike than on partial disruptions of the work process. The need to co-ordinate and give direction to this type of action leads to the develop-ment of new forms of inter-union co-operation, the suppression of traditional rivalries, and the creation of permanent inter-union committees.[47]

Given the aspirations of the work force, the unions in the ad-vanced sector will necessarily focus their attention on demands for control over the whole range of decision making — from the technical organization of the immediate work process to the determination of the most crucial elements of economic strategy.[48]

This inevitably means that there will be a rupture between the traditional union apparatus based largely on territorial organization, and the enterprise-centered unions of the advanced sector.[49] The central union instructions for co-ordinated action will appear irrele-vant, and the unions in the advanced sector will move towards an increased autonomy of action. But, Mallet insists, this does not mean that the new working class will be fundamentally isolated from the rest of the working class, or that its actions will become merely categorical. The highly integrated nature of the economies of capitalist societies ensures that the demands made by the new working class will have major repercussions within the wider social system.[50] The control of economic decisions in these key firms will imply a degree of control over global economic decisions at the societal level. Finally, the gains of the workers in the advanced sector will serve as a model on which the workers in the more traditional sectors will come to base their own demands. Far from being isolated, the workers in the advanced sector will initiate a process of social change that will have crucial implications for the wider working class.

Pierre Naville

An alternative version of the thesis that a highly automated technology may lead to new forms of conflict rather than eliminate tension can be found in the work of Pierre Naville.[51] Naville's views on automation are expounded in two principal books. The first, *L'Automation et le travail humain*,[52] published in 1961, is primarily concerned with the implications of automation for employment and the occupational structure. Some 700 pages long, this is a somewhat dry, technical account of two surveys of industrial branches, and eight case studies of automated factories. Two years later, however, Naville published a collection of essays, mostly written during the period of the research, under the title *Vers l'automatisme social?*[53] These constituted a type of free-floating meditation on the effects and implications of automation presumably based on the insights he had acquired in the course of his more rigorous, but more narrowly focused, empirical work. The book is uneven in quality, and the arguments often fragmented and unsystematically developed, but it is here that we find the fullest account of Naville's conception of the effects of automation on the nature and experience of the work situation, and an interesting alternative scenario of the way in which automation may intensify class conflict rather than reduce it.

In sharp contrast to Blauner, Naville suggests that the work task itself in the highly automated setting is inherently unsatisfying. Automation induces the final rupture between the producer and the product. It deprives the worker of any contact with the raw material, and it destroys any residual sense of a personalized relationship with the machine. In traditional industry, for the worker arriving in the factory in the morning, 'his individual machine is a bit like his child.

He goes to work, and when he arrives he gets it working; when he leaves, at the end of the day, it sleeps until the next morning. It is his machine.' The situation is altogether different in a continuous-process industry. There 'when . . . a worker arrives at work and replaces a colleague while the production line continues to operate, he feels that this machine is not really his. He arrives, he checks it over; then he goes away, and the machine continues to go on running without him.'[54] Further, Naville underlines that work in the highly automated plant is frequently boring, lonely, and mentally stressful.[55]

Not only did automation fail to restore intrinsic satisfaction in the work task, but it created a series of new problems that could be important sources of tension. At the most general level Naville describes these problems as a marked increase in mobility. First, rapid technological change leads to more frequent movement of the personnel between different posts, with all the problems this poses for retraining and for the maintenance of the worker's status in the organization.[56] Second, by transforming the work task from one of the supervision and direction of a specific machine to one of periodic surveyance of a whole complex of machinery, automation encourages a multi-functional use of individuals. They no longer have one specific work task, but have to be able to occupy a series of different positions in the work process. This, Naville believes, tends to undermine the worker's sense of having a distinctive occupational identity. Finally, mobility is increased in the form of the use of shift work. This is an inevitable concomitant of a continuous-process technology; but it involves constant changes in the worker's pattern of life, it can pose problems for his physical fitness, and it can disrupt his family life.[57]

Naville is also very much more sceptical than Blauner about the liberating effects of teamwork. He fully agrees that one of the most fundamental characteristics of automation is that it reverses the earlier trend towards an ever greater subdivision of tasks, and creates a system of work in which the small team is the basic unit — indeed, at one point, he refers to this as the most fundamental revolution in the work process that automation brings about.[58] But whereas Blauner sees this change as a critical factor reducing the alienating quality of work life, Naville suggests that it may simply replace the constraints formerly exercised by the machine by a new, but equally objectionable, subordination to the social pressures of one's colleagues.[59]

If Naville is correct, then, automation may not eliminate major grievances deriving from the work situation, but may simply transform them. If this is the case, the level of social tension may be just as great as in the traditional factory, and there is no particular reason to expect that relations between management and the work force will be any easier or will be conducive to a wider form of social integration. Indeed, Naville goes further than this, and develops a series of arguments that suggests that not only will conflict with management not disappear, but that automation may see the development of a new and distinctive pattern of conflict. It is here that Naville's argument comes, by a very different route, to have interesting parallels with Mallet's. The thesis presented is fragmented and unsystematically developed, but the underlying set of ideas is fairly clear.

For Naville, as we have seen, the work task in the highly automated factory accentuates rather than reduces alienation by bringing about the definitive separation of the producer from the product, and eliminating any residual sense of individual creativity. But although in the automated setting it is inherently impossible to resolve alienation at the level of the work task, work can be made more meaningful by reasserting control over the work process at a higher level — namely by developing control over decision making. This, however, necessarily involves an important shift in worker objectives.

Two factors are likely to be conducive to this. First, automation enables the worker to get a better understanding of the real determinants of the pattern of authority relations prevalent in the society. For Naville, the prevailing pattern of hierarchical and authoritarian social organization is to a considerable degree determined by the pattern of power relations between different social groups within the society. However, in the setting of traditional technologies with their high degree of division of labour this pattern of organization is to a certain degree functional and can therefore be legitimated in terms of the inherent requirements of the technology. Automation, however, leads to a clear dissociation of the organization of the machinery and the organization of men, and underlines the high degree of autonomy of the system of social organization. His argument here is interestingly similar to that of Joan Woodward. But, for Naville, the principal importance of this visible autonomy is that it sweeps aside the veil and reveals the nature of the existing patterns of hierarchical organization in their true light — as patterns that are socially, and not technologically, determined.[60]

Second, not only does automation undermine the pseudo-technical justifications for the traditional patterns of social organization, but it makes these patterns positively dysfunctional. Much like Mallet, Naville redeploys the Marxist thesis that, with technological evolution, there is a growing contradiction between the requirements of the work process and the existing system of social relations. Efficiency can no longer be achieved through the division of labour, but through the development of more efficient patterns of co-operation. This requires a closer integration of the social organization of work, an integration not only at the level of relations between workers, but also between the different hierarchical levels. The traditional patterns of social organization with their emphasis on hierarchical differentiation then become a major obstacle to the most efficient use of the technology.[61]

Automation, then, produces a combination of three factors. It accentuates alienation at the level of the work task; it sweeps aside the legitimating basis of traditional patterns of hierarchical organization; and it imposes the need for a new form of social organization. The resolution of the problems both at the individual and at the organizational level can only be achieved through fundamental social structural change. As Naville puts it:

The triple alienation of the worker — his submission to machinery that does not belong to him, to a product from which he is separated, and to an adversary social class — gives way little by little to new types of relations under the pressure of a technology that restores co-operation between the operators and that which is created, that gives once more a communal character to the product, and that strikes a fatal blow to a capitalist class whose last refuge is bureaucracy. (p. 247)

But although Naville sees automation as undermining the legitimacy of, and accentuating the visible contradictions inherent in, capitalist relations of production, he is rather more cautious than Serge Mallet in predicting the implications of this for the immediate pattern of conflict with management. For it is clear from his more general political commentaries that Naville believes that the specific objectives of overt conflict are formulated by the trade unions, and that these are not only influenced by the specific technological setting, but also by their own internal organizational dynamics.[62] Through the policies they adopt the trade unions can hold back, or realize, the potentialities created by the long-term pattern of social structural change. The explicit demand for control by the unions, although favoured by the work situation, and indeed necessary if the unions are to be effective, is not then an inevitable product of the development of automation.

Finally, Naville differs from Mallet in arguing that the unions, in formulating their policy, will need to take into account the immense problems of co-ordination created by a highly-developed economy. Hence their demand for control cannot be restricted to one of self-government within the enterprise, but it will have to aim at the development of a complex institutional system that will be able to strike a balance between the need for worker autonomy within the enterprise on the one hand, and the need for economic co-ordination at higher economic levels on the other.[63]

For Naville, then, automation helps undermine the legitimacy of the capitalist system, and thereby favours and provides the essential conditions for the contestation of existing structures of power. However, it does not by itself guarantee that the primary explicit objectives of conflict will be focused on control, nor does it determine the specific type of control that will be demanded.[64]

There is, then, a remarkably high degree of divergence between existing studies in their interpretations of the implications of automation for relations within the enterprise. At the two extremes we find the theories of Robert Blauner and Serge Mallet. Their conclusions are in almost total contradiction.

For Blauner, automation removes grievances over the work task and provides powerful incentives towards consensus over the existing social structure of the enterprise. It remoulds the very social personality of the worker and gives him a middle-class perspective. He is loyal to the capitalist employer and has little sympathy for trade unions. For Mallet, on the other hand, automation accentuates the contradiction between the forces of production and the existing capitalist relations of production. Increasingly knowledgeable about the firm, and with a new sense of their collective strength, the workers are induced to directly challenge the prevailing structure of power, and this in turn leads to a distinctive form of trade unionism — more democratic, reunified, and centered on the objective of control over the enterprise.

The quality of the evidence

In setting out to evaluate these arguments, we must begin by noting that their interest lies more in their theoretical plausibility than in the evidence brought in their support. Neither view has received anything like conclusive empirical backing.

To take first the thesis of integration, the flaws in Blauner's work emerge the moment we begin to look at the general design of the study. Blauner's primary data source is a reanalysis of a quota sample of 3000 workers first published in 1947. Given his specific interests this data base was inherently unsuitable. The data are analysed in terms of industry, and in most industries there are likely to be a wide variety of different technological situations. It is very probable that continuous-process production is *more frequent* in the chemical industry than in many other industrial sectors, but it is equally probable that a large proportion of workers in the chemical industry are in work situations that are not remotely related to advanced automation. Furstenberg, for instance, in a study based on seven chemical plants in Germany, was able to include in his research design technologies as diverse as continuous-process production, assembly-line production, and batch production.[65] Neither we, nor Blauner, then, can know precisely what proportion of workers in his sample were in fact working in a highly automated setting. The relevance of his industry level data for his propositions about the influence of technology defies estimation.

At a more detailed level, one must again have serious doubts about Blauner's data. He offers us no evidence to convince us that salary issues will no longer be a fundamental source of division and tension between management and the work force. In his analysis of the work situation, his exclusive reliance on closed questions, focused on *common* dimensions of work experience, confined his analysis, in practice, to the question of the extent to which the particular problems typical of earlier technologies were or were not present in the highly automated setting, and provided him with no adequate way of discovering whether or not automation generates its own distinctive problems.[66]

His evidence about workers' attachment and loyalty to the existing social structure of the enterprise is equally unsatisfactory. He cites the low degree of cynicism among chemical workers about the qualities that enable a man to get ahead, the somewhat greater willingness to accept technological change, and the greater tendency to believe that one's company was as good or better than any other place of work in the industry. These indicators are all pretty weak. The point about cynicism fails to hold up for his oil refinery workers; the greater willingness to accept technological change could be consistent with a variety of views about the desirability or otherwise of the prevailing social structure; and the belief that one's company is as good or better than others in the same industry leaves unrevealed both the reasons for this belief, and the general view of industry from which it ultimately derives its meaning.

Thus the thesis of integration receives only very inadequate support from Blauner's data. Moreover, this empirical base is not significantly strengthened by Joan Woodward's work. Woodward's study was primarily designed to examine the relationship between technology and certain aspects of managerial structure. Although her information about social relationships within the factory was presumably drawn from the interviews with management, the data on which she bases her statements are never very clearly laid out. Certainly there was no attempt at extensive investigation among the workers within the firms, and without such data her affirmations that the organizational structure of continuous-process firms suited the needs of the personnel, and was conducive to close relations between management and workers, should be treated with caution. The most we can say is that her argument that the nature of the control system is important for satisfaction with authority relations has received support from a study of three chemical plants by Dorothy Wedderburn and Rosemary Crompton, although these authors are substantially more cautious in the wider conclusions they draw.[67] All in all, the thesis that automation leads to a high degree of social integration within the enterprise must be seen as an interesting hypothesis floating on a minimal data base.

If we turn to the second perspective — that automation leads to the emergence of new forms of class conflict — the evidence is scarcely more convincing. As far as Mallet is concerned, it is difficult to get any impression at all of how he carried out his study. In the second edition of his book we are left with two highly impressionistic case studies much of whose factual material might easily have been extracted from newspapers, company advertising booklets, or reports to shareholders. The only concrete source that Mallet occasionally cites is the opinion of militants of one of the French trade unions — the *Confédération française démocratique du travail*. However, we are given no detail about the way this information was collected, or of any checks for its validity. On the whole, Mallet's methodology is left so obscure that it is difficult to form any opinion whatsoever about the value of his case studies. Equally, the weight of evidence behind Pierre Naville's views is difficult to assess. His insights presumably had the benefit of an extensive experience acquired during his major study of the technical, occupational, and employment effects of automation, but nonetheless one searches in vain in his empirical work for support for his views about the implications of automation for the legitimacy of the capitalist system.[68]

The most impressive source of evidence in favour of the thesis that the advanced sector will generate new forms of class conflict is to be found in the work of Claude Durand, and this therefore needs to be looked at in more detail.

Durand considers the problem in two separate studies. In one he looked for evidence in the strike of May 1968, which Mallet himself regarded as validating his position.[69] Durand compared the nature of the strike in four enterprises in the 'technical' sector with the pattern it took in four enterprises in the 'traditional' sector. At first sight, his conclusions appear to confirm Mallet's argument. Whereas in the traditional sector material demands had predominated, it was the demand for control that was typical of the technical sector.[70]

The study was unfortunately less than conclusive. In the first place Durand's definitions of the technical and traditional sectors conflicted sharply with those put forward by Mallet, and indeed all of his four examples of the traditional sector had been explicitly classified as mixed cases in Mallet's own work. Second, the evidence for the demand for control in the technical sector is extremely vague and is confined largely to impressionistic accounts by union militants of discussions that had taken place in the factories during the strike. Most critically, these accounts give no indication of whether the issue of control was principally raised and discussed by the union militants themselves, or whether the issue was genuinely popular in the work force.[71] This is important because there was a major difference in the types of unions that were dominant in the firms he happened to select in the 'technical' sector compared to those in the 'traditional' sector.[72] Finally, the importance that was in fact attached to issues of control was placed in doubt by the fact that these issues were given very little emphasis when the time came to negotiate with management. Given the spectacularly powerful position of the work force in May 1968, one would have expected the themes of negotiation to have reflected unusually accurately the issues that were of greatest salience.[73]

However, although this study based on May 1968 appears somewhat unrigorous, the thesis of the emergence of new forms of conflict did gain further support from another more carefully designed study by Durand, *Conscience ouvrière et l'action syndicale*,[74] investigating the attitudes of union militants. Here the author makes a genuine

attempt to devise and spell out a methodology for testing the propositions he is concerned with. The study involved gathering information from over a thousand union militants, and the interviews were
designed to enable the militants to be classified into six distinct types
differing in their self conceptions, the way they perceived their
opponent, and their conception of the wider society. On the basis of
his results, Durand concluded that the union militants in the advanced
sector were more orientated to control than those in other sectors.
Thirty-five per cent of the militants in the advanced sector could be
classified under control unionism compared to 20% in the technologically most traditional sector. The main type of unionism on its
way out in the advanced sector was that concentrating narrowly on
the defence of the workers' economic position.

Durand's study is the most sophisticated of those we are concerned
with, and his methodology is complex. We have left a fuller discussion
of his study to Appendix 1. For the present, we will simply note that
the differences he found between the different sectors were not
highly marked, and certain aspects of his methodology are disturbing.
The classification of people into one form of unionism or another is
in many cases based on answers to non-comparable issues, the meaning of the crucial category of control unionism is highly ambiguous,
and the definition of the technologically advanced sector is a very
loose one. Overall, given these problems and the limited nature of the
statistical differences, it would be wisest to assume that the implications of advanced technology for the pattern of unionism remains
an open question.

On the whole, then, it is difficult to avoid the feeling that the data
bases on which these theories rest are perilously frail. If any headway
is to be made in the discussion of the implications of automation for
social integration, clearly the first prerequisite is to obtain a more
detailed and a more solidly based description of the way in which
workers in a highly automated setting experience their work situation, and of their attitudes to the legitimacy of the existing structure
of the enterprise.

Technology, managerial power and the unions

The theories we have been considering postulate technology as the
critical variable affecting working class integration into society. It is
an essential characteristic of this type of theory that it should be

generally applicable. If technology is the crucial variable, the effects imputed to technological evolution should be clearly visible in the highly automated sector of any capitalist society.

This poses an interesting problem. It has been well documented that there are significant variations between the social structures of different capitalist societies. The emergence of a new form of technology occurs, not in some type of social vacuum, but in societies with well-established institutional arrangements, and with distinctive patterns of social conflict. This raises the question of how the social dynamics attributed to the new technology interrelate with those of the previously established institutions. Does the highly automated sector manage in some way to gain a high degree of autonomy from the wider societal institutions? If it does not, what precisely are the implications of the emergence of a given technology in rather different social structural situations? The theorists we have been considering offer us no answer to this problem.

There are in particular two areas in which one would expect the nature of the interaction between the new technology and the wider institutional pattern of the specific society to be especially important for the problem of social integration. The first is the structure of managerial power in the enterprise, and the second is the nature of the trade union movement.

The structure of managerial power

Despite the centrality of attitudes to managerial power to the preoccupations of these theorists, they give us no more than the sketchiest account of the institutions of power to which these attitudes are directed. We are told nothing about the way in which decisions of different degrees of importance to the work force are reached, and there is no indication of the extent to which the workers have effectively achieved some degree of control over their own fate.

Yet there are several studies that suggest that the structure of managerial power is not something that can be just taken for granted, but that there are wide variations in the patterns prevalent in different Western societies. Harbison and Myers, for instance, suggest that whereas Britain and the United States are characterized by a form of constitutional management, in countries such as France and Italy the predominant managerial pattern remains either dictatorial or paternalistic.[75] David Granick concluded from a series of intensive interviews with European managers that there was a major difference between the high degree of control that American trade unions had managed to acquire over managerial prerogatives such as hiring and firing, and the virtual absence of such control in many European countries.[76] Similarly, Arnold Tannenbaum and his team have found major cross-cultural differences — even within capitalist societies — in the way in which the workers perceive the distribution of power in the firm and in their sense of having influence over decision making — differences, they suggest, which fairly faithfully reflect differences in managerial practice.[77]

If these differences between societies do exist, what are their implications for workers in the newly emerging industries of the advanced sector? The total absence of any discussion of the problem in the existing literature makes it hazardous to try to spell out the particular set of implicit assumptions with which the authors were working. We can, however, outline some of the possible theoretical alternatives available to them.

They might have argued that advanced technology, as well as producing major changes in worker attitudes, at the same time produces a distinctive institutional system which is sharply differentiated from the dominant national pattern. This might be because firms in the advanced sector had sufficient autonomy to resist integration into the wider national patterns and were able from the outset to devise their own institutional structures that were particularly well adapted to the requirements of running a highly automated firm. Alternatively these firms may initially have been integrated within the wider national pattern, but may have subsequently developed a distinctive character through progressive modifications of the prevalent institutional patterns. In the highly automated setting we may have been witnessing a move away from traditional national patterns, and the convergence towards some broadly similar model that is best fitted to the technology. This would presumably be the type of picture that would appeal to Clark Kerr with his belief that there is a long term trend towards the institutional convergence of advanced industrial societies; a trend in which the requirements of technology will increasingly require a form of constitutional government within the enterprise.[78] On the whole the literature has not been over kind to the theory of institutional convergence,[79] but clearly if this is occurring in the advanced sector it is of major sociological interest.

A second argument that the authors could deploy is that the formal institutions of power may well vary, but this has little causal importance for understanding workers' attitudes. This argument could take a variety of paths. It could, for instance, be held that in spite of major formal differences in institutional pattern, the underlying reality of power was basically the same. Even if this proved on more thorough investigation to be correct, it would involve the assumption that workers respond to the realities of power rather than to its external forms. Yet, the work of Tannenbaum and his associates appears to indicate that there is a close relationship between the formal institutions of power and workers' perceptions of the reality of power.[80]

Another possible position might be that the structure of power varies both formally and in terms of the effective distribution of power, but that this will simply mean that the workers in the different countries will be loyal to or contest the specific sets of institutions with which they are confronted. This, however, requires us to believe that the degree of power that the workers effectively possess will not influence their degree of satisfaction with the existing institutional system. Workers largely excluded from any say over the decisions that affect their work lives must be as satisfied or as dissatisfied with the decision-making system of the enterprise as workers who have acquired a substantial degree of institutional control. This may be correct; but, if it is, it flies in the face of a growing literature that argues for the positive effects of participation on worker satisfaction with the firm.[81]

There are, then, a number of different ways in which the authors might have conceived of the relationship between technology and the structure of managerial power while remaining consistent with their underlying theory of the predominant influence of technology. However, at first glance, none of these arguments seem to be instantaneously convincing, and this leaves open the possibility that in neglecting the question of the structure of power, the authors were dodging one of the most difficult problems for their theories.

The unions

The existence of important differences in the nature of the trade union movements in Western industrial societies is well documented in the literature concerned with the growth of the labour movement. Union movements differ in their ideological goals, in the pattern of union division, in the relationship between the unions and political parties, in their degree of participation in decision making at industry and state level, and in the extensiveness of shop floor support.[82] It would be a commonplace to historians that the union movements in the United States or in Britain are very different in character from the union movements in France or in Italy, each conditioned by its own historical experience, and each with a distinctive conception of its role within the wider society. While it is true that historical data have tended to concentrate on the ideas and actions of union elites, and our sociological knowledge of the union movements remains relatively weak, the evidence nonetheless suggests that we need to take into account the possibility of considerable variations between one society and another in the ways in which trade unions operate on the shop floor, and in their role in the generation and resolution of industrial conflict within the enterprise.

If this is the case, we need to consider the implications for the workers in the advanced sector of the types of union movement characteristic of their particular society. Woodward offers no views at all on the subject. Naville recognizes the importance of the unions in the formulation of explicit demands on management, but leaves undiscussed the critical issue of whether the unions can significantly influence the relationship between technology and the latent legitimacy of capitalist relations of production. Blauner and Mallet, however, are rather more forthcoming in disclosing their underlying assumptions. It is clear that for both authors the influence of the unions on the attitudes of the work force is negligible. Instead, they assume a rather simple one-way relationship in which the pattern of unionism is determined by the attitudes of the work force. Thus, for Mallet, the centralized and bureaucratized union movement at present dominant in society is simply a reflection of the attitudes and problems generated by the conditions of work in mass-production industry. Technological evolution, however, by enhancing the worker's desire to participate and his concern to contest the existing structure of society, leads to a regeneration and restructuring of the union movement and a major shift in union goals. Blauner uses exactly the same underlying causal model, but necessarily comes to rather different conclusions. As automation leads to the social integration of the work force within the capitalist enterprise, it produces a loss of interest in trade unions, or at most a willingness to join 'company' unions.

It is notable that the attempt to explain the key characteristics of the wider union movement in a society by reference to a particular phase of technological development is not altogether convincing. It seems improbable that the overall distribution of types of technology is so radically different between countries such as France, Germany, Britain, and the United States, that this could possibly account for the profound differences that have been documented in both the ideology and structure of their respective union movements. If, then, one wants to argue that in the advanced sector there is a one-way relationship in which technology determines the form of unionism, one must simultaneously account for the specificity of the causal sequence in the highly automated setting, and it is not readily apparent how this could be done.

If, on the other hand, one makes the assumption that the union movement can have a substantial degree of autonomy from the specific technological setting even in the advanced sector, this raises several interesting problems. We must not only ask, as Naville does, to what extent the unions can themselves formulate and make salient new issues of dispute between management and the work force, and whether or not they may be instrumental in determining whether issues are resolved peacefully, or lead to overt conflict. But, more crucially, we must question whether the workers spontaneously define their work situation, or whether the unions can intervene and influence the way workers interpret their experience. If the unions can indeed have such influence, and if there are substantial variations in the aims and methods of trade unionism in different countries, then it becomes all the more questionable whether a highly automated technology *per se* will lead to distinctive patterns of worker attitudes and behaviour.

Technology, social structure and cultural values

There are, then, several major problems with existing theories. First, it is clear that the data bases, both of the theories that argue that automation leads to a high level of social integration and of those that claim that it leads to a new form of class conflict, are rather thin. Second, if we can give any credence at all to the empirical claims of the different authors, then this is very disturbing for the likely validity of their underlying explanatory theory. For within a perspective which regards technology as the crucial variable there is no conceivable way of accounting for the very striking differences in worker attitudes uncovered by the different studies. Finally, we have seen that this type of theory encounters major difficulties in providing a satisfactory account of the mode of insertion of the advanced sector within the pre-existing institutional structures of the societies in which it has emerged.

These problems raise the possibility that there may be a fundamental flaw in the basic explanatory assumptions of these theories, and suggest that it would be worth considering an alternative view of the implications of automation, based on rather different theoretical premises. It could be argued that while automation may well produce significant changes in the objective work situation, it is nonetheless likely to be indeterminate in its effects on social integration. The degree of social integration in the highly automated sector will more probably depend on the cultural values prevalent in the wider collectivity to which the workers belong, and on the nature of the institutional structures characteristic of the society in which the automated sector emerges.

The assumptions underlying such an interpretation are those of the action frame of reference. The Weberian emphasis on the importance of taking into account the values and beliefs of the actor for adequate sociological explanation re-emerged in industrial sociology with a new force and explicitness in the *Affluent Worker* studies in the 1960s.[83] The argument here was that the worker's reactions to the constraints of assembly-line technology could not be understood without reference to his orientations to work which were themselves rooted in the individual's broader value system. The authors' general theoretical point was that the worker's wants and expectations mediate between the objective work situation and the worker's response. This general approach could be taken a step further. For it could be argued that many of the social values and beliefs of the individual derive from the wider subcultures of the collectivities to which he belongs, and, further, that the historical development of different Western societies may have led to important differences between them in their specific cultural and subcultural patterns. Workers in societies with different cultural patterns will then interpret similar objective situations in substantially different ways. If this is so, the emergence of new forms of technology, with its associated changes in material satisfactions and in the nature of the work environment, will not lead with any remorseless inevitability either to a high level of social integration or to a major challenge to the existing institutional order. The response to the changes involved will depend upon the specific nature of the aspirations, and of the wider conceptions of society current in the working-class subculture of the specific society.

Moreover, it could be argued that differences in cultural pattern between societies will not only make themselves felt through variations in the aspirations and frames of reference of workers; they will also be reflected in the institutional structures characteristic of the advanced sector. For instance, rather than the structure of managerial power in the enterprise and the structure of trade unionism being mere epiphenomena of the technological base, it seems more likely that they will be moulded in significant ways by the values and beliefs of those in key positions in these institutions, and that they will embody the strategies by which these groups seek to obtain their goals. Moreover, these key groups will probably be integrated into wider networks within their societies, and their values and beliefs will not simply be the result of individual choices in the context of the immediate situation, but rather they will be influenced by people's initial socialization into the more enduring cultural traditions of the wider social groups to which they belong. This initial socialization will be reinforced by the constant process of interaction with their colleagues in other sectors of industry encouraged by the conditions of a complex, highly developed economy.

The institutional system prevalent in the advanced sector will not be in some sense insulated from those in the rest of society, but will be highly permeable, and will tend to be assimilated into the dominant patterns of the particular society. If this is correct, workers in the advanced sector in societies with different cultural and social structural patterns will find themselves confronted with very different institutional systems which may well have substantially different implications, both for their life experiences and for their degree of social integration within the existing structure of the capitalist enterprise.

The focus of the research

In the light of these different perspectives, the fundamental questions that need to be empirically examined are these: does the growth of a highly automated sector of industry have major implications for the social integration of the work force, for the structure of managerial power, and for the nature of trade unionism? Or, alternatively, does the highly automated sector become assimilated into the predominant patterns of the wider society in which it emerges, in such a way that the degree of social integration of the work force depends on cultural and institutional factors deriving from the broader pattern of historical development of the specific society?

Clearly an adequate empirical investigation of these questions requires a cross-cultural research strategy. It is a notable characteristic of the theorists who have emphasized the causal primacy of technology that they have carried out their work in a single national setting. Even if we assume that their factual information about workers' attitudes was correct, this type of research design necessarily imposed important constraints on the types of explanatory variable it was possible to consider. In particular, it excluded any assessment of the influences of societal differences in culture and social structure. A convincing evaluation of the relative importance of technological determinants on the one hand, and cultural variables on the other, requires a study in which factors such as national styles of authority and the nature of the trade union movement can be varied while the type of technology is held constant.

To provide a test of the different theses, we decided to examine the implications of advanced technology in two societies — France and Britain. Although these are societies of the same general type in terms of many of the key macro-structural criteria that are usually employed to categorize societies, they have revealed important differences both in their paths to modernity and in their contemporary social structure. Historically, the relatively stable evolution of British society has been paralleled in France by a tendency for social change to be introduced through radical social disruption. Social crises in France such as those of 1789, 1936, 1958 or 1968, arguably both revealed the existence of, and reinforced, much sharper cultural polarization than existed in Britain. Similarly, if we consider the social structure of the two countries since the Second World War, the indications are of a lower level of social integration of the working class, and a higher level of class tension, in France than in Britain. On the one hand, as we have seen, the dominant pattern of managerial authority appears to have remained authoritarian or paternalistic; while on the other, we can note the persistence of ideologically radical forms of trade unionism, and the survival of a powerful Communist Party despite an era of affluence which might have been expected to extinguish it.[84] In short, we are limiting our investigation to two advanced capitalist societies, but societies in which the evidence suggests that the pattern of class relations has been and remains significantly different.

In part two we shall try to provide clearer evidence than is available from previous studies about the nature of the attitudes and aspirations of workers in the advanced sector — looking first at whether the commonly held assumption that automation eliminates traditional grievances about salaries and the work situation is correct, and then turning directly to the question of the way in which workers in the highly automated sector perceive management, and the extent to which they see the existing structure of power as legitimate. In Part three we shall be concerned with the hitherto neglected area of the structure of power in the highly automated sector; in Part four we shall examine the implications of automation for the nature of trade unionism. Throughout we shall be concerned with the relative importance of technological factors as compared to wider cultural and social structural influences. As Serge Mallet and Robert Blauner provide the clearest, the most systematic, and the most contradictory of the theses assuming the primacy of technology, we shall take their arguments as our primary points of reference for discussing the adequacy of theories of integration on the one hand, and of new forms of contestation on the other. In chapter 4, however, we shall be looking closely at part of Pierre Naville's argument, and in chapter 7 at part of Joan Woodward's. In the conclusion (Part five) we shall try to draw together the different strands of the argument, and to reconsider the determinants of the degree of social integration of the work force within the capitalist enterprise.

2

The research strategy

The aim of the research was to study the effects of advanced technology on worker attitudes in two very different cultural contexts —
France and Britain. The choice of the research setting was governed
above all by three requirements: the need to ensure a high level of
similarity of technology in the two countries; the need for regional
diversity within each country so that regional effects could be isolated
from influences at the societal level; and the need for a design that
would enable us to compare very closely the institutional system that
governed relations between management and the work force.

The first problem was technology. The most highly automated
sector of industry is oil refining. It is a pure example of continuous-
process production in which from the moment of its entry to the
moment of its exit the raw material is circulated and transformed
unseen and untouched by the work force. It corresponds to all of the
criteria of advanced automation proposed by Blauner, Naville and
Woodward; and it is significant that one of the two case studies that
Mallet retained in the second edition of his book was his study of an
oil refinery.[1]

Oil refining has the additional advantage that it offers a high probability of technological similarity between one country and another.
The range of production processes is relatively slight, and the techniques used by the different refineries are highly standardized. The
basic process in every refinery is distillation, and the proportionate
fractionation of the crude oil into the basic 'cuts' of motor spirit,
naphtha, paraffin, gas oil, and fuel oil, is highly determined by the
chemical nature of crude oil. Further transformations of the balance
of the products can be achieved by vacuum distillation, cracking, and
reforming; and the products can pass through various processes of
purification — for instance to remove aromatics or to reduce the
sulphur content. But, again, the number of these processes is limited,
they are common to most refineries, and the main variations are in
the precision and processing capacity of the automated units.

39

Given the need, then, for both a highly automated technology and a high degree of technological comparability, the oil refining industry seemed the most likely to meet these requirements.

To take into account the institutions of industrial relations at a detailed level, the research had necessarily to focus on the individual factory as its basic unit. Since the degree of similarity between the pattern of industrial relations of factories in the advanced sector, and the broader pattern characteristic of the society was unknown, and indeed was one of the questions that the research was hoping to answer, it was essential to be able to locate the workers in the sample in specific institutional settings that could be studied independently through documentary sources.

The choice of the refinery as the basic unit of research necessarily involved the sacrifice of breadth of coverage within the industry in favour of intensiveness. We took, then, as the basis of our research two oil refineries in France and two in Britain. The oil refining industry is run by multi-national companies, and our four refineries belonged to the same company. This choice was largely governed by practical considerations. It took over six months to get permission from the head office of the company, and altogether nine months to be sure of the consent of the individual refinery managers — each of whom had to be visited in turn for the project to be explained and approved. The length of this procedure clearly limits the number of companies it is feasible for an individual researcher to study at any one time.

This poses, of course, the problem of the representativity of our refineries within the wider set. Our main approach to this question was to ask the refinery managers and union leaders for their opinion, and to take into account the data that were available in the literature. We shall be looking more closely at the evidence for the representativity of the institutional structure of the refineries in the second half of the book, especially chapter 7. For the present we shall simply note that both managers and union leaders within each country stressed the homogeneity of the oil industry, and the very high level of similarity between the pattern of industrial relations in the individual refineries. There was only one oil company that was singled out as constituting a somewhat distinctive case in France. It was not a French company and it was not the company that we were studying.

Finally, it seemed important to ensure that there was regional diversity, so that it would be possible to single out the factors that could be attributed to local conditions from the factors that were more widely prevalent in the society. In Britain we selected one of the refineries (Kent) in the prosperous, Conservatively inclined, south-east England; and one (Grangemouth) from a region of Scotland that had known substantial unemployment during the inter-war years, and in which the predominant political culture was traditionally Labour. In France, one of the refineries (Dunkirk) was located in the long industrialized region of the North, which had traditionally been a bastion of the Socialist Party, and the other (Lavera) came from southern France in a region that was in the middle of a massive process of industrialization, and that was a stronghold of the Communist Party.[2]

The refineries

Technology

The main technological variables in oil refining are the modernity and hence efficiency of the units on the one hand, and their processing capacity on the other. These factors usually vary together. Within oil refineries there is a fairly constant process of technological improvement in order to make units safer and less liable to closure through mechanical faults. We can assume that — where it was important — this type of innovation would be rapidly generalized throughout the refineries of a company. There were, also, however, important qualitative jumps in oil refinery technology which involved the introduction of much vaster units capable of carrying out a considerably finer differentiation of the components of the raw material. An example of such a qualitative jump is the development of the hydrocracker in the late 1960s, which made possible an increased and more carefully controlled output of the lighter and purer products needed for aviation purposes. The introduction of a major new unit like this would usually involve a substantial expansion of the refinery. Within the overall context of a high level of automation, one can then distinguish between more traditional and more advanced forms of unit.

Two of our refineries, Kent and Dunkirk, represent the traditional refinery technology including the major innovations of the late 1950s and the early 1960s. The two others, the Scottish refinery and the southern French refinery, included a major new complex of the most recent units developed in the late 1960s. We have, then, matching pairs of refineries between the two countries in terms of the degree of modernity of the units.

Size

The British refineries were larger in terms of the number of people employed than the French. However, in terms of any overall scale of factory sizes, they are clustered together at a fairly similar point on the scale as medium large plants. The overall establishment sizes are shown in Table 1.

Table 1   *Size of refineries in terms of personnel employed*[3]

	Dunkirk	Lavera	Grangemouth	Kent
No. employed	1058	1025	1347	1779

Date of establishment

All of the refineries had been in operation for more than 15 years. Two of them — Grangemouth and Lavera — were initially launched on a fairly small scale between the wars, and then underwent major expansion programmes in the immediate postwar period. The other two, Dunkirk and Kent, were both launched in the early 1950s (1952 and 1953 respectively). It is therefore unlikely that any effects that we find can be attributed to the novelty of automation. Equally, we would expect that, given this time period, the influence that automation does have should have made itself perfectly evident.

Turnover, length of service, and age structure

According to management in each of the refineries, they have had no difficulty recruiting new personnel for manual worker posts at any time in the 1960s or the early 1970s; indeed, there has invariably been a large surplus of applicants for any vacant post.

Turnover in both countries was relatively low. In the British refineries, turnover due to voluntary resignation or dismissal was on average under 10% a year. In the French refineries it was under 5%. As we shall see later the French workers were relatively better paid in comparison with the regional average wages, and their salary system included a length of service increment. Together these factors probably explain the differences in turnover.

Table 2   *Length of service*

No. of years employed in the company	Kent	Grangemouth	Lavera	Dunkirk	
11 or more	73	46	69	81	%
6–10	11	26	8	9	
0–5	16	28	23	10	
	(N = 209)	(N = 205)	(N = 201)	(N = 195)	

Data based on the sample. See question 47 in the interview schedule reproduced in Appendix 2. The sample figures have been weighted to correct for varying sampling fractions. See p. 49.

The result of this low turnover was that, despite substantial later expansions in each refinery, a considerable proportion of each work force had been in the refinery for more than ten years. Indeed, as we can see in Table 2, this was true of more than two thirds of the work force in three out of the four refineries. Employment in the firm seems, for most refinery workers, to have been conceived of as something fairly permanent, and they were largely out of any effective labour market.

The more recent expansion of Grangemouth and Lavera is reflected clearly in the larger numbers having spent five years or less in the refinery.

A second consequence of the stability of the work force was that the majority of the workers in each refinery were well out of the 'life cycle squeeze' of the late 20s — a time at which a certain

Table 3   *Age structure of the work force*

Age group	Kent	Grangemouth	Lavera	Dunkirk	
15–24	4	8	13	4	%
25–34	19	31	16	13	
35–44	28	26	29	44	
45–54	27	21	30	33	
55–65	22	15	12	6	
% over 35	77	62	71	83	
	(N = 208)	(N = 204)	(N = 203)	(N = 195)	

Data based on the sample. See question 47 in the interview schedule reproduced in Appendix 2.

amount of evidence suggests that financial pressures are particularly acute. There was no major difference between the refineries in the percentage of workers over 35, although once more the average age is somewhat lower in the two refineries that have had the most recent expansion.

Community structure

The community setting varied strongly from one refinery to another, but there was no systematic difference between the two countries, and the variations within each country were as substantial as the variations between them.

The refinery in the south-east of England was located very much in the midst of nowhere, and the homes of the work force were widely scattered over the local region. About half of the workers in our sample were fairly evenly distributed between three medium-sized towns of between 35,000–87,000 inhabitants — Chatham, Rochester and Gillingham. These towns were situated at a distance of some ten miles from the refinery. The rest of the workers were dispersed in a number of local villages. There was in no sense a refinery community. Most of the workers, however, had been born in the region — 68% had been born less than 60 miles away from where they now lived, and 41% of these had been born less than 10 miles away.[4]

The Scottish refinery was on the edge of a small town of about 7000 inhabitants, and here there was something much closer to a refinery community — 52% of the workers lived in Grangemouth itself, many in company-provided houses. The local town, dominated by a petro-chemical complex, seemed to an outsider abysmally dreary with its one small cinema converted into a bingo hall, and the streets deserted after nine o'clock at night. However, the area had the advantage that with a car a person could be away and into the mountains in less than half-an-hour. Even more than at Kent, it was a local work force — 61% of the refinery workers had been born less than ten miles from where they now lived.

The northern French refinery was part of a large sprawling urban complex which, taken together, included nearly a quarter of a million inhabitants. It was dominated by a vast complex of docks and had recently become a major centre of French steel production. It was the only community setting that was overwhelmingly urban. Altogether 96% of the refinery workers lived in the agglomeration, 46% concentrated in one particular commune. It was also the refinery in which the work force was most purely of local origin — 68% of the workers had been born less than ten miles from there they now lived. It was a town with a busy life, and with a large shopping centre, but it was hard on nature lovers. The countryside around was barren and dreary; there had been little attempt to create parks within the town; there was only the sea, which, for the better part of the year, was cold and uninviting.

The southern French refinery formed a marked contrast. It had been constructed on a rocky ridge overlooking the Mediterranean where the inhabitants of the towns nearby passed the long summer months indulging in the local sport of sailing. Although part of the work force lived in an uninspiring company townlet close to the refinery (12%), the greatest proportion — 57% — lived a few miles away at Martigues. This was a rather lovely town of some 30,000 inhabitants with a centre of seventeenth-century buildings reflecting into the canals like a miniature Venice. It was a town, however, that was in full expansion. In sixteen years its population had doubled. The local area had become one of the major centres of oil refining and petro-chemicals, and it was due to become one of the most important centres of the French steel industry. The town itself, with its Communist municipal government, had been provided with parks, excellent sporting facilities and well-equipped schools, but the countryside around was like one vast construction site. Lavera was the only one of the refineries where the largest section of the work force was non-local. Only 38% of the workers in our sample had been born less than ten miles away, and 46% had come from 60 miles away or further.

Method

We used three methods for the study: a survey of manual workers in each refinery, a study of documentary material relating to industrial relations, and longer and deeper interviews with a certain number of key participants. In general terms, the survey provides the data basis of Part two in which we look at the attitudes and aspirations of the work force, while the documentary evidence and the deeper interviews provided the material for Part three and four where we examine the institutions of industrial relations and the nature of the trade unions.

In practice, however, the division in method was less clear cut than this suggests. Throughout the study, from the design of the inter-view schedule to its interpretation, there was a continuous interplay between the use of interviews with the workers and the use of docu-mentary sources. Most methods, if used in isolation, have substantial and well known pitfalls. The best chance of grasping the reality of the situation is to bring as many types of data as possible to bear on the same problem. Handled in a vacuum, interview schedules may be irrelevantly worded, and receive meaningless replies through fail-ing to specify the institutional contexts, or to connect with the substantive problems, in terms of which workers are accustomed to think. Similarly, it is often difficult from interview data alone to judge the extent to which attitudes have implications in terms of action. On the other hand, documentary sources can be misleading because it may be difficult to know the unwritten rules of the way in which they are compiled, and it is often impossible to assess whether the events they recount are anything other than a specific version seen through the eyes of elites with their own particular interests at stake. It is only by moving to and fro from one type of data to the other that it is possible to form an impression of the character of each taken alone, and this, in so far as it was possible, was the method we adopted.

The survey

The interview schedule. The questions were developed over several months of preliminary visits to the four factories. I was able to probe the questions that interested me in a relatively undirected way, and then try out the questions of the interview schedule infor-mally, and by discussing them, assess their meaning to the workers. This was particularly important as the study involved translating the questions into French. The original translations were carried out by my wife, whose native language is French; and most of the trickier points were discussed with other French friends. But in many cases a true equivalence of meaning could only be established by getting the workers to comment on the questions.

The questions were typed on individual cards, and the respondent was handed a pile of cards and asked to keep strictly to the order. This system seemed to us to combine the advantages of the question-naire and the interview methods. The respondent was able to re-read the question if he had any doubts about his initial grasp of its meaning. On the other hand, we were still able to answer questions about it, and probe for explanations of the individual's answer.

The interviews lasted between an hour and an hour-and-a-half each. The usual procedure was to introduce a specific area of enquiry by using open questions to ascertain what was uppermost in the mind of the respondent and then to follow this with a battery of closed questions to get information on specific points that could be easily compared.

In the early phases of the project I was interviewing on my own, and, then, as it proceeded, I was helped initially by my wife and subsequently by two research assistants. This use of a small team for a longer period, rather than a wave of professional interviewers for a shorter period, was probably crucial to the success of the project, especially in the very tense atmosphere of the French refineries. The team members were able to become known in the factory, and this made the project less anonymous, less institutional, and therefore less frightening in a conflict situation.

For the interviews with the operators, we were usually able to use the snack rooms situated on the units. This was unquestionably friendly territory. For the interviews with the maintenance workers, we were obliged to use offices sprinkled within the factory, usually within a small administrative building serving a sub-area of the factory. This clearly took the worker further from his home ground, although what impact, if any, this had on the responses it is impossible to assess.

The sample. We took as our sample population the total set of operators and maintenance workers in each refinery. We carried out an initial stratification of the work force into the two main categories of workers, and then took a sample from each category using a different sampling fraction. We aimed to get a sample of approximately 125 operators and 65 maintenance workers from each factory. The actual samples we obtained are shown in Table 4.

The most unsatisfactory sample is clearly that of the northern French refinery maintenance workers. An important reason for the high non-response rate here was the fact that our interviews coincided with the onslaught of what was commonly known as English flu — a coincidence which provided the French with an unfailingly funny joke at our expense. The very high level of similarity between the pattern of answers of the maintenance men we interviewed and

Table 4   *The samples and non-response rates*

	Dunkirk	Lavera	Kent	Grangemouth
The operator samples				
Operator sample	150	156	149	140
Operators interviewed	131	138	136	133
Non-response	12.7%	11.5%	8.7%	5%
The maintenance samples				
Maintenance sample	110	90	86	75
Maintenance interviewed	65	65	73	72
Non-response	40.9%	27.8%	15.1%	4%
Overall nos. interviewed	196	203	209	205

that of the very much better operator sample could be taken as suggesting that the non-response was not a distorting factor, but clearly
there can be no conclusive proof of this, and the results for this particular sample should be treated with more caution than those for the
other samples.

Perhaps the most puzzling feature of these figures is that, with the
exception of the Scottish factory, the non-response rates among the
maintenance workers were systematically higher than among the
operators. The most convincing explanation that I can find for this
cross-national phenomenon lies in the procedure that we adopted for
contacting the men to be interviewed. In each case the operators
were contacted directly. We would be told the unit in which he
worked, and then we would personally go in, introduce ourselves,
and explain what we were trying to do. For the maintenance
workers, on the other hand, because the interviews posed greater
problems for the organization of work, we were obliged to contact
people through the intermediary of the foremen. There are three
reasons why this may have been a disadvantage. First, it meant that
we were unable to answer any questions the individual might have
had about the project before he had to accept or refuse. Second, it
was easier for him to refuse through an intermediary than in a face-
to-face encounter. Third, there may have been a tendency for foremen to report as refusals men they did not want to spare from work.
The only direct evidence that we have on the third of these was at
one of the British refineries. Our interviewers at one stage got
directly in touch with certain people who had been reported as
refusals and they appeared perfectly willing to be interviewed. How-

ever, management was clearly reluctant to let us do this systematically as it undermined the position of the foremen. My own feeling is that far more important than any deliberate misreporting was the effect of an intermediary on our ability to state our case personally to the individual.

The statistics. Given the fact that we used a varying sampling fraction for the operators and the maintenance workers, we have weighted these two samples when combining them. In practice, the weighting represents a fairly slight adjustment, the largest correction being at Kent where the weight used was 0.4250: 0.5750. A comparison of weighted and unweighted figures almost invariably revealed a difference of 1% or under.

To facilitate comparison between the refineries, we have presented tables with non-response categories excluded. Equally, the (N) for each table excludes non-response categories and hence, unless otherwise stated, can be used to calculate non-response by a comparison with overall sample numbers. Where non-response to a question was over 5% for any refinery we have indicated this. Tables in which the differences between the French and British workers are significant at the 0.01 level are marked with an asterisk.

General. The main interviewing was carried out between May 1971 and December 1972. We found the research easier to arrange in Britain than in France. British managers looked on the prospect of large scale interviewing with almost total equanimity. As the Scottish Refinery Manager put it: 'You can ask the lads whatever you like.' French management, on the other hand, was decidedly apprehensive about the interviews, and hesitated to let us proceed. At Dunkirk, the Director explained to me that his fear was that he knew that the workers, 'although very reasonable as individuals, could act quite irrationally when they were a group.' He felt that the interviews might well lead to very serious trouble in the factory. Similarly it took several months for the management at Lavera to allow us to proceed.

The study of the institutions and industrial relations

The first approach to finding out how the institutions of industrial relations worked in the four refineries was through fairly lengthy interviewing with management. In the British refineries the Industrial

Relations Officers were a particularly crucial source of information. In France, I received the greatest help from the Secretary General at Dunkirk. Among other things he suggested that I might find it interesting for my study to read a book by Serge Mallet, *La Nouvelle Classe Ouvrière*, although he warned me that, in his view, it was entirely inaccurate, and he doubted whether Mallet had actually spent any time at all inside a refinery. In addition to the Industrial Relations Officers, and Secretary Generals, I interviewed each of the Refinery Managers and approximately twenty other managers in each country.

The second approach was through refinery documentation. There appeared to be a substantial difference between the conception of the 'secret' in the French and British refineries. Perhaps because I failed to ask for the right things, I found that there was virtually no documentation in the British refineries that people hesitated to allow me to see. The single occasion when I was told that a document was secret was when the Grangemouth Refinery Manager expressed regrets that he could not show me a paper that he had written on the Productivity Agreements because it was apparently secret. Judging from his brief description of the paper it seemed possible that it had already been in my possession for over a year.

In France, a good deal more information appeared to be highly secret, but it was difficult to predict exactly what would fall into the category. As a general rule, the lower managers believed that all documents were secret, and the higher managers believed that only some were. But there was little consistency even among the higher managers, and the information that one manager would say that it was quite impossible to give would often be handed over voluntarily by another. In Dunkirk, for instance, I was given detailed breakdowns of strike propensity by sector, and management volunteered to provide me with copies. At Lavera, when I asked for copies of the same information, I was informed that it was secret. On the whole management had rather less to offer at Lavera than at Dunkirk, but it was difficult to know how much this reflected a reluctance to reveal what they had, or could be accounted for simply by the fact that they took less trouble to analyse events in the refinery. At Dunkirk, for instance, there were very interesting managerial studies of strikes dating back to the mid-1960s, and reports on specific industrial relations issues; at Lavera we were told that such material did not exist. It is, of course, difficult in this type of work not to be more sympathetic towards the attitudes and motivations of people who are more helpful and forthcoming with material that explains their point of view. This is clearly a potential source of bias that the researcher needs to watch closely.

The main documents on which we relied for constructing a picture of industrial relations in Britain were the managerial files covering the meetings between the trade unions and management. These covered from 1961 to 1971 at Kent, and from 1965 to 1971 at Grangemouth. The earlier Grangemouth files had apparently been lost and there were periodic gaps in the years that were covered. The Grangemouth collection was put together specially for us from a variety of different sources, and the incompleteness seemed largely attributable to the fact that the Personnel and Industrial Relations Departments were set up later than at Kent, and that in the earlier period no systematic effort had been made to retain records. The Kent collection was apparently complete, and when requested was simply pulled out of a filing cabinet on the spot, and handed over to us.

In France, the main source of information was the official minutes of the Works Committees from 1965 to 1972. At Dunkirk these had all been publicly released, and had, therefore, gained the agreement of both management and the representatives that they constituted a reliable account of the discussions that had in fact occurred. At Lavera there had apparently been failure to agree on many of the minutes of the meetings and these had not been released. The collection to which we had access, however, included both released and unreleased minutes.

A third, major, source of information on industrial relations was the union militants in France, and the stewards and branch officials in Britain. In all of the refineries we were able to draw on experience dating from the mid 1960s, and at Kent and Dunkirk from rather earlier.

In France we were also able to make use of the union tracts. These often provided a vivid, if clearly partial, commentary on events in the lives of the two refineries. We were eventually able to build up a collection going back to the early 1960s, and taking us up to the summer of 1975. The eventual collection of several hundred tracts comes from a wide variety of sources, and only for highly specific periods can we be reasonably sure that the collection is complete. It seems probable that the tracts that people kept from the earlier period, and were able to give us copies of, were mainly the more interesting and more important ones that they had thought it worth while to put on one side, but we simply cannot be sure of the precise basis of collection. The tracts, however, give us useful additional commentary on particular issues of industrial relations in the refineries. They often contain verbatim copies of letters addressed by the unions to management, they give us an account of the negotiations at industry level, they tell us a good deal about the unions' own views on different questions, and they provide a fair amount of information about the unions' relations with the workers themselves.

Part two

The attitudes and aspirations of the work force

3

Salaries

Although Mallet and Blauner reached diametrically opposed conclusions about the implications of automation for the level of the worker's integration into the firm, curiously enough they arrived at their respective positions by following very similar types of argument. For both, automation prepares the ground for a shift in consciousness by eliminating the traditional sources of working-class grievance. For Mallet, the transcendence of traditional preoccupations makes it possible for workers to aspire to higher things — namely self-determination and control. For Blauner, it abolishes the main sources of friction between management and workers and allows a new, harmonious relationship to develop. In this and the next chapter we shall be concerned to see whether this assumption that traditional issues are no longer of importance in a highly automated setting is a correct one.

If Mallet's and Blauner's arguments were to have force the first question that they had to deal with was that of salaries,[1] since pay has been both the major working-class preoccupation, and the predominant source of industrial conflict, in the traditional sectors of industry. In fact, however, both authors are curiously cursory in their treatment of the problem. Both explicitly state that pay is no longer a central concern, and Mallet goes so far as to make this one of his principal points of difference between the 'old' and the 'new' working class. The new working class is the standard bearer of 'qualitative' demands, the old of 'quantitative'.[2] However, neither author presents us with more than a fragmentary account of why salary issues should have lost their importance in the advanced sector. It is very much left to us to piece together the bits.

It is clear that the firms that Mallet and Blauner were concerned with paid higher than average wages.[3] Why should this have been the case? Both authors give us a fairly coherent argument about why highly automated firms have a special interest in doing everything possible to secure the long term attachment of their workers. They tell us that advanced technology requires from its workers a type of skill that can only be acquired through long acquaintance with the particular complex of machinery, and also a type of person who can be trusted with a high level of responsibility and initiative.[4] Management's aim must then be to try to keep the men that it has selected. But if turnover is to be kept low, then clearly it must be prepared to offer salaries that would reduce to the minimum the chance that workers would leave in search of higher pay. It is relatively easy for it to do this, because in a capital intensive firm labour costs are less critical for the firm's economic viability, and at the same time such firms tend to be highly profitable. Capital intensive firms then need a highly qualified and stable labour force and can afford to pay for it.

But to say that technologically advanced firms have the will and the capacity to pay high salaries does not altogether dispose of the problem. Why should the fact of high salaries mean that workers are satisfied with them? The nearest answer that we get from Blauner is this: 'The integration in chemicals is not based primarily on traditional attitudes but is an outcome of continuous process technology, favourable economic conditions, and worker satisfaction *with superior wages and employee benefits*'.[5] I take it from this that Blauner is assuming that workers essentially assess the adequacy of their own income in terms of their position in relation to other workers. Workers in capital intensive industries are then satisfied quite simply because they are earning more than they would be earning if they were employed in most other factories.

Mallet's position seems to be rather different. To begin with he seems to be committed to the view that the interest shown by workers in the traditional sector in salaries is to a large extent due to the fact that they have been misled from their true interests into an illusory world of consumption values, which has been fostered by the employers as a means of selling their products and enriching themselves. For Mallet, then, the move away from salary demands represents an escape from alienation, a return to the true nature of the worker.[6]

Mallet offers two explanations of why the new working class will in fact be able to throw off the shackles of consumer society. First, he suggests that by participating in the most advanced sectors of the economy one is in a better position to understand the way technical civilization alienates the individual. Second, he seems to believe that it is necessary to overcome one's elementary needs before one is able to focus on higher order problems such as self-determination. The crucial passage in which he sums up his ideas is this:

Precisely because it is placed in the center of the most complex mechanisms of organizational capitalism, the new working class is brought to realize more quickly than in other sectors the contradictions inherent in this system. Precisely because its elementary demands are largely satisfied, the new working class is led to pose itself other problems which cannot be resolved in the sphere of consumption (p. 42–3, see also p. 24).

These, as far as we can reconstruct them, are the reasons for which Blauner and Mallet believed that salaries would fade from the foreground of working class concern. On the one hand, capital intensive firms could afford to pay more and had an interest in doing so. On the other, high salaries satisfied the workers either because, as Blauner believed, they put them in a relatively better position than other workers, or because, as Mallet argued, they enabled them to transcend their elementary needs, and thereby raise their sights to their real objective interests — namely self-determination and control.

The salience of salary grievances

On the face of it, the argument seems reasonable enough. It is perfectly correct that salaries represent a very small proportion of the total running costs of the major oil companies, and that the salaries they pay are well above the average manual worker salary in industry. To give some idea of the advantages that refinery workers have, it is probably best to compare their salaries with those of other workers in the same region, since these are the people with whom they are likely to have most contact. In 1970 the average Kent operator was earning about 14% more than the average male manual worker in the south-east region and the average Grangemouth operator 22% more than the average Scottish manual worker. The advantage was real, if unspectacular. When we turn to France, however, we find much more decisive corroboration of the argument. The Midi operator was getting 79% more than the average manual worker in his region, and the Dunkirk operator was getting as much as 89% more. The extensiveness of income differentials in France (which has been frequently noted[7]) is reflected not only in the overall income structure, but in the differentials within the working class itself. In financial terms at least, affluent workers in France form much more clearly a worker aristocracy than their equivalents in Britain, largely because of the very low pay of unskilled workers.

Mallet and Blauner then, were correct that automation was linked to high salaries. But were they also correct in linking it to a high level of satisfaction with salaries? As far as the British refinery workers were concerned, they seem to have been perfectly right. When we asked people how satisfied they were with their standard of living over 90% of the British workers said that they thought that it was very or pretty good. But when we look at the two French cases the picture changes completely. The great majority of French workers were dissatisfied with their standard of living — 62% of the workers at Dunkirk and 72% of the workers at Lavera said that it was not very good or very bad (Table 5).

The first point to note is that these differences in attitude did not reflect differences in salaries paid. On the contrary, the French were paid rather more than their British equivalents. If we take pre-tax incomes, the French were being paid, on average, 20% more than the British workers; and, because income tax rates were rather lower in France, this advantage increased to around 38% once tax had been deducted. Equally, we have seen that the French refinery workers were very much better off than the British in relation to average manual worker wages in their region.[8]

It might, of course, be argued that dissatisfaction with one's standard of living is not the same thing as dissatisfaction with one's salary. For instance, one might believe that one's company pays well, but that one's standard of living is undermined by government policies that lead to rapid price inflation.

One way of testing whether dissatisfaction with the standard of living is linked with dissatisfaction with the level of salaries is to examine the extent of, and reasons for, overt industrial conflict within the factory.

When considering strikes in oil refineries it is important to remem-

Table 5   *Satisfaction with standard of living* (Q.1)[9]*

	Dunkirk	Lavera	Kent	Grangemouth	
Considers his standard of living to be:					
Very good	2	3	13	14	%
Pretty good	37	25	84	80	
Not very good	58	68	2	5	
Very bad	4	4	0	0	
	(N = 196)	(N = 203)	(N = 209)	(N = 205)	

ber that they have an altogether different significance from strikes in the traditional sectors of industry. Given the immense pressures and temperatures at which units in the refinery work, closing them down either frequently or rapidly is likely to weaken their fabric, and may involve a long-term risk to the workers' own physical safety. A strike in an oil refinery is not then something to be embarked upon lightly.

In our British refineries, at the time of writing there has been only one strike in which the workers stopped operating the units, and this took place at only one of the two refineries. This strike was not designed to put pressure for an increase in basic salary, but was aimed specifically at the shift allowance. It was felt that there was an insufficient differential between shift and day workers, given the major disruptions that shift work caused to family and social life.

In contrast, in France, at least since 1963, the strike has become a fundamental feature of refinery life. At Dunkirk there were 13 strikes that brought the refinery to a halt between 1964 and 1972, and at Lavera there were 11 between 1963 and 1972. What motivated the French workers? We can get an idea of the order of importance of different problems by analysing the types of demands that were made by the factory unions as they were organizing the strikes. What is immediately apparent is the salience of salary demands. In 7 out of the 13 strikes at Dunkirk salaries formed the leading strike demand. Of the 11 strikes at Lavera, salaries were the leading issue in 4 of them, and the second most important issue in 4 others. The main issue that competed with salaries for first place at Lavera was that of the reduction of the working week (see Table 6). In short, it is clear that the French refinery worker's dissatisfaction with his standard of living led directly to discontent with his salary, and that the issue had sufficient importance to induce him to strike, despite repeated warnings by French management about the risks for physical safety in the longer term that this might well lead to.

We can go one step further than this and try to find out just how salient these grievances were within the total field of the worker's grievances about his society. To do this we asked people what they thought were the main types of disadvantage that a manual worker had in his life because he was a manual worker. Once more the French and British workers revealed markedly divergent patterns. In France, far and away the most frequently mentioned source of disadvantage was the worker's standard of living — 59% of the Lavera workers and 46% of the Dunkirk workers gave it as their leading

Table 6   *The main demands in strikes in the French refineries*

Type of demand	No. of strikes Dunkirk 1964–1972	No. of strikes Lavera 1963–1972
1. Leading strike demands		
1. Salaries	7	4
2. Reduction of the working week	1	3
3. Against internal reorganizations within the refinery	2	1
4. Against 'special powers' for the government	1	1
5. For a 'true democracy'	0	1
6. In support of the students	1	1
7. Union rights	1	0
	—	—
	13	11
2. Second strike demands		
1. Salaries	10	4
2. Reduction of the working week	0	1
3. Against internal reorganizations	1	0
4. Early retirement	0	3
5. The protection of union rights	1	1
6. Against the level of unemployment	0	1
7. Against changes in the social security system	1	1
	—	—
	13	11

N.B. Salary demands could take several forms. It was perfectly possible for them to be both the first and the second priority demands in the same strike.

source of resentment. The next most frequently mentioned source of grievance was, interestingly enough, education, but it was given first place by only 14% of the workers at Lavera, and 16% of those at Dunkirk.

In Britain, no very clear pattern emerged. The things that people gave priority to ranged across a very wide spectrum. At Kent, the most frequently mentioned problem was that of work conditions, but this was given by only 26%. At Grangemouth, the most salient issue that emerged was that of status. People resented the fact that because they were manual workers they were treated with less respect. But, again, it is difficult to treat it as in any sense a dominant

Table 7   *The primary disdavantages of being a manual worker* (Q.6)*

Types of disadvantage	Lavera	Dunkirk	Kent	Grangemouth
1. Standard of living	59	46	19	21 %
2. Lack of career oppor- tunities	6	4	9	12
3. Difficulty of getting a good education	14	16	9	4
4. Disagreeable conditions of work	5	12	26	16
5. Treated with lack of respect	10	12	12	23
6. Lack of influence	5	6	6	12
7. Don't get advantage of fringe benefits	0	3	19	10
8. Other	1	0	0	2
	(N = 155)	(N = 152)	(N = 144)	(N = 119)

(Percentages are based upon respondents believing that there were disadvantages. Among these non-response was: Lavera 7%; Dunkirk 8%; Kent 7%; Grangemouth 17%. These people were unable to specify the disadvantages they considered most important.)

issue, as it was given first place by only 23% of those who mentioned disadvantages (see Table 7). What is interesting is that only 19% of the Kent workers and 21% of the Grangemouth workers mentioned the worker's standard of living. Our data here then confirm very clearly the pattern that has emerged before. The British were largely satisfied with their standard of living, and salaries did not constitute a major source of tension within the factory. In France, on the other hand, salaries and the standard of living were not merely issues that were still very much alive, they were the central preoccupations of the refinery workers, and the single greatest source of tension in factory life.

Sources of dissatisfaction with salary levels

It is clear that the French case fundamentally contradicts the argument advanced by Mallet and Blauner that automation leads to the disappearance of major grievances about salaries. Where exactly did their arguments go wrong?

To begin with it is important to recognize that they were both perfectly correct in their belief that technologically advanced companies were likely to give higher salaries and more advantageous fringe benefits than most other companies. Where they were mistaken is in their arguments about how the workers would react to such salary advantages.

It will be remembered that Mallet had argued that there is some type of hierarchy of needs, and that once the more elementary needs had been satisfied then the workers' consciousness would change its focus and come to concentrate on the satisfaction of higher needs such as the need for control. Blauner, on the other hand, appears to have adopted the position that workers would be happy so long as they were *relatively* better off than other workers.

Mallet's theory, of course, runs into the objections that have so frequently been made about Maslow's theory of the hierarchy of needs. It has never been satisfactorily shown that there is any hierarchy of needs *intrinsic* to the nature of man. It seems more probable that the ordering of human goals will be set in accordance with the values prevalent in the culture. If a certain limit *is* set by people to their economic ambitions, and if after they have reached this limit, they turn their attention to other goals such as control, then both the existence of the economic limit and the nature of this other goal will be a product of the particular culture of the particular society. Mallet's theory then, is underpinned by a psychological theory which has never seemed to be very firmly grounded. It might be, of course, that he misjudged the level of income at which elementary needs would be satisfied, but it seems more likely that he was simply wrong in his assumptions about human psychology.

Equally, Blauner's assumption that workers will be happy if they are relatively better off than other workers seems a curiously limited appraisal of the options open. People may primarily compare their salaries with those of other workers in the area, or they may use a totally different type of comparison, such as the relation of their salaries to the wealth of the company and its capacity to pay.

In France this seems to have been an important element in the situation and, of course, once this comparison is adopted, capital-intensive companies are peculiarly vulnerable. Certainly rich companies can give more, but who is to know that they have given as much as they can give. The very knowledge that a company is wealthy, and that salaries are only a very small part of its running costs, could lead to a marked shift upwards of aspiration.

If the French workers were slow to grasp the implications of advanced technology for salaries by themselves, it was soon pointed out to them by the unions as their activity and organization increased.

In the tracts circulated around the French refineries we find arguments like this:

Step up the Action over Salaries   April 1972

The fact that salaries in the oil industry are higher than those in some other sector of industry in no way signifies that its employees are less exploited. The rate of exploitation lies in the comparison between salaries and surplus value, or — if it is not possible to know the latter — in the comparison between salaries and profits.

The tracts harp relentlessly on the enormous profits of the company, on the minimal effect of salary increases on its costs, on the continuous increase in productivity per worker that can be so easily achieved in continuous-process production.

In short, there were a number of ways for workers not to draw the particular conclusions that Mallet and Blauner drew from the capacity of technologically advanced companies to pay high salaries. We shall be suggesting, in a later chapter, that in order to understand the way in which workers in fact react to any given level of salary, it is essential to take into account both their aspirations, and the extent to which they regard as legitimate the procedures by which decisions about salaries are reached.

The salary structures as a focus of discontent

Blauner makes no mention of the structure of the payment system, and we can only assume that he considered it irrelevant. Mallet, on the other hand, argues that automation transforms the salary system and that this is an important factor making for the objective integration of the work force. The crucial development is that the conception of an individual salary is eliminated, since the worker can no longer hope to increase his income uniquely through an increase in his own effort. His share of the overall resources allocated to salaries is now solely determined by his grade, and his only strategy for increasing his income lies through trying to influence decisions at the level of the collectivity.

Although he anticipated that automation would have major implications for the payment system, Mallet did not believe that the structure of the system itself would become a focus of resentment. While this appears to have been perfectly correct for the British workers, it was altogether incorrect for the French. The British, generally speaking, regarded the way in which salaries were distributed between people and posts as fair. The French workers, on the

Table 8   *The fairness of the salary system (Q.23)**

The salary system is:	Dunkirk	Lavera	Kent	Grangemouth	
Just	6	11	76	66	%
Not very just	50	54	17	22	
Rather unjust	24	20	4	7	
Very unjust	20	15	3	4	
	(N = 195)	(N = 199)	(N = 209)	(N = 204)	

other hand, overwhelmingly considered their salary structure as illegitimate. Of the Kent workers, 76% and of those at Grangemouth, 66% thought that their salary system was just, whereas this was true of only 11% of the workers at Lavera and 6% of those at Dunkirk (Table 8).

Why this difference? What was it that made the salary system such a deep point of resentment among the French workers?

The two salary systems

In some respects Mallet's thesis that automation would have important implications for the salary system was perceptive. A piecework system does appear to be inherently unsuitable to a highly integrated production process, and the workers in the four refineries were paid on a time rate basis. What is more, in all of our refineries a system of hourly wages had been transformed in the 1960s into a stable monthly (or, at Kent, weekly) salary; and this both gave the work force a higher degree of security of earnings and eliminated one of the major traditional distinctions between manual and white-collar employment. While it is true that there was a widespread movement in this direction in French industry in the early 1970s, the oil industry anticipated it by a decade. This unquestionably reflected the fact that it was an industry in which manning levels were highly predictable, and in which there was little relation between the level of manning needed and the level of output. There was therefore much less incentive for management to maintain the traditional hourly-wage system than was the case in industries in which it provided a useful flexibility for meeting variable labour requirements.

But what Mallet seriously underestimated was the range of payment systems that remained compatible with automation; and equally he was mistaken in his assumption that advanced technology necessarily involved the elimination of any form of 'individualization' of salaries. In fact, we found that the French and British payment systems were radically different, and that one important element of this difference was precisely the degree of individualization.

The British system was by far the simplest. The skilled craft workers, whatever their particular skill, were all grouped into a single grade and paid an identical salary. The shift operators were still classified into several grades, but over the years there had been a steady reduction in the numbers of grades used. At Grangemouth, at the time of our study, there were seven operator grades and at Kent only five. The grades were related purely to the responsibility (or skill) level of the post, and in Grangemouth, the fairness with which posts had been allocated to given grades was surveyed by a joint committee of managers and shop stewards. The really important aspect of the system to remember was that all workers in a given grade were paid an identical basic salary.

Moreover the only addition to this basic salary was the shift allowance. This mainly affected the operators and compensated them specifically for working the unusual hours involved in the three-shift system. The shift allowance was a fixed amount and was simply added to the basic salary of each grade.

In France the situation was very much more complex. The basic salary, which was called the *salaire réel* consisted of three separate components.

First, each worker received a minimum salary for his skill grade. Both operators and maintenance workers were classified in a common hierarchical grading system that was determined at national level for the whole of the oil industry, by a collective agreement between representatives of management and representatives of the union.

If we leave aside the fact that it was determined at industry level, the grading system was not very different in structure from that of the British operators. However, where the real difference came was that, in contrast to the situation in Britain, you could not move directly from the knowledge of a person's grade to a knowledge of his salary.

The second component of the individual's basic salary was the length of service bonus. A worker became eligible for this after three years' service. After that the length of service component of his salary increased regularly each year, but the maximum that could be obtained in this way was 18% of the guaranteed minimum salary that derived from the person's grade.

The third component could be termed, for the sake of avoiding controversy, an 'individual bonus'. This went under a variety of names. The workers habitually called it the 'Mafia' or *la prime à la tête du client*. They saw it as a bonus for good behaviour. Management tended to term it an allowance for 'the harmonization of salaries'. The meaning of this is not self-evident and we shall look at it more closely in a moment. For the present it is sufficient to remember that this element of the salary, which could be added to each year, could rise to a maximum of 22% of the minimum salary of the grade.

These three elements, taken together, formed the individual's basic salary. It was partly determined by his skill, partly by his length of service, and partly by the accumulated amount of his 'individual bonuses'. There was no way of knowing a person's salary with any precision from a knowledge of his skill level. Theoretically at least, it was possible for two people at an identical level of skill to differ in their basic salary by as much as 40%.

In addition to this basic salary there were several special bonuses: the shift allowance, a termly or 'holiday' bonus, and a productivity bonus. The really important thing to remember about these three additional bonuses is that they were calculated not on the basis of the skill-grade minimum salary alone, but on the basis of the *whole* of the individual's basic salary — that is to say, the grade minimum plus the length of service bonus plus the individual bonus.

Three differences between the British and French salary systems immediately stand out. The first is that the French system was very much more complex. The second is that it led to a marked individualization of salaries, whereas the British system grouped people into a few broad salary groups. The third is that in the French system the individual's salary was much less closely related to his skill level.

Sources of dissatisfaction with the salary structure

The real problem that we have to explain is why dissatisfaction was so extensive in France. If we look at the reasons that French workers gave for why they thought the system was unfair, it is clear that far and away the commonest criticism is the lack of relationship between skill and pay. At Dunkirk 62% complained that people who did the same work received different salaries, and this was true of 44% of the complaints at Lavera. Of these, roughly half explicitly tied the issue to the 'individual' element in the salary structure.

To grasp what was at stake, we need first to look more closely at how the system worked. I mentioned that this 'individual' bonus tended to go by a variety of names. This difference in terminology was not merely accidental, but reflected a certain obscurity about the basis upon which the bonus was given. Even very senior managers within the refineries were sometimes inconsistent in their description of it.

It is perhaps best to start by looking at the official explanation that was given of the bonus in a meeting of the Dunkirk *Comité d'Etablissement* on 9 December 1968.

The Annual Revision of Salaries

As at the end of each year, the services responsible for Personnel Administration are at the moment engaged in the annual revision of the salaries of the personnel of the refinery, in liaison with line management. We take advantage of this occasion to recall a certain number of the rules which are applied for this revision.

First of all, it must not be forgotten that it is not a question:

— either of an end of the year increase,
— or of a merit increase,

but it is an annual revision of salaries the objective of which is to bring about a harmonization of salaries within the framework of the Company's salary policy.

The Company's salary policy . . . consists of ensuring the firm's employees an evolution of their basic salary which takes into account:

1. Age.
2. Length of Service.
3. Experience.
4. Efficiency.
5. Behaviour . . .

The revisions of salaries at the end of the year consist then — after taking into account the personal factor of each of those concerned and his career possibilities — of examining his salary level within the framework which is set out above and in the light of his grade.

The last paragraph, here, still appears to have caused some confusion, and in the meeting of the *Comité* on 12 November 1969 it was adapted to the following:

The yearly examination of salaries which is carried out at the end of each year consists then of examining the salary level of each employee taking into account:

— his grade
— his personal factor (competence, efficiency, behaviour)
— his career possibilities.

When I was first introduced to the salary system by a senior member of the personnel department in December 1970, I was told:

At the end of the year we give salary increases according to various criteria, such as: the quality of a person's work, the quantity, the effort the worker has made to widen his range of skills, the effort he has put into training, the types of relations he has with his colleagues at work, and the manner in which he has carried out his duties.

There are, of course, very important differences between these various explanations. As we move from one to another we get steadily nearer a definition which in all but name is a merit bonus. In practice, French managers had to fill in reports on their subordinates for the purposes of the bonuses under two separate headings, general comportment and promotability, and both sets of comments apparently affected the final decision. We were told that the aim of the second criterion was to enable management to move those individuals that it intended eventually to promote up the salary scale gradually, so that if they did change grade there would not be too radical a jump in their salary. Why this should have been considered intrinsically important remains obscure.

The complexity of the system was enhanced by the fact that the resources allocated by higher management for the individual bonuses varied from year to year; moreover, in different years, different categories of the personnel were chosen by management to be the prime beneficiaries. This variation in the resources that were made available from one year to the next clearly reduced to a minimum the extent to which the workers could predict on the basis of their performance alone whether or not they stood some chance of getting a salary increase.

The amount of conflicting information that we received at one time or another about the true objectives of the scheme was so substantial that it would be dangerous to hazard a guess as to what, if anything, was the prime intention of French management. However, what was quite clear was that as far as both the workers and the unions were concerned it was regarded simply as a merit bonus.

Whatever the actual criteria were which were used to move people about on the salary scale, the structure of the system can be perhaps best grasped by studying Fig. 1.

There are two points to note here. First, at any given coefficient (or grade) there can be a difference of up to 40% between the salaries of different workers at that grade. This is in sharp contrast with the British system, where two operators at the same grade would get an identical salary. Second, although the system of length of service bonus leads to an expectation of an annual salary increase, this may not in fact occur, because the person may have fallen on the marking system for 'harmonization'. For instance, if we take a hypothetical worker who in his 20s was in position X, and in his late 30s was in position Y, we can see that, despite his advantage through greater

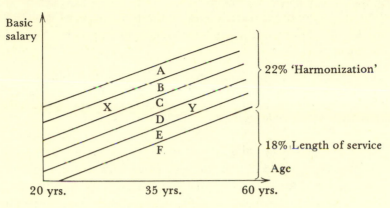

Fig. 1   Structure of the salary system in the French refineries

length of service, his salary level has remained virtually unchanged
(in relative terms).

Whatever the real intentions behind this process of 'harmonization' of salaries, the workers saw it as a merit system open to the
worst possible type of abuse. They found managerial explanations of
the system incomprehensible and assumed that they were an elaborate cover-up of a system which left the worker at the mercy of the
arbitrary preferences and prejudices of his hierarchical superiors.
One Dunkirk operator explained his feelings about the system in the
following terms:

A worker with the grade of 'highly skilled worker class b' can have a lower
salary than someone with the grade of 'skilled worker class a' or 'skilled worker
class b'. Each time that they talk to me about my salary, I can't make any sense
at all of these graphs. The management engineer says: 'On the basis of your age,
you should be there, but with your level of knowledge you should be at this
point'. And then he shows me that my position is below the one he was pointing
to. I ask him why I am below the position I should have on the basis of my
knowledge, and he explains to me that it's because of my age. It's just unacceptable. This favouritism bonus is really lousy. If you are in the foreman's
good books you get an increase. This can add 40 francs a month — that's 360
a year. Really, it's much more because it's incorporated in your basic salary.

This last point is, of course, a very important one. The effect of
the yearly individual increase went far further than appeared at first
sight because it had repercussions on both the termly bonus and the
productivity bonus, which together represented a good additional
10% of a person's salary.

But worry was not confined to the arbitrary nature of the assessment. There was in the minds of many a much darker feeling that

the salary system represented a deliberate managerial strategy to divide the workers and increase management's power. As one Lavera operator put it:

It's a strategy of the employers — they divide us — that gives them authority . . . You never know why one fellow gets more than another, even though they're doing the same work. You never know — they like you or they don't like you. It has an effect on your professional conscience — a chap doesn't care any more if he is earning less than the next person.

If it was management's intention to divide the workers, they appear to have achieved some success. I was frequently told about the atmosphere of mistrust which reigned in the French refineries. Rightly or wrongly many workers believed that their colleagues had betrayed them. Some people felt that if they had made a mistake at work, other workers in the team would deliberately mention it when the foreman was within earshot. In this way, or in secret meetings with the foreman out of hours, it was felt that certain workers quite consciously aimed to undermine the reputation of their fellows, so that they would have less competition when the time came round for the annual merit increase. It was only a short step from a failure to understand the rationale of why increases had been given to a belief that the increases were gained by invidious means.

It's done by favouritism. There's nobody who understands the system because each year they change the theme. They're incapable of explaining it frankly. They do everything to set the workers against each other, and the result is that people aren't very fond of the managers. The comradeship among the workers is false. Each person tries to make known the mistakes made by the others. It's all tied to this favouritism bonus.

Or:

We call the salary system the Mafia. There's a great deal of jealousy because of the end of the year assessment. The chap who has received less leaves all the work to the one who got more.

The French salary system, then, by virtue of the provision that it made for increases for specific individuals, at the discretion of management, was a fertile source of ill-feeling in both the refineries that we studied. Moreover, it is quite clear from reading tracts from other refineries that the problem was not limited to the particular company that we studied, but was common to the whole oil industry. Indeed, the fact that the basic structure of the salary system was decided at national level virtually ensured that this would be the case. Different companies varied as to the emphasis that they put on the productivity bonus or on the termly bonus, but the essential structure of the salary system was identical. Even the maximum differen-

tial of 40% at any given grade or coefficient formed part of the
national agreement.

But crucial as the question of the individual bonus was, it was not
the only source of dissatisfaction with the salary system. A second
major source of resentment was the difference between managerial
and worker salaries. The difference here between the attitudes of
British and French workers is especially interesting because it is not
a difference that can be attributed simply to the structure of the
system itself. Very few British workers questioned the management/
worker differential. It was mentioned by only 2% of those at Kent
and 3% of the workers at Grangemouth. The British workers seemed
to justify management salaries on the grounds, either that managers
were better educated and deserved the fruits of their perseverance as
adolescents, or on the grounds that managers' jobs involved much
greater responsibility, and that they were being paid for the burden
of having to take problems home with them in the evening, and
having their work life overflowing into their leisure time.

Criticism of the extent of differences in pay between managers
and workers was, in contrast, the second most frequently mentioned
source of dissatisfaction with the system in France. It was mentioned by 39% of the Dunkirk workers, and 29% of the Lavera
workers.

Why the French and British workers should have interpreted a
broadly similar situation in such drastically dissimilar ways is an important question, but one that cannot be answered in isolation. We
could suggest that it can only be understood in terms of the broader
context of the workers' perceptions of their societies, and of their
reference groups and aspirations. This, however, takes us beyond the
immediate problems with which we are concerned here, and we shall
be leaving a more detailed analysis of the social imagery of the French
and British workers to a later publication.

Our evidence suggests, then, that Mallet and Blauner were incorrect
in their assumption that salaries would necessarily lose their centrality as a grievance in the conditions of advanced automation. They
were right that technologically advanced firms could pay more and
had good reasons to do so. But they erred in oversimplifying the
possible reactions that workers could have to this situation.

The principal feature of our data was the sharp difference between
the French and British workers in the extent to which they were
satisfied with their salaries. Among the British workers, it is true,

satisfaction with the level of salaries was relatively high. But the French workers, in contrast, were dissatisfied with their standard of living; this was their foremost grievance about their position as manual workers, and it led directly to strikes — despite the difficulties these involved in the conditions of continuous-process technology.[10] Similarly, we found that automation proved compatible with very different types of salary system, and that whereas the British workers were overwhelmingly satisfied with the salary structure, the French workers regarded the principles used for determining the allocation of salaries, both between workers and between workers and management, as fundamentally unjust.

4

Work and work organization

For the majority of the theorists of automation, the nature of work and of work organization in continuous-process plants is considered unproblematic. Whereas with assembly-line production the very nature of the work is supposed to generate powerful sources of frustration and antagonism, providing much of the fuel for industrial conflict, in process production the relationship between managers and workers is thought to take a much more direct form, unmediated by friction arising out of the work situation itself. However, Pierre Naville has seriously questioned the validity of this picture of the implications of automation, by suggesting that it may not so much eliminate problems at the level of work organization as generate its own specific sources of tension. Which of these views best characterized the situation of our refinery workers?

Sources of dissatisfaction

As an initial approach to the problem of how satisfactory people found the conditions of life in a continuous-process plant, we can look at the answers that they gave to a question about the way the refinery was organized. We used this question to open our investigation into people's attitudes to the firm, and it was deliberately worded in a very general way to try to get a picture of the problems people felt most strongly about. The question asked was this:

Q.21 What do you think about the way the refinery is organized? Do you think that:
1. It is the best possible and should be preserved at all costs.
2. It is rather good and should be preserved.
3. It is quite good, and might as well be preserved.
4. It could be better, and certain changes could be made.
5. There are many things that need changing.
6. The whole system needs changing.

After establishing the level of satisfaction or dissatisfaction, we

Table 9   *Level of satisfaction with the way the refinery is organized* (Q.21a)

	Lavera	Dunkirk	Kent	Grangemouth
The way in which the refinery is organized is:				
1. The best possible	4	4	4	8 %
2. Rather good	16	10	9	22
3. Quite good	19	16	10	11
4. Could be better	48	51	60	48
5. Many things to change	12	17	14	9
6. Whole system needs changing	2	3	4	3
	(N = 194)	(N = 195)	(N = 207)	(N = 204)

then asked those who were dissatisfied what they would most like to change.

The first point to note is that only a minority of workers in each of the refineries fell into the three most satisfied categories. In contrast to their responses on the questions of standard of living and salary structure, there was no clear distinction in the *level* of satisfaction between the French and British refineries. For instance, we can see from Table 9 that satisfaction was greatest at Grangemouth and Lavera, and least at Kent and Dunkirk. However, although a clear majority of workers expressed some measure of dissatisfaction, only a fairly small minority wanted to see really extensive changes. Only 18% of the Kent workers and 12% of the Scottish felt that many things needed changing, or that the whole system needed changing. The picture was very similar in France. Only 20% of the Dunkirk workers chose the two most extreme options, and at Lavera the figure fell to 14%.

The type of things that people criticized fell into five main categories. First, there were what could be termed 'relational' criticisms. These were complaints about the way in which management treated workers in interactional situations. They mainly focused on the lack of respect that was shown to workers when orders were given, and the coldness and distance in management/worker relations.

Second, there were 'technical' criticisms — complaints about the lack of efficiency with which management ran the refinery. Whereas the previous type of criticism viewed the work force and management dichotomously, here the worker effectively put himself in the place of management, and criticized the organization from a managerial point of view.

Third, we have a set of complaints about the treatment of shift workers. These were either direct criticisms of the hardships involved in shift work, or complaints about the fact that shift workers were not receiving greater advantages in compensation for their abnormal hours of work.

Fourth, there was a set of criticisms focusing on work conditions. This has been fairly narrowly defined to include only complaints about the unpleasantness of the work task itself, or about the physical environment in which work takes place.

Finally, we have a group of complaints that relate to the level of manning. These typically criticize managerial reorganizations that have resulted in reductions in the size of work teams on the grounds that these have increased the difficulty and danger involved in the work.

The first and second of these sources of criticism refer to the role of management in the organization, whereas the third, fourth, and fifth refer to the nature of work and of work organization.

If we look, first of all, at the overall distribution of criticisms in Table 10, we find that the commonest type of criticisms are those referring to the role of management. However, we also find a considerable number of complaints about the work situation itself.

When we inspected the data more closely, it was clear that it was essential to distinguish between the operators and the maintenance workers, since there was a substantial difference between them in the frequency with which the various types of criticism were mentioned.

Table 10 *Sources of dissatisfaction with the way the refinery is organized* (Q.21b)*

Type of criticism	Lavera	Dunkirk	Kent	Grangemouth	
1. Relational criticism	34	27	18	25	%
2. Technical criticism	22	15	48	36	
3. Shift work	12	17	9	12	
4. Work conditions	13	16	15	5	
5. Manning	7	16	1	2	
6. Grades	5	0	3	4	
7. Inter-worker relations	1	5	1	3	
8. Other	8	4	6	13	
	(N = 107)	(N = 129)	(N = 158)	(N = 112)	

(Percentages are based on respondents who were dissatisfied with the organization and who mentioned specific changes they would like to see.)

Whereas the criticisms of the maintenance workers were overwhelmingly concerned with the role of management, either in terms of its efficiency or of its way of treating the workers, this was not the case for the operators for whom other problems had a relatively high salience.

This is readily seen by a comparison of the two sets of criticisms in Table 11. Among the maintenance workers 75% of criticisms were focused on the role of management at Lavera, 66% at Dunkirk, 91% at Kent, and 75% at Grangemouth. If, on the other hand, we turn to the operators, the corresponding figures are 49%, 31%, 53%, and 50%.

For the maintenance workers, the assumption that the work task and the pattern of work organization do not in themselves generate important sources of frustration seems a valid one. The same does not, however, appear to be true of the operators. Not only do we

Table 11   *Comparison of the sources of dissatisfaction among operators and maintenance workers* (Q.21b)

Type of criticism	Lavera	Dunkirk	Kent	Grangemouth	
Operators					
1. Relational criticism	30	16	17	18	%
2. Technical criticism	19	15	36	32	
3. Shift work	19	25	14	22	
4. Work conditions	16	16	20	3	
5. Manning	9	22	2	3	
6. Grades	3	0	4	6	
7. Inter-worker relations	0	5	1	3	
8. Other	7	2	7	12	
	(N = 71)	(N = 88)	(N = 101)	(N = 65)	
Maintenance workers					
1. Relational criticism	45	51	21	33	%
2. Technical criticism	30	15	70	42	
3. Shift work	0	0	0	0	
4. Work conditions	6	15	5	8	
5. Manning	0	5	0	0	
6. Grades	9	0	0	0	
7. Inter-worker relations	3	7	0	2	
8. Other	6	7	3	15	
	(N = 33)	(N = 41)	(N = 57)	(N = 48)	

(Percentages are based on respondents who were dissatisfied with the organization and who mentioned specific changes they would like to see.)

find a considerable number of complaints about work conditions, but we find that the problem of shift work occupies an important place within the overall set of criticisms. At Dunkirk it was the most important issue of all for the operators, and in two of the other refineries it occupied second place. Finally, in one of the refineries we find a remarkably high level of criticism under the category of manning.

Figures like these are necessarily crude indicators of the nature of problems in work life. They are difficult to evaluate without a more precise idea of the types of criticism that lie behind them, and they give us a snapshot of feelings at only one point in time. In the rest of this chapter we shall look more closely at the problems of work conditions, shift work, and manning, and try to locate them in a rather longer perspective in the history of the refineries. Then, in the following chapter, we shall turn to the criticisms made of management.

The work task and the immediate work environment

Blauner suggests that automation enables the worker to regain a sense of personal control over the work process, that it makes work once more meaningful, interesting, and involving, and that it breaks down social isolation in work by integrating the individual into a work team that provides him with a sense of community.

The picture that Serge Mallet gives us of work and work conditions in the highly automated factory, although very much less systematic than Blauner's is nonetheless identical in its essential points. Like Blauner, Mallet stresses the responsibility involved in the operator's job and the discretion he is allowed;[1] the wider understanding that he gets of the overall affairs of the firm;[2] and finally, the more human and less anonymous work atmosphere that results from teamwork.[3]

How well did these descriptions match up to the pattern of work life that we found in our refineries?

From our observation of the work process for a period of more than three weeks in each refinery, the first point that emerged was that a person's experience of work was likely to vary considerably according to the particular section of the work force that he happened to be in. Broadly speaking there were four main sections among the workers permanently employed by the refinery. First, there were the operators in the central processing units. Second, there were the operators that had responsibility for the tank fields where the supplies of crude oil and refined products were kept. Third, there were the maintenance workers that were attached to the mobile teams that carried out maintenance on the units themselves; and finally, there were the maintenance workers that worked in the workshop, repairing pieces that had been brought to them. Each of these groups had a fairly distinctive type of work and a fairly distinctive type of work environment.

The tank fields and jetties

About 20% of the French operators and about 30% of the British operators worked in the tank fields. These workers certainly moved around — probably more than they wanted to, because of the very extensive distances that they had to cover. On the other hand, they had little opportunity of observing what was going on in the heart of the refinery where the processing units were, and their physical mobility was of pretty limited value for their capacity to grasp the overall process. Moreover, there was little scope for the operator to use his own discretion if he was allocated to the tank fields. His work mainly consisted of checking instruments indicating the amount of oil in the tanks, and opening and closing valves controlling the flow of the products. At one time it appears to have been true that people typically worked in pairs, but in recent years reductions in manpower had led to the job being increasingly an isolated one, in which for long periods of time the operator would be working on his own. Trying to track these operators down for interview often posed quite a problem.

The central processing units

The operators in the central processing units certainly had a much better chance to use their own discretion in carrying out their work than those in the tank fields. Although, as Blauner himself noted,[4] they appeared to have little grasp of the underlying chemical processes, they had often learned through trial and error how to make things happen on the units, and could work away to try to bring the product more into line with the prescribed specifications. The main drawback was that any individual operator was in control for a limited period of time, and since the sampling and analysis of the product was only carried out at intervals, he might well have left before he knew whether his work had in fact had any effect. Moreover, the

settings on which one operator had laboriously worked during his
shift might be immediately reversed by the man who took over from
him, who might well have his own pet ideas on what made things
work. There were limits then to the satisfaction that derived from
discretion. We can get some sense of the frustration that could build
up from the comment of a French operator: 'You never see any
progress in your work. You never see if, at the end, you've worked
well or not. You begin to work at a problem, you make some changes
as an experiment, and then the next fellow who comes along changes
everything.'

The overall experience of work in the central processing units
varied very much according to the position that one held within the
team. The 'responsible' operator, or the leader of the team, did have
very substantial scope for using his initiative. Equally he could move
around as he wanted, and he could concentrate on the things that
interested him most at any given moment of time. Blauner's description of the work of the operator is really only a description of the
work of the 'responsible operator'.[5] None of the other operators
possessed all the advantages he mentions. The control room operator, for instance, was physically tied. He had to keep a constant
watch on his dials, in order to spot immediately any problem that
arose. As the job was difficult, and needed considerable experience,
he was a difficult man to replace. The other operators — those who
looked after the pumps and the furnaces — were in a much less
enviable position than their two seniors. Their jobs were less interesting, they were dirtier, and they involved working a good part of the
time out in the open — which could be less than comfortable in the
rain, or in the winter. On the other hand, they did have considerable
freedom of physical mobility.

As for the operator's chance of getting a wider understanding of
the overall work process in the refinery, this depended very much,
as Blauner recognizes, on the degree of mobility between posts, both
within a given unit, and more importantly, between units. In practice,
this depended to a considerable degree on the personality of the
responsible operator, and on the policy of management towards
personnel training.

Within any given unit, the responsible operator in Britain, and the
shift supervisor in France, had considerable freedom in the allocation
of tasks within the team. They could simply put a chap in a job and
leave him there, or they could encourage him to learn new jobs by
rotating the personnel through the various posts available. The official

policy of management in all four of our refineries was to increase
this sort of flexibility, but in all four cases it was recognized that the
efforts had not been very successful. One problem was that jobs like
that of the control room operator were difficult to learn. Another
was the existence of different operator grades. If a person had proved
capable of carrying out a job above that of his grade, there was a
problem as to what he should be paid; and if he was to be paid more,
there was a problem of incentive to learn. This question of how
flexibility skills should be rewarded had proved a major obstacle in
all of our refineries.

The problem of *inter-unit* mobility was even more intractable.
There was clearly good reason for management to encourage people
to develop skills at handling jobs on different units. It made it much
easier to cover illnesses, and the manpower shortfalls due to holidays.
In each refinery there was a small group of workers that were officially polyvalent, that is to say whose job was to fill holes in different teams as the need arose, and they had to possess the range of
skills necessary to do this. But the real aim of management was to
create a much more general capacity for flexibility among those who
were normally attached to a particular unit. This seemed, however,
to have run into a number of problems. On the one hand the question
of payment for new skills once more reared its head in an even more
acute form, on the other there seems to have been some reluctance
on the part of older operators to actually pass on their knowledge
to other people. Finally, management itself accepted a considerable
degree of responsiblity for failing to provide enough time for adequate training. What seems to have happened is that the size of the
work force had been reduced to a point at which it was difficult to
spare people from their everyday work.

In practice, then, frequent experience of work in different units
was confined to a fairly small number of people who were officially
polyvalent. For the majority of workers, inter-unit flexibility remained an ideal that was far from becoming an actuality at the time
of our study. This imposed fairly strict limits to the amount of knowledge that people could have of the overall process of the factory.
What was fairly common was a reasonable knowledge of the work-
ings of a particular unit; for the rest, there was no particular reason
why they should have known more than the average automobile
worker. Moreover, when we say that they had a greater understanding of the overall process within a given unit, we must bear in mind
that there was an important sense in which the job was probably less

meaningful than many jobs in traditional industry. The increased
technical complexity of the work process imposed barriers to meaning that to a certain degree undermined the effect of increased
physical mobility within the plant.

As far as the physical comfort of work was concerned, Blauner
was unquestionably correct that the work did not involve a great
deal of physical effort. The only tiring part of the exercise was the
need to climb up and down the tall ladders that led to various parts
of the units. On the other hand conditions in the control rooms
seemed to us rather variable. Some control rooms were spacious, well
equipped, and impeccably tidy. Others were small, noisy, and rather
squalid. Much seemed to depend on when the unit had been built.
The newer units undoubtedly had very much better facilities than
the old. Generally, the level of noise in the central process area struck
us, as outsiders, as uncomfortable; and in the power stations it was
often positively painful. If we take a general view, however, the
physical conditions of work imposed no important hardships, although the work environment remained, in most cases, inferior to
that of the office workers.

Again, it was in the central units that we found the clearest
examples of the team work which forms such a prominent part of
many descriptions of work in the automated plant. There is no doubt
that team work was important, but there were indications that its
importance was on the decline. There was an increasing tendency
in the refineries to reduce the numbers in work teams as much as
possible — even to the point where units or sections of units would
be manned by a single person, who, if in difficulty, could call for
help by telephone. This trend was regarded with considerable apprehension by the workers, and was clearly the source of a certain
amount of soul-searching within management. It was not simply a
question of the isolation that a man might feel, staying in a unit
entirely on his own in the middle of the night, but of the possibility
that a combination of this isolation with a critical emergency might
lead a person to panic.[6]

The main disadvantage of working in the central units was the
slight uneasiness that accompanied the knowledge that something
might go wrong with the units, and that in such cases they became
highly dangerous. The managements of all our refineries clearly took
safety issues very seriously, but managers and workers alike were well
aware that there were some things that it was difficult to predict. At
one level this consciousness of danger emerged in the very tight

security precautions that involved, for instance, an absolute ban on smoking in the units. To be caught smoking on the units meant instantaneous dismissal.

At a deeper level the consciousness that people had of the dangerousness of the units emerged every time that a warning light flashed or an alarm bell rang. These devices were clearly highly sensitive, and normally indicated relatively minor problems, but it was striking how each time the atmosphere on the units changed. Within seconds the person you were interviewing would have vanished, and the operators could be seen rushing around the units with a sense of urgency that left one in no doubt as to the seriousness with which any disturbance in the running of the unit was regarded. While we were interviewing, this could easily happen two or three times a day. Some units were notoriously more volatile than others. For instance, it was generally recognized that you needed strong nerves to enjoy working on the 'Cat Cracker'. There seemed, indeed, to be a certain paradox involved in the work. The greatest job interest was to be found on the most dangerous units, and the safer the unit the more routine and monotonous the work was likely to be.

The maintenance workers

If we turn from the operators to the maintenance workers, we find that one of the most curious points is how little attention has been paid to them in the literature. For instance, although both Mallet and Blauner emphasized that they wished to take the factory as a whole as the unit of their analysis, without differentiating between the component elements of the work force, in practice most of their explanation is related simply to the process operator. Moreover, in so far as they mention maintenance workers at all, their comments are confined to only one section of them. In reality, as we saw earlier, there were two distinct components to the permanent maintenance force: those who worked in the workshop, and those who serviced the units. These two groups had substantially different work experiences.

The workshop workers had conditions of work that strongly resembled those of skilled workers in traditional industry. They worked in a large hangar-like building, where they could be supervised without much difficulty, and they carried out their job at a bench. Although people could obviously talk to their bench neighbours, the atmosphere was noticeably less relaxed than among the operators. Their work was usually laid out for them by the supervisor, and the initiative that they could use was no greater, and no less than that of the usual skilled worker.

The maintenance workers that serviced the units were in a rather different position. During routine periods they worked either on their own or in small groups. Unless they were coping with an emergency, they were freer to plan their own schedules, and, as their activities were so widely scattered across the refinery, they were less closely controlled by supervisors. They were able to cash in on the more relaxed atmosphere of the process units, and they could join the operators for one of their frequent cups of tea or coffee. They were often subjected to sustained bantering about the inadequacies of maintenance work on the refinery, but this was a price which they appeared willing to pay. They had the disadvantage of sometimes working in the rain and the cold, but, if things got too bad, they could always take shelter in the control rooms.

There were, however, indications that the freedom of these workers was becoming increasingly curtailed. In all of the refineries, the 1960s had witnessed a growing concern on the part of management about the efficiency of maintenance. In France, this had led to a fairly drastic reduction in the numbers of maintenance workers. In Britain, the main drive for efficiency lay in increasing flexibility between crafts, in planning work much more systematically, and in trying to develop yardsticks of how long the work should take, so that pressure could be put on people to carry out the work in reasonable time. In Kent, where outside consultants had advised management that the maintenance force was working at about 40% of its potential efficiency, there was an attempt to institute a formal control system with work measurement, and with job cards on which people were supposed to indicate the amount of time they had taken over specific jobs. Just as increased planning was reducing the area in which the maintenance worker could use his own initiative, this new control system threatened to take away much of his discretion over the pace of work. The job card system in fact collapsed, partly because of the opposition of the maintenance workers themselves, and partly because of resistance to the scheme among some of the foremen, but the general aim of management to streamline maintenance in one way or another remains unaffected, and the workers are likely to find themselves increasingly controlled.

Moreover, it is important to remember that this small-group work was only one part of their work experience. Periodically, entire units or groups of units were closed down for a major overhaul, and then the maintenance workers set to in a way that resembled a military operation. The work was much more closely supervised, it was planned out from above in considerable detail, and there was little room for the use of initiative. When the units were closed down, there was invariably very considerable pressure to keep the work on schedule since the cost of each additional day in which the unit was out of action was so enormous in terms of lost product. For these large-scale operations, the permanent force would usually be joined by workers lent by outside contractors, so the sense of working with a known group was sharply diminished. In short, even for the workers that usually serviced the units, only part of their work experience fits the type of description given by Blauner of the conditions of work in a highly automated plant.

The use of contractors for major overhauls raises a further complexity for any description of work experience in a refinery. As they were only temporarily employed in the refinery, we excluded workers hired by contractors from our samples, on the grounds that we would not expect them to be deeply influenced by the overall refinery environment, and this made them less valuable for testing the theories with which we were concerned. Nonetheless, they were a very important section of the maintenance work force and they are not to be forgotten. Usually, they worked for high cash with very low job security. Their relations with the permanent work force were often problematic. The permanent maintenance workers believed — possibly accurately — that the contractors were a potential threat to their jobs. Moreover, the contractors' work force was not integrated into the culture of the refinery work force, and there was the constant risk that it might, through lack of knowledge of the traditions of the factory, undermine advantages that had been secured from management. The tendency has been (though it is not perhaps irreversible) for refinery managements to rely increasingly on contractors and to reduce the home maintenance force to the minimum. In this sense the advanced industries harbour large numbers of workers who in no way share the types of advantages that Mallet and Blauner emphasize in their descriptions of the permanent force. Mallet quite acutely appreciated this in connection with the dependence of advanced firms on smaller subfirms that might retain all the worst conditions of employment associated with traditional industry, but he failed to appreciate that the same process could penetrate even into the tasks performed within the advanced factories themselves.

In their analysis of work in highly automated firms, Mallet and Blauner have concentrated very heavily on a very limited section of the work force. They have generalized from the role of the 'responsible operator' in the central processing units to the rest of the workers in the factory. While they do appear to have been largely correct in suggesting that automation removes many of the actual hardships that can be found in more traditional manual work settings, this has led them to give an exaggerated picture of the positive aspects of work life in a continuous-process factory.

The elimination of traditional hardships emerges clearly if we look at the types of complaints about work conditions that are made. People do not complain about the work being physically exhausting or about being ground down by monotony. Rather, we hear complaints like these:

Work conditions here are bad. They've cut down the locker room in size. There's not time to sit down properly for a meal. We should get the mobile canteen back at least. They should provide transport to and from the refinery. (British)

If I'm working in the tank field I have to walk a mile for lunch, and I'm not allowed to leave the job early to compensate. (British)

Work conditions are really lousy. There are far too few workers. You have to go across enormous distances. It's especially hard in winter. There's only one car, and the foreman disappears with it if his own breaks down. The lighting is very, very, poor. (French)

The quality of life isn't what it used to be. Previously, the control rooms were painted every year. Now, never. And they've cut down on the personnel. Before, there were eight of us working at the Bitumes, now there are two. (French)

These are not the complaints of desperate men. They reflect an irritation with inconveniences, and very commonly a sense that life is not as good now as it was at an earlier period.

But although many of the hardships of work conditions characteristic of earlier technologies are largely eliminated, this in no way implies that continuous-process production provides, as Blauner suggests, a totally new type of creative, absorbing, and meaningful work. When we asked people whether they looked forward to an interesting day at the refinery, or were indifferent or fed up at the idea, we found that most people were indifferent. There were more people who were enthusiastic in Britain than in France, but the overall pattern was broadly similar across the four refineries. (See Table 12.)

Nor was there any sign that the work of the operators in the central units was particularly conducive to a deep sense of satisfaction,

Table 12   *Satisfaction with work (Q.20)**

Q. Generally speaking, when you come to work, do you feel:
  1. Rather happy at the idea of an interesting day (or night) in the refinery
  2. Nothing in particular; not particularly happy or unhappy
  3. A bit fed up at the idea of having to pass the day (night) in the refinery.

	Lavera	*Dunkirk*	*Kent*	*Grangemouth*	
1. Happy	26	18	34	43	%
2. Indifferent	64	73	58	46	
3. A bit fed up	10	10	8	10	
	(N = 202)	(N = 195)	(N = 208)	(N = 204)	

although this came nearest to the type of work that Blauner was describing, For instance, if we compare the central unit operators with the maintenance workers, we find no consistent pattern. If we look simply at the Grangemouth data, we find that the operators are indeed the more satisfied group — 45% of them, compared to only 31% of the maintenance workers, looked forward to an interesting day. However, in two of the other refineries there is no difference at all between the two types of worker, and in the fourth refinery (Lavera) the relationship was completely reversed. There it was the maintenance workers who were markedly more satisfied in work (36%) than the operators in the central units (19%).

Curiously enough, however, there was one group of workers that did find work considerably more satisfying than any of the others. These were the operators in the Tank Field area — the men who were the least like the 'new' type of operator characterized by Blauner and Mallet. They were the men who were the most isolated from the central life of the refinery, who were the most likely to be working on their own, and who had the most straightforward and least creative jobs.[7] (Table 13.)

Advanced automation, then, has not fundamentally altered the significance of work in the worker's life. The question we asked was intentionally rather more demanding than the traditional type of question designed to discover whether a person finds turning knobs a little more interesting than work on an assembly line. I think few would dispute that in this very narrow sense the work is a little more interesting.[8] However, what we were concerned to see was whether work has become a central life interest, a source of self-realization,

Table 13 *Comparison of work satisfaction of different categories of workers* (Q.20)

% of workers happy at the idea of an interesting day

Type of worker	Lavera	Dunkirk	Kent	Grangemouth	
1. All operators	20	18	36	50	%
2. All maintenance	36	14	32	31	
3. Central unit operators	19	14	33	45	
4. Tank field operators	38	31	43	62	

and of self-fulfilment. This is really the only meaningful sense in which we can talk about an overcoming of alienation. From this point of view, we have seen that the development of highly advanced forms of automation does not make work a source of deep satisfaction. What it does do, and this is certainly not negligible, is to remove many of the traditional hardships of work.

People were not physically tied for hours to one particular place in the factory, the work was not unbearably monotonous, and people were not working in conditions that were either exceptionally dirty, or unhealthy. However, while it is important to bear these major improvements in mind, we must also remember that operators in continuous-process industry were faced with an element of the work situation which is largely absent in the traditional sectors of industry. We must now turn to the problem of continuous-shift work.

Shift work

One of the most curious features of Mallet's and Blauner's accounts of the effects of continuous-process production is their almost total neglect of shift work. Yet the problematic nature of continuous shifts had already been frequently noticed in the literature. For instance, in an article published in 1953, Wyatt and Marriot concluded from their research that: 'There is not the least doubt that night work is unpopular and, in the long run, is detrimental to health, efficiency, and the enjoyment of life.'[9] In the most substantial American empirical study of the effects of automation on the conditions of work at the time that Blauner was writing, Mann and Hoffman wrote that: 'Among shift workers and others connected with shift operations, an extensive "folklore" has developed about the effects of working nights. There is widespread belief that shift work shortens workers' lives, that night workers have more illnesses, and that men age more rapidly doing shift work.'[10] They summed up their findings in the following words: 'We found that a majority of workers actively and strongly disliked working afternoons and nights'.[11] Since Blauner and Mallet published their respective theses, shift work has come under considerably more searching scrutiny, but, with very occasional exceptions, the conclusions have been the same: shift workers find that working shifts is a major burden in their lives.

We have seen that in our own samples shift work was the main source of grievance among the operators in one of our refineries, and that it was the second most important grievance among the operators in two of the other refineries. In fact, most of the operators in all of the refineries that we studied found shift work intrinsically undesirable. When we asked people whether, given the same pay and the same work, they would choose shift or day work, around two-thirds of the operators in each refinery said that they would choose day work. Shift work was disliked most at Dunkirk and Grangemouth (72% and 68%), and least at Lavera (64%). But the differences are remarkably small. In their general dislike of shift work our samples then reinforce findings that have emerged repeatedly elsewhere.

In two of our refineries (Grangemouth and Lavera) we asked people what precisely it was about shift work that they disliked. The same set of problems emerged in both refineries, but there were some interesting differences in what was considered to be most important.

Broadly speaking, complaints about shift work fell into three main categories. The first concerned the effects of shift work on physical fitness; the second, the way in which shift work disrupted family and social life; and the third, the sheer irregularity of life that shift work involved, the lack of a stable life routine. If we take the first complaints that people mentioned as the ones that are the most salient to them, it is notable that the French workers are significantly more concerned about the effects of shift work on their physical fitness, while the Scottish workers are more concerned about the way in which it affects their social and leisure life. (See Table 14.)

If we look first at the complaints about the effects of shift work on physical fitness, we can distinguish between those that dwell on the feeling of tiredness that shift work induces, and those that go further and describe it as a source of ill-health. What really distinguishes the French workers from the Scottish, is their emphasis on shift work as a source of tiredness. Very similar proportions of opera-

Table 14   *Sources of dissatisfaction with shift work* (Q.24)*

Source of dissatisfaction	Lavera	Grangemouth	
1. Health	10	11	%
2. Tiredness	33	7	
3. Leisure life	2	32	
4. Family life	27	19	
5. General irregularity	27	30	
6. Other	—	1	
	(N = 139)	(N = 137)	

(Percentages are based on operators who disliked shift work.)

tors in the two refineries refer to problems of health — 10% at Lavera, 11% at Grangemouth. In contrast, when we come to the problem of tiredness, we find that this accounts for 33% of complaints at Lavera, but only 7% at Grangemouth. This problem of tiredness was in fact common to both of the French refineries. Due to their growing concern about the extent of resentment about shift work, the company asked its doctors for a report on the sources of the problem at the refinery of Dunkirk. In their report the doctors made the following comment: 'It seems that the quality of sleep is very much affected by continuous shift work, . . . many workers are haunted by the need to get up very early in the morning or find it difficult to wake up. They are tired when they wake up and feel drowsy for a period during the morning.'[12]

The Scottish workers, on the other hand, were mainly concerned with the way in which shift work disturbed family and leisure life. Of these two, it was leisure life that seems to have been the main worry — 32% of complaints bore on the way shift work made it difficult to visit friends, carry out regular sporting activities, and such like, compared to 19% which referred to the problems it posed for family life. Interestingly, this order of importance was entirely reversed within the French sample. Here, complaints about leisure life amounted to only 2% whereas 27% were concerned with family life.

There are, then, three problems that we must look at. First, why is it that shift work generates the major themes of complaint that we have found in both of the refineries? Second, why should there have been some difference of emphasis between the two refineries? And third, what are the implications of these problems of shift work for the nature of social relations in the highly automated factory?

Tiredness and health

As we have seen, the most frequently mentioned source of dissatisfaction among the French workers was tiredness. This may have been partly due to the timing of the shifts. In France, the morning shift started at 5 am, the afternoon shift at 1 pm, and the night shift at 9 pm. At Grangemouth, on the other hand, the shifts started at 6 am, 2 pm, and 10 pm; and, at Kent, yet another hour later. The French company doctors attributed the tiredness of their workers to the very early start for the morning shift at 5 am. This meant waking up at 4 am at the latest. Most of the shift workers recognized that the way to make this less strenuous was to get to bed early the night before, but this effectively meant getting to sleep at 8 pm. Given the fact that their evenings were totally disrupted on both the afternoon and night shifts, the temptation to extend these evenings for going out, meeting friends, or simply watching television, was very great. For the younger workers, these evenings represented virtually the only time when they could join in the party life of the youth around them. The very nature of shift work tended to make regular dating difficult, and they were reluctant to lose this chance for the sake of a few hours sleep.

A second important source of tiredness was the night shift. Here, the crucial problem was that of trying to get to sleep during the day. Most of the workers lived in fairly small houses or flats, and their families had the unenviable task of trying to carry out their daily activities in such a way as not to make any noise. Clearly, when there were small children around, sustaining an environment conducive to sleep verged on the impossible. Even if the family was prepared to make exceptional efforts, there was always the problem of the noise generated in the day time by a busy town. On the whole the Grangemouth workers seem to have been fairly lucky in their environment, since the town that most of them lived in can only be described as sleepy. This, together with the fact that they benefited from a system which gave them a rest from shift work in the middle of each cycle, probably explains why complaints of tiredness were comparatively rare. The French workers seem more typical of the problems of shift workers generally in the difficulty that they had with sleep. Mann and Hoffman, for instance, found that adjusting to changes in sleeping times was the most frequent source of trouble mentioned by both their weekly and their monthly rotating shift workers.[13] A Swedish study by Bjerner, Holm and Swenssen found that on night shift, workers averaged only 5½ hours sleep, compared to an average of 7½ hours for day workers.[14] Mott *et al.* conclude a comprehensive review of the literature by saying that: 'Most authorities on the subject agree that the central problem of working shifts is getting adequate sleep.'[15] Moreover, with their own samples, only 23% found that they adjusted right away to the problem of sleeping after night shift, while 20% found that it took four days or more. Roughly a quarter of their workers got as little as 5 hours sleep, or even less when they were working night shift.[16]

Although there is general agreement about the problems shift work poses in the way of tiredness, there has been considerable disagreement about whether it has more serious implications for health. Mott *et al,* although recognizing that there were certain problems with their data, nonetheless believed that it showed a link between shift work on the one hand, and upper gastrointestinal complaints, ulcers, and rheumatoid arthritis on the other.[17] P. J. Taylor, however, argued from his work at Shell Haven refinery that there was no evidence at all that shift work had serious implications for health. He pointed out that shift workers were less likely to be away from work with illness than day workers, and that if one compared the pattern of the illnesses of those who did have to take time off with those of the day workers there was no significant difference.[18]

We made no systematic investigation into this problem, but there were indications in our data that tended to reinforce Taylor's position. We obtained, for instance, sickness figures for one of our British refineries (Kent) and the pattern that emerged from these was almost exactly the same as the one that Taylor had found. The maintenance workers at Kent were almost twice as likely to be away sick as the shift workers. The same tendency seems to have been true in the French refineries. The French company doctors, after analysing the refinery illness statistics, reported:

Using the statistics of the refineries of Dunkirk and Lavera, we have tried to compare absenteeism, sickness rates, chronic ill-health, and deaths between continuous shift workers and day workers. The results we obtained, comparable in all respects to those in other refineries or industrial plants, do not reveal a sufficient statistical difference for the four categories studied: absenteeism, serious illness, length of life, and chronic ill-health. We should, in addition, underline that the average duration of absence for illness and of absenteeism in general are lower in the shift worker groups than among the day workers.[19]

At a less serious level, however, the French doctors did suggest that there was a relationship between shift work and certain digestive difficulties. This has been confirmed in other studies. The shift workers interviewed by Mann and Hoffman found difficulties with eating the second most important source of trouble in adjusting to shift changes, and Mott *et al.* report that their shift workers had a greater tendency to suffer from stomach discomfort and loss of appetite.[20]

Family life and leisure

Just as the rotating shift cycle poses a set of important problems in relationship to the normal physical body cycles, similarly it presents difficulties in terms of its relationship with the social cycles of the communities within which the worker lives. We find for instance complaints like these:

Shifts disrupts your whole social life. You can't go to a dance or go fishing at the weekend. The family have to be quiet on Sunday mornings so that Dad can sleep. I'm only on shifts for the money.

Shifts means that you are a social outcast — you cannot arrange anything. From a family man's point of view, it's your children and wife who suffer.

Your home life begins with the normal working day. On shifts you don't see your wife for a day at a time, and then at odd hours. You don't see your children for a week on some shifts. You're a stranger to them.

The French had similar problems:

You lead a ridiculous life working shifts. It's not normal. One is made for working in the day time. Leisure activities are organized for the weekend and the evening. The people I know, my friends, work during the day, and it is only from time to time that I can get to see them.

Working shifts, you have to come during the night and sleep during the morning. If my wife makes just a little noise, I wake up and quarrel with her.

Presumably many of the social disadvantages of shift work could be alleviated if the family as a unit could move onto the shift system. But, in practice, this is rarely possible. Throughout most of their working lives most shift workers have children at home, and this effectively forces the wife onto the ordinary day routine so that the children can be sent to school and fed. Within the family, then, two totally different cycles are juxtaposed, and there is a very real possibility of incompatibility between them.

Each shift poses its own peculiar set of problems for family life. On morning shift the worker has the difficulty of getting up early without disturbing his wife's sleep. By the evening he is probably tired, and he is under pressure to avoid any sort of entertainment that will keep him out late, since this will mean a short night's sleep in preparation for the next morning and hence a mounting accumulation of tiredness.

When he is on afternoon shift, the main problem is that he is away for a good part, or even all, of the evening. The French worker would get home between 9.30 pm and 10.00 pm, and the British worker even later. Either way, it is likely to be a week in which he will see little or nothing of his children, and it will be a week in which, if the wife wants an evening out, she will have to go out alone. The shift worker's loss of contact with his school-age children, when he is on afternoon shift, would not in itself be so serious were it not for the fact that he will also be working at weekends, and will have difficulty taking his holidays at the same time as his children are on holiday.

Finally, when he is on night shift, the problem of sleep disturbance is reversed. This time it is the wife who faces the problem of getting up and of getting her children off to school without disturbing her husband's sleep. As we have seen, most shift workers sleep badly when on nights and this fatigue can easily lead to irritability and a strain on family relations.

Shift work, then, provides the family with quite an array of points of possible friction. It also effectively disrupts much of the possibility of maintaining the traditional ritual of family life, and at least to some people this seemed to be quite important. The shift worker is absent from many of the shared family meals. Especially in France, people felt the loss of most of the Sundays of the month since this was habitually regarded as the day of the family. And, of course, the shift worker was rarely at home for Christmas Day, or the New Year.

Perhaps more important, he tended to see less of his wife than the normal person, since he was sleeping when she was awake, and he was awake when she was sleeping. Times together had to be fitted in at odd and irregular moments. If the wife stayed at home this was feasible, but the situation became very much more difficult if she herself was on a daywork job. If this was the case, free time was necessarily confined to the evenings and could not be made up at other times of the day. The seriousness of this varied with the type of shift system. With the French systems, the workers had almost no full evenings at all. If they were on morning shift they ought to have been in bed at 8 pm; if they were on afternoon shift they did not arrive home until 9.30 to 10.00 pm; and if they were on night shift they had to leave home to go to work between 8.0 pm and 8.30 pm. Thus if his wife worked days the French worker hardly saw her. I did meet occasional people for whom this was one of the great attractions of shift work, but there were others who were embittered by it. The British systems were more advantageous from this point of view and the worker could have a relatively full evening when he was on both morning and night shift.

The fact that the French workers were relatively more concerned about the impact of shift work on their family life may in part reflect a greater cultural value placed on family activities. But it is difficult to avoid the conclusion that the shift systems that they adopted were genuinely more disruptive of family life, especially in cases where the wife worked.

The disruption of the evenings also had important consequences for the social life of the worker. Most entertainment is geared to the cycle of the normal day. The shift workers at Dunkirk gave vivid descriptions of their attempts to follow the *Forsyte Saga* on television. Equally, the cinemas catered for those free in the evening. Some of the younger workers regretted their inability to attend evening classes and felt that shift work was making it impossible for them to have any sort of career. Others were mainly concerned about the fact that most organized sport was timetabled for weekends and once more they were necessarily excluded.

It was difficult to maintain contact with friends — unless they happened to be shift workers too. One could not meet frequently enough to make the relationship a close one, and the shift workers found themselves getting gradually left out of things as their friends found it difficult to predict when they would be around. People were afraid simply to drop in, in case they were met at the door by a bleary-eyed man in pyjamas. Again, this problem of making and maintaining friendships was not something specific to the shift workers we happened to be studying. Mann and Hoffman write about their power plant workers: 'In both plants the frequency of visiting friends was less among shift workers than among non-shift workers.'[21] In a similar vein, Mott *et al*, report: 'One clear finding that emerged from the analysis was that the rotating shift workers reported far fewer friends than either day workers or other shift workers.'[22]

Shift work and conflict in the factory

In the 1950s, the French shift workers were mainly remarkable for their passivity. The unions found it impossible to get them to strike. This was perhaps partly due to a certain apprehension about the

dangers inherent in any sudden closing down of the units, and indeed
doubt on the part of the workers about whether they were technically capable of doing it without the active help of their supervisors.
But it was also felt among older workers that I spoke to, and among
union militants, that the shift workers were simply not very interested in militancy, and on the whole felt that they were being adequately paid for their work.

Then in the mid-1960s things began to change. The shift workers
began to join in some of the more partial measures of protest: one
shift for instance would demonstrate in front of the factory gates
for half an hour while the previous shift covered their posts for them
by working on overtime. Management responded by ordering the
buses that were due to pick up the shift workers that had stayed on
overtime to leave at their usual hour, and the shift workers had to
plod home on foot. But the experience did not seem to discourage
them, and the shift workers were soon fully participant in the union
demonstrations, and proved themselves both able and willing to
repeatedly close down the units to join in strikes.

When later the Secretary Generals of the various refineries came
to put together a formal report on the growth and causes of shift
worker militancy, they placed their major emphasis on the way in
which the unions had created a new consciousness of the disadvantages from which shift workers suffered.

For some time now, the unions have been creating an awareness of the problems
of workers on continuous shift work, — this gives fuel to their demands. The
response of the base has been all the sharper in that this type of work involves
real constraints. The reduction of the working week below 42 hours necessitated
a change in a shift cycle that had been almost universally adopted and that had
been practised for a very long time. The discussions for drawing up a new shift
cycle which took place within each factory created sharp differences, led to
disputes over the terms to be adopted, and so produced a deterioration of the
social climate throughout the industry. The demands concerning the continuous
shift workers are growing steadily more numerous.[23]

The analysis given to me by the union militants in many ways
resembled that given by management. They, too, regarded the creation of a militant consciousness among the operators as very much
their own work. Certainly, in the mid-1960s the unions turned their
efforts much more decisively towards the problems of shift work.
At Dunkirk, for instance, the CGT set up a special section for organizing the shift workers, and in October 1966 launched a new internal
factory journal, '*Le Posté*'. In their tracts the unions ceaselessly
evoked, and no doubt to a certain degree reinforced, the sense that

the operators had of the way shift work disrupted their lives, and of the extent of their social marginality. To take just one example from Dunkirk refinery's shift worker journal '*Le Posté*':

What is the life of a shift worker?

The nights, which are made for the human being to sleep, are spent in the factory. Sundays, public holidays, instead of being devoted to the family, for outings, celebrations, or family reunions, are spent at work.

How many times have we said: 'to think that we must give this beautiful day to the employer'. How often we have regretted not being able to take advantage like everybody else of the sun and the public holidays.

When the shift worker has passed his night in the factory, he sleeps for a good part of the day; he gets up dazed, very often with a headache, which makes him more irritable, and if by ill luck the children make a bit of a row, he gets angry, shouts, and loses his temper more easily.[24]

If the CGT seemed most skilful at evoking the sense of frustration of shift workers, the CFDT took the lead in turning the shift worker problem into a coherent set of goals that could be achieved by negotiation or by industrial action. In 1966 the CFDT Chemical Federation produced a remarkable document, called the *Statut du Travailleur Posté*, which was circulated in the form of tracts around the factories. The *Statut* was a statement of a great number of the demands that were to emerge over the following years as leading sources of contention.

From 1966 onwards, then, there developed a specifically shift worker programme of action: aiming at the reform of the holiday system, the right of transfer to day work, the provision of hot meals during shifts, an increase in the number of shift workers to provide better cover for absences and illnesses, and most important of all, the lowering of the retirement age for all shift workers to fifty-five.

In our British refineries there was no equivalent to the systematic campaign that took place over shift work in France. The main issue of contention was quite simply the amount of the shift allowance. This was often hotly disputed in negotiations, but it never seemed a real threat to industrial peace in the refineries. For the British managers, the shift workers remained a group of reasonable men, who preferred discussion to force. It was generally recognized that in negotiations the greatest pressure was coming from the craft side, and the completion of an agreement with the crafts was normally seen as a matter of more urgency than finalizing negotiations with the shift workers. And yet, as we have seen, shift work was as widely disliked among the British operators as among the French, and at Grangemouth at least, it was as salient an issue as it was for the operators at Lavera.

However, by 1972, some of the British managers were detecting a greater feeling of impatience among the shift workers. The Industrial Relations Officer at Grangemouth told me: 'Now I get the feeling that some of the younger workers feel that they are second class citizens because they have never really used the power that they have got. By stopping the refinery they could, after all, cause chaos to the Scottish economy.' In the summer of 1974, the Grangemouth shift workers did indeed go on strike for the first time; and significantly, it was specifically for an increase of their shift allowance.

Resentment over shift work then undermined any strong sense that refinery workers might have of being an especially privileged element of the working class. It neutralized the effect of the relatively easy job and a relatively comfortable environment of work. Moreover, it meant that high salaries were not seen as an unexpected windfall, but as the direct pay off for substantial discomfort.

Shift work is inherently problematic. Most shift workers in most countries find it intrinsically undesirable. It seems unlikely that any amount of experimentation with different shift systems will give a long-lasting solution to the problem. It is possible that our French workers were involved in a particularly arduous system that increased their sense of physical tiredness. But what is interesting about the Grangemouth example that we studied is that it seems that, even if it is possible to reduce to a relatively low level the tiring quality of shift work, this may only switch the focus of attention to the social disadvantages that it brings.

Quite how salient shift work is as a focus of overt conflict between managers and workers depends on the level of satisfaction with the financial rewards it brings, on the degree of explicitness with which people have formulated their own sense of the disadvantages that it entails, and on the readiness of the unions to formulate specific plans of action for improving shift work conditions. Once it has emerged as a major issue, management can no doubt take the heat out of the problem for given periods of time by well-timed concessions. But it is unlikely that it will remain submerged for very long, and if the emphasis on leisure values increases we would expect the price that is demanded for shift work to be raised.

Reorganization, manning and security

The theorists of advanced automation have been virtually unanimous in seeing it as the source of an entirely new degree of job security for the manual worker.[25] This was confirmed by our own data. Over the twenty year period that we were able to study, there was not a single instance of people being compelled to leave on the grounds of redundancy. This was true both for the 1950s when competitive pressure was slight, and for the 1960s when it became very much more intense and management became substantially more cost conscious.

This high degree of security of employment clearly meant a major advantage in conditions of work for workers in the advanced sector compared to their equivalents in industries such as the automobile industry where insecurity is chronic. It did not, however, mean that insecurity as such was no longer a problem. Rather, what had happened was that aspirations for security had come to focus at a different level. People were now primarily concerned about security in their particular job within the organization, about security of their hierarchical rank, and about security in the way of work to which they had become accustomed.[26]

A major threat to all of these came from management's efforts in both countries in the 1960s to increase productivity by technological improvement, and by reductions in the work force. The essential point to remember is that security of employment for the individual is by no means incompatible with a considerable reduction of the work force over time. As we shall see later, it is a question of how precisely it is done. In fact, in three of the four refineries that we studied there had been a major fall in the number of workers employed in the course of the 1960s; and in all of our refineries the question of manning levels had been at one time or another a central focus of industrial relations.

At Dunkirk, between 1961 and 1970, the number of workers employed had fallen from 897 to 672, a reduction of 25%. At Lavera, the work force in 1957 had consisted of 675 workers. By 1970 it was down to 458 — a reduction of 32%. After 1970 the numbers began to increase again with the construction of several large new units and by March 1972 there were once more 512 workers employed. However, I was told that this was probably an inflated number that would be once more reduced once the difficult period of the inauguration of the new units was over.[27]

Nor were the reductions confined to France. At the refinery in Kent, a work force of 1955 workers in 1960 had been cut down to 1396 by 1971, a reduction of some 28%. It was in fact only at Grangemouth that there had been no absolute decline over the decade, and even there, there had been a period of cutting back in the early 1960s when the craft force had been reduced, and a major relative decline because the work force was now operating a substantially expanded refinery.

Management in all of our refineries was committed to a policy of no forced redundancy. The essential technique that they relied on for reducing the work force was to exploit natural wastage.

The main trouble about natural wastage was that it did not necessarily free the posts that management wanted to dispose of. It also tended to be distributed fairly evenly around the refinery, whereas effective reorganization was usually best done by drastically reconstructing and reducing particular sectors at a time. The obvious method for clearing manpower out of a sector at a faster rate than was possible with natural wastage was through redeployment. The personnel of a particular sector could be redeployed into the variety of vacancies that had appeared naturally at different points of the refinery.

But here again, things were less simple than they appeared, because, if people were to be redeployed, what was one to do if the posts that were free were not of the same hierarchical level as the person's previous post. Management tended to take the view that the skill hierarchy was sacrosanct, and refused to commit itself in either country to permanently maintaining a person's grade irrespective of the effective position in the organization that he eventually filled in the aftermath of reorganization. Hence, although people had security of employment in the sense of being guaranteed some sort of job, they had no guarantee against demotion in the course of a restructuring of the work force.

While there can be no question but that, in comparison with other industries, drives to cut the cost of labour through reorganization were relatively painless, they were nonetheless not without their problems. And precisely because security of employment in the traditional sense was something that people took for granted, these problems could assume an importance which was possibly rather greater than they would have had in the traditional sectors of industry. For people who had come to expect both a predictable salary and a predictable evolution of salary, and who had come to base their budgeting upon this, the threat of demotion was clearly a very serious one.

Manpower reductions, moreover, not only had an impact on the individual's career and status, but they also had an effect on the ongoing pattern of life of the teams running the units. First of all, it had an effect on the sense of pressure at work. If manning levels were reduced, each individual tended to have an increase in his task duties, his work schedule became tighter, and his sense of freedom began to diminish. As Blauner correctly pointed out,[28] the ability to experiment depends on having time. What he did not point out was that the amount of time that one had was itself determined by the tightness of manning levels. With less men, the job also tended to become a more isolated one. Whereas previously it was often feasible for people to carry out part of their work in pairs, now increasingly they would be operating on their own. Their sense of belonging to and participating in a team would begin to give way to the increasingly individual character of their work. Finally, as manpower was reduced, the level of anxiety about whether or not people would be able to cope with crisis in the units began to grow.

One of the factors that makes the level of manning particularly problematic in process industry is that it is extremely difficult to establish criteria for assessing the technically necessary level of manning for running the units. This is due to the highly irregular pattern of work. When the units are running smoothly, the work load is relatively light. The moment, however, that the units are in crisis the work load escalates. If the units are manned in such a way as to keep to a reasonable level the degrees of work pressure on people at moments of crisis, then it is virtually certain that in periods of normal running there will be a substantial manning surplus. Conversely, if the units are manned so that people will be kept reasonably busy during normal running, then the operators are under very severe pressure in times of crisis. There is, then, no single ideal level of manning that will cover the two extremes of operating conditions.

The policy adopted in all of the refineries to handle this problem was necessarily a compromise one. Manning levels were fixed at a point at which there was some surplus in normal running, and some degree of pressure in times of crisis. The precise nature that this compromise took, however, was obviously a potentially explosive issue, for there was a clear divergence between the interests of workers and management. Management's main interest lay on the side of reducing the surplus during normal running as far as was compatible with the preservation of safety on the units; whereas the operators' main interest lay in maintaining a level of surplus that would reduce as much as possible the pressure on them during crisis.

Process production, by creating an irregular pattern of work load, makes the level of manning inherently problematic. But the situation is further complicated by the fact that the technical requirements of running the units are far from the only criteria for assessing man-power needs. Most importantly, the level of manning could have a major influence on the degree of constriction imposed on workers' lives by the continuous shift system. In particular, reduced manning levels could pose problems for the coverage of absences due to sick-ness, and for people's ability to take their holidays when it was most convenient to them.

In all of the refineries, a reserve group of workers was kept on each shift to cover the inevitable absences due to sickness and holidays. The real question was one of how large this reserve should be. The reserve needed to cover sickness was rather difficult to calculate because sickness rates went through sharp fluctuations. The problem was that if there were a large number of illnesses the units still had to be fully manned in order to remain safe. Apart from the reserve force, the only other means of coping with absences was to ask workers to break their normal routine and work unusual hours. For instance, people could be asked to stay on at the end of their shift to cover absences in the shift that was due to be taking over from them. Alternatively, they could be asked to come out to the refinery on one of their rest days. Either way, it was likely to disrupt the worker's family and leisure life in a situation in which this was already one of the most important sources of grievance about the form of work. For the operators, then, the larger the reserve force for cover-ing illnesses on each shift, the less likely it was that they would have to be called out to meet emergencies, or would have to work double shifts.

As far as holidays were concerned, the size of the reserve force was linked to the flexibility that the system allowed for people to take their holidays when they most wanted them. Given the require-ment that the units must always be fully manned, the number of people who could have their holidays at any one time was strictly a function of the availability of replacements. This did not appear to be a great problem in the British refineries where workers were pre-pared to accept the establishment of a strict holiday rota which guaranteed that over a period of years each individual would receive an equal share of the best holiday dates. However, in France, there was a strong feeling that a holiday was only a holiday when it was taken in the summer, and everybody wanted their holidays at about the same time. Perhaps this reflected a certain cultural unfamiliarity with the principle of the queue, but it was generally attributed by the workers themselves to their desire to have their leave during the long school holidays when they could be with their children. At all events it led to considerable problems for manning, and substantial frustrations among the workers. As one French operator put it: 'It's a war to get people to replace us for the holidays. You have to grumble and badger people. In our team there are three people who want to take their leave in August. If there are no substitutes, or if a substitute falls ill, we have to put off our holidays.'

Manning and conflict

The question of manning levels was central to industrial relations in each of our refineries during much of the 1960s. However, although the problem arose in each of our refineries, it led to very different degrees of confrontation between management and the work force. This can be partly explained by the situation of each refinery at the time, partly by the way management handled the problem, and partly by the nature of union objectives.

In each of our refineries management's goal was to reduce labour costs. As we have seen this threatened the security of refinery workers in two principal ways. It could undermine the individual's career expectations and lead to demotion, and it could have a sharp effect on the quality of life of the work team. However, the degree of threat posed by a reorganization depended on whether a refinery was static or expanding. If it was static, then both the threats at the individual level and the threats at the team level were relatively strong. If, however, the refinery was expanding, the threat to the individual's career was much weaker. Reorganization could be timed so that the reduction in the numbers manning the older units was carried out at the same time as the inauguration of new units. Since the grades in the new units tended to be higher, redeployment could be carried out in the form of promoting people from the old units into the new. This association between individual promotion and reorganization, in turn, made it much easier for the operators to swallow the effects of the tightening up of work at the team level. Hence, although reorganization threatened the traditional way of work life in all of the refineries, it was only a potentially explosive issue in refineries that were static.

The two most vulnerable of our refineries were, then, those of Kent and Dunkirk. In both of these the process of increasing efficiency proved much more difficult to handle than in the expanding refineries of Lavera and Grangemouth. However, Kent management, despite prolonged and at times tense negotiations, managed to carry through its reorganization without open conflict. At Dunkirk, in contrast, relations deteriorated sharply, and in January 1971 the refinery workers came out on strike over the issue. Kent management's success in avoiding conflict must, in good part, be put down to its willingness to interpret managerial prerogative flexibly. But this leads us into the complex field of the structure and use of power in the factory, which is best left to later. A more detailed analysis of the two cases is given in chapter 8.

Of the two expanding refineries, the problem of manning produced a markedly higher level of confrontation in Lavera than in Grangemouth. At Grangemouth a very extensive process of reorganization was carried out with minimal friction. At Lavera, in contrast, management and the unions remained locked in stalemate over the problem of manning levels from 1968 to the summer of 1971 when Lavera management cut short the dispute by imposing its own preferences by fiat. This higher level of confrontation at Lavera was again partly due to management's strategy for handling the issue, but it also in part reflected an evolution in union objectives. The case is interesting in that it may indicate the pattern that is likely to develop in the future.

As we have seen, there are two main criteria by which people may assess the adequacy of manning levels: the criterion of technical efficiency, and the criterion of the quality of life of the work force. Management initiatives are likely to be based on the first of these, but it is possible that the unions, on their side, will initiate action on the basis of the second. This is certainly what appears to have happened at Lavera.

The unions used the opportunity provided by the need to adapt the prevailing shift system to the new 40 hour week gained in the strike of May 1968 to try to force management to increase the numbers employed in the refinery. There were several types of shift system that could be adopted to cover the new hours, but some led to a greater surplus in manning over the technically minimum requirements, while others involved a much smaller surplus. The unions were fully aware that the greater the surplus the more comfortable would be working life, the less likely it was that people would be called out from home to cover unexpected absences, and the easier it would be to arrange holidays. In terms of their longer-range strategy, they realized that, if a fairly sizeable surplus could be established in the refinery, it would be easier to put pressure on management for a further reduction in working hours, since part of the additional manpower that this would require could be provided from the surplus. The unions and management then pushed for quite different shift systems with considerably different implications for manning.

This shows the way union thinking in France was developing, and the potential that exists for widening the manning debate very much further. If the refinery workers come to adopt the position that efficiency criteria are not legitimate bases for assessing manning needs, but the criteria should be related to the quality of work life, then clearly the field for expanding aspirations becomes almost infinite. If the problem of defining the technically necessary level of manning is already unusually difficult, the problem of defining the level needed for an adequate quality of work life in a way that would be acceptable to both management and workers could clearly become truly formidable.

In this chapter we have been looking at the question of whether the nature of work and of work organization associated with continuous-process technology are inherently conducive to harmony between management and the work force.

Generally speaking, it seemed that Mallet and Blauner were correct that many of the specific grievances associated with the work task in traditional mass production industries are of little importance in a highly automated setting. In particular, the work was not unbearably repetitive and monotonous, people were not tied for long periods to a specific work post, and work conditions were relatively good. On the other hand, Blauner appears to have been somewhat over-optimistic in his description of the positive rewards deriving from the work task. The commonest attitude towards work in all of our refineries was one of indifference.

Both authors, moreover, failed to take into account the possibility that automation would generate a different, but equally important, set of problems in relation to work organization. The first of these lay in the fact that automation necessitates continuous shift work. Shift work imposes powerful constraints over the worker's entire life pattern, and was resented by workers in both countries as a source of tiredness and ill-health, and as a source of disruption of family and social life. Our samples were not peculiar in this respect. Shift work has been shown to have these consequences in many countries, and at many different points in time.

A second major problem that automation poses for work organization is that it makes correct manning levels unusually difficult to assess — largely because of the highly erratic nature of work loads. Management and workers have opposed interests in the definition of adequate manning levels, and the issue is a particularly delicate one because the level of manning affects the danger involved in the work, the quality of work life on the job, and the degree of inconvenience that can be caused by the shift system.

Here, then, our data strongly confirm the suggestions of Pierre Naville. Automation does not eliminate sources of friction in the work situation; rather, it transforms them.

However, although these problems were inherent in the technology, and were central to industrial relations in all of our refineries during the 1960s and early 1970s, their implications for management/worker relations differed sharply between the two countries. In the British refineries the major issues about work organization were settled without imposing a serious tension on management/worker relations, whereas in the French refineries they led to confrontation and a substantially higher level of militancy.

5

The perception of management

The clash between the view that there would be consensus on the social structure of the enterprise, and a high level of harmony between management and workers on the one hand, and that the legitimacy of managerial power would become a central object of contestation on the other, was clearly so absolute that it was essential to get direct data on the way in which workers viewed management and their own position in the decision-making structure of the firm. We shall approach the problem in two ways. First, we shall look at the spontaneous criticisms that were made about management. This should reveal the assumptions about management involved in the workers' everyday thinking, and particularly the salience to them of the problem of the distribution of power. Second, we shall look at a set of closed questions bearing directly on the problem of power in the enterprise. These, of course, will tell us nothing about the salience of the issue, but they will tell us a considerable amount about whether or not, at a latent level, the decision-making structure is regarded as legitimate.

Types of criticism of management

In chapter 4, we introduced a question that was designed to obtain a picture of the types of dissatisfaction with refinery life that were most salient in the workers' minds. It asked people whether they would like to see changes in the way the refinery was organized, and if so, what types of changes they attached most importance to. Although we found that there was considerable criticism of work conditions, of shift work, and of manning levels, the commonest type of criticism focused on the role of management in the organization. At Lavera, this accounted for 51% of all criticisms; at Dunkirk for 42%; while in the British refineries of Kent and Grangemouth it represented as much as 66% and 61% respectively of all complaints.

These criticisms of management fell into two broad types. The

106

Table 15   *Types of criticism of management* (Q.21b)

Type of criticism	Lavera	Dunkirk	Kent	Grangemouth	
1. Technical	39	35	72	59	%
2. Relational	61	65	28	41	
	(N = 59)	(N = 54)	(N = 105)	(N = 69)	

Table 16   *Types of criticism of management*

Type of criticism	Lavera	Dunkirk	Kent	Grangemouth	
1. Technical	39	33	67	61	%
2. Relational	61	67	33	39	
	(N = 80)	(N = 79)	(N = 134)	(N = 93)	

first, which we have called 'technical' criticism, is essentially a critique of the efficiency with which management is carrying out the technical side of its duties. The second, 'relational' criticism, refers to the worker's subjective experience of authority relations, to the way in which the management/worker relationship affects his own identity. If we take the first criticisms that people gave, there was a marked difference in the relative importance of the two types of criticism in the two countries. Technical criticism was the dominant type of criticism in the British refineries, relational criticism in the French. (Table 15.)

It is notable that the pattern remains highly stable if we take the wider section of the sample for whom criticism of management was either the first or the second criticism. (Table 16.)

To assess the significance of this difference between the two countries, we need to look more closely at what the two forms of criticism involved.

Technical criticism

One major theme of technical criticism was the inefficiency of communications within the organization. Slowness of communications was seen as an important source of reduced organizational effectiveness. To take some examples. Information that was crucial to a unit about what was happening on other units on which it depended was said frequently to arrive so late that corrective action had to be taken in a crisis, and at a point in time at which it was already impossible to avoid a substantial wastage of materials. Requests for maintenance work took so long to be processed that faults that could easily have been repaired before they caused a breakdown were allowed to develop to the point at which the unit had to be brought to a halt, with a loss to the company of thousands of pounds in lost output. The slowness with which the results of the laboratory analysis of the product were communicated back to the units meant that for hours the unit could be quite unnecessarily producing an inferior quality of product. Workers had to wait months for new equipment that would enable them to carry out their work swiftly and more efficiently.

Criticisms frequently took the form of tirades against the increasing formalization of the communications process as earlier patterns of direct communication were replaced by written documents. The picture that often accompanies these criticisms is one of an organization gradually being submerged under a mountain of paperwork.

One of the complaints about the formalization of the communications system was that it acted as a screen between management and the reality of the situation. It led to a form of decision making that was divorced from a real knowledge of what was going on on the shop floor, and of the problems that people were encountering with their work.

There's too much pen-pushing. With less administrative staff and more people who knew the job with direct contact it'd be better. It was better with a charge-hand — everyone was more interested in the job then. It all takes too long now — too much paperwork. They have to by-pass the system to make it work. Your so and so has a graph on the wall. All he wants is to see that it's a straight line and he's happy. But if he went out and saw what was actually going on, he'd be less happy. (British)

Sometimes, however, it was difficult to avoid the impression that the criticisms reflected a belief that paperwork was intrinsically a bad thing, because it represented an entirely artificial form of work. The bureaucratic hierarchy was seen as parasitical on the people who were doing the 'real' work. There was a feeling that members of staff were simply generating new paperwork in order to keep themselves in a job. If only the Company would be prepared to ruthlessly root out all the dead wood in the staff, it would both make an enormous saving in salaries and, at the same time, make possible a simpler and more direct form of communication that could enable the whole organization to operate in a more co-ordinated and efficient way.

Too many chiefs, not enough Indians. Too many people in high places trying to justify their existences. One man in the field working, three people looking on (bosses), and three clerks to do the paperwork. (British)

There are too many people doing too much paperwork for one job. They are all fighting over it. (British)

It's the century of red tape. To get anything you have to go somewhere to get hold of a form, and then you've got to go and get the signature of two or three chaps. You lose hours because of paperwork. (French)

There are heaps of useless papers. We had to ask for a year to get our slide rule. There are so many bits of paper for a tiny repair. I think it's something special to France. (French)

Another important type of technical criticism concentrated on the selection and training of managers. In contrast to the complaints about communications, which were comments about the organization as a whole, these were often very specific criticisms of people's immediate superiors. The common thread of the complaints was that the managers in question were unable or unwilling to take decisions crucial to the effective running of the job, or to advise the workers adequately on how they should proceed when they encountered difficulties in their work. Some attributed this to the fact that their managers had grown doddery; others felt that their managers had simply lost interest in the job, or were bone idle by nature. Some of the replies were little more than a statement that the immediate manager was a half wit.

The efficiency is abysmal. I'm not a management hater but the management here is inefficient. If I'm doing a job and want a decision made my immediate fore-man is incapable of making it — especially if it's technical. He asks the next one up who doesn't know either (the engineer), and the engineer has to ask a fore-man lower down again. A job came in and lay on the ground for six months. After six months the foreman said it should be done, but he hadn't yet ordered the new part for it. (British)

Those in charge don't take enough interest in the job, they depend too much on the men to do it correctly. (British)

There are too many foremen who are not tradesmen. They have not served an apprenticeship and don't know what they are talking about. (British)

First of all, the managers are no good. We are led by people who know much less about things than we do ourselves. (French)

There was a rather more complex variant of this type of criticism. It was pointed out that whereas previously the ranks of lower management tended to be filled by the most experienced and skilled of the workers, now increasingly lower managers were being selected from young graduates who were destined for higher posts. This was

seen as leading to a situation in which the managers had a very extensive theoretical knowledge of the work process, but little understanding of how their theoretical ideas should be translated into practical
activity. It might be that this type of criticism is partly indicative of
a growing difficulty of communication between managers and
workers. The new pattern of recruitment to management may mean
that there is less of a common language between lower managers and
the men doing the work.

In the refinery they have brought in graduates with paper experience, but no
practical experience. They have education, but they can't help an ordinary
engineer. In the boilers, the engineer in charge hasn't the experience to understand the problems of the men under him. (British)

Technical criticism was, as we have said, primarily to be found in
the British refineries. And among the British workers, by far the
commonest criticism of all concerned the organization of maintenance work. This accounted for about half of all technical criticisms,
and was over three times more frequent than its nearest rival.

There was a fairly wide consensus that maintenance was the British
managerial problem. In the early 1960s one of the refineries had gone
to the trouble of bringing in an outside consultant to advise on the
best way of improving the efficiency of maintenance. The consultants came to the startling conclusion that the maintenance work
force was operating at about 40% of its potential efficiency. Both
workers and management in Britain saw it as a really major problem.
They had, however, very different ideas as to the causes of inefficiency. British management tended to blame the inflexibility of the
craft stewards, their reluctance to abandon more than the most
marginal demarcations, and above all their implacable hostility to any
form of work measurement. The explanations given by the workers
on the other hand varied substantially according to whether they
were operators or maintenance workers.

The operators clearly attributed part of the blame to what they
saw as the idleness and carelessness of the craftsmen. But the major
responsibility they placed squarely on the shoulders of management.
If the craftsmen were allowed to get away with substandard work, it
was because management was failing in its job of supervision. If the
maintenance department was failing to cater adequately for the needs
of the units, it was, at least in part, because of the way in which
management had deployed the work force in the refinery. If demarcations were allowed to persist and hinder the efficiency of work,

this showed that management had not invested sufficient effort in its attempts to persuade the craftsmen that a more efficient refinery was in the interests of everyone. So while for the operators the source of the problem was located in the quality of work of the craftsmen, the assumption was nonetheless that it was management's job to manage, and that the onus fell on management to be both more forceful and more imaginative in driving up the quality and speed of maintenance work.

Nothing gets done that needs to be done. There's a lot of neglect on the management's side. Take maintenance and repair work. Management gives the impression that it couldn't care less whether things get done or not.

A lot of maintenance jobs are left undone; the maintenance men just leave their mess behind them. Management just lets this go by the board.

Maintenance is disgusting — our favourite subject. I've been a technician in the army for 18 years, and the organization of maintenance here just makes me weep.

It's a question of utilization of manpower. We seem like two firms, as though we were a customer of the maintenance department which should be simply an ancillary service. It's a question of the tail wagging the dog. We don't get the service we should. We need an integrated force.

The maintenance workers took a rather different view of the problem. They were even more critical than the operators of the appalling state of maintenance, but unlike the operators they did not attribute this to management's failure to put sufficient pressure on the craftsmen, but rather to management's organizational bungling. There were two main things they emphasized. The first was management's inability to organize the stores properly. Whenever you got down to do a job, you found that the equipment you needed wasn't available. Nobody had seriously thought through what would be needed for the job, or if they had, they had simply forgotten to order it.

The system of work needs changing. I'm a machine fitter and I get a job stripping down pipes, but I can wait days for spares and I lose interest in the job. No one seems to bother. The foreman says wait till the spares arrive. Sometimes they never come, and the foreman says: 'Put it back as it was and don't bother'. They train you to do a job right and then you don't have to do it. It seems wrong.

Getting spare parts — it takes such a long time. They wait for an item to run out before reordering.

There's hopeless co-ordination between the stores and what the men need. The men are losing all interest, although they are wonderful craftsmen. The men come to work but just hang around in huts. The work is very badly organized.

The second target of the maintenance workers' criticism was the way the work was planned. Management didn't bother to make sure that the equipment one would be using would be actually brought to the place of work when it was needed. Even more seriously, there was no real effort to work out the phases of the job. When you arrived at the job you would find that some crucial piece of work, that had to be carried out before you could actually do anything, had been forgotten about. The maintenance teams would often be constructed without the right balance of skills to do the job efficiently.

The people in charge need changing. They are inefficient. We've got planners here that couldn't plan a light. When you go to a job everything is supposed to be ready but they just tell the foreman what job needs doing, and nothing is there waiting for you.

I would like to see better planning as regards the jobs. It's very poor here. For example, if I have a job to do, and the planner knows I have a job to do. If this job needs scaffolding the planner should have arranged it beforehand. Here you are issued with a card to do a job and you find there is no scaffolding when you get there and you have to go and get your own. The planning is non-existent.

The organization here is chaotic. They brought in consultants and then made the foremen's rise depend on performance figures, so the whole thing was sabotaged. Management doesn't iron out unnecessary delays by getting the right crafts on the spot at the right time, or even the right equipment. The average bloke does what he is told, but he has just given up now.

The refinery is a shambles. It's 80% management's fault that the men only work 4 hours. It would make you cry. We tell them that for an overhaul they are manning the job wrongly. But the foremen won't swop men between teams. They always get the wrong mixture of crafts. The foremen have a pre-productivity mentality.

The main objects of technical criticism were: the slowness of the communications system, the poor selection or training of managers (in particular of lower managers), and above all the pitiful way in which maintenance work was organized. But what conclusions can we draw from these criticisms?

One interpretation might be that this criticism represents, in some sense, a demand for greater control by the workers over the way decisions are made. But this would definitely be going further than the data itself warrants. There was only a single instance in which criticism of the inefficiency of management was explicitly linked with the need to develop some type of organization through which workers could express their criticisms, and even here the type of organization suggested was to be purely consultative. In all other cases the criticism was limited to an expression of dissatisfaction, and there was no suggestion whatsoever that the source of this dissatisfaction could be best cured by a change in the decision-making structure in the direction of greater worker participation. When we consider the issues involved this is not altogether surprising. The single most important source of technical criticism concerned maintenance work, but a crucial feature of this issue was that it pitted one section of the work force against the other. It would have been difficult to use inefficient maintenance as a basis for demanding greater control since the operators and the maintenance workers were sharply divided in their explanations of this inefficiency. Indeed a good part of the operator's solution to the problem lay in a much tougher supervision of maintenance work by management. They believed that the maintenance workers had already achieved too great a degree of control over the work process, and they wanted an increase and not a decrease of managerial power.

It is very unlikely, then, that the predominance of technical criticism in the British refineries is an indication of a desire for greater control. What is probable is that it reveals that there is an important area of consensus between management and workers about the main objectives in running the refinery. The British workers were assessing the organization in terms of the maximum possible efficiency of production, and, in doing this, they were essentially looking at the organization from the same point of view as management itself. They were judging management in terms of management's own yardsticks for the assessment of work. The workers were urging management to do their job better; they were not seeking to displace management. Clearly this did not mean that they were indifferent to their own self interest. The efficiency of the firm was undoubtedly seen as critical to its ability to raise the workers' standard of living. But the important point is that the organization was basically seen as a unity in which everybody rose or fell together. An increase in the efficiency of the enterprise was seen to be in the interests of everybody.

Relational criticism

The commonest form of direct criticism of management in France was relational criticism, that is to say criticism referring to the subjective experience of authority relations. Since it was this category that included explicit complaints about the degree of power that workers had over decision making, it is here that we come to the heart of the problems posed by the Mallet thesis. Does the importance of the category of relational criticism mean that, in France at least, aspirations for control had become central to the preoccupations of workers in continuous-process industry?

The answer is quite definitely no. If we examine the category of relational criticism we find that only a small proportion of the answers refer to the problem of control of decision making. At Kent they represent 3% of relational criticisms, at Dunkirk 5%, at Lavera 15% and at Grangemouth 21%.

Moreover, if we look more closely at the answers and distinguish between those who merely felt that greater consultation was needed and those who followed the pattern that Mallet indicates of wanting some stronger form of control over management, we find that aspirations for control in the stronger sense were almost entirely confined to the French factories. In Britain, some three quarters of those who wanted increased control were thinking strictly in terms of increased consultation. In France, on the other hand, aspirations were more radical and nearly two thirds of the people concerned seemed to want at least a right of veto over managerial decisions.

Only a small group of workers, almost entirely located in the French factories, showed signs of possessing the type of consciousness that Mallet had predicted. Moreover, the most precise formulations of the demand for control were in themselves fairly vague. The most explicit comments that we were able to find were these:

There should be participation by the workers — in the widest sense — in the running of the firm. (French)

The system of management must be changed. The workers ought to have a say in things. If the employer can fire someone — then the whole system is a dictatorship. One must have a director, but the unions should be able to control the director's power. There ought to be nationalization, but the firm shouldn't be run by the state. It's necessary to leave the firm some autonomy. (French)

To begin with the unions and the workers should be consulted more in discussions with top management. They should have a power that is more than consultative. Top management should take your ideas, and what you say, into account. (French)

The system of command should be a democratic one, organized with the agreement of the unions and the representatives. When they set up the Topping 5, we could have intervened over questions of safety. Double glazing ought to be put in against the noise, and there should be more men on the unit to make life better. We would like to make agreements with the Company — for instance over a sliding scale for pay. It's the Company that doesn't want to. (French)

Finally, it is interesting that the majority of French demands for greater control turned out on closer inspection to come from men who were actively participant in the shop floor union organizations

— including three out of four of the people quoted above. In Britain, on the other hand, the demand for greater consultation seems not to have come from the shop stewards in the sample but from ordinary shop floor workers.

If Mallet was incorrect in suggesting that advanced automation leads to a preoccupation with major organizational decisions, what were people concerned with?

There were complaints about lack of discretion and information in the immediate work task, about favouritism, and about confusion in the lines of authority. But by far the most important source of relational criticism concerned the degree of social distance between managers and workers. This accounted for 51% of relational criticisms at Lavera, 81% at Dunkirk, 69% at Kent and 43% at Grangemouth. It was felt that the managers had no real interest in the workers as human beings: relations were distant and formal, there was no contact at a personal level, and there was no effort by management to build a sense of community.

It's a waste of time training foremen to take a personal interest in the workers, because they don't put it into practice. (British)

There should be a better relationship between top management and the workers. The manager used to come round and talk to you individually. The top management are getting away from the workers. (British)

We're not very satisfied with the management engineers. They've a bad way of giving orders. There's no humanity at the level of the area supervisors. No human contact. Between us and those people there, there's a gulf, and that comes from money. (French)

Relations between the workers and middle management could be improved, and between the workers and top management. The middle managers have a work load that isolates them. It's no longer as it was before. We used to see the area supervisor every day. Now we see him once in two days. You never see the Director. Globet (a former director) used to come round every Sunday, and he could solve problems on the spot. For instance, problems about housing. If the middle managers had lost it among their papers, you could put your question straight to the top manager of the refinery, and in three days it was resolved.
(French)

Several factors may have contributed to a deterioration in the personal quality of the relationship between managers and workers. In all of the refineries there had been reductions in the ratio of lower managers to workers as part of the drive for greater productivity, and one price of this is that managers had less time to spend to get to know their workers in a personal way. There was also a shift in the type of person who was being recruited into lower management. Whereas previously foremen and section heads had been chosen from the shop floor, now, especially on the operations side, people were being increasingly selected on the basis of their formal qualifications. Lower management which had previously been the top of the career ladder for workers was now often little more than a starting off point for men who were to be quickly whisked upwards in the managerial hierarchy. This change of recruitment pattern may well have increased the social gulf between workers and management. The managers were no longer people who had known their subordinates for years as former colleagues. They had a very different educational background, with its implications for difficulties of communication and differences of interest, and finally the very fact that they were not likely to spend long in the post may have made it less pressing to establish satisfying personal relations than would be the case for someone who was likely to be spending a good part of his life with the same group of men.

But although there seem to have been certain general factors that may help to account for an increase in social distance between managers and workers, these can at best only offer us a partial explanation of the problem. For we must not lose sight of the fact that relational criticism was much more important in France, representing a higher proportion both of criticisms of management and of overall criticisms of the organization.

The point is reinforced if we look at a closed question that we asked, bearing on the problem of social distance in the factory. In order to obtain a common reference point we decided to focus on a particular level of the managerial hierarchy. We selected middle management because it was both a group with real power and at the same time one which had a regular pattern of interaction with the work force. The precise question that we asked was this: 'Would you say that in their relations with workers in the refinery, middle level staff, that is to say members of staff between your immediate supervisors and top management, are: very distant, quite distant, quite friendly or very friendly?'

The answers are very revealing. The French were twice as likely as the British to feel that relations with middle management were distant. 58% of the workers at Dunkirk, and 54% at Lavera saw them as distant compared to only 21% of the men at Kent and 19% at Grangemouth (Table 17).

Some French workers attributed this strain in management/worker relations to the authoritarianism of management, and the coercive form of control exercised in the factory.

Table 17   *Social distance between workers and middle management* (Q.27)*

Relations are:	Lavera	Dunkirk	Kent	Grangemouth	
1. Very distant	5	12	3	3	%
2. Quite distant	49	46	18	16	
3. Quite friendly	44	39	63	72	
4. Very friendly	3	3	16	9	
	(N = 196)	(N = 192)	(N = 198)	(N = 205)	

There's a lack of peace. If you make a mistake, you are immediately denounced by your superior who informs the whole management hierarchy. It's too disciplinarian.

You are watched over too much. They tell you: Do this; do that; what are you doing? They should be more flexible.

From the human point of view, you're treated very badly here — it's the foremen as well as the higher managers. I was in prison in Germany during the war, and I was better treated over there than here.

The strains in personal relations in France were clearly compounded by the recurrence of strikes. When a strike was threatened, it was often very difficult to anticipate how far-reaching the support for it would be, both because of the difficulty that the different unions found in co-ordinating their action and because of the somewhat problematic relationship between the union militants and the work force. This uncertainty undoubtedly provided management with a strong enticement to throw into the scales whatever weight it had in order to limit as far as possible the scope of the strike. An example of the way in which the workers could feel the coercive hand of management in a period of tense relations in the factory can be seen in the following three quotations. The first two come from young workers who had been drafted to a new important unit, where the question of how their posts should be graded was still under consideration. They complained that management used the question of grading to penalize them for their participation in a strike. The third quotation comes from one of the older workers. It both reinforces the point and shows how certain strategies of control could play on generational tensions within the work force.

As for relations with management, we don't have any. D. (a middle manager) told me that the decision over my grade was very much held up by top management because of my position during the strike.

We don't like to talk about politics because of the bosses. I was being trained for the post of control room operator with a grade of 200 (a very high worker grade). Then, in June, I joined the strike. The Director nominated me for safety duty during the strike, but I stayed outside the gate. We received disciplinary letters. They withdrew them after the second strike. The day foreman told me that as I had gone on strike I would be given grade 185. The management engineer told me that it was because of the strike. Everybody's afraid to go on strike. I know a chap who took four days leave to get round the problem. It's the young workers that are the most frightened.

The young are more frightened to go out on strike. They're afraid for their careers. And then the older workers are afraid that the younger ones could take their places, and some of them go back to work as well.

Two very different patterns of attitude emerge, then, from the British and French data. In the British refineries there was considerable criticism of management, but it was primarily devoted to an attack on management's technical inefficiency. Decisions were made too slowly, management training was inadequate, maintenance was chaotic. There were no signs that the workers wanted an increase in their power over the decision-making process. Their criticism was a demand that management should do its job better, and not a demand that it should surrender part of its power. The prevalence of technical criticism in the British refineries indicates a fundamental agreement between management and the workers about the criteria that should be used in assessing good management.

In France the dominant form of criticism was relational criticism. Above all, it focused on the social distance that existed between managers and workers, on the coldness and formality of relationships, and on the lack of any personal interest in the lives of the workers. The factory was conceptualized as involving a sharp social dichotomy between rulers and ruled.

In contrast to the situation in Britain, there was no broad agreement between management and workers on objectives, but rather there was a sense of contradiction. Instead of sharing management's concern for higher technical efficiency, the French workers were highly suspicious of it. They saw the drive for greater productivity as being carried out in a way which increased the burden on them to the advantage of management. They viewed it primarily in terms of the way it affected their human experience of work, and in this perspective it appeared as a negative factor disintegrating the community spirit of the factory, formalizing worker/management relations, and increasing the atmosphere of compulsion.

That there was this contrast between a greater sense of common objective in Britain, and of conflicting interests in France, is clearly

Table 18   *The motivation of management* (Q.25)*

	Dunkirk	Lavera	Kent	Grangemouth
Management is most concerned with the:				
1. Interests of workers	2	5	5	5 %
2. Interests of shareholders	75	62	39	29
3. Interests of everybody	23	34	56	66
	(N = 194)	(N = 202)	(N = 198)	(N = 205)

borne out by the answers to a closed question that we asked about the motivations of management. We asked the workers in each refinery whether they thought that management was most concerned with the interests of the workers, of the shareholders, or of everybody. Whereas, in Britain, a clear majority of the work force answered that management was concerned with the interests of everybody, in France, an overwhelming majority thought that management was only concerned with the interests of the shareholders (see Table 18).

On the basis of our data so far, then, we are obliged to reject both the hypothesis that advanced automation leads necessarily to a high degree of consensus between workers and management, and the hypothesis that it leads to an overt contestation of management control over the decision-making process. We found that the issue of control was not a salient problem in any of our refineries, and there were signs of consensus in only two of them. The evidence suggests that the situation is much more complex than existing theory would allow. What we have discovered is sharply contrasting patterns of attitude between the British and the French workers. The British did appear to have identified with managerial objectives, but this was not the case with the French. While not openly contesting the power structure of the enterprise, the French workers saw the enterprise as socially dichotomized and they felt that there was a fundamental contradiction between their interests and those of management. Whereas the British workers were urging on management to greater technical efficiency, the French workers felt that technical efficiency was being imposed upon them. The British workers, then, had an image of the firm that was essentially 'co-operative',[1] while the French workers had an image that was essentially 'exploitative'.

6

The legitimacy of managerial power

Problems of method

Our data so far have shown that control was not a *salient* aspiration among workers in continuous-process industry. What weighed most on the minds of the British was the need for management to increase its technical efficiency, while in France people were principally troubled by the coldness and distance of authority relations.

But to say that the issue of control was not salient is by no means to say that it was without importance. People may regard the formal structure of power as illegitimate, while not placing an alteration of the distribution of power at the forefront of their demands. Even though discontent may be relatively latent, it may still play an important part in determining the way people react to crises in industrial relations. Where legitimacy is high, we would expect management to be able to exert greater moral pressure for tolerance when it is failing to meet workers' expectations about salaries, or when it wishes to carry out fundamental changes in the organization of work. Where legitimacy is low, then we would expect the workers to react more sharply and more defensively to threats to their prosperity, or to their traditional working practices.

It was clear, then, that we needed some direct measure of the legitimacy of the formal structure of power. The problem was how to get one. Despite their concern with the problem of the legitimacy of management neither Blauner nor Mallet had offered the slightest indication of how one should measure it. The methodological problem, is, as ever, one of trying to unravel complex sets of attitudes with relatively simple and unambiguous tools. Whatever procedure was used, it was clear that it would need to involve a comparison of the way people actually perceived the decision-making structure with the way they would ideally like it to be. Given the sheer complexity of power phenomena, the hiddenness of the decision-making process and, sometimes, the interest of the main participants to give distorted accounts of it, it was more than likely that there would be a certain amount of divergence of opinion, even between workers within the same organization, about the exact way in which decisions were made. If indeed there was variability of perception, this would make unreliable any measure of legitimacy that consisted simply of a comparison between the way decisions were objectively made with the views that workers had about the ideal way of making them. Therefore it seemed essential both to examine perceptions and ideals and to make the measure of legitimacy depend on the difference between these.[1]

The technique we adopted was to offer people a set of three different systems of decision making which seemed to us to offer qualitatively different degrees of control to the work force. The first was one in which decisions were made by management alone; the second was one in which decisions were taken by management after asking the opinion of the representatives of the workers; and the third was one in which decisions were taken with the agreement of both management and the representatives of the workers. The first, then, was a system of unbridled managerial prerogative, the second gave the workers' representatives a right of consultation, and the third gave them a right of veto. We first of all asked people which method most closely corresponded to the way a particular type of decision was made at present, and then we asked them which they thought was the ideal way of making this type of decision.

A familiar problem in power studies is to decide what issues to select, given the fact that it is manifestly impossible either to investigate all possible types of issue or to meaningfully sample an overall set of issues. The only viable strategy lay in finding criteria for the selection of 'key' issues on the grounds that these were likely to have the greatest psychological weight in people's thinking about management. Thus we were looking for those decisions that would have the greatest impact on the workers' well-being — on the security of their future, and on their present experience of work.

It was first of all essential to include strategic level decisions that governed the long term economic future of the firm. These were the types of decisions that Mallet believed would come under attack. Two types of decision seemed of particular importance. The first was the basic process of financial budgeting — how much of the surplus was to be allocated to salaries, how much to dividends, and how much was to be reserved for investment purposes. This type of decision clearly conditioned all others. The second strategic level decision that we selected related to the more specific problem of the set of decisions involved in investment in new units. This was the type of investment that was likely to have the most immediate and direct consequences for the workers' lives. The construction of new units in a refinery meant an important increase in the level of opportunity in the factory, since it increased the number of high level posts. In refineries where no expansion was taking place, promotion chances were restricted to the vacancies that arose through retirement and death. Even more important, in a period when the emphasis was on increased productivity through the diminution of labour costs, expansion guaranteed security since it usually implied the need to maintain at least the existing strength of the work force.

The choice of middle level decisions, or decisions that governed people's more immediate experience of work, was rather more difficult because there was a greater range of possible candidates. The best grounds for choice seemed to be to select issues which the workers themselves had consistently regarded as of major importance. We based the choice on a reading of the documentation on industrial relations gathered from the four refineries. The documents covered the discussions between the worker representatives and management between 1965 and 1971. Three issues emerged as of predominant importance. These were (1) the organization of the three-shift shift system, (2) changes in the size of the work force, and (3) salaries. The shift system was, of course, specific to the operators. The nearest functional equivalent to it that we could find for the maintenance workers was the provision made to cover work outside the normal working day. In all of the refineries there was a need for an emergency maintenance force to cover the operation of the units during the night, and there was a need for special working hours to cope with the unusually heavy work load involved in the overhaul of major units. These needs could be met either by the institution of a form of shift system, or by the use of overtime, or by a combination of both. Whatever was the case, the arrangements were disruptive of normal work and leisure routines, and thus shared some of the characteristics of the operators' shift system.

Perceptions and ideals of power in the five issue areas

We set out then with five issue areas: financial budgeting, investment in new units, salaries, manning, and work time schedules. For each issue area we first asked people how they thought decisions were made at present, and then we followed this up by asking how the decisions should be made.

Work time schedules

In Britain there was a high level of unanimity about the way in which this type of decision was taken. Over 80% of the workers in both refineries thought that it was by agreement (Table 19). In France, however, there was less certainty. The commonest opinion was that management consulted the representatives of the workers, but maintained its right to put into force the system that it preferred. But this answer accounted for less than half the work force. If we look, however, at the overall pattern of answers there is an important contrast to the British cases. A substantial majority of the French workers believed that decisions were not made by agreement, whereas in Britain the reverse was the case. At Lavera 74% believed that these decisions were made either by management alone or by management after consultation, and the figure was 64% at Dunkirk.

This difference between the countries can be fairly readily explained. Decisions about work time schedules, in Britain, were indeed made by agreement. Grangemouth management, for instance, although deeply unhappy about the shift system in operation, limited itself to an attempt to change it through productivity negotiations. The proposals put forward by management were thrown out time and again, but there was not the slightest sign that management had seriously contemplated trying to change the system unilaterally.

In France, however, the situation was more ambiguous. In Dunkirk, in the 1960s, management had once changed the shift cycle of part of the work force unilaterally. The unions counter-attacked by taking the question to the State Inspector of Work, but the Inspector simply confirmed management's right to determine the hours of the

Table 19 *How decisions about work time schedules are made* (Q.28a)*

	Lavera	Dunkirk	Kent	Grangemouth	
Decisions are made by:					
1. Management alone	32	25	5	5	%
2. Consultation	42	39	13	9	
3. Agreement	26	37	82	88	
	(N = 197)	(N = 195)	(N = 209)	(N = 205)	

Table 20   *Ideal system for decisions about work time schedules* (Q.28a)

Decisions should be made by:	Lavera	Dunkirk	Kent	Grangemouth	
1. Management alone	2	4	4	2	%
2. Consultation	15	19	13	7	
3. Agreement	83	78	83	90	
	(N = 202)	(N = 195)	(N = 209)	(N = 205)	

work day. On the other hand, when a new shift system had to be set up to operate the new 40 hour week gained in the strike of May 1968, a joint management/worker representative committee was set up to discuss the new shift cycle, and agreement was reached on the system to be adopted. At Lavera, in contrast, the new shift system became one of the most central elements of contention between management and the unions. There was certainly consultation, and management even held a referendum to find out grass roots opinion. There was fairly continuous negotiation between management and worker representatives on the Works Committee. Ultimately, however, agreement proved impossible and management imposed its own system unilaterally in the middle of the summer holidays.

What is mainly remarkable about the French answers, then, is that relatively few people at Dunkirk seemed aware of the fact that agreement had been reached on the issue in the last major change of shift system. A possible explanation is that the unions were not eager to stress examples of agreement, since this conflicted with their desire to underline the incompatability of interest between management and workers. Hence, whereas the earlier failure to reach agreement had been widely publicised, the later agreement over the 40 hour week system was concluded with little union comment.

When we turn away from the present system to the ideal system that people wanted, there is little ambiguity in the picture that emerges. The great majority of workers in both countries believed that decisions like these should be negotiated.

Manning levels

For the question of manning levels a dominant consensus emerges in both countries about how decisions are in fact made. But, significantly, the consensus in France is to be found at the opposite pole to the consensus in Britain. A majority of the French workers (62% at Lavera, and 72% at Dunkirk) believed that management made its decisions about manning entirely on its own, without so much as consulting the workers' representatives. In contrast to this, a majority in Britain believed that this type of decision was made by agreement (68% at Kent, 60% at Grangemouth).

In their overall pattern, the answers accord fairly well with the way this type of decision was actually made in each country. In Britain, manning had on the whole been the subject of productivity agreements. The pattern was least clear cut at Grangemouth where management had adopted two principle strategies for reducing the maintenance force. The first of these involved offering individuals extremely favourable terms to leave. The second, which was adopted to eliminate chargehands and mates, was placed squarely within the productivity deal framework. The first case obviously gave less organized control to the work force, whereas the second required the consent of the collectivity. This duality of method was reflected in the relatively low figure for agreement among the Grangemouth craft workers (50%), if we compare them either with the Scottish operators or with the craft workers at Kent.

In France, management made no attempt to secure the prior agreement of the workers' representatives. The determination of manning levels, was regarded very much as part of managerial prerogative. What is much trickier to determine is whether or not there was consultation. The French managers were obliged by law to consult the Works Council over matters of organizational change. But, as we shall see later, the term 'consultation' can be interpreted in different ways.

The answers to our question by the French workers show that, by and large, they discounted the form of consultation that management was prepared to engage in as being largely a façade, and that they felt that decisions were taken by management unilaterally. There was, then, a complete break between the 'official' procedure for

Table 21 *How decisions about manning levels are made* (Q.28b)*

Decisions are made by:	Lavera	Dunkirk	Kent	Grangemouth	
1. Management alone	62	72	7	25	%
2. Consultation	23	21	25	16	
3. Agreement	15	7	68	60	
	(N = 198)	(N = 195)	(N = 207)	(N = 205)	

Table 22   *Ideal system for decisions about manning levels* (Q.28b)

	Lavera	Dunkirk	Kent	Grangemouth	
Decisions should be made by:					
1. Management alone	3	3	5	7	%
2. Consultation	16	18	23	15	
3. Agreement	82	79	72	78	
	(N = 202)	(N = 194)	(N = 209)	(N = 205)	

decision making, which was laid down by the law as one of consultation, and the workers' perception of decision making.

The sharp differences in the way in which the French and British workers saw the present way of making decisions in their factories contrasts with the high level of similarity in the nature of their ideals. Over 70% of the workers in each of the refineries believed that changes in manning levels should be decided upon only after prior agreement with the workers' representatives. The numbers seeing this as an area which should be by right one of unilateral managerial control are minimal.

Salaries

As with manning levels, the French and British workers differed sharply in their assessment of how decisions were made about salaries. The majority of French workers saw them as remaining within management's prerogative (80% at Lavera, 84% at Dunkirk), whereas in Britain the overwhelming majority believed that salary levels were arrived at by agreement (78% at Kent, 86% at Grangemouth).

In Britain salary negotiations were carried on at the refinery level. There were two main forms they could take. They could either be

Table 23   *How decisions about salaries are made* (Q.28c)*

	Lavera	Dunkirk	Kent	Grangemouth	
Decisions are made by:					
1. Management alone	56	65	10	9	%
2. Consultation	24	19	13	5	
3. Agreement	20	16	78	86	
	(N = 201)	(N = 194)	(N = 207)	(N = 205)	

uniquely concerned with salaries and in that case the discussion usually bore on the relationship between refinery salaries and those in local industry, or between the proposed increases and the movement of the cost of living index, or alternatively they could form one aspect of a much more complex productivity deal. Either way the end product was always a signed agreement. Very few workers seem to have adopted the position that these agreements were merely formal or that they hid the underlying power of management to determine the terms of the agreement. Indeed it appears to be a characteristic of the British perceptions of the power structure that they conform closely to the picture that one would get from a study of the formal procedures.

In France, on the other hand, responses seem to imply a rejection of the formal procedures as hollow and the positing of a 'real' structure of power which underlies them. We have seen already that few of the Dunkirk workers accepted that the shift system had been the subject of agreement, and equally there was a tendency to dismiss the idea that any form of consultation took place about manning levels. We now find a similar thing occurring over the question of salaries. In the oil industry in France there were formal negotiations at the level of the whole industry between management's representatives and delegates sent by the union federations. In contrast to the British system, negotiations were highly centralized. The discussions were often protracted, but they most commonly failed to end in agreement. The usual pattern was for the two sides to separate in disagreement, for the unions to publish their tracts to explain why management's terms had been wholly unacceptable and for the individual company managements to apply the increases that had formed the last offer of the management negotiators in the industry level meetings. Clearly there was little about these proceedings to suggest agreement, but it might be thought that they involved an element of consultation. The majority of the French refinery workers, however, regarded them as mere charades. It was often explained to me that the various managements had agreed long before the meetings on the final offer that their representatives would put forward, and that it was an entire illusion to believe that their position had been in any way affected by the arguments put forward by the unions.

In their ideals French and British workers were again remarkably alike. Only a very small number felt that management had the right to dictate salaries unilaterally. The great majority held that the decision-making process should be one of agreement.

Table 24   *Ideal system for decisions about salaries* (Q.28c)

Decisions should be made by:	Lavera	Dunkirk	Kent	Grangemouth	
1. Management alone	2	6	4	4	%
2. Consultation	11	21	14	4	
3. Agreement	87	73	82	92	
	(N = 201)	(N = 195)	(N = 207)	(N = 205)	

Strategic level decisions

The answers to the two sets of questions about financial budgeting on the one hand and investment in new units on the other were so similar in pattern that they can be handled together. They present us with a fairly consistent picture of people's attitudes about strategic level decision making.

The vast majority of workers in both countries recognized that these types of decisions were, at present, solely the province of management. This was true for over 70% of the workers in the French refineries for the question of financial budgeting, and for over 80% of the workers in the British refineries. It was even more the case for the question of investment in new units. Here over 85% of the French workers believed that management made these decisions unilaterally, and the same was true for over 90% of the British workers.

The real interest when we come to the strategic level of decision making lies in the ideas that people had about the way in which decisions should be made. This brings us back to the core of the Mallet thesis. We have already seen that Mallet was incorrect in asserting that demands for control over long term economic decisions were salient in the minds of workers in the technologically advanced sector

Table 25   *How decisions about company financial budgeting are made* (Q.28d)*

Decisions are made by:	Lavera	Dunkirk	Kent	Grangemouth	
1. Management alone	73	77	81	84	%
2. Consultation	13	15	8	4	
3. Agreement	14	7	11	11	
	(N = 198)	(N = 191)	(N = 196)	(N = 204)	

Table 26 *How decisions about investment in new units are made*
(Q.28e)

Decisions are made by:	Lavera	Dunkirk	Kent	Grangemouth	
1. Management alone	87	89	91	95	%
2. Consultation	6	7	6	2	
3. Agreement	7	3	4	3	
	(N = 201)	(N = 195)	(N = 205)	(N = 205)	

of industry. But presumably we could reformulate his thesis in a
weaker way and pose the question of whether, at a latent level, there
might not be a greater questioning of management's right to make
this type of decision on its own. In its new form the theory would
simply propose that advanced technology provides conditions that
weaken the legitimacy of managerial authority over high level
decision making.

In this form we find that the theory fits the French data well, but
poses considerable problems with the data from Britain. In the French
refineries, a substantial majority of workers believed that crucial
decisions about the Company's financial budgeting and investment
plans should be taken by agreement with representatives of the
workers. For budgeting this was true of 70% of the Dunkirk workers
and 80% of those at Lavera; for the question of investment in units
it was the view of 58% of the Dunkirk workers and 62% of the Lavera
workers. The French, then, questioned the legitimacy of managerial
authority in areas that were at the very heart of traditional managerial prerogative.

When we turn to Britain, however, we find a rather different picture. In contrast to the French case, only a minority of workers
believed that the work force should have a right of veto over the
really long-term decisions of the Company. The greatest support for
the idea was over the issue of financial budgeting. Here we find that
opinion is highly fragmented — 48% of the Grangemouth workers
and 32% of the Kent workers favoured making this type of decision
subject to agreement, but on the other hand 36% of the Grangemouth workers and 40% of the Kent workers thought that the
workers should have no say at all and that it was management's job
to manage. There is clearly an interesting difference here in the
legitimacy of the authority structure in the Scottish and English
refineries, but this difference nonetheless pales to insignificance the

Table 27   *Ideal system for decisions about financial budgeting* (Q.28d)*

Decisions should be made by:	Lavera	Dunkirk	Kent	Grangemouth	
1. Management alone	5	8	40	36	%
2. Consultation	15	22	28	16	
3. Agreement	80	70	32	48	
	(N = 201)	(N = 194)	(N = 209)	(N = 205)	

Table 28   *Ideal system for decisions about investment in new units* (Q.28e)*

Decisions should be made by:	Lavera	Dunkirk	Kent	Grangemouth	
1. Management alone	18	22	69	73	%
2. Consultation	19	20	18	11	
3. Agreement	62	58	12	16	
	(N = 202)	(N = 195)	(N = 207)	(N = 205)	

moment we compare the British data with the French. If we turn to the question of investment in new units, the contrast becomes even stronger. Here there is general agreement in the British refineries that this is management's job — 69% of the English workers, and 73% of the Scottish said that it should be solely management's responsibility.

For the French, then, the ideal system of decision making at the strategic level would be one in which the workers had a right of control over company policy, while in Britain the majority are in favour of a division of labour in which management retains its full powers over the most crucial decisions.

If we take an overview of this phase of the analysis there are four things that emerge as particularly important.

1. The British and French workers felt that they were faced by very different structures of power. The most crucial difference was that the French were much more likely to stress the concentration of power in the hands of management in the middle-level decision making areas. Unlike the British they saw themselves as largely excluded from decision making over questions such as the time scheduling

of work, the choice of manning levels, and the determination of salaries.

2. Whereas the account of the power structure given by the British workers reflected fairly faithfully the formal procedures for decision making, this was not the case in France. The French workers tended to brush aside the formal procedures as a charade and emphasize what they saw to be the underlying reality. In particular, there was a marked tendency to deny that consultation had taken place in situations where consultation was supposedly institutionalized.

3. In their view of what the ideal decision-making system should be for middle-level decisions the French and British workers were remarkably alike. In both countries it was felt that decisions of this type should be the subject of agreement between management and the representatives of the workers.

4. However, in their ideals for strategic-level decision making we find a marked contrast between the two sets of workers. A clear majority of the British workers felt that it was inappropriate to insist that financial budgeting and investment decisions should be subject to agreement, whereas in France the reverse was the case and a clear majority would have been prepared to see the extension of worker control into the heart of the traditional area of managerial prerogative.

The level of allegiance

By scanning the data presented above we can only get a very rough picture of the degree of discontent with the formal structure of power. Although a comparison of the 'perceived present system' and 'ideal system' tables gives us the general tendency to correspondence or difference for each decision area, it is difficult to get a clear overall impression of the extent of divergence between perceptions and ideals for the whole set of decision areas. Similarly we have little idea of how the pattern is composed. Are we dealing with a consistent group of people who are radical over each decision area, or is it a question of different individuals feeling strongly about different issues?

We can, however, go a stage further and construct a measure that summarizes an individual's attitudes over the set of decision areas and that would give an idea of his overall radicalism. This will also enable us to get a sharper picture of the differences between the refineries. We constructed our measure of allegiance in the following way:

1. We compared a person's perception of the actual decision-making system for a given type of decision with his ideal.

2. If the 'actual' and the 'ideal' were identical we gave the person a score of 0 for that type of decision.

3. If the person believed that at present the decision was taken by management alone, but wanted it to be taken by consultation, he was given a score of 1.

4. If the person believed that at present the decision was taken by consultation, but wanted it to be taken by agreement, he was given a score of 2. This type of discrepancy between 'actual' and 'ideal' was deliberately given a higher weighting to reflect the fact that it marks a much more decisive change in the level of control desired.

5. If the person believed that at present the decision was taken by management alone, but wanted it to be taken by agreement, he was given a score of 3. This involves a simple addition of the two previous types of score.

Diagrammatically the principles of the score construction can be shown in the following form:

Actual		*Ideal*
1. Management alone	score = 1	1. Management alone
2. Consultation	score = 3 / score = 2	2. Consultation
3. Agreement		3. Agreement

6. If the person — as occasionally happened — wanted a decrease in the level of control, and an increase in managerial power, then the arrows are simply reversed, and the score is recorded with a negative sign.*

7. The index of allegiance is then finally composed by the addition of the individual's scores for the five decision-making areas.

* (People who either did not know how a given decision was made, or had no opinion on how it should be made, were classified as wanting no change for that type of decision. If they had no opinion on more than 2 items, they were excluded from the index.)

Table 29   *The index of allegiance**

	Level of allegiance	Lavera	Dunkirk	Kent	Grangemouth	
1. − 15 to 0	High	8	7	49	40	%
2. 1 to 5	Medium	17	26	42	41	
3. 6 to 10	Medium low	28	23	9	16	
4. 11 to 15	Low	47	44	1	3	
		(N = 202)	(N = 195)	(N = 209)	(N = 205)	

(In each refinery the vast majority of the people in the high allegiance category were people who were completely content with the status quo, that is to say people whose overall score was 0. The percentages of the samples that actually wanted an increase of managerial power were 2% at Lavera, 1% at Dunkirk, 6% at Kent, and 4% at Grangemouth.)

Since the maximum score for each type of decision was 3, and the minimum score was − 3, the index provided an overall range of scores from − 15 to + 15. This is rather unwieldy and for presentation we have collapsed the index into four categories. The zero and minus scores have been placed in a single category, and the positive scores have been divided into three equal sections. In Table 29 we show the way in which people were distributed across the index in each of the four refineries.

If we look at the index we can now get a global view of the degree of satisfaction with the formal structure of power. The difference between the British and the French scores is striking.

In the British refineries the great majority of the work force fall into the high or medium allegiance categories. This is true of 90% of the Kent workers and 80% of the Scottish workers. Of these, about half are completely satisfied with the present methods of decision making. The percentage of people who completely reject the existing structure are minimal − 1% at Kent, and 3% at Grangemouth.

In France, on the other hand, we find a completely different picture. Very few people indeed are completely happy with the present way of making decisions. At Lavera only 8%, and at Dunkirk only 7% can be classified as high allegiants. Instead, what we find is that the largest single category of all among the French workers is the category implying the most extreme rejection of the existing structure. At Lavera 47% of the workers and 44% of the Dunkirk workers clearly want very major changes in the way in which decisions are made.

Although aspirations for control were not among the major pre-occupations of the workers whom we interviewed in either country it is clear that there were very important differences in the extent to which the French and British workers regarded the formal structure of power of the enterprise they worked in as legitimate. The British were relatively satisfied with the way in which decisions were made, whereas the French believed that power was far too massively concentrated in the hands of management.

Attitudes to industrial authority: a closer look

The method that we have used so far has clear advantages in terms of the ease with which it can be understood by respondents, and the speed with which it could be used.

It seemed, however, important to try to get an idea of how the more differentiated picture would look for at least one of the decision areas that we had previously studied. We therefore decided to use the more complex apparatus of the Tannenbaum control graph to investigate in greater detail people's feelings about the way decisions were made about manning levels. As we have seen earlier, there is considerable evidence that manning was an issue that mattered a great deal to workers in each of our refineries. Thus it probably gives us a fairly good indication of the type of changes in the decision-making structure that people regarded as most pressing in the general area of work organization.

The control graph method involves dividing the organization into a number of strata, and asking people how much influence each stratum has over the way in which decisions are made. The choice lay between four levels of influence: very great, quite great, fairly small and very small. It is probably easiest to grasp the technique by looking at the question we asked the English operators:

Q.29 In a decision such as whether or not to reduce the number of workers in the units, how great is the influence of:

1. The general manager — very great, quite great, fairly small, v. small
2. The assistant works manager
3. The section heads (day supervisors)
4. The shop stewards meetings with departmental heads, and with the works manager
5. The union
6. The workers

After establishing the amount of influence each stratum had over the making of this type of decision, we then proceeded to ask people what influence they would give each stratum in an ideal system.

The greatest difficulty in the use of the method was to set up a comparable set of strata in the two countries. While there was a reasonable degree of similarity between the structures of the organizations within each country, there were substantial differences both in the managerial structure and in the formal institutional machinery of representation between the countries. The critical task, then, was to find *functional* equivalences.

If we take first the managerial strata, we could equate the British General Manager with the French Director without difficulty. For our second level we took the highest level manager responsible for *one* of the major departments, i.e. the maintenance or operations departments. This gave us the Assistant Works Managers in Britain, and the Heads of Department in France. For lower management we decided to take the immediate day supervisors in both countries. These went under a variety of names in Britain, and were the *contremaîtres de jour* in France.

When we turn to the non-managerial strata our aim was to distinguish between those representatives that derived their power primarily from the fact that they were elected by the shop floor, and those whose power was based on the fact that they were the official representatives of one of the major national unions. The problem was that elected shop floor organization differed considerably between the two countries. In Britain the shop stewards had multi-functional roles, while in France their activities were distributed between the *délégués du personnel* on the one hand, and the representatives to the *Comité d'Etablissement* on the other. It was clear, however, from a reading of the minutes of these two bodies that it was the Works Council that provided us with by far the best equivalent to the British stewards as far as the problem of manning was concerned.

Once the data has been collected the procedure is to give scores to the answers for each stratum. Of the four choices given — very great, quite great, fairly small, and very small — it seemed to us that the interval between the second and third was greater than the interval between the other adjacent pairs. We, therefore, took this into account in the scoring which took the following form:

Very great	Quite great	Fairly small	Very small
5	4	2	1

The scores for each stratum are then averaged to provide a score for each refinery. The averages for each stratum are then plotted on

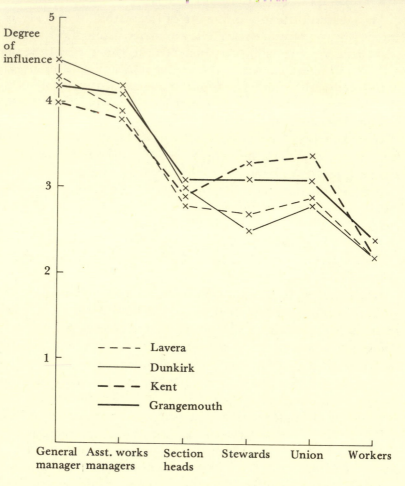

Fig. 2   Perceptions of influence in the four refineries

a graph giving a pictorial representation of the structure of power in each factory. In Figure 2 we show the way in which the workers in the four factories perceive the existing distribution of power; in Figure 3 we show their ideals; and in Figures 4 to 7 we compare for each refinery the perceived with the ideal structure of power.

We can see from Figure 2 the overall picture that people had of the power relationship between management on the one hand, and the workers and their representatives on the other. The level of control is equivalent to the differential between the power attributed to the refinery manager, and the power attributed to the workers' representatives. In three out of four of the refineries the union was

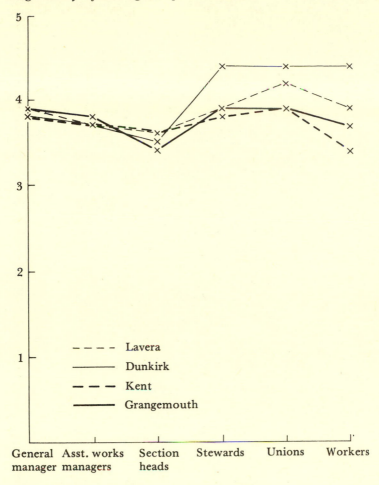

Fig. 3   Ideals of influence in the four refineries

seen as more influential than the stewards, and in the fourth the two
sets of representatives were seen as equal. For our measure, then, we
can take the difference between the power of the refinery manager
and the power of the union.

If we look at Table 30, which sets out these differences for
each refinery it is clear that the French workers felt that they had
much less power to control management decision making than did
the British workers. This reinforces the conclusion that emerged by
using our previous method. There was, however, a difference between
what the two questions measured. Our earlier technique focused on
whether or not people felt that they had *institutionalized* control.

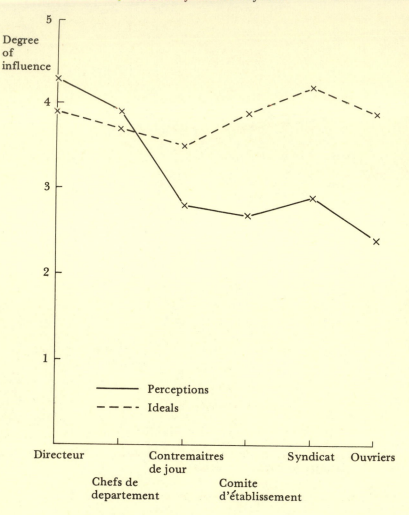

Fig. 4   Perceptions and ideals of influence at Lavera

Table 30   *Degree of control by the work force over manning decisions*

	Lavera	*Dunkirk*	*Kent*	*Grangemouth*
Refinery manager/ union differential	1.4	1.7	0.6	1.1

N.B. the higher the figure the lower the level of control.

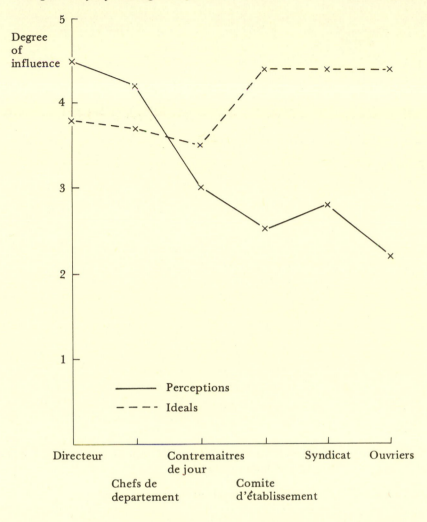

Fig. 5 Perceptions and ideals of influence at Dunkirk

The phrasing of the Tannenbaum question on the other hand allows the respondents to assess the power relationship in terms of all the types of influence available to them. It might, for instance, be the case that a group of workers felt that they had no institutionalized control but that they could effectively make their influence felt all the same — say by the threat of force. What the data here suggest is that not only did the French workers see themselves as formally excluded from the decision-making process, but they also felt a greater degree of overall powerlessness. The influence that derived

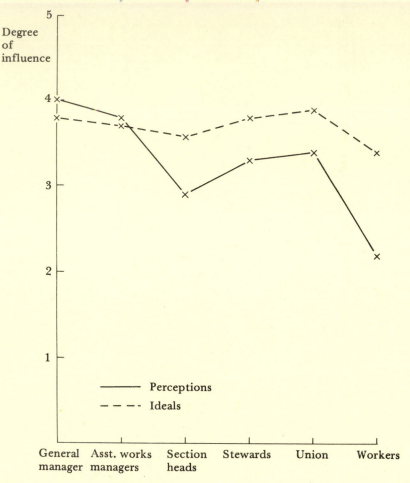

Fig. 6   Perceptions and ideals of influence at Kent

from their ability to go on strike did not seem to compensate for the lack of the type of institutionalized power that the British representatives possessed.

What type of power structure would the French and British workers have preferred? The overall pattern is quite clearly one of a much more even distribution of power across the different strata. In neither country did there appear to be any serious contemplation of eliminating the influence of either the refinery manager or the departmental heads. Rather it was a question of substantially boosting the power of the work force and its representatives so that there was an effective level of control. The pattern that emerges in France,

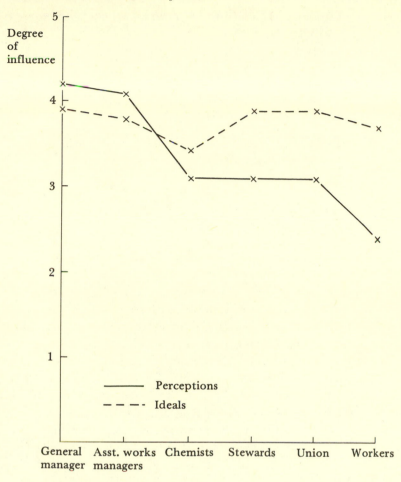

Fig. 7   Perceptions and ideals of influence at Grangemouth

however, is distinctly more radical than the one in Britain. Whereas
in the British refineries the pattern suggests a balance of power
between management and the unions, in the French refineries it
rather indicates a system in which the work force itself would have
the decisive say in case of dispute. This appears clearly if we take
as our measure of the ideal level of control the differential between
the level of power attributed to the refinery head in the ideal system
and the level of power attributed to the unions. In three of the four
refineries the index figure becomes negative, revealing a pattern in
which the work force is dominant, but it is only in the French refineries that the pattern is clear cut.

Table 31   *Ideal degree of control by the work force over manning decisions*

	Lavera	Dunkirk	Kent	Grangemouth
Refinery manager/ union differential	− 0.3	− 0.6	− 0.1	0

Table 32   *The level of allegiance to the decision-making system control graph Index 1*

	Lavera	Dunkirk	Kent	Grangemouth
Difference between management and union differential in present and ideal systems	1.7	2.3	0.7	1.1

The French workers, then, stand out as having a particularly low sense of their own power within the present system, and at the same time as having a particularly high level of aspiration. The tension between these two leaves them with a much lower level of attachment to the prevailing system of authority than is the case with the British workers. We can develop a measure of allegiance by comparing the management/union differential in the perceived present system with the management/union differential in the ideal systems. If we look at Table 32 the contrast between the two countries emerges clearly. The greater the discrepancy that exists between real and ideal, or in other terms the lower the level of allegiance, the higher the figure in the Table

We can refine the analysis a stage further by moving from the comparison of means, which is necessarily a somewhat crude indicator, to a measure of satisfaction with the structure of power based on a comparison of perceptions and ideals at the individual level. The construction of this index took the following form:

1. The aim was to measure the extent to which workers wanted to reduce the power of management and increase their own power. We decided to base the index on five of the six strata in the graphs — the refinery manager, the departmental heads, the stewards, the union, and the workers. We omitted the stratum of lower management because for this specific purpose the meanings of the answers were difficult to interpret, i.e. a belief that the power of lower management should be increased might simply mean that power should be

brought down to a level at which the workers could more effectively exert their influence.

2. For each of the strata, we derived a *stratum score* for the individual by subtracting the ideal score that he had given the stratum from the score that he had given for the present power of the stratum. Diagrammatically the score construction looks as follows:

Stratum — General Manager

Power	Present system score	Stratum score	Ideal system score
Very great	5	0 → 1 →	5
Quite great	4		4
		3	
	———	4	
Fairly small	2		2
Very small	1		1

The point to note is that the score was positive if the respondent wanted a reduction in the power of the stratum, and negative if he wanted an increase in its power.

3. As we wanted to measure an individual's desire to reduce the power of management and increase the power of the workers and their representatives we took the positive scores for the two managerial strata and the negative scores for the strata of stewards, union, and workers. The scores were then added reversing the sign for the scores of the last three strata so that the overall index score was cumulative. To take a hypothetical individual's score:

Stratum	Present	Ideal	Original score	Converted score
General Manager	Very great	Quite great	+ 1	+ 1
Departmental Head	Very great	Quite great	+ 1	+ 1
Stewards	Fairly small	Quite great	− 2	+ 2
Union	Fairly small	Very great	− 3	+ 3
Workers	Very small	Fairly small	− 1	+ 1
		Individual's index score		+ 8

The maximum score for each stratum was 4, the maximum possible overall index score was therefore 20. To have achieved this an individual would have had to attribute very great power to both sets of higher managers in the present system and very little in the ideal system. Equally he would have had to attribute very little power to each of the three work force strata in the present system and very great power in the ideal.

4. For presentation we have collapsed the scores into four categories. The first three represent equal divisions of the scores up to and including 11, the fourth includes the remaining scores from 12 to 20.

This more carefully constructed measure confirms the conclusions that emerged from the earlier measure derived from the average scores from each refinery. The French come out as considerably more radical than their British equivalents. Whereas over half the British workers fell into the lowest scoring category (59% in Kent, and 53% in Grangemouth), this was true of only 27% of the Dunkirk workers and 39% of the Lavera workers. If we turn to the highest scoring category we find that it contains 26% of the Dunkirk workers and 11% of the Lavera workers, but only 3% of those at Kent and 5% of those at Grangemouth. It is noticeable that the rank order of the factories remains exactly the same as on our previous measure. The highest level of disaffection is at Dunkirk, followed by Lavera, and then by Grangemouth. Kent remains the refinery in which there is the highest level of satisfaction with the existing structure.

While it is important not to oversimplify the picture, and to recognize that we find people with very different levels of allegiance to, and disaffection from, the structure of power in both countries, nonetheless the overall tendency comes out quite clearly. Whether we use crude measures, or more refined ones, we find that the French appear to regard the present way in which decisions are made in the factory as less legitimate than the British.

Table 33   *The level of allegiance to the decision-making system control graph index 2**

		Level of allegiance	Lavera	Dunkirk	Kent	Grangemouth	
1.	0 – 3	High	39	27	59	53	%
2.	4 – 7	Medium	28	25	26	29	
3.	8 – 11	Medium low	22	23	12	13	
4.	12 – 20	Low	11	26	3	5	
			(N = 190)	(N = 190)	(N = 200)	(N = 203)[2]	

Implications for the theories of Mallet and Blauner

In this chapter we have been looking at the question of whether workers in an advanced technological setting regard the formal structure of power of their enterprise as legitimate or whether they come to question its fundamental principles. The answer that has emerged from our data is that an advanced form of technology is in itself indeterminate in its effects on people's attitudes to authority. We found that two fundamentally different patterns of attitude existed. While the refineries within each country were relatively consistent in pattern, there was a sharp contrast between the attitudes of the British workers on the one hand, and of the French workers on the other.

The British workers felt that they had a fairly high level of control over decisions that affected them in the medium term. Decisions about the timing of work, manning levels and salaries were all seen to be reached by agreement between management and their representatives. Agreement was not seen as implying an equal level of influence between the parties, and the British workers would have liked to see a more equal balance of power. But, nonetheless, what is of fundamental importance is that the British workers were satisfied with the basic form of the institutionalized mechanisms of negotiation that had been established.

As far as long term or strategic decisions were concerned they were fully aware that these were outside the range of the influence of their representatives. But, while there was no unanimity about this, the majority felt that this was a legitimate sphere of decision making for management to keep under its own wing. The feeling was that it was management's job to manage.

The French workers, on the other hand, appeared to be fairly deeply alienated from the system of authority that prevailed in the enterprise. They felt that they were confronted by a highly centralized form of management that remained sovereign over the entire field of decision making. They regarded the institutions of participation provided by the law as largely a façade, and they tended to reject the idea that the discussion that did take place between management and their representatives even amounted to consultation. The predominant feeling was one of powerlessness.

If their perception of their present power was substantially lower than that of the British workers, their aspirations on the other hand were considerably higher. They believed that the work force should have the right to veto not only the whole range of medium term decisions over which the British unions had already achieved a considerable degree of control, but that it should also have the right to veto the very highest level economic decisions.

What are the implications of this for a theory of the social effects of advanced automation? On the one hand we have two refineries that seem to resemble the picture drawn by Blauner of a high level of consensus both about managerial objectives and about the authority structure of the enterprise. But on the other hand we find that the French refineries are much closer to the picture drawn by Mallet, although contestation remains at a latent level, and control is by no means at the forefront of worker objectives. It is clear from the very fact that we have found such highly contrasting attitudes in very similar technological settings that technology itself can have at best very little influence over people's attitudes to authority. We could, however, make a final reformulation of the available theories and ask whether or not technology might enhance or reduce aspirations for control within a given national context. This is in fact rather a difficult hypothesis to examine because at the time we were formulating the study there was little data on attitudes to authority onto which we could latch for purposes of comparison. We can, however, push the analysis one stage further in the case of France.

In their survey of the French working class carried out in the summer of 1969 and published somewhat curiously as *L'Ouvrier Français en 1970*, Adam and his colleagues included a question on the way people would like to see their enterprise run.[3] They were given a choice between control by the State, control by the unions, control by the whole personnel, or finally the preservation of the existing system. Our own experience with this question was somewhat unhappy. From the beginning of the pilot survey we found that people regarded the choice as rather crude and felt that they were selecting the least objectionable option rather than expressing their own feelings with any precision. Nonetheless, the question seemed to us to give a rough indication of the degree of people's satisfaction or dissatisfaction with the existing structure of their enterprise, and we decided to include it in the main survey to give us a reference point.[4] In fact the comparison between the answers that they obtained and the answers that we obtained is rather interesting.

We can see from Table 34 that, in the national sample of 1969,

Table 34   *How the enterprise should be run* (Q.22)

	Lavera	Dunkirk	National sample*
It should be run:			
1. By the state	10	11	17 %
2. By the unions	12	5	12
3. By the whole personnel	24	21	22
4. As it is	54	63	48
	(N = 184)	(N = 189)	

* Data from Adam *et al, L'Ouvrier Français en 1970.* To make comparability easier the non-response has been distributed proportionately. The total sample was 1116, and non-response for this
question was 5%. Non-response for our samples was 9% at Lavera,
and 4% at Dunkirk.

48% of French workers wanted broadly to maintain the present way
of running the firm.[5] If we turn, however, to our French refinery
workers we find that the same option was chosen by 54% of the
Lavera workers, and 63% of the Dunkirk workers.

Far from the contestation of the existing authority structure being
more marked in continuous-process plant, it appears to be reduced.
This reduction does not appear to be at the expense of that section
of the working class that has opted for some form of workers' control. Roughly the same percentage of the refinery workers chose a
system of control by the whole personnel as we find in the national
sample. Whereas nationally 22% of workers favoured control by the
whole personnel, this was the case with 21% of the Dunkirk workers,
and 24% of the Lavera workers. What we do find is that there is
considerably less enthusiasm for nationalization. Only 11% of our
workers thought nationalization would be a good thing, compared
to 17% in the national sample. In this Mallet appears to have made
a correct prediction. There are signs that workers in the advanced
sector are deserting the traditional goals of the working-class movement. But far from this swelling the ranks of those aspiring to some
direct form of self government it seems merely to have led to an
increase in those who have thrown their support behind the capitalist
system.

The question used by Adam and his colleagues probably under-
estimates the percentage of people who want fairly fundamental
changes in the authority structure of the French enterprise since it
fails to allow for an option providing for a higher degree of control

within the capitalist system. But it has helped us in two important ways. First it suggests that the pattern of relatively low legitimacy of authority that characterized our French refineries is one that characterizes the French working class more generally. This suggests that we need to look for explanatory factors outside the specific enterprise. Second, it indicates that within the French pattern the effect of advanced automation is not to strengthen but to weaken the level of contestation of the existing formal structure of power. Thus the Mallet thesis appears to be contradicted even in its weakest possible form, while there is slightly more evidence in support of the view that advanced automation increases the level of integration within a given national context.

Nonetheless, the clearest feature of our data remains the divergence between the refineries in the two countries, and the relative insignificance of the technological factor in determining attitudes to authority. One is above all struck by the essential legitimacy of the formal structure of power in Britain and its lack of legitimacy in France. Part of this difference can be traced to the fact that French management retained tight control over many key areas of decision making which British management had opened up to detailed negotiation. To this extent the higher level of dissatisfaction in France can be seen not as deriving from specifically French working class norms, but from a desire by the French workers to secure a level of participation which had been the objective of workers in both countries. But it is clear that this is far from the whole story. The French were not merely concerned to achieve the level of control that had already been achieved in the British factories, nor indeed did they limit themselves to the existing aspirations of the British workers. The French workers contested the legitimacy of unilateral managerial control at all levels of decision making, and even at the medium level the evidence suggests that they were more extreme in their ideals than their British equivalents. The particular characteristic of our French workers' attitudes to authority lay precisely in the tension between their present sense of powerlessness and their comparatively high level of aspiration.

Part three

The structure of managerial power

7

The machinery of participation

The second major objective of this study was to examine the implication of automation for the formal institutions of power within the
enterprise. We have already seen that the major divergences in the
legitimacy of management in the two countries were associated with
differences in the way in which crucial decisions were taken. In this
chapter we shall see that these differences can themselves be seen as
a product of fundamental differences between the institutional system
prevalent in the French and British companies. We can then turn to
examine the extent to which these institutional systems form part of,
or diverge from, the wider patterns within French and British society.

The French pattern

In France we found a three-tiered pattern of industrial relations. The
workers and their representatives had access to decision making at
the level of the factory itself, at the level of the company, and at the
level of the whole industry. Each level was specialized; it had its own
domain of activity and its own particular mode of relations. As we
shall see, French management was deeply committed to maintaining
this specificity. The French unions were dissatisfied with the overall
structure of the system and felt that it had been devised by management to serve its own interests. Their participation was reluctant and
distrustful, and they agreed to play according to the rules of the game
only for want of an immediately viable alternative.

Plant level

A striking characteristic of intra-plant relations in France is that they
are highly codified, and that this codification is to a large extent
provided by the law. The law lays down the ground rules by which
the representatives are to be elected, and specifies the field of their
activity. It ensures that the representatives have regular contact

with management and to a certain extent protects them from victimization. However, this extensive legal underpinning of the representational system by no means ensures that the personnel has a high level of influence in the factory. In the first place, the range of the issues that the law brings within the scope of the factory institutions is fairly narrow. Most conspicuously, it does not make any provision for the discussion either of salaries or of salary structure. Second, the powers granted to the representatives are highly restricted.

There were three principal channels through which some degree of influence could be exerted within the plant: the delegates of the personnel (*les délégués du personnel*), the Works Committee (*Comité d'Etablissement*) and the Union Section (*Section Syndicale*). The least controversial of these were the *Délégués*.

The 'Délégués'. The institution of the *Délégués* derives from the law of 16 April 1946 which made it obligatory in all establishments employing more than ten people. The delegates are selected each year by a secret ballot of the personnel. The unions were intended to have a strong grip over the choice of delegates, and the law gives them the right to put forward the candidates for the first ballot. Only if the union candidates are explicitly rejected by the personnel does the competition become open to all comers.

Their legally defined area of action was to bring to the attention of the employer grievances among the personnel about the failure to implement either the legal regulations governing work, or the clauses of collective agreements that had been reached between the unions and employers. Their primary job was to ensure the implementation of existing rules. In reality there was somewhat more flexibility than this suggested. The delegates could try to expand the interpretation of a rule by playing on ambiguities left by the regulations. It was also generally accepted by refinery management that they had a right to base their demands on the customary conditions of the refinery, and this considerably extended their range of action. In practice, they used their position to push for improvements in work conditions in specific areas of the refinery, and from time to time they used meetings as a sounding board for grievances that fell well outside the strict scope of their permitted activities. But management was determined to prevent them wandering very far from their rule-protecting function, and the weight of the law was fairly unambiguously in its favour.

Even within the recognized area of their activity, the powers of the delegates were limited. If there was a clear case of a breach of a legal regulation they could take action by calling in the State's Inspector of Work. In most other cases management was, in effect, its own judge.

The importance of the delegates' work in defending cases of individual injustice, and maintaining the standard of work conditions in the refineries is incontestable, but the scope of their activity was fairly strictly limited and they had almost no powers to ensure that their views were taken into account.

The Works Committee. The second and more important set of plant level institutions that could be used to bring pressure on management were the Works Committees. Like the delegates, the representatives to the Works Committee were selected by the work force from lists of candidates provided by the unions, only this time the elections took place every two years. The Committees similarly owed their existence to legislation in the immediate post-war period,[1] and the legislators seem to have intended the Committees to play a complementary role to those of the delegates. Whereas the delegates were to contest the employer over breaches of the rules, the Works Committee was to be a forum of co-operation which would draw together employer and employed. It was to do this in two ways. First, it was to administer and foster the firm's social welfare provisions for its personnel; and second, it was to be a setting in which the major organizational problems facing the enterprise could be discussed.

The management of the firm that we were studying believed that, in comparison to many other French firms, it adopted a very liberal attitude towards the Works Committees. For instance, in reply to union criticisms in a meeting in November 1970 the Director at Dunkirk made the following comment:

The Director reaffirms that at the Refinery of Dunkirk the participation of the Works Committee in the examination of organizational problems is extremely wide-ranging and active, much more so in any case than in many other firms that he is acquainted with. He underlines that he has formally included this participation among the general objectives of the refinery. (Managerial Minutes. 'Entrevue avec les Organisations Syndicales le 20 novembre 1970', p. 4.)

There were, indeed, certain indications that the firm's management was comparatively progressive. In the first place, there were regular monthly meetings of the Committee. While this might seem fairly natural in the light of the law, it was an improvement on the position in many firms where the provisions of the law were simply ignored.[2] Equally, the Company was relatively generous in the time allowances it gave to key representatives so that they could carry out their functions. In both refineries the secretary of the Committee — who was in each case also a leading member of the refinery's CGT union organization — was allowed to overrun by far his legal allowance of hours, and was at times virtually a full-time official.

The social welfare and leisure activities of the committees were also quite clearly flourishing. According to French law, French employers are obliged to give the Committee a grant which the representatives can choose, within limits, how to spend. Above a certain legal minimum, company management is fairly free to decide how generous a grant to make. By all accounts the Committees were fairly prosperous and they organized a wide range of activities. They provided recreational facilities from basketball to photography, they ran libraries, they organized holidays for the children of the personnel, and they even arranged trips for the employees themselves. Their oldest function of all was the traditional distribution of presents at Christmas. It was moreover a sphere in which the representatives were self-governing, and there was only an occasional sign that management wanted to interfere with the way they spent the money.

However, for questions that touched more important spheres of managerial prerogative, French management took a rather more conservative interpretation of the law and, in both of the refineries, we found that the Committee's role in questions affecting the internal organization of the factory had become a major area of dispute between management and the representatives. Legally the refinery manager was obliged to *consult* the committee over questions concerning the organization of the factory. However, the representatives of the personnel felt that management was consistently devaluing the concept of consultation, either by by-passing the Committee completely, or by starving it of the information it needed and by failing to take any serious account of their views. This was just as true at Dunkirk where relations were relatively good, as it was at Lavera where they were substantially more difficult. Time and again in the minutes of the Committees we find the following types of complaint:

M. B. intervenes to regret that the elected representatives are consistently confronted with decisions that have already been taken over questions of reorganization. The President contests this affirmation and recalls that the Committee has been extensively informed of the anticipated modifications in the structure of the organization.[3]

The Secretary regrets that the Committee has been neither informed nor consulted about the project for reorganization.

The President wishes to make it clear that the recent reorganization of Sector
D 532 was part of a larger operation: the setting up of an operational center in
Zone 1 about which the Works Committee has already been informed.

The CGT notes yet again that the Director has informed the Works Committee
after a change has been put into effect. We think that the representatives should
be consulted beforehand, so that they can give their opinion as was intended by
the law on the Works Committee (18 June 1966). Yet again, you have by-passed
us. (Dunkirk CE 27 Jan. 1969.)

At Lavera it was very much the same story, as witness the following scene in the Works Committee on 23 May 1969. The representatives have just been listening to the replies of the Director to their
questions about a proposed reorganization. After a brief suspension
of the meeting, they ask for the Works Committee to be reconvened
at a later date so that they can have time to formulate their own
proposals.

On the resumption of the meeting, the Secretary expresses the regrets of the
Works Committee that the suspension of the meeting, which was too short, has
not allowed the members of the Works Committee to make a judgement on the
reorganization after a detailed examination of the Director's replies to the question on this subject, and he requests that a special meeting should take place
fairly soon taking into account that the new organization is to be set up in the
near future.

The President [the Director of the refinery] declares that he is not opposed
to a special meeting, but that he does not see the point of it. Furthermore, he
points out that he will be very busy in the month of June, and that he has no
intention of discussing matters that go beyond those that he has to discuss.

The Secretary is of the opinion that the meeting could be very short because
it is uniquely a question of letting the President know the Works Committee's
position.

The President declares that he cannot guarantee his presence at this meeting
as it is a matter of taking note of the decision of the Committee, and that he
will send someone to represent him if it is necessary. He considers that as far as
the practical side is concerned, the reorganization has been studied and carefully
reflected upon.

The Secretary remarks that the words of the President seem to signify that
he does not intend to take into account the Committee's remarks.

The amount of power that management was prepared to allow
the Committees did indeed appear to be very small. At the very most
they were allowed to discuss the implementation of management
decisions and secure certain alterations of detail. They were entirely
excluded from the strategic choice that lay at the roots of management's plan. On the whole, as one departmental manager at Lavera

put it, management interpreted its obligation to inform and consult primarily as an obligation to inform.

The union section. The French unions only obtained the legal right to organize within the factory in December 1968, when, in the wake of the general strike of May, Parliament passed the law on the union section. The effect of the law in our refineries, however, was almost entirely an indirect one. The oil companies in France had long taken a relatively lenient attitude towards the activities of union militants on the shop floor. Most of the specific rights ensured by the law had already been acquired *de facto* in both of the refineries.

Where the law did have a certain impact was in heightening, and to a certain extent reformulating, the long standing controversies over the existing plant-level institutions. This was possible because it had remained silent over the crucial question of the role to be attributed to the union section in the factory, and the way it was to fit in with the institutions already in existence. This meant that the French employers and unions were able to confront each other with equally sound, but mutually contradictory, interpretations of what the legislators had intended to do.

The unions claimed that the law was clearly designed to bring about a major modification of the representational system, in which the elected bodies would now come to play a secondary role while the unions took over the discussion with management of all the really important issues affecting factory life. Management, on the other hand, claimed that, if the law had intended to give such powers to the unions, this would have been made explicit. The true aim of the law, it argued, was simply to extend to less fortunate workers the advantages that the oil companies had already voluntarily given. As such the law had no relevance at all for refinery relations.

In practice, it was management's view that prevailed, although it did go some way towards granting the unions an enhanced representational status by agreeing to hold occasional meetings with the union representatives to hear their grievances.

Despite, then, the importance with which it was initially greeted by both management and union spokesmen at the national level, the law on the union section had made no appreciable difference to the pattern of plant relations in the refineries we were studying. Management treated its occasional meetings with the union representatives as little more than another channel for the exchange of information,

and it insisted that the Works Committee should have formal priority
for the purposes of discussion.

At plant level, then, the main institution through which the workers
could hope to exercise a certain degree of influence over decision
making was the Works Committee. The *Délégués* were confined
effectively to contesting breaches of existing rules, and management
firmly rejected the claims of the unions to any form of control
within the plant.

Management was concerned that the Works Committee should be
a going concern. It met regularly, time allocations were relatively
generous, and the representatives were allowed to use it as a sounding board for their grievances. But for questions of work organization,
management interpreted the law conservatively. It tended to inform
the Committee of its plans in fairly general terms, and it withheld
the information which would have allowed more effective contestation. Management remained sovereign within the plant and the control
exercised by the Works Committee was slight.

Industry level

Although French management rejected the right of the unions to
negotiate at plant level, it was prepared to meet them and negotiate
at industry level. Here, in the vast assemblies of the Parity Commissions, the oil company employers grouped in their union — the *Union
des Chambres Syndicales de l'Industrie du Pétrole* — confronted the
five unions representing the personnel (SCIP, CGT, FO, CFDT and
CFTC).

There were principally two types of meetings. The first, and least
frequent, concerned the modification of the *Convention Collective
Nationale* — the industry's collective agreement. This was in many
ways the centrepiece of industrial relations in the oil industry, and
represented the accumulated rights that had been acquired by the
employees in their terms of employment. The basic formula of the
collective agreement was again heavily conditioned by the law which
laid out in detail the range of issues with which it had to be concerned. But its importance lay in the fact that its provisions were
often substantially more favourable to the workers than the rights
they derived from general labour law, and it gave them one of their

most powerful means for containing the range of managerial prerogative. It covered issues as diverse as the conditions governing recruitment and dismissal, retirement, holidays, absence for illness or acci-
dents, maternity leave, work conditions, the institutions of representation, and the structure of the salary system. At its heart lay a
complex scheme in which the entire range of jobs available in the oil
industry were classified and given a coefficient which determined
their minimum salary. Much of the negotiation centering on the collective agreement was focused on this system of classification, in an
attempt to keep its unwieldy structure in some degree of conformity
with the realities of the demands of work posts that were constantly
evolving under the pressure of technical change.

Discussions over change in the collective agreement were notable
for the length of time over which they extended. Negotiations to
simplify the classification system appear to have taken some eight
years before they were finally brought to fruition in 1971.[4] At least
three years had been taken over the discussions about the re-evalua-
tions of work-post classifications that resulted in an agreement in
1973. In April of 1975, we find Force Ouvrière dismally recalling
that a whole series of negotiations covering security of employment,
the use of contracting enterprises, and the treatment of shift workers,
that had originally been started between March 1968 and December
1970 had still produced no tangible results.[5] While, then, there did
appear to be some room here for positive results, the sheer length of
the negotiations ensured that agreements were few and far between.

The most frequent type of meeting of the Parity Commissions
dealt with salaries. It was here and here alone that French management was prepared to negotiate salaries. Although the discussions
concentrated not only on the minimum salaries of each grade but also
on what were termed 'real' salaries, this apparent comprehensiveness
was somewhat an illusion. The negotiations that took place only
affected a proportion of what would have been regarded as the overall
salary in the British refineries. The chief management negotiator in
1972 was reported to have said that whatever management gave in a
Parity Commission was invariably at least doubled within the enterprise itself.[6] The remaining part of the salary was made up of a wide
variety of bonuses that were determined by the individual companies
and that remained entirely discretionary. French management, by
adopting the position that it would only discuss salaries in the Parity
Commissions effectively excluded the right to negotiate on the overall
pay packet.

The meetings were usually held two or three times a year. There was no fixed timetable for calling them. The usual procedure was for the unions to demand that a Parity Commission be called and for management to determine when the meeting should be held, although there were cases when the employers themselves took the initiative. When they were finally held, most meetings failed.

The very high failure rate of the meetings can be seen from Table 35 where we have used union tracts to analyse the results of Parity Commissions on salaries between the beginning of 1967 and June 1975. Sixteen of the twenty-four meetings ended with the two sides entirely unable to agree with what was a reasonable offer. In these

Table 35   *The results of salary negotiations 1967–June 1975*

Date of negotiation	Agreement	No agreement
8 février 1967		X
1 juin 1967		X
18 janvier 1968		X
13 mars 1968		X
9/10 mai 1968		X
29/31 mai 1968	X	
22 janvier 1969		X*
26 mars 1969		X
26 septembre 1970		X
19/20 février 1970		X
22 septembre 1970	X	
1 avril 1971		X
2 juillet 1971		X
21 septembre 1971		X
2 mars 1972		X†
14 avril 1972		X
19 septembre 1972	X	
6 février 1973		X
6 septembre 1973	X	
8 février 1974		X
6 avril 1974		X
7 juin 1974	X	
18 février 1975		X
10 juin 1975	X	
	—	—
	6	18

* Blocked by dispute SCIP/CGC.
† Blocked by dispute   FO/CFDT.

cases the President of the Employers' Delegation simply recommended a figure to the managements of the different companies, and they applied this unilaterally. Two more of the meetings failed to get off the ground at all because of disagreement about who were legitimate negotiators on the employees' side.

Six of the negotiations ended in signed agreements. On closer inspection, however, these are rather less successful than they at first appear. The crucial point to remember is that in French law an agreement is valid if it is signed by any one of the unions that are officially classified as 'representative', even if the union in question represents only a very small section of the work force.

The first of the agreements in the list was the nearest to an agreement in the usual sense of the word. It was signed by all the major unions representing the work force. It was one of the agreements that brought to an end the nationwide strike of May 1968, when the government was putting immense pressure on all employers to try to stem what looked at the time like a possible threat of revolution.

The agreement that followed — in September 1970 — represented a real achievement in that it involved a more flexible and creative approach to bargaining, and saw the first major innovation in the type of agreement the employers were willing to consider. It accepted the principle that the CFDT had been struggling for — namely a system of pay increases that would reduce the differential between the higher and the lower paid posts in the job hierarchy. The main drawback was that by far the most powerful union on the shop floor — the CGT — disapproved of the principle and refused to sign, and this clearly undercut a good deal of the moral weight of the agreement.

The four remaining agreements on the list were even flimsier. They were signed by FO, which is the smallest of the unions and represents only a very small fraction of the work force.

In sum, four of the six agreements between 1967 and 1975 were signed by unions that could by no stretch of the imagination be seen as really representative of the work force. If we were to take as an indicator of genuine agreement negotiations that gained the consent of the most powerful of the workers' unions — the CGT, we would be left with one solitary agreement between 1967 and 1975. Moreover, it is clear from the tracts of the period that there had been no signed agreement by any of the major unions (including FO) in the whole period between the summer of 1963 and the strike of May

1968, which leaves us in all with only one successfully concluded negotiation in a time span of twelve years.

Company level

For the unions, the major disadvantage with industry-level negotiations was that they were fundamentally concerned with establishing minimum standards and gave little control over what was actually being practised within the enterprise. Most of the major companies had granted 'privileges' to their employeees that substantially exceeded the provisions of the collective agreement, and, as we have seen, the industry-level negotiations over salaries related to only a part of the overall salary a worker received. These benefits over and above what was obtained at industry level represented then a series of rewards that were entirely at the discretion of the Company managements, and to the unions they represented a formidable lever of power with which management could control the work force. For the unions it was essential to gain some degree of control over this discretionary power, and to do so required the opening up of negotiations directly with the Company.

In the 1960s, the only channel through which the unions could influence central Company policy was the Central Company Committee (*le Comité Central d'Entreprise*). The members of this Central Committee are selected by the Works Committees in the individual plants.

The principal function of the meetings of the Central Committee was that they provided an occasion when management informed the personnel of the economic fortunes of the firm during the year. Actual discussion, however, of the Company's economic strategy was very limited indeed. For instance, when crisis did apparently face the Company in the winter of 1974, the representatives declared that they were simply not able to obtain the type of information that they needed to make any serious analysis of the crisis. Equally management was fairly cagey about the measures it proposed to take. Having explained that one of the principal strategies it intended to adopt was a rapid diversification of the Company's activities, it immediately swept these proposals out of the scope for discussion:

In a whole series of fields, we have undertaken an effort to develop our existing activities and to explore new possibilities, and this is beginning to bear fruit. In the very interest of the success of these operations, I must be discreet about our objectives. Each of our achievements will be announced when the time comes. (CCE. Réunion Ordinaire des 10 et 11 décembre 1974.)

The Central Committee meetings did also provide a forum in which the representatives could demand extensions of the existing social benefits provided by the Company. But the amount of weight behind these demands was pretty slight. Management was not obliged to enter into prolonged discussions over the issues raised, and its replies to questions about social benefits tended to be short and to the point. It certainly made concessions, but these remained acts of managerial generosity, and the unions had a hard time trying to convince the workers that they had in some sense been forced out of management in meetings of the CCE.

As with the Works Committees, the Central Company Committee was inimical to efforts by the representatives to control decision making, and the legislation in force could be, and was, interpreted by management as an obligation to do little more than to inform. For the unions, then, a central aim was to by-pass the Central Committee and increase their influence by opening up an area of real negotiation between Company management and the union organizations. (We will see in chapter 10 that this was a union objective in both the traditional and the advanced sectors of industry.)

The law of December 1968 on the Union section gave an added impetus to their demand. Whereas previously they had requested negotiation with the Company largely on the grounds that the Parity Commissions were paralysed and were clearly not fulfilling their correct function, now the justification became one of legal right. As we have seen, the law was in fact wholly unspecific about the rights of representation to be accorded to the unions, but it could certainly be seen as putting a certain moral pressure on management to increase their involvement. The Company had traditionally opted for a relatively progressive industrial relations policy, and its response to the new law was wholly in character. The essence of its strategy was to exclude the unions from any form of plant-level bargaining, but to make a move in the direction of the law by enhancing their role at Company level. The crucial limitation to the extent to which this could be done was the Company's determination not to infringe any of the major powers that had traditionally been reserved to the Parity Commissions. The new level of negotiation had, then, to be introduced in a way that left the old fundamentally intact.

The first opportunity for the unions to play a more direct role at

Company level came over the issue of profit sharing. This had its
origin in the Ordinance of August 1967 — one of the centrepieces of
de Gaulle's scheme of creating a new type of participatory society
that would avoid the 'twin evils' of capitalism and socialism.[7] Although the Company fell outside the provisions of the ordinance
(its taxable profits were too low), its management decided to volun-
teer a scheme. Management laid down unilaterally the amount that
it was prepared to put into the scheme (approximately 2 million
francs, or the equivalent of 1.20% of its overall salary bill), but it
agreed to allow the unions to negotiate some of the details of its
application.

But these negotiations had a somewhat exceptional character. It
was a once and for all type of negotiation that did not in itself establish much in the way of a new principle. What it did do was to build
up a certain practice of constructive negotiation that could later be
built upon. This reaped its fruits in 1971. Faced with a steadily rising
wave of shift worker discontent since the mid-1960s, Company
management decided that it needed to make a decisive gesture to
bring the situation under control. To do this, it offered the shift
workers a substantial number of concessions and, in an effort to
ensure the maximum consent, it invited the unions to negotiate on
them. The result was the *Protocole D'Accord* of July 1971[8] This
marked a more decided break with past practice. It involved a more
positive recognition of the position of the unions within the Company than in the past, by conceding them the right to negotiate over
a limited problem area that was likely to re-emerge in the future.
Whether management realized it at the time or not, it had established
a precedent, and the unions moved on to consolidate the breach
with another, if more modest, agreement concerning the problems
of shift work in the summer of 1973.

The early 1970s did, then, see a certain evolution in the industrial
relations system that had prevailed in the 1950s and the 1960s. But
the change remained a limited one. Indeed, compared with the wide-
ranging system of negotiation within the Company that the unions
would like to have seen, it represented little more than a minor first
step. The crucial pillars of the traditional system remained intact.
Management's authority within the factory was untouched, salary
negotiations were still only allowed within the context of the Parity
Commissions, and the Company retained its discretionary power
over its share of the employees' salary.

The British pattern

In contrast to the three-tiered pattern in France, the British system was highly decentralized and based almost entirely on the individual refinery. There was no national agreement, and there were no negotiations at company level. The formal responsibility for all discussions with the workers' representatives — whether they concerned the grading system, the hours of work, holidays, work organization, or salaries, lay with the general manager of each refinery. The system departed sharply from the classic two-tier system that characterizes much of British industry,[9] but it conformed to the dominant pattern within the oil industry itself.[10]

The institutions of industrial relations within each refinery had developed in a relatively informal and ad hoc way, and drew their legitimacy from a very loosely defined body of traditional customs and practices in the workplace. This contrasted strongly with the situation in France where institutions both at company and at plant level mirrored the legal provisions that defined in detail their structure and mode of operation. One consequence of this is that, in Britain, we found a greater degree of variation between the institutions of the two refineries than had been the case in France. The specific traditions of each refinery had a dynamic of their own that affected the relative weight of the key participants in the system, and the types of institutional adaptation that took place to cope with new problems. It was principally a question of variations around a given theme, but it makes the pattern more complex to describe.

Moreover, the high degree of decentralization and informality of relations seems to have encouraged greater flexibility and openness to change. In each of the British refineries we found a fairly continuous process of institutional modification and experimentation. Indeed, as we shall see, in the course of the 1960s there were quite fundamental changes in both refineries in the underlying pattern of industrial relations.

The shop floor representatives

In both of our refineries the 1950s saw the growth and consolidation of a powerful shop floor organization. This seems initially to have been accepted more easily at Grangemouth than at Kent. At Grangemouth, from very early on, management seems to have made an effort to come to terms with the stewards, and to recognize them as a major power within the industrial relations system. At Kent, on the other hand, the older stewards remembered the 1950s as a difficult time when they had to struggle to be recognized. By the 1970s, however, management in both refineries had a very considerable respect for the stewards and saw them as a power it would be foolish to ignore. But, to a certain degree, these initial differences in the degree of managerial recognition lingered on. At Grangemouth the elected representatives had easier access to the higher levels of management than at Kent, and they had a more important role in negotiations.

Whereas in France the elected personnel delegates and members of the Works Committees had represented the whole of the work force, in the British refineries shop floor organization was split in two. The operators and the maintenance workers were separately organized.

The operators were members of a single union — the Transport and General Workers Union — and were organized in a refinery-based branch. As employees, they elected a set of shop stewards; and as branch members, they elected a group of branch officers, of whom the most important were the branch secretary and the branch chairman. Although management had only formally recognized the stewards as spokesmen of the shop floor, in practice it treated the branch secretary and chairman as the equivalents of shop steward convenors. Equally the branch secretary and chairman worked hand-in-glove with the shop steward committee. There was, then, a two-level system of representation in which the branch officers were the spokesmen of the shop stewards' committee to higher management.

The craft workers, on the other hand, belonged to a variety of unions, and the branches of these unions were located outside the factory and grouped together workers in a number of different industries. Since the stewards were responsible to a diverse set of external branch authorities, the problem of their co-ordination within the refinery itself presented rather greater difficulties than on the operators' side. The main organizational means for trying to overcome this was the Joint Shop Stewards' Committee in which the different crafts had equal voting power independently of their strength in the work force. The Joint Shop Stewards' Committee elected a chairman and a secretary, thus creating a two level representational system broadly equivalent to that among the operators.

The shop floor representatives, on both sides, saw themselves as ultimately governed by the expressed wishes of the workers they represented. On the T&GWU side the sovereign body was unmistakeable; it was the branch meeting which could be attended by the entire body of operators. On the craft side the situation was somewhat more ambiguous. In a strict sense the craft stewards were obliged to give priority to the particular set of craftsmen who had elected them. However, most of them were aware that if they held rigidly to this position it must lead to the total paralysis of the craft stewards as a coherent negotiating body with management. At times, the stewards could claim to be responsible to the wishes of the craft force as a whole, as institutionally expressed in the mass meeting. It was clear that there was a certain possibility of tension between these two different sources of sovereignty, and the issue was never worked out in any very clearly formulated way. The craft stewards had to steer somehow between the wishes of the sectional group and the wishes of the collectivity, and their method of doing this was largely *ad hoc*, and required not insignificant political skills.

The influence of the shop floor representatives pervaded to a greater or lesser degree most of the major areas of industrial relations. But we can distinguish between those areas in which their influence was predominant and those in which they either played a supporting role to, or shared their power with, the full-time union officials. Here we shall look at the areas in which they were the main parties to the discussions with management, and later we shall come to consider the other spheres in which they could make their influence felt.

The longest-standing role of the stewards had been to struggle for the protection and improvement of work conditions. The stewards directed their campaign for better working conditions on a wide variety of fronts. They put pressure on management to obtain protective clothing, to improve lighting and heating, to keep the toilets working, to provide adequate facilities for cooking meals when on shifts, to make sure that overalls were returned clean from the laundry, to increase the supply of bicycles, to improve the changing rooms, and so the list could continue.

In both refineries there were regular meetings in which grievances about work conditions could be aired. In Grangemouth the main setting was a central Works Committee chaired by the Works Manager. In both of the refineries the channels provided were consultative, but the stewards felt that they were reasonably efficacious. A former branch secretary of the T&GWU summed up the stewards' influence in the following terms: 'The unions now control work conditions in the sense that changes cannot be introduced without their agreement, and they can also get most of what they want — in the long run. But it's not a 100% certain.'

Like the French personnel delegates, another major role of the stewards was to ensure that the system of job grading was applied fairly. As a major determinant of salary and status, a grading system can easily generate rivalries between individual workers and between groups of workers; and in both the French and the British refineries the representatives were anxious to reduce as much as possible management's freedom of manoeuvre, and to rationalize rules governing the way the system was applied. On the craft side the solution had been drastic. The grading system itself had been abolished, and the craft workers had been placed in a single grade with a single salary. The operators, on the other hand, were still graded hierarchically, and the constant process of technological change and manpower reorganization was continually undermining the validity of the existing grade structure by altering the work loads of particular posts.

At Kent, for much of the 1960s the role of the stewards in the negotiations over grades was a limited one. They could raise cases where they felt that an injustice had been done, but the negotiations rapidly passed into the sphere of the full-time official. With the increased pace of organizational change, however, the burden on the full-time official grew steadily heavier, and there was dissatisfaction on the shop floor with the length of time that decisions were taking. In June 1969, urged on by the full-time official, management agreed to decentralize negotiations about grading and to carry out virtually all the discussion with the shop floor representatives, leaving only the occasional case in which agreement had proved impossible to the full-time official.

At Grangemouth this had already been the case for some time, and indeed Grangemouth management towards the end of the 1960s went a stage further and gave the elected representatives a powerful degree of institutionalized control over the allocation of grades, through the creation of a Joint Evaluation Committee on which there were three main union representatives and three representatives of management. These analysed the contents of each job in terms of a thirteen factor job evaluation scheme. As there was no casting vote, and as decisions had to be reached by agreement, the committee gave the shop floor representatives a genuine degree of control.

The craft stewards did not have to worry about the problem of grading, but on the other hand they had preoccupations specific to themselves. They were considerably more involved than their equivalents among the operators with keeping an eye on the everyday organization of work. Even more central, however, to the work of the craft stewards was their concern to control the demarcation boundaries between crafts. As early as 1920, Carter Goodrich had predicted the gradual disappearance of this aspect of the stewards' work with the development of more advanced technologies.[11] Over fifty years later, and in the most advanced technological setting, there was still no evidence that this was coming about.

There were, then, important areas in the life of the refinery — such as the grading system on the operators' side and the deployment of labour on the maintenance side — where the shop floor representatives had secured important independent powers to control management's actions. But this was far from the limit of their influence.

Formal plant level negotiations

Whereas in France the crucial negotiations over the terms of employment — salaries, holidays, and the length of the working week — were highly centralized and carried on in the industry-level Parity Commissions, in Britain they were dealt with at the level of each individual refinery.

Virtually simultaneous, but almost entirely independent, negotiations were carried on on behalf of the members of the Transport and General Workers' Union on the one hand, and of the craft unions on the other.

One important characteristic of the negotiating system was that management was represented not by the head of the refinery — the General Manager, but by his immediate subordinate the Works Manager. This gave a considerably greater flexibility in negotiation and prevented the risk of the managerial negotiator becoming over-identified with the particular position he was defending. When the negotiations became deadlocked, the meeting would be suspended, and the Works Manager would go away to consult his superior, who had remained outside the heat of the discussion and could authorize a new negotiating position without any loss of face. In this way, the head of the refinery could always present himself in the role of conciliator, and the possibility was minimized that the inevitable tensions of negotiation would lead to personal hostility.

Although the General Manager had the formal responsibility for carrying out the negotiations, in practice there were outside pressures that could be brought to bear on him. He would have to justify an exceptionally large pay increase to the head office of the Company, but his opinion on what was necessary would still have a great deal of influence. He was also caught up in a fairly intricate system of inter-company relationships in the region, but these had mainly moral weight, and at a crunch the refinery could adopt a policy even if this put its neighbours in a difficult position. Refinery management's freedom of manoeuvre was, then, subject to certain constraints, but they were fairly broad.

On the union side, the formal negotiators were the full-time officials, but these co-ordinated closely with the shop floor representatives. They would usually meet the stewards before the negotiations began, and provisions had been made for shop-floor representatives to be present during negotiations in an observer capacity. If, in the course of the negotiations, a difficult decision had to be made, the full-time officials would normally ask for a suspension of the meeting so that they could get together with the stewards to discuss the issue. There was no sharp dichotomy between the area of influence of the stewards and the area of influence of the full-time officials. The wishes and opinions of the stewards were an ever present factor even when management was formally negotiating with the external union officials. As we shall see, the extent of the stewards' influence varied according to the type of negotiation, but during the 1960s the general trend was for it to increase and indeed, at Grangemouth, the stewards took over much of the negotiating role of the full-time officials.

Another crucial factor that the full-time officials had to take into account was the mass meeting of the workers.[12] There was a well established tradition that the proposals for an agreement should be presented to the mass meeting and receive the consent of the men themselves. The consent of the mass meeting was by no means a foregone conclusion. Sometimes, the full-time officials would return almost apologetically to the negotiating table to announce that the proposals had been rejected. They had, in fact, the power to sign agreements on their own authority, but it was a power that they were on the whole reluctant to use. A full-time official who signed over the head of his membership took the risk of open rebellion and the loss of any real control. In both of our refineries the situation had arisen in which, after repeated rejections by the mass meeting, they had taken the plunge and signed. In each case the move led to an upsurge of discontent on the shop floor, and an attack by the stewards on the full-time officials' negotiating rights.

The most frequent issue handled in the formal plant-level negotiations was pay. The usual expectation was for an annual pay settlement, and the two sides would often begin negotiations several months in advance. Unlike the negotiations in France, these were concerned with the overall salary a worker received. Equally, in contrast to the French situation where the majority of negotiations over salaries failed, in the British refineries there was not a single case of a pay negotiation which had not led to agreement between management and the full-time officials. Both management and the full-time officials, then, negotiated in the expectation of eventually agreeing; indeed it was stronger than this — they regarded the achievement of an agreement as an obligation, and any prolonged deadlock of negotiations would be felt as a failure. Both sides were proud of their ability to maintain good relations, and both sides were anxious to retain their reputation for reasonableness.

In the course of the 1960s there was a significant shift in the pattern of formal negotiation. In the first place there was a major extension in the range of issues that came to be handled in the negotiations. Faced with the growing competitiveness of the oil industry and a more acute awareness of the highly inefficient use of labour in the refineries, management felt the need to carry out a fundamental transformation of the system of work organization. Very much spurred on by the example of Fawley, it decided to carry out these changes through the employment of comprehensive productivity bargaining. This involved seeking the explicit agreement of the unions to specified changes in traditional working practices, in exchange for a substantial increase in salaries. It thereby brought into the arena of the formal negotiations the whole sphere of work organization. From the early 1960s to the end of the decade, these productivity negotiations became central to the industrial relations systems of the two refineries leading to four fully fledged productivity agreements at Kent and six at Grangemouth.

Productivity bargaining and relations of power

The implication of productivity bargaining for relations of power in the factory has been a subject of substantial controversy. Alan Flanders, whose study of the Fawley negotiations did much to stimulate initial interest in productivity bargaining, argued that one of its major virtues was that it involved a simultaneous increase in the power of both management and the representatives of the work force. Drawing the lessons of productivity bargaining for British industry, he wrote: 'The paradox whose truth managements have found it so difficult to accept, is that they can only regain control by sharing it'.[13] In contrast, Tony Cliffe has argued that '"productivity" is part of a major offensive by the employer class of this country to shift the balance of forces permanently in their direction.'[14] For Cliffe, the essential feature of productivity bargaining is that it destroys the traditional resources available to shop stewards to win the loyalty of their own workers and to coerce management.

Neither of these arguments gives a very accurate account of the impact of productivity bargaining on the refineries we were studying. To take first Cliffe's thesis, it is notable that his central argument is that it weakens stewards' power by reducing their control over the payment system, through the abolition of piecework systems and the introduction of measured day work. This argument has little weight in the refinery situation, because the technology makes piecework systems impossible to operate, and hence this was never a basis of steward power. The main ways in which the stewards could influence earnings was through their role in negotiations over job grades on the operators' side, and through the control of overtime on the maintenance side. Productivity bargaining certainly did affect steward power with regard to job grades — but in the direction of greater control. At Kent, the enhanced pace of organizational change led to the decentralization of negotiations over grades from the full-time officials to the shop floor representatives, while at Grangemouth it led to the introduction of a job evaluation system. Cliffe argues that such schemes are invariably detrimental to the workers because they tend to be entirely under management's control. In the refinery we were studying, however, this was not the case, for the stewards were given equal weight in decisions to management in the joint committee that ran the scheme. The greatest apparent threat that productivity bargaining posed to steward power was on the craft side, where the stewards lost control of overtime when this was abolished. However, when questioned about this, the stewards appeared altogether undisturbed. They had apparently never regarded it as one of their principal power resources, their primary worry had been to secure a fair distribution of overtime to prevent discontent against themselves, and they felt that the abolition of overtime had in fact been an important factor enhancing unity among the craft stewards, since it removed resentments between the crafts over variations in earnings due to the differential availability of overtime work.

In addition to loss of control over earnings, Cliffe suggests that productivity bargaining weakened shop-steward power by enabling management to by-pass the stewards over individual grievances, through increasing the number of supervisors and formalizing grievance procedure, and by making it possible for management to undermine local steward power bases by moving militants around the factory under new provisions for flexibility.

None of these fears seemed to have been borne out in the refineries we were studying. Management's policy about supervision was largely governed by the desire to save costs by reducing the number of supervisors and decentralizing responsibility to the men themselves for their everyday work.[15] Grievance procedure was indeed formalized, but the shop stewards remained central to it, and the full-time officials continued to have responsibility only for the rare cases in which agreement could not be reached. Equally, management would have found it difficult to use the flexibility provisions to undermine the stewards that it regarded as militant. On the operations side, the high degree of specialized knowledge that was needed to work on a unit meant that flexibility could only take place within a unit or between a very limited set of units. On the maintenance side, the type of flexibility that was bought was a craftsman's flexibility in the use of his skills, and this had minimal implications for his degree of geographical mobility within the plant.

It is perfectly possible that the effects of productivity bargaining on the stewards' position vary depending on the technological setting. In the refinery situation, however, Cliffe's arguments carry little conviction. The support of the stewards did not depend to any important degree on the work practices that productivity bargaining eliminated. In terms of negative sanctions their power lay primarily in the closed shop. On the more positive side their influence derived in part from their ability to defend individual cases of injustice, and in part from their capacity to improve work conditions — safety, and the physical environment of work. But above all it came from their ability to represent the work force in the crucial negotiations between the full-time officials and management over general salary levels and over changes in work organization, and in this, as we shall see, productivity bargaining heightened rather than diminished their status in the work force.

Turning now to the argument that productivity bargaining enabled the stewards to 'share' managerial power, assessment becomes rather more complex. The overall effect of productivity bargaining in both refineries was clearly to make the stewards more central to the bargaining process, and hence to make their co-operation more important to management, and their services more critical to the workers on the shop floor. The reasons for this are fairly straightforward. So long as the main criteria for determining wage increases were the retail price index and comparisons with other firms in the neighbourhood, the full-time officials could feel reasonably confident about their own ability to assess the reasonableness of management's offer. But once pay negotiations involved changes in work organizations, they became much more dependent on the stewards to give them an idea of how drastic the proposals were and how much value the work force attached to the practices involved. The very extensiveness of the changes now proposed put it quite beyond the capacity of the full-time officials to personally check up on their implications. Far more than before, then, the stewards became the crucial link between the full-time officials and the shop floor. The full-time officials relied on the stewards both to assess and predict the reactions of the work force, and to carry out the bulk of the work of actually presenting the concrete proposals to the workers. Equally, the stewards were brought into much more frequent contact with the higher reaches of management, and were involved in discussions on a much wider set of organizational problems. They had to shift their focus from being primarily concerned with the immediate issues of the sector in which they worked to dealing with the longer range organizational problems of the refinery.[16]

In addition to increasing the influence of the shop-floor representatives in negotiations, productivity bargaining probably involved a small but significant increase in the overall amount of control over management decision making.

First, it led management to recognize formally that questions of work organization had to be negotiated and agreed. Some issues — such as job evaluation and works study (which the stewards eventually rejected) — were new, and the productivity negotiations were therefore important in setting precedents for the future. For others there was a subtle, but important, shift from an informal tradition of co-operation to a formal recognition of a right of control. While not all formalization is necessarily advantageous to the work force or its representatives, formalization of the right of control indisputably is.

Second, it was intrinsic to the nature of comprehensive productivity bargaining that management put forward in a fairly explicit way its objectives over a period of years. In the earlier system of negotiations the representatives had been confronted with a series of apparently isolated changes, and, given the pressures of the moment, it was likely that these would be handled largely in terms of their own specific merits. It was, then, perfectly possible for the representatives to be unaware of the cumulative effect of the changes that they were accepting. Productivity bargaining, on the other hand, by its global character, pushed the problem of cumulative effects into the very forefront of the scene, and the representatives were able to judge individual issues in the light of the overall picture. To the extent that they were now making decisions with fuller information, their effective control was greater.

Thirdly, and closely allied to the previous point, productivity bargaining provided better institutional machinery for vetting management proposals. Under the earlier system, hard pressed full-time officials, with little knowledge of the life of the refinery, had to rely on brief contacts with their stewards and with the workers immediately affected. Productivity bargaining, on the other hand, was usually accompanied by the setting up of joint productivity committees which could discuss the proposals in greater depth, and which had the time to examine alternative proposals. The result was that it was possible to give a considerably more thorough examination than before to the implication of changes for work life. Again, although this produced no formal alteration in the powers of control, it probably made existing powers considerably more effective.

Productivity bargaining consolidated and made more effective the powers of control that the representatives already had acquired, and it extended their formal right of control to the entire sphere of work organization. It would, however, be wholly unrealistic to adopt Flanders' view that productivity bargaining enabled the workers' representatives to 'share' managerial power in the more profound sense of the term.

First, the initiative in designing the proposals for changes came predominantly from management. This predominance of managerial initiative is not altogether surprising. Management had considerably superior organizational means at its disposal for meditating on the design of proposals, and it alone really knew of the possible technical changes that could be introduced to simplify work tasks and enable manpower to be redeployed.

The power of the representatives was, then, largely one of vetoing or of suggesting modifications of proposals designed by management, and then negotiating for a fair distribution of the economies that could be achieved. But even here the relationship was fundamentally one between unequals, and this was largely because of management's reluctance to reveal the way it costed proposals. Once a detailed list of suggestions had been drawn up, the usual procedure was for management to simply propose a salary increase which it claimed represented half the value of the proposals (the other half going to management). At no point was it prepared to go into detailed discussions about how it had calculated this value. Requests for further information were invariably met with evasiveness:

Mr. W. (the Works Manager) explained that direct costing was difficult since a number of changes in working practices had been grouped together to justify the agreement, and that if the costing had been on concrete proposals alone the wage increase would have been very low.
(Grangemouth Meeting with T&GWU Dec. 1967)

Mr. R. (the branch secretary) said branch members had requested that they be provided with details of the financial savings resulting from each individual productivity item in the proposals. Mr. M. (the Works Manager) said that this was a 'Package Deal' and he did not consider it desirable to break it down.
(Grangemouth, Meeting with T&GWU Sep. 1969)

A long discussion on the costing of the 1967 agreement then took place, and Mr. D. (the branch secretary) quoted figures purporting to show that the Company had gained the majority of benefits arising from the crew reductions in Operations Department. Mr. C. (the Industrial Relations Officer) gave earnings figures showing that the earnings had been shared equally between the two parties. He emphasized that the agreement and its costing had been made on an overall basis, and no breakdown between various sections of the community had been attempted.
(Kent, Meeting with the T&GWU, Oct. 1969)

The representatives could therefore reject management's figures as unrealistic, or they might take them as a starting point for bargaining, but in either case they had to rely mainly on intuitive judgement.

Productivity bargaining then unquestionably shifted influence away from the full-time officials, and into the hands of the shop floor representatives. Equally, it strengthened the control that the workers could exercise over management decisions, by making existing powers more effective and by formally extending the scope of control to the whole sphere of work organization. But the type of power it gave the stewards remained essentially negative. There were times when the representatives took a more active role in proposing changes but they were relatively rare. Moreover, their ability to assess management's own proposals was restricted by management's reluctance to reveal its costing procedure. The discussions remained, then, discussions between unequals, and although productivity bargaining strengthened steward power it can hardly be said to have led to a 'sharing' of power.

The fundamental effect of productivity bargaining in the 1960s was to consolidate and strengthen the pattern of industrial relations that emerged in the British refineries in the 1950s. This pattern was characterized by the highly decentralized level at which formal bargaining took place, and by the central role of the elected shop-floor representatives. These not only had important independent powers in certain areas of refinery life, but they also exercised a major influence over the negotiations between management and the full-time officials.

The refineries and the national patterns

In both countries the institutions of the refineries shared common characteristics with those prevalent in many other industries in the same society, and indeed, the traditions of industrial relations in each country appeared to be an overwhelmingly stronger factor than pressures deriving from the technology in explaining the pattern of relations.

The unity of the French industrial relations system derived in part from the extensive intervention of the law. The law laid down in detail the form that the elected company and plant level institutions should take. It provided rules that governed the process of election, the frequency of meetings, and the hours management was to allow the representatives for carrying out their functions. In a less clear-cut way it also regulated the scope of discussions and the nature of the powers of the different institutions. The two French refineries that we studied were remarkably similar to each other in their institutions, and indeed the same basic pattern can be found in all of the other French oil refineries.

If we compare the oil industry with the more general pattern in French industry, it emerges as relatively progressive in the way it operated its plant-level institutions. In 1975 the Sudreau Report noted that, in nearly half of the firms that fell within the terms of the law, there was no committee at all.[17] The Company that we studied both had regular meetings and extended the formal provisions of the law by increasing the time allowances available for key representatives to fulfil their functions. The social welfare and leisure activities of the company were flourishing, and management, at least, believed that the level of information it gave the committees was superior to those in many other French firms.

On the other hand it is clear that the Company had made no dramatic institutional innovation, and that in terms of conceding influence to the committees it went no further than was strictly required by the law. The discussions were limited in scope, and management tended to interpret the obligation to consult as an obligation to inform. In this it appears to have been wholly unexceptional among those firms that did comply with the law. Although much of the evidence in the literature is impressionistic, there is a quite striking degree of consistency in the various accounts provided by informed observers of the French labour scene since the war. The unambivalent picture that emerges is that, where the committees existed at all, they functioned inadequately, and provided the workers with only a minimal degree of influence over the factors affecting their work lives.[18]

The Company, like other companies in the oil industry, must also be seen as relatively progressive by French standards in its attitude to the unions in the workplace. Years before the law of December 1968 was passed, most of its key provisions had become *de facto* realities within the refineries, and management left the unions relatively unhampered in their efforts to organize the work force. This contrasts with the more rigid anti-union attitudes of many French employers, and indeed there are well-known examples of French managements that have been quite ferociously repressive.[19] On the other hand, this liberalism had no important impact on the institutional structure of management/worker relations, and there was no effort to experiment more radically. Management upheld the traditional policy of French employers of refusing to negotiate with the unions at plant level.

The Company's attitude to negotiations with the unions at company level was fairly cautious and mainstream. It decided not to participate in the upsurge of company agreements in the second half of the 1950s, but this upsurge itself proved to be a temporary phenomenon, and affected only a small section of French industry. On the other hand, it did begin to move towards company negotiations on a small scale in the early 1970s. In this it seems to have kept pace with more widespread developments in French industry. Its negotiations over profit-sharing, for instance, were part of a more general movement that followed the Ordinance of 1967, and the extension into unsystematic negotiations with the unions on restricted topics appears to have been common in the aftermath of 1968.[20] At all events, there was no major initiative here that was in any way comparable with the precedent setting moves taken by the leading car firm — Renault.

Where the companies in the oil industry were rather less characteristic of French industry was in their preference for very highly centralized negotiations over the terms of employment. The traditional preference of French employers has been to carry out negotiations at regional or departmental level, where they could take into account the specific conditions of the labour market and resist pressures to generalize the advantages that had been conceded in areas where labour was scarce. The oil industry, however, was not alone in its system of national negotiations; the pattern was the same in both the chemical and the textile industry. Moreover, there are indications that national-level negotiations are becoming more important for French industry as a whole.[21] It is possible, then, that the pattern prevalent in the oil industry may be to some degree prototypical of the direction in which the French industrial relations' system will develop.

The degree of centralization apart, the essential formula of negotiation is identical in the great bulk of French industry. The negotiations are external to any given factory, they are concerned with minimum salaries, and they leave company management with an important degree of discretionary power.

The Company we were studying was then distinctive in two main ways. First, it was probably a little more liberal than most firms in its handling of the Works Committees, and in its tolerance of union organization of the work force. Second, it was linked in with a more highly centralized system of negotiation than was traditional in French industry. But what is very much more remarkable is the very high degree of similarity between the fundamental features of its institutional system and that prevalent more widely in French industry. Its essential aspects — the unilateral nature of managerial control in the factory, the centrality of the industrial branch for negotiations with the unions, and the restricted scope of negotiations over salaries — are all fundamental characteristics of the general French industrial relations system in the private sector of industry.

In the British case, there are also important parallels between the pattern in the refineries we studied and developments in the wider industrial relations' system. The growth in power of the stewards in British industry in the course of the 1950s has been the subject of widespread comment.[22] The Royal Commission Survey of establishments in manufacturing and construction found that 78% of Works Managers in their sample negotiated with their shop stewards. These negotiations ranged not only over work conditions and many aspects of work organization, but also frequently concerned wage issues as well.[23] There was nothing particularly remarkable about the pattern of shop floor organization that had grown up in the refineries by the early 1960s. Where the refineries were uncharacteristic was in the level of formal bargaining. Unlike the dominant pattern in British industry, the Company was not a member of an employers' federation, and hence it was free to develop its own rules and carry out its own negotiations entirely as it pleased. In fact, like most of the other oil companies in Britain, it decided to decentralize negotiations to the level of the individual refinery. In doing this, it to some degree intensified and at the same time formalized a widespread tendency for a shift in the effective level of collective bargaining in British industry. In the traditional sectors of industry, the main institutional development since the war has been the lessening relevance of the system of regulation at industry level, and the growing importance of workplace bargaining.[24] However, in our refineries, it was not merely a question of an informal system undermining the formal, it was that the workplace had become the formal bargaining unit itself.

There can be no doubt that non-federation was a considerable asset in that it made possible greater negotiating flexibility, and allowed the decentralization of the bargaining process to a level at which it was possible to involve in a much fuller way the workers on the shop floor while preserving the benefits of a formal agreement. But non-federation does not appear to have any clear cut connection with a specific technology. The reasons why firms are non-federated appear to be very diverse. The majority are small firms, and their main motive seems to be to avoid dealings with the unions.[25] Some of the larger firms seem to have been primarily affected by their links with the United States where there is a much greater emphasis on formal plant-level bargaining. At all events, we find among the non-federated firms not only companies that rank among the advanced sectors of industry, but equally companies like Ford and Vauxhall that are firmly in the traditional sector.

This brings us finally to the question of productivity bargaining. How far can this be seen as a form of institutional adaptation that reflected the particular needs and problems of the advanced technological sector? One thing is clear — the movement started in a continuous-process plant — Esso's refinery at Fawley. Equally, it spread rapidly through the other major refining companies — Mobil, Shell and BP. The capital intensive industries were unquestionably among the pace setters of the new system of negotiation.

A variety of factors have been put forward to explain why productivity bargaining was initiated at Fawley.[26] Some relate directly to characteristics of the technology. The British oil refineries are particularly exposed to pressures to increase efficiency, because their technological similarity with those abroad and their integration into international companies made international comparisons relatively easy. Refinery management's attention was particularly focused on finding ways of making savings through increasing manning efficiency, since this was the main element of costs under their control. Other factors refer to the particular system of industrial relations in which Fawley was already involved. Management found it easier to adopt a new pattern of negotiation because it was unrestrained by belonging to an employers' federation. And the fact that it was involved in formal plant-level bargaining meant that particularly close working relations had developed between management and the fulltime officials, which provided a climate of mutual confidence and understanding that favoured innnovation. Once the initial breakthrough had been made at Fawley, its technological similarity to other refineries was an important factor in explaining the speed with which productivity bargaining spread throughout the industry.

But while technology did play some role in explaining why the new system of negotiation was originally conceived in the advanced sector, this did not mean that productivity bargaining was a response to problems that were specific to technologically advanced industry, or that it represented a form of negotiation that was any more suited to the advanced sector than to other sectors. As Flanders has convincingly argued, what Fawley management had discovered was the solution to a much more general problem in British industry — namely how to introduce major organizational change when confronted with a powerful shop floor organization that could effectively resist changes to which it objected.[27] At a time when general economic prosperity made the risk of lost production a very costly one, the only viable way of doing this was to win agreement, and this was unlikely to be achieved without major financial rewards and extensive discussions with the shop-floor representatives. Thus the method adopted was to a very large degree, determined by the fundamental characteristics of the wider industrial relations system.

That this was the case was shown by the speed with which productivity bargaining was adopted by industries that were very different in their technologies and capital structure. When McKersie and Hunter came to analyse the characteristics of firms that had taken up productivity bargaining during the period 1960 to 1966 — that is to say when it was spontaneous and uninfluenced by the general rush to dodge incomes policy — they found no relationship at all between productivity bargaining and capital intensiveness.[28]

It would, then, be a mistake to see productivity bargaining as particularly characteristic of advanced technology. Although technological factors, in combination with a particular system of industrial relations, can help explain why it got off the ground fairly early in several capital intensive firms, the shift in the structure of bargaining is much more realistically seen as a fairly natural outgrowth of the pre-existing national system of industrial relations, once the problems of industrial efficiency and the need for major organizational changes became major issues.

The institutional structures through which relations between management and workers were conducted in the two countries were then intimately linked with the wider national systems of industrial relations. Their distinctiveness was in somewhat accentuating the dominant characteristics of each system. In France, negotiations with the workers' representatives were usually external to the workplace and relatively remote from the workers in any given establishment. In the oil industry the very high degree of centralization of negotiations made this remoteness particularly evident. In Britain, the overall tendency was for a shift of the true locus of negotiation from industry level to the workplace. The oil refineries represented an extreme case of this development with the formal negotiations being carried on at the level of the plant.

There was, moreover, no sign of a tendency of the two systems to converge over time. The French system had remained remarkably static over two decades, and the small scale extension of company-level negotiation in the early 1970s left unaffected the main pillars of managerial power. In Britain, there had been substantial modifications in the negotiating system in the course of the 1960s, but these had largely involved an extension and formalization of union rights of control, and an increase in the influence of the work-place representatives. If anything, there had been a tendency from the early 1960s for the differences between the two systems to become more marked.

8

Participation and the image of management: interpretation

Managerial strategies and the institutional system

Firmly locked into the wider institutional patterns of their societies, the institutions of the French and British refineries reflected fundamentally different conceptions of management. Broadly speaking, French management's strategy was paternalistic while British management's was semi-constitutional. These two widely diverging conceptions of management both proved perfectly compatible with a highly automated technology, but they implied substantially different experiences of factory life for the work force. It seems very possible that the tendency of the French workers to think of the firm as exploitative, in comparison to the prevalence of a co-operative image among the British workers, can be in part explained by typical differences in their experience of relations of power.

French management's strategy was to maintain the maximum degree of managerial discretion while seeking to tie the workers directly to the firm. The two elements of this strategy were complementary. The preservation of a high level of managerial discretion over the rewards that members could hope to derive from membership of the organization was the prerequisite for the development on the part of the workers of a sense of direct dependence on the generosity of management.

Three aspects of the specific form of paternalism practised by French management are particularly noteworthy. First, it paid its workers substantially higher wages relative to the regional and national manual worker averages than British management, but it took care that a considerable proportion of the worker's income should remain, and should be seen to remain, entirely within management's discretion. Second, it 'individualized' members of the work force by making their financial status in the organization not merely a product of their skill or market position, but dependent upon their seniority in the 'family', and management's view of their degree of

182

commitment and loyalty to the firm. Finally, it is notable that paternalism was extended to the worker's family as a whole through the
activities of the Works Committees. The firm provided the children
with Christmas presents, and holidays, while the mothers were provided with useful local facilities for minding the children. While the
representatives decided on the precise distribution of funds, management kept its entire discretion over the overall amount that would
be made available.

The efficacy of the strategy depended on management's ability
to emphasize the non-obligatory nature of its actions, and the tight
relationship between the privileges the worker and his family received
through membership of the Company and managerial good-will. The
implication of this was that management was necessarily highly committed to the preservation of an institutional system that guaranteed
and, indeed highlighted, its discretionary power by the formal restrictions it placed on the rights of the workers' representatives to participate in decision making.

The institutional system itself expressed a unitary conception of
the firm in which problems were held to be harmoniously resolvable
through discussion, and which emphasized representation of the
community as a whole and denied the legitimacy of separate organized interest groups.[1] Within such a conception, trade unions could
be easily defined as external and divisive agencies seeking to sow
discontent within a community that would spontaneously achieve
consensus.[2]

Management's rigid adherence to the letter of the law in its interpretation of its obligations towards the company and plant committees did not, then, reflect legalism *per se*, but rather the fact that
a more liberal interpretation of the law — which might have provided
the representatives with a real degree of control — would have
imperilled quite fundamentally its overall strategy by undermining
both the material and the ideological means by which it hoped to
secure the loyalty of the work force.

British management, in contrast, adopted a semi-constitutional
strategy. Its aim was to win the loyalty of the work force by making
sure that the terms of employment and the rules of work organization
had secured the explicit consent of the workers' representatives. In
contrast to French management, British management de-emphasized
its discretionary power. The worker's salary was negotiable in its
entirety, and there was no system of bonuses that tied the worker's

income directly to management's good-will. Financial status in the firm depended purely on occupational skill level, and management had largely abandoned the capacity to use the reward system to create a sense of the direct dependence of the individual worker on the Company.

Instead, it had adopted an institutional system that recognized the central role of the unions as mediators between the Company and the workers, and that implicitly legitimated the organized expression of the collective interests of the workers as a distinct category within the firm. The institutional system, then, represented a definition of relations as pluralistic,[3] and hence an acceptance that management/worker relations could only be stabilized on the basis of procedures that allowed the expression of divergent points of view, and the negotiation of compromises that could obtain 'consent', and hence morally bind members to the system of organizational rules.

At one level, this could be seen in management's constant affirmation of an 'open-door' policy, of being prepared to meet and discuss with the stewards the moment any problem arose on the shop floor. But, most importantly, it was expressed in management's concern to maintain and reinforce the 'agreement' — the formally agreed set of rules that laid down the rights and obligations of the work force. As the years pass, we see the agreement becoming steadily more complex and more extensive. It was the lynch-pin of the semi-constitutional system, symbolizing consent to the existing normative structure.

The institutional systems governing management/worker relations in the two countries were not, then, mere products of institutional traditionalism, or patterns of social organization imposed from outside and reluctantly accepted. Even in France, where institutions were more specifically governed by the law, management, had it wished to do so, could have treated its legal obligations as minimum provisions, and adopted a substantially different system. Rather, the institutional system is best seen as the mechanism by which management implemented its specific strategies for securing the loyalty of the work force.

There is, of course, no necessary equivalence between intent and result. Our evidence suggests that, on the whole, British management was substantially more successful than French management in securing the involvement and identification with the Company of its workers. To understand why this was the case, we need to look at the implications of the institutional systems for the experience of work life of the personnel.

Salaries

Whatever the variations in the degree of instrumentalism of different groups of manual workers, there is an overriding consensus in the literature that pay is central to most workers' evaluation of their job.[4] It is therefore probable that the way in which salaries are determined will be particularly important in structuring a worker's image of his firm and his attitude to management. Different institutional systems, we would suggest, tend to shape distinctive patterns of interaction between management and the work force, and are therefore conducive to rather different perceptions of management.

If we compare the French and British systems for negotiating salaries, a first feature that emerges is the sharp difference in the degree of centralization of the negotiations and, hence, in the degree of collectivization or differentiation of the key parties to the nego-tiation. In the French refineries, the workers were spectators to a very distant set of negotiations at Paris. The negotiators would not usually be people they personally knew, but the representatives of the impersonal bureaucracies of the employer federations and the trade unions. Moreover they would not be the representatives of the specific community of workers and management of the firm, but of larger collectivities. The negotiations represented in their very formula, an impersonal confrontation between organized big business and organized labour, and as such could be easily comprehended in terms of the extensive categories of a class definition of society. Given such a system of negotiation, the use of terms such as *le patronat* and *la classe ouvrière* to describe the ebbing and flowing of the discussions seemed not inappropriate.

In the British refineries, the critical salary negotiations were at plant level. The managerial negotiator was a known individual who would have been seen walking around the units, and who, in many cases, was well-known from his earlier experience as a more junior line-manager. The General Manager at Grangemouth, for instance, was clearly a very familiar figure on units, due to his previous practice as Works Manager of walking around and getting to know the men by name. The formal representative of the work force — the full-time official — was a more anonymous figure, but, as we have seen, his role was diminishing, and the work force was directly represented at the negotiating table by the shop floor representatives that it had elected and that it knew well.

In contrast, then, to the impersonality and collectivization of the

French negotiatory system, the British negotiations took place between known individuals and were confined to the individual plant. The fate of the negotiations was more easily seen as determined by the personalities of the individuals involved. Evaluation in terms of general class categories fitted less easily. The General Manager and the Works Manager might well be seen as the employers, but it was less self-evident that these familiar figures were the representatives of the employer class.

In addition to the varying degrees of conduciveness of the two negotiatory systems to different descriptive vocabularies with their attendant associations, it is also noteworthy that the handling of the negotiations had somewhat different personal implications for the individuals involved. In the British system, the parties to the negotiation were involved in a multiple role relationship. The Works Manager was the front-line negotiator over salaries, but he was also the critical technical co-ordinator for the functioning of the factory. The stewards were representatives, but they were also workers, who, after the negotiations, would revert to their usual position in the hierarchical chain, and who might well have average, or even higher than average, career aspirations in their roles as workers. In France, in contrast, the parties to the negotiation met infrequently and might well never see each other outside the specific negotiating arena.

The implication of this is that, in the British setting, the pressures for smooth and successful negotiations were more substantial, since the activities of the actors in one of their roles might have important implications for their capacity to perform successfully in their other roles. If the Works Manager proved too decisively that he was intransigent in the negotiations over salaries, he might find life decidedly uncomfortable if he had later to walk round the units to try to whip up enthusiasm in a moment of production crisis. Equally shop floor representatives who proved totally uncompromising in their attitudes over negotiations had to bear in mind that in doing so they might well be convincing management that they lacked those qualities of responsibility and impartiality that were considered essential for people who were to be promoted.

The fact that the parties had to live together on a day-to-day basis unquestionably imposed important penalties if negotiating relationships became too embittered, or if negotiating rhetoric became particularly ferocious. The system tended to lead to a playing down of inherent conflicts, and to a wariness of allowing tensions to mount too high. It was conducive to a presentation of negotiatory differences to the work force in dry, technical, and unemotional terms, un-embroidered by the jabbing asides about class greed and exploita-tiveness that was typical of the accounts that reached the workers in France.

A third difference between the French and British systems lay in the time spacing of negotiations. The British negotiations took place annually, and their results were applicable to the following twelve months. This meant that the tension generated by the climax of a negotiation occurred only once in the year, and the remaining months were relatively undisturbed by issues of contractual dispute. The French system was rather different. Given the centralized and collectivized pattern of negotiation, meetings tended to be highly formal and had to be planned well in advance. There were usually three meetings to negotiate salaries, spaced out across the year; and, most importantly, it was usual for *each* meeting to lead to some concrete result — either an agreement or, most commonly, a uni-lateral decision by management. This meant that, in France, salary disputes were on the agenda over a much greater part of the year. The French worker was typically in a position either of anticipation of, or in the immediate aftermath of, an important negotiation.

For the French worker the issue of his contractual relationship with his employer was a major preoccupation throughout the year, and the psychological separation between management/worker relations in their contractual mode and in their technical mode was likely to be minimized. For the British worker, it was more likely that the year would be experienced in terms of successive phases in which for a restricted period contractual relationships became pre-dominant, while for the rest of the year the focus lay on co-operative technical relationships. The British system encouraged a differentia-tion of the modes of management/worker relationships, the French system their mutual interpenetration. By enhancing the salience of contractual disputes with management across the year, the French system made it more likely that the overall image of management would be coloured by the experience of economic conflict.

The time spacing of negotiations also affected their character. Within the British system the negotiators could take their time. The typical pattern was for the stewards to forward their demands, and then for a series of meetings to be held at which proposals and counter-proposals would be put forward, studied, and discussed. The important point is that no particular meeting was regarded as crucial. The breakthrough to agreement could occur unexpectedly at any time. There was little feeling that it was critical for a decision to be reached there and then. This reduced the pressure on the discussions, and it meant that, where there was fairly deep disagreement, there was the time to expand arguments more fully and to try to negotiate acceptable compromises. It made possible a process of mutual socialization into the role perspectives of the other; and this, in turn, was conducive to greater flexibility and tolerance.

In France, the fact that each meeting in the course of the year was expected to produce a result tended to increase the atmosphere of tension that surrounded it. The size, impersonality, and brevity of the meetings ensured that they could be the scene of little genuine discussion. It was understandable for the workers to feel that, if management was going to make major concessions, it would have to decide on them in the crucial informal discussions between employers that preceeded the meeting, in which a common negotiating position was drawn up. Once that had been established, then the sheer diffi- culty of obtaining the co-ordination between employers necessary to determine which compromises would be generally acceptable made it likely that the employers would be relatively inflexible. But, if it was correct that the employers had to be influenced before the meeting, then the only effective method of communication with them lay through overt expression of discontent in industrial action. There was, then, a pattern by which crucial meetings came to be *preceded* by strikes. The rationale behind this was clearly expressed in a CFDT tract of February 1968:

A Parity Commission is far removed from an idyllic encounter of people who meet for the pleasure of seeing each other. Every Parity Commission is situated in a highly determined context — that of the relationship of power that exists at the moment that it is being held.

If there exists throughout the industry a SUFFICIENT PRESSURE (as after 17 May 1967) we can hope for sufficient *concessions by the employers* to justify an Agreement. In the absence of such pressure a Parity Commission cannot bring any very tangible concrete result.[5]

This had two effects. First, it poisoned the mood of the negotia- tions — partly because management felt that the strikes were un- reasonable given the fact that negotiations had not even begun, partly because the union delegates, arriving fresh from mobilizing the base, were still wrapped in the emotional fervour of contestation and were in little mood for compromise. Second, it meant that whatever gains were achieved at the meeting were immediately attributed by the workers to the success of their militancy, and concessions on the part of management simply reinforced the belief that management/

worker relations were determined by power and power alone. There was a vicious circle in which the failure of genuine negotiations in the meetings led to an emphasis on the shop floor on the importance of a display of power before meetings which, in turn, made it less likely that the meetings would see genuine negotiations.

A fourth difference between the French and British systems was the fact that the negotiations in Britain led to a signed agreement whereas in France they usually ended with a unilateral decision by management. This accentuated the types of problems that emerged from the time-phasing of negotiations. The signing of the agreement — almost invariably with the explicit consent of the mass meeting — created a clear point of closure in the phase of contractual dispute. Perhaps the work force had not obtained satisfaction on certain issues, but in formally accepting the compromise it invested the *status quo* with a certain degree of legitimacy, and it was implicitly understood that unresolved areas of contractual dispute should not be allowed to interfere with the work process, but should be reserved for the next negotiating round when they would be brought forward following the normal procedure 'at the proper time and place'.

With the French system, there was simply no equivalent to this. At the end of each round of negotiation the representatives would leave angry and embittered; they would come out of the meeting denouncing the employers' miserliness, and their lack of any real willingness to enter into discussions:

It was on Wednesday 15th June, then, that the different representatives met around the negotiating table in the Avenue Kléber, Paris; and our representatives from Dunkirk had high hopes of being able to bring back to their comrades a substantial increase in minimum rates.

Alas . . . the meeting began at 3 p.m. and ended about 4.30 p.m. After various proposals had been put forward by the Unions, the Employers offered us to raise the value of the 'point' to 1 franc 55. [The 'point' formed the basis of a formula for calculating minimum salaries. D.G.]

We had the choice: *1,55 or nothing.*

Faced with such a ridiculously low figure, the Comrades refused to sign, and with good reason.

. . . the Representatives of our Federation wanted absolutely to engage in a serious discussion, but given the intransigent attitude of the Employers, your Delegates were unable to hide their anger.

(Tract. 'Syndicats CGT–CFTC–CGT–FO. — de la Raffinerie de Dunkerque' *Juin 1960*.)

NO DISCUSSIONS ABOUT SALARIES

This, in reality, was the astonishing declaration made by the President of the Employers' Federation . . . at the 'Parity Commission' of 19 January.

The extraordinary brevity of this meeting, held under the auspices of the

National Parity Commission and called at the initiative of the Employers themselves, shows that they were only looking for a pretext to pursue a reactionary social policy.

In effect, the employers' delegation did nothing more than let the union representatives know of its refusal to examine their demands, and of its decision to increase salaries by 2% and not to reduce the length of the working week.

(CGT Tract, 'Fédération Nationale des Industries Chimiques' 20.1.1966.)

THE EMPLOYERS HAVE AGAIN REFUSED ANY SERIOUS DISCUSSION
The Employers' Delegation takes little trouble to discuss our demands . . . *A quarter of an hour* was enough for the Employers' Federation to explain that it was unable to go further than:

> — 2% on basic salaries.
> — and an equivalent increase of minimum salaries.

The question of the reduction of the working week was disposed of in *3 minutes*: they do not intend to modify the existing hours.

And just to be certain that no illusion lingers on, the President of the Employers' Federation hastened to declare that *these proposals will not be modified*. In other words, 'You can say whatever you like, put forward all the possible arguments, we're not interested. It's 2%, and that's that'.

(Tract 'CFTD Pétrole' 18.1.1968.)

Faced with the employers' unwillingness to make any reasonable concession, there was no choice, the unions argued, but immediately to intensify industrial action, since only the exercise of power would make management listen. The spreading out of the formal contractual negotiations across the year was, then, accentuated in France by the fact that the negotiations themselves tended to accelerate rather than diminish the growth of antagonisms, and that each negotiation — far from bringing the curtain down on unresolved issues — simply unleashed a new wave of industrial action in protest against them.

The formal procedure of agreement in Britain both gave an aura of legitimacy to the prevailing social order of the factory, and clearly 'marked-off' the phase of economic conflict with management. The absence of such agreements in France meant that there was no psychological closure to economic conflict with management, and this made it more likely that this conflict would be more salient to the life-experience of the workers, and more central to their overall image of management.

In the highly salient area of pay negotiations, then, the French and British workers were likely to have fundamentally different experiences of the nature of power relations. The typical experience of the French workers was more likely to be conducive to a feeling of the relevance of class categories of thought, with their implications of a permanent conflict of interests between an exploitative capitalist class of employers and a class of wage labourers, while the British

system was more conducive to a perception of particularized relationships in which contractual conflict was only one element.

Organizational change

It has frequently been recognized that organizational change is one of
the most powerful generators of conflict between management and
the work force. This is because it frequently involves a fundamental
threat to the workers' security. It may undermine traditional working
practices, and lead to the disintegration of well-established patterns
of relations, both among workers and between workers and supervisors. It threatens the intensification of work loads and poses tricky
problems about the grading and rewards attributable to new types
of jobs with their implications for the traditional status structure of
the organization. For some, it threatens demotion, loss of income
and status, and even redundancy. Organizational change is typically
associated by the worker with the threat of a sharp deterioration in
working conditions, the loss of work satisfactions gradually accumulated over the years, and acute job insecurity. Given such a potentially inflammable situation, it could be expected that the way that
management handles organizational change will be of particular importance in determining its image among the workers.

The French and British institutional systems led to typically
different methods of handling organizational change, and as a consequence of this change implied a substantially different type of experience for the workers.[6] We can best illustrate this by comparing
the attempts by Dunkirk and Kent management to reduce and
restructure the work force in the light of the growing competitiveness of the oil industry in the 1960s. We have chosen Kent and
Dunkirk because our data is most complete and detailed for these
two cases (see chapter 2). However, the basic differences in procedure
for introducing organizational change would have emerged equally
from a study of Grangemouth and Lavera.

The comparison is an interesting one in that we can watch the
way that management of two very similar factories faced an almost
identical problem in the two countries. In both Kent and Dunkirk
management was faced with the need to carry out a reduction in
manning levels in the situation of a static refinery. The implication of
this was that it was unable to carry through the reductions simply
by redeploying workers into better paid jobs in newer units. On the
other hand, in neither case was management faced with a crisis

situation in which personnel would have to be laid off rapidly. Management had the room for manoeuvre to plan carefully, and to phase its restructuring of the work force over a period of years. The strategies that were adopted do not reflect the pressures of the moment, but reveal the logic of the normal institutional mechanisms of power.

Organizational change at Dunkirk

1. The initiation of the phase of radical reorganization in the French Company came from the Paris head office. It was first announced by the President of the Company at a meeting of the Central Company Committee in 1965. The process of reorganization was announced as inevitable — a necessary concomitant of the economic situation. The President warned: 'From now on, and irreversibly, we are involved in a future of struggle and *permanent* change.'[7]

Although the refinery Directors were individually responsible for working out and implementing the process of change within the refineries, the pressure from above was never far under the surface. As the Dunkirk Director explained to his Works Committee on 12 January 1967: 'The Director of the Refinery has pledged his word to the Director General that he will satisfactorily carry through the reorganizations, and again, it would then be desirable to pass without delay to the application of the measures which are envisaged.'[8]

Hence, although discussions about refinery level reorganizations were restricted to the refinery's own institutions, the representatives were made aware that they were not discussing with a free agent. The driving force behind the process of change remained out of their reach at Paris.

2. In planning the reorganization, the managerial machinery for considering the human relations problems that might arise was relatively weak. The French Director, himself, was deeply embroiled with the daily activity of his major departments which were all individually responsible to him and to him alone. This high level of involvement with the technical running of the refinery on a day-to-day basis clearly made it difficult for him to spend much time on strategic planning. This was compounded by the fact that his departmental machinery for analysing industrial relations problems was highly inadequate. The main burden for advising management fell on the shoulders of the Secretary General. But the Secretary General's

task seemed truly mammoth. His sphere of responsibility covered the entire financial and personnel activities of the refinery, quite apart from his role as industrial relations adviser. Which of these many activities under his formal responsibility he actually spent time thinking about seemed to depend in good part on where the most immediate pressure was coming from. Even if the Secretary General was genuinely concerned about industrial relations problems — as was certainly the case at Dunkirk — it was difficult for him to handle them in anything but a discontinuous and *ad hoc* way.

It seems probable that this weakness of advisory machinery at refinery level was an effect of the highly centralized pattern of negotiations with the unions, and the reluctance to engage in meaningful plant-level discussions.

3. The drawing up of the proposals for change was placed entirely in the hands of managerial study groups. When completed, the studies — which would lay out the feasible options for restructuring a given sector — would be handed to the head of the relevant department, and to the Director. Access to the studies was restricted to management.

The study groups tackled the different areas of the refinery in a piecemeal fashion starting with the more peripheral services in 1966, and ending with the central area of the production units in the period 1970/1971. The overall sequence of the studies was never clearly defined to the representatives. In 1966, for instance, we find the Director assuring the Works Committee that he had no intention of reducing manning levels in the production units, and that indeed these could be considered as already undermanned.[9] In practice, manning reductions in the production units came both to be planned and implemented.

In carrying out a reorganization, the refinery Director was legally obliged to 'consult' the Works Committee. The key article of the law defining the Committee's rights reads as follows:

The Committee 'studies the measures envisaged by the Director and the suggestions put forward by the personnel with the aim of improving the production and productivity of the enterprise and it proposes the items which it has retained . . . It is obligatorily informed and consulted about questions concerning the organization, the management, and the general running of the enterprise, and notably about measures that affect the volume or the structure of the work force, the length of work time or the conditions of work or employment of the personnel. It can formulate what it would like to be done about these different points. The committee is obligatorily informed with good notice of any projects for compressing the number employed; it puts forward its opinions on the projected scheme and the details of its application.'[10]

In practice, however, the representatives played no meaningful role whatsoever over the whole period of reorganization from 1966 to 1970. Their influence over proposals was minimal, and, indeed, for the greater part of the period constructive discussions were blocked by a sharp clash over the interpretation of the legal rights of the Committee.

To understand why this was the case it is important to realize that the apparent precision of the law is illusory. The Committee is to be 'informed' about organizational changes, but in just what detail is it to be informed? It must be informed in good time, but what is good time enough? The answers to these questions can make all the difference between the Committee being in a position to formulate effective counter-proposals that could influence management's decisions, and its having little option but to reject or rubber-stamp pre-determined decisions. The obligation on management to consult the Committee is even more problematic. The interpretation of 'consultation' could vary from the most formal pretence of listening to the views of the Committee when the entire project has in fact been already finalized, to a genuine attempt to take into account the opinion of the representatives.

The amount of prior warning that management gave the Committee varied sharply according to the period under consideration. Between 1967 and 1971 there appear to have been three principal phases.

In the initial phase, management presented its proposals before implementation, and in January 1967 a special commission of the Works Committee was set up to examine them.[11] By June of the same year the commission had collapsed with bitter recriminations. The representatives claimed that they had not been allowed to have contact with the people who had carried out the studies, that management refused any information on the long term grading of the new posts, and finally that management was already beginning to implement changes without waiting for the commission to express its view.[12]

In a second phase, management appears to have proceeded by ignoring the Committee altogether. When challenged on the legality of this, the Director justified his position in the following terms:

The method adopted about two years ago, by which the studies for the reorganizations were carried out by cost reduction study groups whose conclusions were presented to the Works Committee for information and consultation, was unsatisfactory. The examination of the conclusions of the studies gave rise to sharp discussions between the Director and the representatives only to invariably arrive at statements of disagreement. As a result, the Director has judged it preferable for certain studies to ask management itself to proceed with the studies for the reorganization of its services, it being understood that when the conclusions are being put into practice there will be room for dialogue between management and the representatives of the personnel belonging to the sector.[13]

In the third phase — from the beginning of 1969 — the Director reverted to the earlier procedure of giving the Committee management's proposals before implementation. However, it would appear that management engaged simultaneously in direct discussions with the workers of the sector concerned, and the members of the Works Committee clearly regarded this as an attempt to cut the ground from under their feet as representatives.

A representative of the personnel notes that since the decisions have already been made, it is difficult for the Works Committee to formulate comments. The people concerned have been directly informed by management about the measures which were going to involve them, before the Works Committee has been put in the picture.

The Secretary feels that the reactions that each person concerned might have had, as an individual, are not necessarily in agreement with the interests of the personnel taken as a whole.[14]

In so far as it allowed discussions to take place management made it clear that it took a literal interpretation of the law and that it alone had the responsibility and the authority for making decisions. This was made clear from the very first meeting at which proposals were presented to the Works Committee for consultation.

The President asks the Works Committee what remarks the elected representatives might have to make now that they have seen the information that has been communicated to them.

However, he recalls beforehand the procedure that is followed over questions of cost reduction:
— each group responsible for a study can only submit its proposals to management.
— management itself, and on its own responsibility, applies the recommendations that it has decided to retain at the end of the study.[15]

Management, then, regarded its prerogative in decisions over organizational change as absolute and this conditioned the type of information it was prepared to make available to the representatives. In management's view the role of the Works Committee was confined to examining the implications of changes for the welfare of the individuals who would be immediately affected. The technical decision about the specific form the reorganization was to take, it regarded as outside the Committee's competence. In consequence management was prepared to allow the Committee to examine the final proposals for change, but not to see the original studies in which the range of different possible options was discussed. For their part, the representatives maintained that they had a right to look at these original studies since it was only if they could see the technically feasible options that they could meaningfully discuss and influence the reorganization proposed. The two parties were unable to overcome their disagreement on this question and in consequence the discussions remained paralysed from the outset.

4. The absence of meaningful discussions in the Works Committee makes it difficult for part of the period in question to know how this gradual and piecemeal process of organizational change was experienced on the shop floor. It is notable, however, that already by September 1966 the Secretary General had drawn up a private memorandum for Company management, arguing that the problem of manning levels had become the predominant preoccupation of the unions in the refinery and suggesting that this reflected deep worries among the workers themselves.[16] The situation became clearer in the autumn of 1970 when management began to prepare to implement its plans to reorganize certain sectors of the production units. As we have seen, these had hitherto been left untouched, and indeed in 1966 management believed that they were already undermanned. They presented a particular problem in that the determination of adequate manning levels on the units is inherently very difficult and because undermanning greatly increased the level of danger in the work. Management's proposals were announced to the Works Committee in the summer of 1970, and led to the now familiar conflict over the definition of the powers of the Committee. Then, suddenly, in November, taking both management and the representatives by surprise, the shift workers came out in revolt against the proposed measures. A private managerial report gives the following account of what happened:

Taking advantage, it seems of the weekend of the 7/8th November, and the absence of the principal union officers, members of the hard-line ('Maoist', 'red', or 'gauchist') faction of the CGT set about inflaming the feelings of the personnel of the sector affected by the reorganization in particular, and of the shift work personnel in general. The union officers were informed of the high feelings that had built up on Monday 9th November, and in order to get an accurate measure of the extent of the problem, and equally, so at least it seems, to calm people down, they called the personnel to a meeting that took place on Friday 13th November at 15 h . . . That meeting, it seems, was extremely stormy, and the union officers were overwhelmed by their troops.[17]

The unions now decided to take over the leadership of the protest movement, and, after a sharp intensification of their demands in

December, finally brought the work force out on strike against the proposed reorganization in January 1971.

The process of reorganization in the French refinery, then, culminated in a revolt of the base that appears to have been spontaneous, and that took both management and the representatives by surprise. At first sight, the suddenness and violence of the revolt is puzzling given the relatively minor nature of the specific change at which it was directed — a regrouping of the workers in one sector on to a flying squad basis. Management seemed genuinely at a loss in trying to understand what had gone wrong, and tended in conversation to put it down to the fundamental irrationality of worker action. What seems probable, however, is that the specific incident sparked off a much deeper anxiety about the future that had gradually been accumulating in the face of creeping organizational change.

Organizational change at Kent

1. In contrast to the French case, the initiative for reorganization at Kent came primarily from refinery management, and throughout the process of change the Refinery Manager clearly possessed considerable freedom to decide on the tactics to deploy, the specific set of changes to press for, and the pace at which changes should be introduced. While the general economic factors that influenced French management clearly played their role, the immediate inspiration for change seems to have been the success of Esso management at Fawley in carrying through quite fundamental changes in the deployment of the personnel. This led Kent management in 1961 to call in a firm of consultants to assess the efficiency of its maintenance department. The consultants came to the somewhat disturbing conclusion that the work force was operating at only 40% of its potential efficiency. At roughly the same time, management was coming under increasing pressure from the craft unions to follow the example of Fawley, and to negotiate changes that would make possible a substantial rise in salaries.[18]

2. For most of the period of drawing up and carrying through its proposals for change, refinery management could draw on a substantially more developed industrial relations machinery than existed in either of the French refineries. This can probably be attributed to the fact that under the British system, management was carrying on regular negotiations at plant level both with the shop floor representatives and with the full-time officials.

In the first place, the General Manager himself had largely withdrawn from the problems of the everyday technical running of the refinery,[19] and was able to spend a good part of his time thinking about longer term issues. As the General Manager at Kent put it: 'I see my job as one of trying to get people to think about things in a new way.' Moreover, in both of the British refineries there were industrial relations officers who had the full-time job of getting to know shop floor problems inside out, and who had direct access to the Refinery Manager. While there was no question of either of these being neutral, they did clearly have a very good understanding of the viewpoint of the stewards, and they had a perspective on the organization that differed markedly from that of many of the line managers.

Underneath the industrial relations officers, there were two employment relations officers — one for the Operations Department, and one for the Maintenance Department. These men constituted management's front line for handling industrial relations problems, and it was their job to soothe the stewards in the first flush of anger. Three out of four of these officers had previously been either union branch officials or shop steward convenors. They had been appointed largely because of the skill they had shown in leading negotiations for the shop floor. They had a formidable knowledge of shop floor politics, and there can be no doubt that they were highly effective as trouble handlers. Indeed, their combination of managerial authority and knowledge of the shop floor sometimes risked leading to a concentration of power at this level that management found positively alarming.

3. Management clearly took time in making up its mind on the exact strategy it was going to adopt. In a curiously oblique reference to the Fawley agreement, an internal management memorandum of 1962 makes it clear that an attempt to introduce a certain amount of change through the use of existing managerial prerogative was still on the cards. 'We feel that the need to negotiate an Agreement of the type concluded elsewhere is not entirely proved, as it should be possible to obtain many of the advantages outlined in the Agreement under consideration by good organisation, and "infiltration", thus establishing helpful local customs and practices without cost.'[20]

However, in the course of 1963, union pressure clearly mounted and the strategy management eventually decided to deploy for carrying out the reorganization was that of comprehensive productivity bargaining. This meant that management sought change by obtaining

the explicit agreement of the work force to a complex set of proposals in exchange for a substantial rise in salaries. The basic principle
adopted was that savings made through the reorganization would be
split 50 : 50 between management and the work force.

In thus accepting the principle of comprehensive productivity
bargaining, management committed itself not only to laying out its
plans to the unions for a period of several years, but it also *de facto*
surrendered its formal prerogative to unilaterally control substantial
areas of work organization, and this correspondingly led to an important increase in the *formal* extent of union control.

The constraints implicit in this procedure were evident in the
negotiations with the craft unions that began in April 1964. Management was concerned to secure manpower reductions through the
elimination of mates and chargehands, and to increase the efficiency
of the craft force by introducing greater inter-craft flexibility, and
eliminating paid overtime which it regarded as an important force
behind the preservation of restrictive practices. From the very
beginning of the negotiations, the craft stewards were brought into
the centre of the discussions, and the full-time officials repeatedly
made it clear that all proposals had to pass through and receive the
acceptance of the stewards. Between May 1964 and May 1965, the
stewards were given some 7000 hours of paid time for discussions
with their members. The final agreement was concluded and signed
in March 1966. A second round of negotiations began in November
1967 and led to a second agreement in December 1969. In the course
of these agreements management achieved substantial gains in terms
of the relaxation of demarcations, but it is important to note that in
both sets of negotiations critical issues had arisen on which the two
sides disagreed intensely. In the first series of negotiations, management had wanted the introduction of a detailed record system of the
time taken over maintenance jobs; and in the second, one of its
principal objectives had been to establish provisions allowing a much
more extensive use of contractors for maintenance work in the
refinery. Both of these proposals aroused substantial opposition
among the craft workers who saw them as posing a direct threat to
their conditions of work on the one hand and their job security on
the other. The important point here is that, having adopted a strategy
of negotiating change, management had to drop both of these crucial
proposals when it failed to win the craftworkers' consent to them.

4. On the T&GWU side — mainly affecting the operators — the
procedure of negotiations changed substantially over time, and the

course of this development is revealing about the implications of different methods for experience on the shop floor. The first round of negotiations started in December 1964, and management's objectives were to secure substantial crew reductions, the introduction of a simpler grading system to facilitate flexibility, and a series of smaller scale economies such as the abolition of the internal transport system and the existing provisions for the delivery of meals to shift workers. In the initial phase management drew up a series of proposals for crew reductions, and negotiated with the full-time officials a salary increase in exchange for an acceptance of the general principles involved.

The immediate reaction of the operators appears to have been one of considerable anxiety. Poorly informed, the operators seem to have feared that the reductions would necessitate widespread redundancy. At a meeting with the full-time official, management told the union representative that: '. . . when the crew reductions on the Crude Distillation units were due to take place, there appeared to be grave doubts amongst the operating personnel regarding what, if anything, had been agreed between Management and Union Representatives'.[21]

The full-time official replied that the trouble had arisen because the workers were worried about the implications of the proposals for their job security, and he added: 'the rapidity of the Company's proposals had denied him the opportunity of discussing this point fully. Within hours of the meeting on the 13th January, rumours of redundancy affecting 90 people were current throughout the refinery.'

The senior shop floor representative made it clear that the workers felt that the Company's proposals had not been laid out in sufficient detail, and had not been adequately discussed with the work force itself:

Mr. N. (the branch secretary) also commented on the ambiguity of the Company's statement. Management were talking of crew reductions affecting about 90 people by October, and no one on shift foresaw normal wastage of this magnitude. . . . They . . . had accepted in principle Stages 2 & 3 but they could not be expected to accept the full implementation when they were not in a position to know how or when the Company intended to carry it out.[22]

When the discussions for the next, and most important, stage of the agreement reached their critical phase in 1966, management was concerned to avoid a repetition of this panic reaction by the operators, by making sure that much better provisions were established for communication with the shop floor. Management remained the initiator of proposals, but this time it provided the time and facilities for special union-branch subcommittees to be set up to discuss in detail the proposals with members of middle management. Management transferred the shift workers involved in the discussions onto days and continued them on full pay during the period of the discussions. It is clear that both sides felt that this innovation had been a good thing.[23]

In July 1966, however, the national economic crisis and the government's pay freeze cut sharply across the normal development of the negotiations. The pay freeze limited the Company's room for manoeuvre, while the shift branch was still dissatisfied with two of the proposals in the existing offer. The negotiations remained deadlocked until the spring of 1967. Throughout this period, the full-time official had been showing signs of increasing impatience with his own members. In a meeeting of 22 September 1966 he declared himself completely 'nonplussed' by the position the branch had adopted, and on 18 October he explicitly refused to take up with management the grievances that the branch had expressed over the proposals.[24] He regarded the existing draft agreement as a good one, and felt that the branch members were making a fuss over trifles. Then, in May 1967, he finally used his own authority to sign the agreement over the head of the branch.

It is notable that the branch did not explicitly attack the legitimacy of this move, and there was no resort to unofficial action. On the other hand, it made its discontent very evident. The branch officers were rapidly deposed and replaced by people who were believed to be more radical. The full-time official himself clearly came in for a certain amount of personal abuse. On 4 December 1967 he told management that 'he was now being accused of being a traitor and a Company stooge'.[25]

It might have been thought at this point that the prospects for successful future negotiations were decidedly dim. The atmosphere in the refinery had been embittered, and the operators had clearly become suspicious of management's methods of handling the negotiations. In fact, however, not only was a new round of negotiations launched, but it was brought to a highly successful conclusion with the full support of the branch membership.

The way in which management got out of the impasse that had been created is interesting. It involved a substantial revision of the original institutional procedures by which responsibility for constructing the new proposals was delegated to a Joint Committee

composed of an equal number of management and branch representatives. The Committee provided its own account of the problems it
faced, and the initial reaction of the work force.

It soon became apparent that, throughout the union membership dissent continued to prevail over the outcome of the 1967 Productivity Agreement. Some
members were exceedingly suspicious of the 'new approach' towards greater
productivity by way of a Joint Working Party. Many were of the opinion that
Management were solely responsible for the 'new approach' and that they were
delegating their responsibility to manage. This attitude was quickly changed,
however, when union members were informed that the original suggestion of
Joint Working Parties was made by their District Officer and that management
had agreed to his proposal. The Company representatives of the Joint Working
Party were invited to a Shop Stewards' meeting. At this meeting the efforts of
all four members of the J.W.P. appeared to further relieve the perceptible
tension that existed.
   During the following weeks the general attitude of union members changed
from that of suspicion to one of pleasant surprise to know that their views,
ideas, and suggestions were being sought. The knowledge that their own contribution could affect the proposals in this report instilled a greater confidence
in the 'new approach'.
   In the course of this project, dozens of employees have contributed their
own ideas and/or assisted in assessing the practicability of other suggestions.[26]

The proposals forwarded by the Joint Working Party became the
principal basis of the subsequent negotiations, and led to a new
agreement in December 1969.

A comparison of organizational change in the two refineries

In comparing the process of organizational change in the two refineries, the following contrasts appear particularly fundamental:
   The strategies deployed by management differed sharply. French
management regarded organizational structure as part of managerial
prerogative, and essentially imposed change by managerial fiat.
British management followed the logic of a semi-constitutional
strategy, and sought to carry through organizational change by
consent.
   The retention of a conception of managerial sovereignty in France,
and the preference for a consensual strategy in Britain were linked
to differences in the nature and visibility of rewards for change. This
was not accidental. Once British management had accepted the principle of change by consent, it was probable that it would have to buy
consent. In the French case rewards were limited to the upgrading of
certain individuals in the sector immediately affected to compensate

for the increased complexity of work tasks.[27] In the British case, rewards for organizational change were shared by the work force *as a whole*. Moreover, the basis of the rewards was not just the nature of the new job definitions (although the British workers benefited from this too), but the overall increase in productivity. Through the negotiations a direct link was established between the organizational change in question and enhanced salaries. In the British case, then, the link between change and reward was both more substantial and more visible.

The information made available to the representatives about the long term perspectives of management differed sharply in the two cases. In the French refineries, management announced its proposals piecemeal, and replied to questions about its long term intentions with somewhat vague formulas about the fact that the industry was entering an era of *permanent* change. In the British case, management laid out its proposals for several years in a detailed document that formed the basis of negotiation.

It is notable that these different methods of deciding upon and implementing change were associated with substantially different reactions from the work force. What is interesting is that in both countries there is clear evidence that organizational change was easily regarded as highly threatening by the work force, and could lead to anxiety and a reaction of panic. This came out quite clearly in the early phases of the British case when management was still largely confining its discussions to the full-time officials of the T&GWU. There is, then, no reason to think that the changes *per se* were intrinsically more likely to be regarded as threatening in one country than in the other. And yet in the French case the process of organizational change culminated in a spontaneous eruption of the base which took management completely by surprise, whereas in the British case the process of change culminated in a relatively high degree of consensus, and the maintenance of harmony between management and the work force.

It seems probable that an important factor in explaining the difference in overall response to the potentially threatening situation of organizational change lay in the degree of participation in the process of decision making.

The French workers had no power to veto decisions they strongly disliked, and they were confronted by piecemeal changes whose long term implications were not spelt out to them. This created a situation which might be termed one of 'institutionalized insecurity'. Having only fragmentary information on longer term managerial plans, and little ability to influence the decisions being made, it seems probable that the French workers lived in a fairly permanent state of anxiety about what the future held in store for them. In a situation of institutionalized insecurity, a relatively small move can mobilize much deeper sources of worry. It was above all what changes in the present signified for possibilities in the future that led to the apparently irrational intensity of the French workers' action.

In the British refineries the institutional system guaranteed a considerably higher level of security, and as the process of negotiation continued it grew steadily higher. By the final stage of the negotiations, the work force could be pretty sure that proposals that they felt strongly against would either be modified, or abandoned altogether. As this process of participation increased, we can see a constant diminution in the level of anxiety of the work force from an initial state of anxiety and panic, to one of ambivalence and restrained dissatisfaction, to finally one of overt legitimation of the process and procedures of organizational change. Once a relatively high level of control had been achieved, a given move did not start a wave of worry about the future, because there was a feeling that any future developments could be controlled as and when they arose.

Organizational change and the image of management

It seems likely that the different experiences of power produced by the French and British institutional systems on issues so central to the quality of working life were conducive to different images of management.

For the French workers, the fact that organization change was imposed from above could lead easily to an interpretation of management's actions as uniquely concerned to maximize its own advantages rather than to seriously take into account the possible impact of such changes on the quality of work life. Institutionalized insecurity led to a free play of speculation about management's intentions, charged with the emotional intensity generated by anxiety. Together with the piecemeal method of introducing change, this led easily to an almost obsessional concern to divine the secret long-term intention behind every move that management made, and it led to a vision of management as devious, manipulative, and exploitative. Rather than run the risk of being tricked on issues as crucial as these, it was safer to immediately define relations as oppositional and hostile, and to react to each measure with distrust. Knowing that there were no institutional safeguards that would protect their interests, the workers tended to be preoccupied almost exclusively with the threat implicit in organizational change. Organizational change, then, in the French setting sharpened the awareness of a fundamental conflict of interest between management and the work force, and emphasized the decisive importance of relations of power.

Given the nature of their experience of the factory, it is, then, understandable that we found in chapter 5 that the French workers' image of management was sharply distinguished from that of the British workers by its tendency to regard management as exploitative, and that the criticisms that the French workers made of the organization were primarily focused on the way in which their interests and rights as workers were threatened by the existing system.

The relatively high level of security possessed by the British work force was conducive to a rather different image of management. In contrast to the types of criticism expressed by the French workers, the British workers tended to emphasize technical inefficiency in the running of the plant. This could well be seen as representing one of the longer term effects of the productivity negotiations. With a higher guarantee for its security, and a greater say in decision making, the British workers were more easily able to move away from a purely defensive attitude to organizational change, and to come to view it in terms of a mechanism that could serve the interests of all parties. As such their criticisms focused on the failure to carry through measures that would maximize productivity, and by adopting this perspective they were essentially viewing the organization from the same viewpoint as management.

At the same time, the willingness of management to subject its proposals to detailed scrutiny, and to drop proposals for which it was unable to gain consent, suggested that management did not operate altogether without regard for the implications of its actions for the well-being of the work force.

This combination of a closer identification with managerial objectives, and the belief that the planning of organizational change was taking into account the welfare of the work force, encouraged a blurring of the sense of irreconcilable conflict between management and workers, and was conducive to an image of management as concerned to maximize the advantages of all parties.

The level of participation, cultural values and the image of the firm

Many of the factors we have been considering in this chapter could be seen as in part deriving from a critical underlying structural difference between the institutional systems governing the refineries in the two countries — namely, the level of participation in medium-level decision making. In looking for a more generally applicable explanation of attitudes to the firm, a theory that included the effects of differential levels of participation would, then, appear to hold some promise.

Although market economies involve similar objective conflicts of interest between employers and employed, these contradictions appear to have different implications for the workers' perception of the firm in different societies. We need, then, to locate the intervening variables that account for the workers' image of the firm. Tentatively, we would suggest that the image of the firm is the product of the experiences of workers with specific aspirations and expectations within given types of institutional system. The effects of institutional structure are not, then, mechanical, but are conditional upon certain cultural contexts. This clearly makes explanation more complex, and reduces the range of feasible generalizations. Some degree of generalization, however, is likely still to be possible, since it is improbable that cultural values vary randomly, and there is probably a reasonable degree of homogeneity at least within the major strata of a given society. Indeed, historically, major new cultural currents seem to have swept across a variety of different societies at once, although the degree of penetration of the new values may have varied from one society to another.

In the course of the nineteenth century, the value of equality became increasingly salient in most Western societies, and it seems probable that this cultural change sharply increased tension between employers and employed given the prevailing principles of unilateral managerial power within the firm. In the twentieth century, however, a divergence began to occur between various Western societies in the pattern of institutional development within large-scale industrial enterprises. One aspect of this was that the institutional systems came to vary substantially in the degree of access to decision making that they allowed to the workers and their representatives over issues that were immediately important to them; and this, in turn, has led to rather different experiences of employment for workers involved in different types of institutional structure. In elaborating the reasons why this should be the case, we shall for the moment simplify the argument by assuming that the workers in these societies have roughly the same commitment to the value of equality.

The most general thesis is that, in cultures in which the value of equality has salience, the less participative the decision-making system — in the sense of the effective capacity of both workers and their representatives to influence the formulation of decisions and to veto proposals through the formal institutional machinery — the greater will be the tension in management/worker relations,[28] and the more likely it is that the firm will be viewed as exploitative. There are several reasons why this is likely to be the case:

(1) The less participative the decision-making system, the less will workers regard it as legitimate. A lower degree of legitimacy will in turn be associated with a higher degree of generalized distrust of management's motives. Since:

(a) In societies in which the value of equality has salience, workers will have expectations for a certain degree of control over decision making, as a derivation of more general expectations of equal treatment.

(b) The less participative the system, the more will these normative expectations conflict with the explicit or implicit normative structure of the formal institutions, and hence the less these will be regarded as legitimate.

(c) The lower the level of institutional legitimacy, the more workers will distrust the motives of management, since it will be assumed that the refusal to adopt an institutional system more congruent with prevailing cultural values is due to the fact that the system defends the fractional advantages of those in power.[29]

(2) The less participative the decision-making system, the less will workers with any given level of relative deprivation over substantive issues feel committed to specific decisions taken. Decisions, then, are likely to appear as imposed and hence lend support to an exploitative image of the firm. Since:

(a) The lower the legitimacy of the institutional procedures for decision making, the less likely it is that specific decisions will be acceptable.[30]

(b) The less participative the system, the less it will provide conditions conducive to attitude change when proposals conflict with workers' initial beliefs about what is a fair or correct course of action.[31]

(c) The less participative the system, the greater will be the temptation for management to increase its own advantages by exploitation of its power position rather than through a process of exchange. Conversely, in higher participative systems, where the work force can veto proposals, management will be more likely to try to achieve its goals through a process of exchange. Put crudely, to a certain degree, consent will be bought. The advantages acquired by workers in this process of exchange will increase the acceptability of a decision both because they will be intrinsically satisfying and because they will satisfy norms of reciprocity.

(d) Where commitment to important decisions is not achieved this will increase the likelihood of lasting hostility to management because there will be no temporary psychological closure over issues of dispute. Particular decisions will be judged primarily and continuously in terms of the extent to which they conflict with long-range worker goals. Even beneficial decisions will be judged less in terms of what has been acquired than in terms of what has not been acquired.

(e) Lack of commitment to decisions leads to the likelihood of greater hostility to management because decisions must be implemented primarily through the use of external constraints. Conversely, commitment activates internal controls. Decisions are, therefore, self-enforced, and are less likely to be experienced as coercive. Successful implementation of decisions will contribute to the individual's own sense of achievement, and will generate satisfaction.[32]

(3) The less participative the decision-making system, the less likely it is that the system of work organization will be well adapted to the needs and expectations of the work force. Dissatisfaction with the system of work organization will, in turn, contribute to an unfavourable image of management. Since:

(a) When management can impose decisions unilaterally, it is less likely to try to anticipate the problems that specific decisions will create for the lives of the workers, and hence, in the longer term, work organization will be determined principally by management's priorities, rather than by a compromise between the interests of management and the interests of the work force.[33]

(b) When management does wish to take account of the needs of the work force, it is less likely to have the relevant information for effective decision making. Low participative systems are likely to be associated with patterns of communication heavily biased towards a downwards flow of information and in which upward information is often distorted.[34]

(4) The less participative the decision-making system, the more it is likely to generate a generalized sense of insecurity in the work force. Insecurity is likely to lead to anxiety, and anxiety will find expression in enhanced suspicion of management's intentions and a higher level of hostility to management. Since:

(a) Less participative systems of decision making are likely to be associated with the piecemeal announcement of plans to the work force. Since management will regard decision making as its own prerogative, it will feel under less obligation to explain the long-term thinking behind specific proposals.[35]

(b) Where the work force is confronted by discrete decisions unrelated to a longer term perspective, it is more likely to react to individual proposals in terms of their *possible* implications for the future. This is likely to increase anxiety because the work force has no assurance that it will be able to prevent future developments if they do come to seriously threaten the quality of work life. Where future proposals can be vetoed, immediate proposals arouse less anxiety because workers feel they have the possibility of arresting management's longer-term strategy at a later date.

(5) The less participative the decision-making system, the more *intense* will be overt conflict between management and workers. Such conflict will be conducive to a conflictual image of relations with management. Since:

(a) Low participative systems generate greater frustrations, but provide less possibility for resolving them through the existing institutional machinery. There will, then, be a greater tendency for grievances to accumulate over time.

(b) In low participative systems, effective attempts to influence necessarily involve overt displays of coercive power; but in the context of a high level of managerial power coercive action also involves substantial personal risks for those who undertake it, and will only be undertaken when feelings of resentment have reached a very high level.

(c) Strike action will not then necessarily be more *frequent* than in more participative systems (indeed, it may be less so), but when it occurs it will be much more intense — that is to say, it will reflect higher levels of aggression against management.

(d) The highly-charged atmosphere of strikes in a low participative system is conducive to the use and acceptance of a high-keyed rhetoric in which the opponent is viewed in terms of a relatively simple, but emotionally charged sterotype.

(e) Intense conflict over a specific issue provides an experience that can act as a model for highlighting the relevance of a more general interpretation of management/worker relations as consisting of a fundamental conflict of interests in which the relative advantage obtained by each party is determined primarily by the power resources each can command.

A low participative system, then, by enhancing normative conflict, by increasing the likelihood that major decisions will be experienced as coercive, by reducing satisfactions derived from the work environment, by creating a generalized sense of insecurity, and by enhancing the intensity of overt conflict, will tend to generate an alienative attitude to the firm. Management will be viewed with distrust, and will be regarded as exploitative.

These propositions are explicitly culturally relative. Moreover, in order to simplify the presentation of what is in reality a complex pattern of interaction, we have assumed that the level of commitment to the value of equality is constant. Within a given society, the range of variation may not be sufficient to require serious modification of the theory in this simple form. Between societies, however, variations may well be greater. We need, then, to take into account the fact that at any given level of participativeness, tensions will be greater and the image of the firm will be more alienative, the higher the level of egalitarianism. This is because the level of egalitarianism will affect both procedural expectations and the degree of relative deprivation over substantive issues. It is our guess that in Western societies variations in the structure of institutions will prove of more causal significance than existing variations in commitment to the value of equality. But this is an empirical problem, and we would expect both to have some degree of causal efficacy. We return, then, to our earlier point that in the explanation of concrete situations, it is the interaction of cultural values and institutional structures that is crucial.

Our data cannot, and were not designed to, establish the validity of these propositions in any precise form. This would require a different programme of research. The argument, here, is simply that, if it is correct, such a theory would offer an economical explanation of several features of our data. There are some indications that the French workers were more committed to egalitarian values than their British equivalents — for instance, they felt they had a right to a higher degree of control over decisions, and they were less satisfied with their standard of living although they had higher salaries. On the other hand, they were involved in organizations that were substantially less participative. These two factors, then, reinforced each other and would help account for the fact that we found that the French workers: (1) regarded the formal structure of power of the enterprise as less legitimate than their British equivalents, (2) were more dissatisfied with important features of organizational structure — such as the salary structure, the manning levels, and the shift system, and (3) were more likely to have an 'exploitative' image of the firm.

9

The control of work performance

An important theme in the work of both Robert Blauner and Joan Woodward is that automation profoundly transforms the nature of the control system within the factory, and in so doing eliminates many of the worst sources of friction between management and workers. As Joan Woodward has put forward the most extreme version of this theory in arguing that control has been incorporated to a substantial degree into the machinery itself, we shall start by looking at her argument, and then examine the way in which it differs from Blauner's.

Mechanical control?

Types of control system can vary substantially between different organizations, Woodward argues, in their degree of impersonality.[1] At one end of the scale there are systems in which all the various aspects of control are carried out directly by managers, and in which it is highly probable that employees will feel the weight of personal power. Further along the scale one encounters systems of impersonal administrative control where the penalty for unsatisfactory performance — although mediated by human beings — is awarded very much as the result of the operation of an impersonal set of rules. A classic example of this form of control is to be found in the various systems of incentive payments. Finally, at the other extreme of the scale we find systems of mechanical control where control is built into the machinery itself, and where once the machinery has been designed and put in place, there is almost no need for managerial intervention to assure the required standards of performance. The specific form that a control system takes, Woodward believes, is closely linked to the dominant form of production technology, and continuous-process firms have highly mechanistic systems.[2]

The concept of mechanical control is in fact a tricky one. It is open to two rather different interpretations, and elements of both can be found in Woodward's own work. The first is that the machinery itself comes to control the production process automatically, and increasingly eliminates the need for human intervention. This seems to have been what was in her mind when she stressed the importance of the built in sequencing of operations, and when she discusses the development of automatic mechanisms.[3] Presumably the implications of this for management/worker relations is that direct hierarchical control becomes less important as the quality of the operator's work performance becomes less essential to the quantity, quality, and cost of the product. The incorporation of control into the technology itself leads, then, to a reduction of the need to control the operator's own behaviour, and hence reduces the potential for friction.

Now this is surely to make a confusion between a change in the mode of intervention of a worker in continuous-process production and the significance of his role in the productive process. Indeed, the whole tenor of the argument would seem rather strange to anybody coming fresh from a reading of Mallet or Blauner. For there we find precisely the opposite assertion — namely that the operator's role is now much more crucial, involves much greater responsibilities, and requires a much higher level of individual discretion. While we have argued earlier that it would be wise to take some of Blauner's more extravagant statements with a pinch of salt, there can, I think, be little doubt that the operators do still have a crucial role and that the quality of their work performance is critical to the quality of the product, to the time it takes to produce, to its cost, and perhaps most important of all to the physical preservation of the plant and of the work force itself.

Even in the everyday running of the units the operators were usually responsible for maintaining the specific quality of the product that was required. Given the volatility both of operating conditions and of the input products, this could involve persistent effort at adjusting the controls in order to keep to the required specifications. Moreover, at irregular intervals the operators had tasks where the cost of error was particularly high. When changing the flow of a product to a new storage reservoir, if an operator turned the wrong valve, he could mix products of very different qualities, and ruin hours of previous production. The entire supply could be recycled but the consequences for production time and cost can be easily imagined. The consequences of error were particularly serious at the difficult moments when units were started up or brought to a halt. What made errors particularly costly in a refinery was the high level of integration of the different units. An error on one unit had immediate implications for many others.

But it was not only in avoiding error that the operator's work performance could save the Company the immense costs of lost production. Critical too was his ability to anticipate problems in a way that could not be formally defined as part of his duty. The really skilled and experienced operator was renowned as having a sixth sense, an ability to hear almost imperceptible changes in the sound of the units which would enable him to detect a coming problem. If a difficulty could be anticipated, one could often take action that would avoid altogether the need to close down the unit. It was the unexpected breakdown that could prove so costly.

Although, then, a high level of automation certainly incorporates into the machinery many parts of the work process that with other technologies might be carried out by management and its employees, it does not reduce the significance of the operator's work performance for the quantity, quality, or cost of the product. He is unquestionably less directly related to the production process and his interventions are more irregular, but the consequences of poor work are enormous, and the need for a highly efficient control of operator performance remains crucial.

A second interpretation of the term mechanical control is that the machinery in some way regulates the worker's performance. Personal and impersonal administrative controls were after all forms of control over people, and the typology would remain most consistent if mechanical control were seen in the same light.

This is certainly what Blau and Scott had in mind in their discussion of impersonal controls.[4] They take the assembly line as their prime example of the way in which machinery itself can exercise control. There is clearly a sense in which the assembly line imposes mechanical constraints on the rate of production of the worker — at least if one focuses on the short term, and puts on one side the fact that the speed of the assembly line can itself be a central question of industrial relations. In assembly-line production the worker must carry out his specialized task within a given time, otherwise the next item will be upon him.

There is clearly no direct correspondence to the impact of an assembly line in a continuous-process firm. One of the most central characteristics of advanced automation is that it breaks the link between the rhythm of the machine and the rhythm of the operator's work. In comparison with the situation in other technologies, the worker is comparatively free to plan his own work schedule, and can be flexible in his choice of when to carry out specific operations. There is relatively little mechanical control of the rhythm of his work. The question, then, must be one of whether we can find rather different but comparable forms of mechanical control in a continuous-process setting.

The main attempt to develop the argument along these lines can be found in Wedderburn and Crompton's article 'Technological Constraints and Workers' Attitudes'.[5] Although the authors believe that the quantity of output is unaffected by the operators' performance, they do recognize that the quality of the produce may still be influenced by the way the workers do their job. They suggest, however, that their purest form of continuous-process production — their Works A — was highly distinctive in that the workers' performance was regulated by mechanical control rather than by the direct intervention of the managerial hierarchy.

Their argument is an interesting one, and it is worth looking at closely. Describing the quality control system in Works A, they write:

In Works A it was mainly built into the production system, in that dials showing the continuous analysis of the product were to be read as an integral part of the operator's work. If the continuous analysis showed that the quality of the produce was veering outside the prescribed limits, the operator concerned had to adjust his equipment to bring the quality back within the limits. Increasingly stringent quality specifications meant that the operator had to make adjustments more frequently, as the area of slack in the productions system was systematically eliminated. More detailed quality checks carried out by the laboratories were communicated directly to the operator. He acted on these results if necessary and, if he encountered any serious difficulties, called on his supervisor for help.[6]

Summarizing their argument a little later, they conclude:

Works A was a classic example of the operator's task becoming the 'control of control', and of control being almost completely mechanical.[7]

The assumption behind this argument appears to be that the dials control the operator by giving him information about the state of the product directly. But this is surely to confuse the problem of the communication of information with that of control. After all in many other forms of production the operator or worker can directly find out whether the quality of the product is good or poor simply by looking at it, but this hardly meets the problem of quality control. The crucial problem is what the worker does once he knows that the quality is deficient — does he immediately try to improve it, or does he simply shrug his shoulders. The dials in a continuous-process plant, then, can tell the operator when action should be taken; they can in no way ensure that he does act.

The same applies to their example of the direct communication of the results of laboratory analysis. This provides essential information but it does not ensure the quality of the operator's performance. And even if we confine ourselves to the question of communication, it is doubtful whether the pattern observed by the authors is really a direct result of the technology. Whether information is communicated directly to the operators or through lower management will be influenced both by the degree of technical competence of the work force and by management's beliefs about the best way of running an organization. But this is something that we will return to later.

It seems, then, doubtful whether the concept of mechanical control explains very much whether we take it in the sense of the elimination of the operator's responsibility or in the sense of the machinery regulating the worker's performance. The first argument involves a confusion between a change in the mode of the operator's intervention and the degree of importance of his intervention, whereas the second confuses the provision of information with the regulation of behaviour.

The status structure

Like Woodward and her team, Robert Blauner was convinced that advanced automation necessitated a fundamental break with traditional forms of control, but he approached the problem in a rather different way. His point of departure was that any attempt by management to impose a rigid system of surveillance would prove completely ineffective in a continuous-process setting. This was in part due to the physical mobility of the workers, and to the fact that the operators worked shifts. But it was also due to the nature of the work itself. The increased importance of the operator's own initiative and discretion on the work process implied a relationship of mutual dependence between management and the operators which made counterproductive any strictly hierarchical system of command.

In Blauner's view the only system of control that would work effectively under the conditions of continuous-process production was one in which control was no longer imposed by management on the workers but was internalized by the workers' themselves. But this immediately begs the question of why workers in continuous-process plant should be prepared to control their own performance.

One suggestion that Blauner puts forward as to why a system of internalized control is likely to be effective is that advanced automation leads to the development of a highly elaborate status structure. This has important implications for the assimilation of organizational norms. The nature of the technology, he believed, required an unusually wide range of skills, and this in turn brought about a highly differentiated system of job classification. This provided the worker with a promotion ladder that strongly encouraged him to have high career aspirations, and thereby motivated him to produce the best work performance that he was capable of. He writes:

An elaborate system of superior and inferior ranks supports a normative structure because those in higher positions have presumably internalized the goals of the enterprise and more clearly express its values. The existence of achievable higher positions also serves to motivate those of lower status to accept the goals of the organization and to act in accordance with its norms.[8]

In its general form, one must have serious reservations about the validity of this argument. In the first place such promotion as does occur is nearly entirely confined to grades within the blue-collar work force. One of the most characteristic features of the developing organizational structure of continuous-process industries is the increased tendency to recruit highly qualified engineers into lower management positions and the consequent reduction of the ambitious operator's hopes of moving into management.[9] This sharp restriction on promotion chances for the highest status operators necessarily blocks mobility at lower levels, and it undermines the value that is likely to be attached to the highest operator post because this can no longer be seen as a jumping off position for the real promotion prizes.

Just how frustrating the situation can be for somebody who did start off with high aspirations is clear from these comments by one of the French operators:

Ten or fifteen years ago a worker could hope to be promoted into supervision. Most of the supervisors were former workers. But the new policy of the Director is only to allow into supervision people with high formal qualifications. What's more, they've been suppressing foreman posts. They abolished the shift foreman and gave his work to the operator. It was the same work but with a smaller salary — it's the devaluation of a job. My hopes for promotion were crushed then. After that, I decided to learn all the posts in the Power Station — which I did. And at the moment that I had another possibility of being promoted it was again crushed because they gave the position of shift foreman to a completely new fellow with formal qualifications, who didn't know a thing. Now, I'm no longer interested in anything.

In one important sense the overall promotion range was decidedly restricted. But if we confine ourselves to the internal stratification of the work force itself, there is at first glance a little more support for Blauner's view. Within each refinery there was a hierarchical grading system with about seven different operator grades.

The moment we look more closely, however, the picture rapidly becomes more complex. If we look first at the operators as a whole we find that far from the pattern being one of equal distribution across the various operator grades, there was in fact a high degree of clustering. Two of the grades in each refinery accounted for 50% or more of the operators employed.

The classification system was designed to cover all operator posts within the refinery, but each refinery had major internal subdivisions, and each subdividion tended to employ a rather more limited stretch of the overall grading scale. The primary division among the operators was between people who worked on the Tank Farm and Jetties on the one hand, and people who worked on the Central Production Units on the other. Posts on the Tank Farm were usually drawn from a lower stretch of the scale than posts in the Production Units. For instance, at Kent all of the Grade E posts were to be found in the Tank Farm/Jetty area, whereas the base operator grade in the Production Units was Grade D. This was important because careers almost invariably took place within the major subdivisions. It was rare for a Tank Farm operator to transfer later to the Production Units, and hence operators in the two areas were faced with considerably different career possibilities.

Even the range of the scale used within one of the major subdivisions of the refinery did not really represent a career ladder up which a successful operator would climb step by step.[10] To illustrate, we can take the case of a Kent operator in the Central Production Units. The posts in the central units fell into one of four categories — A, B, C and D. But this did not mean that there were typically four steps in an individual's career. What was decisive for the career path was usually the structure of posts on the particular unit on which the person worked. Promotion tended to be internal to a unit because the skills needed for the higher posts could only be learned through long experience with the particular complex of machinery. Within a unit at Kent there were in fact usually only two or three grades. A and B were both top operator posts, and were never to be found together on any one unit. Grade C (which was usually allocated to an official stand-in for the Responsible Operator) simply did not exist on many of the units. All other operators were assigned to Grade D. The successful operator would then either move directly from Grade D to a Responsible Operator post, or he might pass through one intermediate position. The simplification of the grading system within units had been carried furthest at Kent, but the situation was not radically different in the other refineries. At Grangemouth the commonest pattern was for a unit to have three grades, and at Lavera for it to have four.[11] In neither case was the range of the classification system equivalent to the real career paths available to individuals. Blauner's picture, then, of an elaborate career ladder, along which the work force was spread out evenly, and up which people advanced step by step, was a rather poor description of the situation that we encountered in our refineries.

Finally, under normal conditions, promotion in a refinery tended to be pretty slow. This was largely because of the low turnover rates. As both Blauner and Mallet correctly pointed out, people tended to join a refinery to stay. Given the virtual impossibility of a Responsible Operator being promoted to a higher position, posts tended to become vacant only when the incumbent died or retired.

In its general form, Blauner's argument about the nature of career opportunities in continuous-process plant is untenable. Promotion into management is unusually restricted, the career ladder is not a particularly elaborate one, and mobility under normal conditions is fairly slow.

It is very probable, however, that Blauner's picture was considerably more adequate for the situation of the 1950s. In both France and Britain there had been a progressive simplification of the grading system on the units in the 1960s and early 1970s. The primary drive behind this came from the fact that management was finding a highly stratified system an obstacle to efficiency. The emphasis in managerial thinking in both countries came increasingly to lie on the importance of manpower flexibility. Work roles in a continuous-process plant are difficult to define with any precision, and in practice what is needed is a willingness to lend a helping hand where it is required rather than any rigid adherence to a specific set of operations. A complex hierarchical system, and clear status differentiation between the occupants of different work roles, are likely to make it much more difficult to develop a co-operative team in which people would be prepared to define their roles loosely.

While Blauner may have correctly perceived the situation at the particular time he was carrying out his study, he was incorrect in believing that a high level of status differentiation was a necessary corollary of a highly automated system of production. On the contrary, continuous-process technology requires manpower flexibility, and flexibility was hampered by a high level of status differentiation.

The work team in the control system

The second, and rather more persuasive, argument that Blauner deploys is that, in the continuous-process setting, many of the traditional control functions of management are handed over to the work group. His most explicit statement of his view is in the following passage:

> the work team which runs an individual plant takes over many of the functions of supervision in other technological contexts. A worker will come to work and do his job well, not out of fear of a particular boss, but because he feels the other operators in his crew are depending on him to do his part of the total work. Many of the co-ordinating and administrative functions of supervision fall to the head shift operator, the leader of each plant's work crew. Since the head operator is an hourly blue-collar employee, his guidance is not felt to be oppressive supervision. (p. 147)

The links between the new technology and team control are not elaborated in detail, but in their broad outlines they are clear enough. The operators' work in a continuous-process plant is collective in the sense that no individual team member produces something that can be seen as deriving uniquely from him. He is responsible for one of several processes that must be carried on simultaneously if the work is to be successful. Since these processes are interdependent, the failure to adequately supervise one of them will both have immediate repercussions for the work of other people and lead to a poor performance by the team as a whole. This close interdependence of roles becomes especially salient in moments of crisis, when the failure of one individual can mean the death of his colleagues. Where success or failure is determined by the performance of the team as a whole, each individual has an interest in making sure that his colleagues pull their weight. A person, then, who is careless or lazy in his work is likely to find himself very soon subject to fairly intense group pressure.

Broadly speaking, the argument that control functions are decentralized onto the work team seemed to us the most persuasive of the various propositions that have been put forward about the transformation of the control system with advanced automation. Nonetheless, in the specific way in which it has been formulated, the argument is rather simplistic, and it fails to take into account the important differences in the ways in which control systems can operate in a given technological setting. In our refineries control was partly in the hands of management, and partly in the hands of the work team. The frontiers of the two spheres of control were often unclearly delineated, and this ambiguity could generate tension within the organization. Moreover the degree to which decentralization actually occurred was influenced by managerial philosophies that seemed to be rooted in rather different national cultural traditions.

There were clear signs in both countries that automation is conducive to a certain degree of team autonomy. In all of our refineries there had been a long-term trend in which management drew back from trying to regulate in a detailed way the particular pattern of activity that the work team adopted in order to fulfil the objectives that it had been set. This was clearly reflected in the reduction of the intensity of supervision. In the early 1950s when the workers had been only recently recruited, management's policy was to safeguard against risks by manning the units heavily, and at the same time ensuring close supervision by lower management. However, over the years, as the workers' experience of the units grew, the policy switched to one of reducing the ranks of lower management and devolving greater responsibility for the routine running of the units onto the workers themselves. It would seem then that Blauner was incorrect in believing that the technology made intense supervision impossible. It was perfectly feasible and had in fact been practised. What appears to have been decisive was that management found it increasingly unnecessary as the training of the work force improved, and, in a period when it was becoming increasingly cost conscious, decided that manning cuts at the supervisory level were an easy way of making savings.

This process of decentralization of control over routine operations had been carried furthest in the British refineries where the Responsible Operator — while remaining a full-time worker on the units — was also almost entirely responsible for organizing the work activity of his team. It was his job both to allocate tasks among members of the work team and to make sure that they were carried out properly. It was his business to ensure that the members of his team acquired the training that they needed to work effectively. He was the main mediator between the work team and outside expertise, and laboratory reports requiring corrections in the setting of the unit controls were transmitted directly to him. In France, although there were clear signs that a similar process of decentralization had been initiated, it had been pushed somewhat less far. Many of the tasks which had been placed fully within the sphere of the British Responsible Operator were still supervised by the lowest ranking stratum of management — the Shift Supervisor. This was partly reflected in the different ratios of First Line Supervisors to workers. If we look at the French refineries we find that at Lavera there was one First Line Supervisor to every five operators, at Dunkirk one to every nine. In the British refineries the ratio was considerably lower. At Kent a typical process supervisor controlled fourteen men, and at Grangemouth eighteen.

The growing sense of autonomy that the work teams experienced with the reduction in first line supervision was powerfully reinforced by the effects of the shift system. The bulk of the managerial hierarchy worked during the usual daytime hours, while the teams of operators rotated through the three shifts. What this effectively meant was that for long stretches of each month, there was no contact whatsoever between the main managerial hierarchy and its process workers.

This becomes clear if we look at the case of a specific shift cycle. At Dunkirk the cycle ran as follows:

	Sat	*S*	*M*	*T*	*W*	*T*	*F*	*Sat*	*S*	*M*	*T*	*W*	*T*	*F*
First and second weeks	M	M	M	M	M	M	M	O	O	O	O	N	N	N
Third and fourth weeks	N	N	N	N	O	O	A	A	A	A	A	A	A	O

M = Morning shift; N = Night shift; A = Afternoon shift; O = Rest day

The managerial hierarchy was absent when the worker was on night shift, and equally it was absent when he was working over the weekend. Out of twenty one working days in each cycle, then, the worker was in the factory without the hierarchy for eleven — or for just more than half the working month. In addition to this, it is important to remember that even when his shift did coincide with the presence of management, the overlap was only partial. When he arrived for morning shift, it was at 5 o'clock in the morning. Day management only appeared at 7.30 a.m. When he was on afternoon shift, management left the refinery at 6 p.m., but the work team continued at the job until 9 p.m.

French management had begun to realize that this posed an important problem for communication by the time that they started their investigation in 1971 into the dissatisfaction of the shift workers. In their report on the problem, the Secretary Generals made the following comment: 'The information coming from the Director (as well as from the unions it seems) does not get through: no doubt because it is not backed up by verbal comment. It's an important problem. Should we consider a sacrifice of management, such as visits of the units outside the normal day hours?' (*Etudes du travail en Service Continu*. Groupe des Secrétaires Généraux)

They were perfectly correct. For half their working life the operators were totally outside the reach of day management. They could feel themselves masters of the factory. During these periods there was a noticeably greater atmosphere of freedom and relaxation in the refinery. People discussed more and the topics of discussion were more controversial. In the night, the cold and darkness outside gave the control room a home-like quality that was almost entirely lacking during the day. There was a feeling of being cut off from the outside world that both knit people together more tightly and sharpened their sense of responsibility. It was in these periods of the shift cycle, then, that there grew up a feeling of solidarity between the workers, and that the teams developed their own patterns of activity and their own informal methods of social control.

Certainly, then, the shift system contributed a good deal to strengthening the sense of autonomy, and to developing the capacity for self-regulation of the work teams. But it was far from being unambiguous in its effects. For the implication of the shift system was not so much that it ensured a system of team control as that it created an essential discontinuity of control systems. We can see the reason for this if we continue to follow the team in the course of its shift cycle. When, after the period of virtual self-government on the night shift, the team came to work on the afternoon shift, it found the refinery transformed. The units would be buzzing with members of the managerial hierarchy that had arrived to take notes, make suggestions and check that everything was in order. The atmosphere was more alert, stiffer, and more controlled. Such a transition inevitably posed a delicate problem of relations. It was easy for the operators to feel that the area of their discretion had been abruptly narrowed. From feeling masters of the refinery, the operators were suddenly turned back into subordinates. If the situation was clumsily handled it could give rise to a feeling that the manager's intervention was simply an effort to throw his weight around.

The experience of self-control that the workers had during night shift and the weekends was to a certain extent an illusory one since they had only been running the refinery in a very limited sense. They were able to maintain a pre-set cycle of production, but not to initiate a new one or to cope with important problems.

The discontinuity in the control system paralleled, then, a discontinuity in the level of activity of the refinery. During the night shift and at weekends the refinery was set for purely routine running, while important changes in the operation of the units were only carried out when day management was present. If the night shift encountered difficulties in maintaining the quality of the product, then it would be a matter of the operators holding on and doing their best until the experts arrived. In cases of crises — if for instance a unit had to be shut down in an emergency — then the alarm signal would be given and key members of day management would rush from their beds to the refinery. Few operators, then, would have doubted that periods of active middle management intervention on the units and supervision of work team activity were essential. The experience of work team autonomy on the night shift and at weekends did not mean that management was seen as dispensable, and was unlikely to lead to the growth of any neo-syndicalist feeling that the workers could run the factory themselves.

The disciplinary system

Finally, we must remember that everyday control over the ongoing work process is only one aspect of the broader control system. We also need to take into account the mechanisms that existed for handling more serious breaches of work rules, or protractedly poor work performance. In neither country had control been so fully devolved onto the work team that management had felt able to abandon its arsenal of sanctions against deviance. If we take the case of Kent where manager/worker relations were outstandingly amicable, we find that for the period 1952 to 1970 there were on average thirteen formal disciplinary measures taken against individuals each year, and again on average six of these involved dismissal. Partly this reflected problems that would be found in any type of factory, but also it in part reflected the fact that faults that in other technological conditions might have been regarded as relatively minor, came in the conditions of refining to assume a very high level of importance because of the danger inherent in the production process. The classic instance of this is that smoking on the units led to instantaneous dismissal. On the whole the number of rules governing behaviour was small, and this in part produced the feeling of a relatively high level of freedom that observers have noticed. On the other hand, the rules that did exist tended to be treated very seriously, and deviance carried heavy penalties.

British management, consistently with its greater emphasis on team autonomy, made a self-conscious effort to present itself in its disciplinary function essentially as a support of the work team. In a disciplinary hearing that I attended concerning a man who had fallen asleep at work, management made the point time and again that it took the fault seriously not so much because it represented a failure of the person in his obligations to management, but because it endangered the lives of the members of the work team and made their work infinitely more difficult. Discipline, then, was presented not as a form of control over the work team, but as a way of helping it to cope with cases that it would have found embarrassing to deal with itself. Management's interventions came only over incidents in which the infringement of the rules had been sufficiently serious and clear cut for it to be able to be fairly confident of having at least the tacit support of the work force behind it in what it was doing. The procedures for handling disciplinary cases had been negotiated with the unions and cases of dispute were in the last instance to be sent to an independent arbitrator whose decision was binding. Finally, when disciplinary action was taken the form of the sanction was clearly defined. The person might be dismissed, demoted, or warned, but the crucial point was that the managerial sanctions were directly tied to a specific fault, and there could be little confusion about what the sanction involved.

In France, the nature of the disciplinary system was both more obscure and more controversial. If we look first at the formal disciplinary system, it provided management with broadly similar sanctions to those that its British colleagues deployed for the most serious cases. Just as in Britain there was possibility of dismissing a person, demoting him or handing him recorded warnings of different degrees of gravity. The thinking behind sanctioning seems however to have been much more related to a conception of the direct relationship of the employee to the employer, and of the legal right of an employer to keep order in his own house. For instance, in an extended discussion of discipline in a manual provided by the French Company for the guidance of refinery managements, we find that the entire consideration of the rationale behind discipline is cast in the form of a review of legal rights.

The courts have then recognized as sovereign the power of control of the head of the enterprise. They tie this power to the risk that he assumes in a capitalist regime. Vulnerable to sudden difficulties, the head of the enterprise must be in a position to meet them in complete independence and to take in consequence all the decisions which he feels are justified.

Among these decisions is the power of discipline. This is recognized as such by the courts and certain decrees even go as far as to stipulate that the head of the enterprise is 'the sole judge of his decisions'.

The most important decree relating to this is a decree of the Appeal Court of 1945 which laid down that the head of the enterprise has a power that is 'inherent in his position'. He can then, by right, impose a disciplinary sanction even in the absence of any written source of enterprise rules, and hence of any formal procedure for dismissal. (*Guidance Manual to Refinery Managements*: Ch. 4 'Les Sanctions', 44)

It followed from this emphasis on disciplinary power as deriving from the prerogative of the employer that the unions were to be consulted about discipline simply out of management's goodwill and not as a matter of right. In contrast to the situation in Britain where the disciplinary procedure was itself the product of joint agreement between unions and management, and where in cases of dispute management agreed to accept the decision of an outside arbitrator, in France refinery managements were explicitly warned off either giving the unions any power over the disciplinary procedure itself or of surrendering any of management's prerogative in determining the sanction.

The employer can equally, and sometimes it is in his interests to do so, notify the union representatives of an enterprise of the decision that he intends to take.

This dialogue should make it possible to convince the delegates that the decision is fully justified, to study if need be the method of application of the sanction, and to avoid if possible any later action by the employee.

Through this contact the employer must not however give the impression that he is submitting the sanction to the control of the delegates and that a disciplinary procedure is implicitly being created. The employer must conserve his entire authority in this area, and the fact of entering into dialogue with the delegates arises mainly from a policy of maintaining good relations with the delegates.[12]

Finally, there was a difference between the two countries in the mode of application of one of the main elements of the formal disciplinary system. The commonest method of dealing with faults of medium importance was to send the person a formal warning note. A copy of this would be placed in his file, and if he committed another fault within a specified period of time he would either be given a final warning or be liable for dismissal. Clearly the weight of this penalty lay to a large degree in the period of time during which the warning stayed on the person's file. In the British refineries the

time period was twelve months. Quarterly progress reports were sent
by the supervisors to higher management, and if at the end of the
twelve months they were satisfactory the original adverse report and
all copies were to be destroyed. From that time onwards the individual would be working with a clean slate, and subsequent faults
would have to be considered on their own and not in the context of
the person's previous errors. In France, on the other hand, the time
period during which the original warning remained on the file was
rather longer. Refinery managements were recommended to keep the
letter for between three to five years depending on the seriousness
of the fault. It was only at the end of the fifth year that all warning
letters had to be removed from the file and destroyed. Moreover, it
is clear that this represented a comparatively liberal attitude on the
part of French management compared to the one that reigned in the
1960s. At Lavera, at least, management had traditionally adopted the
practice of keeping all warning letters for ten years, and the degree
of resentment this caused became apparent in May 1968 when one
of the main demands in the refinery was for a reduction of the period
to twelve months. Faced with the need to get the petrol flowing
again, management had fallen back to the five year period as a compromise.[13] The signs, then, are that the French disciplinary system
was more severe in the application of its sanctions than the British,
and that in the past this had been even more the case.

Moreover, alongside the formal disciplinary system the French
workers felt that there existed an informal disciplinary system that
was institutionalized in the payment system. In chapter 3 we saw
that there was a considerable difference between the nature of the
payment system in the two countries. In Britain salaries were directly
related to skill levels, whereas in France this relationship was very
much weaker. In part this was because people's pay was related to
their length of service in the firm, but it was also due to the operation of an individual bonus system. This bonus system was highly
controversial, and management and the workers produced rather
different accounts of its function. For our purposes, however, the
crucial factor was the significance of the bonus system for the work
force. The workers regarded it as a merit bonus, and the definition
of merit depended on the individual manager. Some managers, they
believed, used the system to reward those who put special effort into
their work and to penalize bad work. Others would merely favour
the people they happened to like, or those who showed themselves
particularly subservient. For the workers, then, the system enabled

management not only to control work performance, but also co-operativeness in the broader sense.

Control exercised through an annual bonus system has rather different implications for the work force than a system of control that is based on specific sanction for particular instances of poor performance. It is a long distance form of control, and it may be difficult for the person to know precisely what actions are being penalized. This necessarily leaves more room for questioning the justice of the sanction, and makes management highly vulnerable to charges of favouritism. It is moreover a form of sanction which could in principle continue indefinitely. A worker who commits an error can never know precisely when the incident is forgotten. It is understandable that he may feel that his superiors have developed a fixed image of his performance on the basis of one mistake, and this image is influencing their assessments long after it has ceased to be relevant. This type of difficulty was compounded by the pattern of irregular intervention of day management on the units. It was easy to feel that they simply did not have enough contact with the workers to make an accurate assessment of the standard of their work.

The bonus system, then, unquestionably heightened the workers' sense of the coerciveness of the organization, and focused attention more directly on the underlying relations of power. It dichotomized more sharply the relationships between the workers on the one hand, and middle management on the other. For, although the supervisors had to present to middle management reports on the workers' performances for the purposes of the annual review in which the bonuses were allocated, it was the middle managers themselves that made the final decision and announced it to the worker in the annual personal interview. The middle managers, then, gained a particular salience in the worker's mind. As one operator put it: 'It's the Management Engineer in charge of the Sector who is our boss, because he's the one who gives us our end-of-the-year increases.'

In both countries management had preserved a system of sanctions which gave it a means of control of work performance over and above the work team. But the thinking behind these sanctions and the way in which they were deployed differed between the two countries. In the British refineries sanctions were presented as a support for the work team, as a means of helping the team to cope with problems it was unable to cope with itself. The emphasis was on ensuring the consent of the collectivity to the decisions that were taken. In France, on the other hand, the stress was on the individual relationship between management and the particular employee. This is evident in the way in which management justifies its own disciplinary function entirely in terms of its legal rights as employer, and in its reluctance to allow disciplinary questions to be in any way subject to control by the collectivity. Most particularly it is apparent in the individualizing effect of the payment system in which the work team is by-passed, and it is the individual team member who is rewarded or sanctioned. While, then, in both countries the system of managerial sanctions imposes clear limits on the jurisdiction of the team, in the British refinery care was taken to preserve an autonomous area of work team control, whereas in the French refineries the system of sanctions tended to cut right across the team by emphasizing the direct relationship between management and the individual worker.

The control system and social distance

One of the most interesting implications of the argument that advanced automation shifts the control function away from management itself is that this is thought to have a substantial impact on the quality of management/worker relations. Freed from its traditional role of having to put pressure on the worker to make sure that the job is properly carried out, and spared the personal friction that arises out of a system of close supervision, management is able to develop a closer, more equal, and more satisfying relationship with the work force.[14] However, as we have seen, the control system in a highly automated setting is more complex than is generally thought, and indeed between the two countries we have found certain important differences in the way in which control was exercised. In France, management had kept a tighter grip over the control process: more powers were reserved to the supervisors, disciplinary sanctions were more severe, and management had an additional lever of control in the salary system. In the light of this we are faced with the question of whether there is in fact a relationship between the nature of the control system and the closeness of management/worker relations, and if so, what type of relationship it is.

One way of looking at the effect of the control system is to compare the extent to which the operators in each refinery felt that there existed a high degree of social distance between management and themselves with the feelings of the maintenance workers.

The maintenance workers were in many ways a traditional enclave in the heart of the advanced sector. Their work skills were very similar to those of maintenance workers in many other industries. If we examine a breakdown of the Kent maintenance force we find that the principal groups of skilled workers were welders, fitters, boilermakers, pipefitters, instrument mechanics and electricians — groups that one could find in a great diversity of work settings. Part of the work force worked at benches in the workshop, and part operated around the units themselves, but in both cases control of the work process was exercised by direct managerial supervision.[15]

The intensity of supervision, as measured by the average number of workers supervised by a foreman, varied between refineries, but was in all cases sufficiently low to make direct personal control perfectly feasible. At Kent, there was one foreman to every eight skilled maintenance workers, at Grangemouth one to eleven, at Lavera one to four, and at Dunkirk one to ten. Neither the workshop nor the unit overhaul situation was particularly conducive to the development of a self-regulating team. In the workshop people tended to find themselves in a highly complex job that needed a high level of managerial co-ordination, and they were often submerged in a larger work force that included men lent for the specific occasion by contractors. In comparing the maintenance workers with the operators we are then able to compare the effect of a system of personal managerial control with a system of semi-team control.

The question we asked was: 'Would you say that in their relations with workers in the refinery, middle level staff, that is to say members of staff between your immediate supervisors and top management, are: very distant, quite distant, quite friendly, or very friendly?' Table 36 compares the percentage of maintenance workers and operators who thought that middle management was very or quite distant.

Two things stand out in this table. First, generally speaking the

Table 36   *A comparison of operators' and maintenance workers' perceptions of social distance in the refinery*

Relations are: *Very or quite distant*	Lavera	Dunkirk	Kent	Grangemouth	
1. Operators	50	50	24	13	%
2. Maintenance	62	81	17	31	
	(N = 196)	(N = 192)	(N = 198)	(N = 205)	

operators do have a closer relationship with management than the maintenance workers. This was the case in three out of four of the refineries, and even if we look at the deviant case it is clear that relations were outstandingly good.

However, the second point that emerges is that even if we control for type of worker we still find that there are considerable differences between the French and British workers. The French workers are more likely to feel that relations are distant both among the operators and among the maintenance workers. If we look at the operators for instance we find that in France they are still twice as likely as the Kent operators and nearly four times as likely as the Grangemouth operators to feel that management is distant.

A possible explanation of this pattern lies in the nature of the control system. It seems very likely that the more that control is taken off the shoulders of management and is invested in the work team, the closer will be relations between management and workers. Where management personally controls the work process it is brought into a relationship with the workers in which there is a high potential for friction. Management's role is one of issuing direct commands to the workers, and this risks explosive clashes of personality, and a sense on the workers' part of the coerciveness of managerial intervention. It produces a clearly defined relationship of superior and subordinate. Even if management's role is confined to a regular post-factor evaluation and sanctioning of the individual's performance, this is likely to make relations more distant. When managers appear on the scene of work they appear to the workers as judges rather than as advisors, and unless the criteria of judgement are self-evidently fair there is a high possibility that the social climate will become soured by individuals feeling that they have been unfairly treated and that management's rule is guided by the dictates of favouritism.

We have seen that among the process operators in both countries there had developed a form of team control for routine operations, whereas among the maintenance workers the system of control is essentially a personal one. It seems, then, perfectly consistent with this that generally speaking the operators had closer relations with management than the maintenance workers.

However, although there was this general similarity in the salience of the team among the operators in both countries, we also found that there were significant differences between the countries in the exact extent to which the team had been granted autonomy to supervise its own activities. In France management had kept a tighter grip over the team as was evident in the greater powers of first line management, in the greater weight of the middle level sanctions it reserved for itself, and in the operation of the payment system which gave middle managers control over the individual bonus element in each worker's pay packet. If we follow through the logic of the theory of the influence of the control system, then it is only to be expected that the French operators, while having a closer relationship with management than the maintenance workers, should nonetheless find management substantially more distant than the operators in the British refineries.

If we turn to look at the maintenance workers it is clear that there is an even higher degree of variation between the different refineries than we encountered with the operators. Whereas among the Kent craftsmen only 17% saw relations as quite or very distant, at the refinery of Dunkirk this was true of some 81%. How was it that a similar type of work could lead to such very different experiences of relations with management?

Part of the answer, no doubt, lies in the fact that the French maintenance workers were subject to a similar type of payments system to the operators. Indeed, the contrast between the way in which the French and British maintenance workers were paid could hardly have been greater. In Britain the vast bulk of the skilled maintenance workers were paid an identical salary, whereas in France, not only was there a complex system of grading, but, even within grades, workers received different salaries according to their length of service, and the accumulation of their individual bonuses. The payment system in Britain, then, offered management little leverage to penalize poor work performance, whereas in France the possibility of exercising such control was quite considerable.

The second factor that was unquestionably of major importance was the organizational strength of the British craft unions. The craft unions traditionally upheld a high degree of autonomy in work for their members. This was partly reflected in the way in which they made themselves to a certain degree the guardian of work quality through their control of the system of apprenticeship, and it was also to be seen in the traditional practice by which foremen had to be members of the craft union. The effect of this had been to make first line management very much more susceptible to pressures coming from the work force. In our refineries this latter tradition had begun to give way with the creation of mixed craft teams under a common foreman. But in the workshops, and among the electricians and instrument mechanics it still remained very much in sway. In such a situation, management was unlikely to break rapidly with past tradition or to encourage a sharp differentiation between the supervisory treatment of different sections of the maintenance work force. The independence of the skilled worker and the continuation of a loose and informal system of supervision remained then characteristic of the British maintenance work force. The particularly cordial relations at Kent, which provided us in our earlier discussion with a deviant case in which the craft workers were even more likely than the process operators to see relations with middle management as friendly, probably reflects the fact that it was in this refinery that craft consciousness was by all account most sharply crystallized. To give just one instance, the greater power of the craft stewards at Kent was evident in the fact that they had managed to acquire the *de facto* right of being full-time stewards while their colleagues at Grangemouth still worked with their tools.

In some respects the relatively high level of autonomy granted to the craft workers might be seen as similar to the devolution of control to the work team on the process side. However, the situation in the two cases was rather different. The process work team was a highly integrated and stable team that had both the time and the motivation to develop powerful mechanisms of self-control. On the craft side the type of work was more varied, and it rarely required co-ordination by different members of the same craft. Rather the type of team co-ordination needed was one between crafts. But at this level, far from integrating the team, craft traditions disrupted it because of the salience of the problem of maintaining traditional job demarcations. The craft workers were not prepared to maximize team efficiency if this conflicted with the traditions which they believed in the long term guaranteed their job security. The effect then on the craft system was to create a situation in which there was relatively little control rather than to transform one control system into another. This was no doubt part of the explanation of why the consultants at Kent found that the craft force was working at only 40% of its potential efficiency.

British management was fully conscious of its relatively weak control over the maintenance force, and at Kent in the 1960s it made a considerable effort to reassert control. The consultants had recommended a system of payment incentives but management rejected this on the grounds that it would be impossible to impose. Instead they sought to introduce a scheme by which work tasks would be measured, and which would therefore enable management to put pressure on the workers to eliminate delays and meet what would then be the established standards. Despite repeated efforts by management to implement the system it eventually had to back down, partly because the foremen were reluctant to co-operate but primarily because the craft workers were powerful enough to reject schemes that they found threatening.

The situation of the maintenance workers indicates, then, particularly powerfully that the way in which control systems function cannot easily be imputed from a knowledge of the work task. Although in both France and Britain the maintenance workers were primarily under a system of personal control, the way in which this operated differed considerably between the two countries. The French were under a system which we could term one of *high power* personal control. This was partly because of the additional grip provided by the payment system, and partly because there was no organized constraint on the exercise of managerial authority. In Britain the maintenance workers were under a system of *low power* personal control. British management had no powers of control through the payment system, and its capacity to issue instructions to the work force was hedged round by a whole series of constraints that had been originally obtained through the organized power of the craft unions and that had, to a certain degree, become consolidated into the customs of the factory.

The implications of a personal control system for relations with management depended on whether it was a high power or a low power system. In the former case we would expect tensions to run high, and relations to be poor. The type of description of the effects of a personal control system that we find for instance in Blau and Scott are essentially descriptions of a high power system. However, the more we move towards a low power system, the less we would expect the theory to hold because management is essentially obliged to yield its powers to issue commands and penalize poor work performance. Indeed, in the case of Kent, we have found that a low power personal control system can make possible even better relations between workers and management than a system of semi-team control. This, we would suggest, is a fairly rare case. Generally speaking, we would expect personal control systems to pose greater problems for management/worker relations than semi-team systems. This is because the factors facilitating relations in a semi-team system derive from the requirements of efficiently manning the technology, and are therefore in the interests of management, whereas the factors making good relations possible in a low power personal control system are in part due to the organizational power of the workers — which is inherently more difficult to achieve and maintain — and may run against the maximization of efficiency. In the case of a low power personal control system, then, there is likely to be a certain pressure on management in the direction of trying to reassert control, and to the extent that management commits itself to do this, it imperils the good relations that the control system fosters.

The systems of control that we have found among the maintenance workers gives us, we suspect, an indication of the styles of management that are prevalent in a much wider spectrum of French and British industry. This type of work was very similar to the type of work to be found in many other industries, and it was much easier than was the case with process work to import the managerial techniques that existed elsewhere. Just as earlier we made the point that dissatisfaction with the level of control over decision making in our refineries seemed to be part of a more general problem of authority relations in French industry, and that indeed the level of contestation was, if anything, less fierce in the refineries, so too we would suggest here that the central overt source of dissatisfaction among our French workers, namely the coldness and distance of relations between management and workers, is a problem that is likely to be found much more widely in French industry, and that the somewhat novel conditions of control to be found among the operators went some way towards attenuating it.

Our general conclusion, then, is that the writers who have suggested that automation has produced important changes in the control system are correct, although we would disagree with the particular accounts that they give of this change. What we did find was that there had been a distinct move towards a system of semi-team control among the process operators. Broadly speaking, the system was one in which the team had a fairly high degree of autonomy in its conduct of routine operations but was subject to much more intensive managerial control whenever variations were introduced in the running of the units, and in periods of difficulty. However, we also found that there were important differences between the French and British refineries in the extent to which control had been decentralized to the work team, and it was clear that the structure of the control system was a product not only of the technology but of managerial philosophy.

Moreover, we would emphasize that automation transforms the

control system only for the operators. Most discussions virtually ignore the work situation of the maintenance workers in continuous-process plant. This is particularly serious in that maintenance workers represented between 30% and 40% of the work force of each refinery, and were thus a very substantial factor in the overall social climate. In both France and Britain, the maintenance workers were under a personal control system, but we found important differences in the way in which the personal control system actually operated in the two countries. In France we found that it was essentially a high power system, whereas in Britain it was a low power system.

In an earlier chapter we found that one of the most significant differences between the French and British workers was that whereas the French workers were preoccupied about the coldness and distance of relations with management, the British workers mentioned this much less frequently and were mainly concerned with the problem of the technical efficiency of management. This was confirmed by the replies to a closed question focusing specifically on the problem of social distance. The French workers were very much more likely to feel that relations were distant than their British equivalents.

In this chapter we have suggested that this difference in the salience of the problem of social distance can be largely accounted for by the structure of the refinery control systems in the two countries. The growth of a semi-team system among the operators seems to have facilitated better relations in both countries, but management had retained a tighter grip over the control system in France, and this was reflected in the greater sense of social distance among the French operators than among the British. On the maintenance side, the French workers were subject to a high power personal control system and this seems to have led to the coldest relations of all the groups that we studied. The British maintenance workers, on the other hand, were under a low power personal control system, and this appears to have made possible relatively good relations.

We would argue, then, that the greater salience of the problem of social distance in the French factories was due to the tighter grip that management exercised over the control process, and this tighter grip was reflected for the operators in the more limited autonomy of the work team, and among the maintenance workers by the prevalence of a high power system of personal control.

Part four

The unions

10

The theory and strategy of the trade unions

Conceptions of unionism

The principal unions in the French and British refineries had fundamentally different conceptions of the role of the trade unions in the workplace; and this difference had important implications for their method of operation on the shop floor, the nature of the relationship between the workplace and the central union organization, the type of demand that was made on management, and the quality of relations between the unions and the workers themselves. Broadly speaking, the French unions saw their role as one of *mobilizing* the work force for a far reaching structural transformation of society, whereas the British unions saw theirs as one of *representing* the work force; that is to say pushing for objectives that were consciously desired by the workers themselves.

The French unions saw contemporary Western society in broadly Marxist terms, as a class stratified society in which the principal social classes had fundamentally contradictory interests and were engaged in a struggle for dominance that could ultimately only be resolved by a major structural reorganization of society. The most powerful union in the French refineries was the *Confédération Générale du Travail*. In its educational literature designed for militants, we find the following account of its view of the nature of society.

Relations are established between the working class and the capitalist class in the sphere of production which are not relations of equality, but are relations of exploiters to exploited. This is the source of a permanent conflict between the working class and the capitalist class, which constitutes the primary antagonism of society. This confrontation, this conflict which derives from capitalist exploitation is the class struggle . . . It is in this context of the class struggle that the existence and activity of the unions and worker action are situated. There can be no progress for the working class without determined and constant struggles on its part against the capitalist forces and the opposing reactionaries.[1]

For the CGT, union action — in the context of a class society — had the double objective of limiting as much as possible the effects of capitalist exploitation, and at the same time of heightening people's awareness of the underlying structure of society, thereby making them realize that the only definitive solution to their problem lay in the abolition of capitalism as a social system.

Daily struggle is necessary to limit, to act as a brake on the effects of capitalist exploitation.

To cease this daily struggle for the defence of the demands of the workers is, in the first place, to deliver the working class up to merciless exploitation by the capitalists, and it is to strike a blow at its immediate interests. It is also to condemn it for the future to capitalist slavery and immense misery.

It must be a *permanent* struggle because, after each success achieved by the working class, the bourgeoisie returns to the charge to take back what it has been obliged to cede, and if possible even more than this.

Finally, the daily struggle raises the level of understanding and the combativity of the working class and forges powerful organizations, and courageous and able militants.

In this way, the working class lives its own experience which shows it the necessity of abolishing capitalism itself if capitalist exploitation is to be abolished.

The definitive solution lies in the realization of the objective defined in the first article of the statutes of the CGT, the abolition of employed and employers, the suppression of the capitalist regime.[2]

The second most powerful union — the CFDT — had passed through a major ideological transformation between the early 1960s and 1970, in which it had shed its remaining formal ties with Christian doctrine and had come to explicitly adopt a conception of society in terms of class conflict.[3] By 1970 its critique of the existing structure of society had become as fundamental as that of the CGT, although there were important differences between the two unions in the type of repressiveness emphasized and in the strategical solutions proposed. The CGT stressed, above all, economic exploitation, and the ability of the employers to expropriate surplus value. Its solution was to heighten the political awareness of the population until it would be possible for a political party favourable to the working class to capture state power, and eliminate private ownership through nationalization of the means of production. The CFDT, on the other hand, emphasized the alienation inherent in the sharp restrictions that capitalist society imposes on the individual's ability to influence the decisions that affect his destiny. In contrast to the CGT, it believed that the process of structural change could be initiated prior to the capture of power at the level of the state, and that the nationalization of the means of production was only one aspect of the structural change that would be necessary if the alienating qualities of contemporary society were to be eliminated. The essential element of its strategy was the progressive overthrow of the systems of oligarchical control in the main institutions of society, and their replacement with a new form of participatory democracy.

Despite these differences, the CFDT shared with the CGT the underlying conception of a class society in which the central dynamic was the class struggle. Similarly, it saw the role of the union as being one of actively working for the overall transformation of society by intensifying this struggle. The revised ideological position of the CFDT was given explicit and official form in the *Document d'Orientation* adopted by the 35th Confederal Congress in May 1970:

> The strategy of the CFDT is an offensive strategy. To say that the workers are engaged in class struggle is not for the CFDT simply a statement of fact but the affirmation of a will to participate in it in an offensive way.
>
> It is as an anticapitalist organization that we must adjust our behaviour, define our objectives and our means of action, in order to make possible the transition to a form of socialist society. The strategy of the CFDT is an offensive strategy that tends through the class struggle to bring closer the creation of this society.[4]

In the British refineries, the most powerful union was the Transport and General Workers' Union. It not only had the largest membership, but it had a monopoly of the process operators — the only group that could bring the refinery to a halt and thus seriously threaten management. With the T&GWU we find no equivalent to the incessant effort of the French union to place union action within a systematic critique of the structure of society.

If we examine the objectives that the T&GWU sets itself in its rule book, there are elements that could be given a radical interpretation; but they are set out in a piecemeal way, lack precision, and are placed on a level with an immense variety of other aims — many of which are of a purely administrative type. We get some idea of this curious mixture of the everyday and the visionary in the opening paragraphs of rule 2.

Rule 2 — Objects

1. The principal objects of the Union are the regulation of the relations between workmen and employers, and between workmen and workmen, and also the provision of benefits to members.

2. The objects of the Union shall further include: (a) The organization of all members and other persons qualified for membership, . . . and the obtaining and maintaining of just and proper hours of work, rates of wages, and to endeavour by all means in their power to control the industries in which the members are engaged.[5]

Clause 2 of the rule then continues with ten further objectives that include: the settling and negotiating of disputes; the provision of benefits to members; 'the furtherance of political objects of any kind'; the transaction of insurance business; the extension of co-operative production; the establishment of, or provision of financial help to, various kinds of publications; the furtherance of the work of, or financial help to, bodies working in the interests of labour 'including the securing of a real measure of control in industry, and participation by the workers in management'; the provision of opportunities for social intercourse, sport, and social events among members.

When we turn away from the formal statement of objectives to the type of guidance that the T&GWU gives its stewards about the way they should carry out their activities in the workplace, the more potentially radical aspects of the T&GWU programme are firmly subordinated to the immediate task of handling the everyday problems of the workplace. In its *Shop Stewards Handbook* the T&GWU starts out with the following definition of the stewards' job:

The shop steward is the key figure in carrying out the T&GWU's policy for high wages and effective organization. The two aspects of the policy advance together. Our plans for high wages based on the maximum extension of plant and local bargaining depend on workshop representatives who are able to take the initiative and play a positive part in negotiations with management.[6]

A few pages later the order of priorities is re-emphasized:

Your first and foremost responsibility to your members is to help them secure good wages and working conditions. (p. 16)

The emphasis then is firmly placed on the steward's role in securing immediate advantages in the workplace. There is no reference at all to the wider structure of society. There is no discussion of any class struggle; and indeed the words 'class', 'capitalism', 'exploitation', do not appear once. There is no consideration of any wider social changes that the union might be trying to achieve, and there is not the slightest suggestion that the stewards should be seeking to make the workers more aware of their social situation.

In contrast to the French literature, management is not treated as an enemy that is ever ready to manipulate the workers or seize back any advantages that it might previously have been coerced into giving. In so far as the question of the steward's attitude to management is treated at all, the emphasis is on the need to show respect and courtesy:

The workers rightly demand a respected status in industry, and courtesy and considerate treatment. The obligation operates both ways. The workers should themselves show the courtesy to management which they expect to receive. Courtesy applies not only to the manner of speaking; it applies to punctuality and to general bearing as well. If the workers' behaviour sets a good example, they are in a strong position to insist on like treatment for themselves. (p. 11)

There is some indication that the stewards should be interested in extending control over everyday management powers, but the advice is vague and it is kept at the level of suggestion. For instance, the guide-book suggests that management 'might be asked to divulge' information on pay, use of labour, finance and production, promotion, and training. Its advice continues:

On all these topics the shop stewards should be ready to express their point of view. On some issues the organized workers have already gone beyond this. They already effectively share in the control of the policy of labour utilization. Questions about whether to work overtime and the recruitment and dismissal of workers are not left to management. They are subject to joint discussion and join decision.

But the stewards are warned that if they do intervene in such matters, it should be in a constructive way;

Of course, workers should have something constructive to contribute to the problems they raise. They should be able to substantiate any proposal they wish to make or any point they take up with carefully prepared and checked information. This involves time and trouble but it is worth it. It is much safer to say nothing than to wade in before being properly briefed. (p. 23–5)

In short, the T&GWU's advice to its workplace representatives is decidedly low keyed. It stresses the furtherance of immediate objectives, and it depicts management as being worthy of being treated with courtesy and respect. The context of steward action is firmly restricted to the problems and needs of the particular workplace. In so far as wider issues of the control of industry are raised, they are formulated in a hesitant and purely suggestive manner.

Clearly, the shop floor representatives themselves, faced with the immediate pressures of the workplace, may not necessarily share the same conception of unionism as the permanent officials in the central union apparatus. To get some idea of how they did see their role, we asked the representatives with the highest level of responsibility in the workplace organization what they thought were the qualities of a good union.

If we take first the CGT in France. At Dunkirk, the representative of the CGT put his view in the following terms:

A good union is one which follows a philosophy and which adapts it without compromise to the context of the interests of its members. I undertook union responsibilities in the interests of the employees, and in order to bring about a fundamental change in the economic system.

His equivalent at Lavera:

A good union must be a union of class struggle. A bad one practises class collaboration. It must allow for union democracy. One must always ask for the
opinion of the union member. It must not be a union run by three people. But
the problem is that the members show no interest. They say: 'We've elected
you, get on with the job'. It's flattering, but it's not what we want. The union
must take up a position on political questions, but not in favour of any one
party. It has to be political to the extent that it is helping to overthrow capitalism, and influences the standard of living and the conditions of work of the
workers.

Both of the CGT shop floor leaders, then, placed union action
within the context of a long term struggle to transform the social
structure of society. The general impression is of a very high level of
assimilation of the basic conceptions of the central union apparatus.

We found a somewhat greater divergence between the views expressed by the two representatives of the CFDT, and indeed a rather
less close adherence by both to the official formulations of the
Confederation.

One must be honest. You can't allow yourself to lie to the workers. One must
put the emphasis on the workers' problems — their standard of living, but also
their whole situation of dependence. (Dunkirk)

The important thing is effectiveness — and that depends on the work of the
militants. If they are in agreement with the people who are in agreement with
them, they will be effective. Secondly, there must be a doctrine and that doctrine must be communicated to people. That is the educational role of the
union. (Lavera)[7]

The extent of the departure from the image of the union presented
by the Confederation is not great, but in both cases there is a certain
displacement of emphasis. At Dunkirk, the representative started out
by stressing the importance of the ethical qualities of the union. It
represents to a certain degree a flash-back to the priorities of the
union in its officially Christian phase, and it reminds us that it was
in the northern region of France that the evolution of the union's
doctrine to essentially Marxist conceptions met some of its strongest
resistance.[8] Nonetheless, even here, we find in the second half of the
account the emphasis on the need to be concerned with the worker's
total situation of dependence, rather than simply with the immediate
problems of the workplace.

At Lavera, the displacement takes a rather different form. The
initial emphasis is on the need to construct an organization that will
have the power to achieve its ends. This in all probability reflects
the fact that the CFDT at Lavera was fighting for its very existence.
In the elections to the Works Council, only 20% of the workers were
supporting it compared to some 80% backing the CGT.[9] The need to

redress this balance of power had then become a central preoccupation of the CFDT's secretary. Yet, once again, the wider aims of the union are by no means ignored. The union's doctrine must be diffused, and the union has an educational role.

If we turn to the British refineries, we find a very different pattern of answers. There is no mention of the need for a 'philosophy' or a 'doctrine', or of a class struggle or a need for a change in the economic system.

The nearest to the type of conception we found in France came from the secretary of the T&GWU branch at Grangemouth who led the strike of 1974.

A union should be trying to forward the interests of its members in three ways. First, it should look after wages and conditions in the workplace. Second, it should keep a check on the standards of health and safety in the factory. And third, it should try to influence legislation to benefit the workers by influencing MPs and sending delegates to the Labour Party Conference.

The similarity with the French examples lies in the emphasis on a certain 'political' role for the union, on the extension of its activities outside the immediate sphere of the work place. But this said, there is little else in common. The purpose of political action is seen as one of trying to get legislation to benefit the workers, rather than to seek a major restructuring of the social system. The method of political action lay not through educating the work force, but through forwarding trade union views through members of parliament and conference delegates.

At Kent, the emphasis shifts altogether, and the basic preoccupation was with the type of relationship that the union should establish with its base, with the need for the union to assess the attitudes of its members adequately, and act in accordance with them.

You've got to be honest with yourself. The craft unions may be more militant, but I know that I haven't got a militant membership. So when you make a claim it has got to be realistic, and not some hairbrained scheme for which you are claiming strong backing when you haven't got it.

In the course of this discussion we have been primarily concerned with the T&GWU as the most powerful of the unions in the British refineries. But the picture would look little different if we took the case of the craft unions. The two chairmen of the joint craft committees gave the following answers to the same question:

The important thing is for the union to try to improve the conditions of its members — holidays, working conditions, wages, — and even conditions that cover the family as well, like pensions and sick pay. (Grangemouth)

The most important thing is honesty. You've got to win the respect of both members and management. You've got to be skilful at negotiating. If the union was militant it might win one point, but it would lose two or three others. If you have them over a barrel one day, management will get its own back later. The shop stewards must try to convince the others of what they think is best. You shouldn't have a stoppage of work without asking the men. (Kent)

There was, then, a high level of congruity between the views of the workplace representatives themselves, and the views of the central union organizations, about the types of objectives that the unions should pursue in the workplace. In both cases we find strikingly dissimilar conceptions of unionism between the French and the British union organizations.

Union positions could be ranged along a continuum at one end of which the unions would see their role purely as mouthpieces of the views of the workers themselves, and at the other, as uniquely concerned to transform the workers' ways of thinking, by giving them a new consciousness of their society and a new set of aspirations. In terms of such a continuum, neither the French nor the British unions could be placed fully at one extreme or the other. The British stewards unquestionably saw themselves as offering some type of leadership in the formulation of demands in the workplace; and the French unions saw themselves as having a responsibility to take into account the existing views of the work force — indeed, if they had failed to do so, they would have quickly been eliminated. Nonetheless, the French and British unions were located at sharply different points on the continuum. In the French case, the everyday action of the militants was conceived as forming a part of the longer term objectives of the unions of bringing about a radical restructuring of society. Their role was to use the incidents of everyday working life to educate the workers about the degree to which they were exploited and alienated, and to convince them of the need of a class struggle to attain a fundamentally different form of society. In the British case, in so far as the unions were attributed a political role at all, it was seen as sharply distinct from the representatives' everyday work in the factory. The policy of the representatives was to restrict themselves to the type of issues which they felt would gain the ready assent of their members — the improvement of pay and of working conditions.

In this sense, we can speak of two broadly different conceptions of unionism in the two countries: in France, the unions were principally unions of ideological mobilization, whereas in Britain, they were principally unions of representation.[10]

The principles of union strategy

These two rather different conceptions of unionism had important implications for the types of strategy that the unions adopted for trying to achieve their objectives.

The French unions — primarily concerned with the eventual structural transformation of society and its necessary prerequisite, the mobilization of the working class — based their strategy on a sustained ideological onslaught on the system of values and ideas justifying the existing social order. The feeling was that if the working class had failed to appreciate the true extent of its exploitation and to adopt the radical positions that this would necessarily imply, this was largely due to the extent to which the capitalist ruling class was able to manipulate the minds of those they exploited. The ruling class was seen as consciously and actively struggling to ensure the hegemony of its ideas by taking advantage of its controlling position in the enterprises, the mass media, and the schools, to maintain a constant process of ideological indoctrination.

According to the CGT in its basic guidance material for militants:

In order to maintain and consolidate their economic and political domination, and also to turn the workers away from the class struggle, the capitalists attempt to make people believe that this exploitation is inevitable. They conduct their campaign by making use of the powerful and numerous means of education, information, and propaganda that they direct or control.

Equally the bourgeoisie spreads around numerous 'theories' in order to create confusion in the minds of the workers, and to divide and disarm them.[11]

Or as the Bureau of the Union Locale des Syndicats de Dunkerque explained to its militants:

The workers are subjected, whether one likes it or not, to *the intense ideological pressure of the State and the employers* who ceaselessly distort the realities of the situation. They conduct a constant campaign of lies that aims to turn the workers away from their correct path, and to drag them into class collaboration. ... They are aware that the power of resistance and the successful continuation of their system of exploitation of man by man necessarily depends on the ignorance of the masses and if possible on their approval. It is to this end that they create confusion in people's minds. ... They are not mistaken and they devote all the time, means, and money (often fabulous sums) to this ideological pressure. ...

If we want to recruit, to strengthen ourselves in order in effect to strengthen the working class by giving it the strong and powerful mass and class organization that it needs, not merely through sectional spirit but because it is a necessity that is more and more justified, *we must work in such a way that the workers have their ideas clear.*[12]

The CFDT was equally preoccupied with the powerful ideological grip which it felt that the capitalist ruling class had achieved over the minds of workers, but it tended to focus its analysis primarily on the indoctrination of the working class into the values of the consumer society.

Consumption, far from being the result of choice by the consumers, is organized by those who are responsible for the apparatus of production. These use the growing inequalities in income to transform into mass production a luxury production hitherto reserved to a minority of privileged people serving as a model for others. Taking advantage of all the means of pressure that are in their hands (advertising, the press, literature, the cinema) they succeed in making the consumer desire and accept the things that they have chosen to produce. . . . In this way a type of human being that is adapted to the functioning of neo-capitalist industrial society is moulded from outside.[13]

Given this conception of the determinants of worker attitudes, the French unions believed that the mobilization of the working class could only be achieved by making a systematic attack on the worker's consciousness, by shattering the grip of the assumptions of bourgeois culture, and by allowing the workers to achieve a true awareness of the extent to which they were alienated. Ideological warfare, then, became quite central to the preoccupations of the French militants in a way that had no parallel in the British refineries.

In the T&GWU's handbook for shop stewards, there is only one reference to ideology and it is the following:

Don't talk for the sake of talking. There is no need to give management the benefit of your views on social philosophy. They are unlikely to dispose them to generosity.[14]

Compare this to the CGT's advice to its shop floor representatives in its elementary training courses.

Use every means at our disposal to fight the ideas and the theories of the class enemy, to refute erroneous notions, to throw light on problems, to instil the right ideas, the positions of the CGT. 1. Through propaganda by word of mouth (from discussions and committee meetings, to public speeches and assemblies). 2. Through specially drawn up written propaganda with the editing and distribution of the enterprise journal and the use of the union's different services. All that assumes a serious effort of organization and of circulation of our propaganda. (Notes for educators giving the Stage Formation Générale de Base, 2ème degré élémentaire)

Similarly, the CFDT, discussing the necessary strategy for the decisive transition from a capitalist to a socialist society, comments:

The fundamental condition on which this process depends is the growth of a collective consciousness on the part of the workers of the harmfulness of capitalist society and the necessity for a socialist society. It is indeed essential to bring about the transformation of existing power relations in favour of socialism both in the sphere of the unions and in the sphere of politics. . . . Action to modify the balance of power, the reduction of alienation through the development of a social criticism elaborated at the most decentralized level, will develop the social and political consciousness of the workers.[15]

Transposed to the life of the factory, this strategy implied a quite prodigious output of union literature, skilfully intertwining the problems of the workplace with the wider issue of the exploitative character of the capitalist social system. We can get some idea of the volume of propaganda that would descend on the individual worker by examining the collection of tracts received by a member of the CGT over two time periods: November 1970 to December 1971; and September 1973 to April 1975.[16] The person in question had been a CGT militant several years before, but had now withdrawn from active involvement. His collection represents the quantity of literature that would be received by somebody who was known to be sympathetic to union objectives, but who was not collecting the material at its source.

In the fourteen months between November 1970 and December 1971 he received altogether 113 tracts — 56 from his own union, the CGT; 26 from the CFDT; 11 joint CGT/CFDT productions; and 5 from outside organizations — mainly Trotskyist groups, and the Communist Party. If we take away his holiday month, he received on average some nine tracts a month (Table 37). During the second period, he received 197 tracts over twenty months — 80 of these from his own organization. If we take away again his holiday month, he was receiving on average some 10 tracts a month.

A worker in a French refinery then would usually be receiving over a hundred tracts a year, each tract being some one-and-a-half to two pages long. This, of course, by no means indicates the entire union output. Quite apart from the holiday months, there were

Table 37 *The quantity of tracts received by a French worker*

| Time period | Source of tracts: | | | | | |
	CGT	CFDT	CGT/ CFDT	FO	Other	Total
1. Nov. 1970–Dec. 71	56	26	11	15	5	113
Tracts per month	4.3	2	0.8	1.2	0.4	8.7
2. Sep. 1973–April 75	80	38	26	33	20	197
Tracts per month	4.2	2	1.4	1.7	1.1	10.4

Note: In both cases the holiday month of August has been excluded. In period 2 the category 'other' includes tracts from a dissident union organization within the refinery which will be discussed later.

regular blocks of rest days at specified periods of the shift cycle when the person would be at home and would be unlikely to receive the tracts of the period. We can get an idea of the gaps in the collection by looking at the weekly factory journal produced by the CGT. In the twenty months between September 1973 and April 1975 there should have been 80 copies; in this worker's collection there were only 51 — which gives a reception rate of some 64% of the overall output of his own organization. Then, again, he was considerably more likely to receive tracts from his own organization than from the other unions. The output of the CFDT is probably particularly underrepresented. A collection of tracts belonging to a member of the CFDT at Lavera showed that between January and September 1975 the CFDT produced some 40 tracts or an average of 5 tracts a month, whereas in the collection we have been considering the average is only 2 a month.

There was simply no equivalent to this ouput of union propaganda in the British refineries. During the period in which we were carrying out the study, the only union information the workers received was the monthly copy of the T&GWU's magazine *Record*, produced by the union's central office. Quite apart from the relatively low volume of material that this constituted, it was material of an altogether different type. It indicated the union's general policy positions, but it was necessarily very general in its approach, and distant from the immediate preoccupations of the refinery workers. In contrast, the general practice in the French tracts was to fuse the issues affecting the particular workplace with the wider issues of society, and each incident in the workplace was turned into an illustration of the wider social struggle.

This inundation by union literature was only the tip of the iceberg of the overall propaganda effort. The real work of persuasion took place in the day-to-day encounters between the militants and the other people in their work teams. It was in everyday conversation, in the discussions that followed the arrival of any new memorandum from management or any clash between a worker and a member of the hierarchy, that the more involved militants could systematically put across their interpretation of management motives, and their view of the way in which the workers were being exploited. Moreover, in the strategical theory of both the CGT and the CFDT, one of the most efficacious forms of education lay in 'action'. It was through active involvement in struggle that the workers could be brought most clearly to see the class nature of society.

According to the CGT:

The daily struggle raises the level of understanding and the combativity of the working class, and forges powerful organizations and courageous and able militants.[17]

Or in the terms of the CFDT:

The definition of demands of a radical type and their prolongation in action assumes a political dimension, not only because of the consequences they generate in relation to the State, but also, and mainly because they pose an alternative, they aim directly at central state power.

This action, by developing class consciousness, tends to create at each moment the position of power that is most favourable to the workers, to use it to the maximum, and to improve it. In this way, by means of the facts of the situation, events, daily action, the collective consciousness of the workers is progressively realized and the contradictions of the capitalist system are accentuated in a way that is permanent.[18]

Action, then, is seen as a crucial way of developing consciousness — but not *any* form of action. Action can only be effective if it is given direction and meaning by the union militants.

In its more advanced training course for militants, the CGT explains:

It has to be kept constantly in mind that the struggle helps raise the consciousness of the workers all the more if:

1. It is proposed by us, but decided by them.
2. It is preceded by good information, a discussion (the referendum is only an appearance of democracy).[19]

and Edmond Maire, the Secretary General of the CFDT, makes the same point in his discussion of 'spontaneous' action by the working class.

'Spontaneous action', 'basism', which we are often, wrongly, reproached for favouring does not constitute a satisfactory solution either. Action that is carried out depending uniquely on those elements of information that are present at a given moment within the enterprise . . . is no more than a type of activist corporatism. It is short-sighted, if not blind, even when it claims to be 'pure and hard' . . . In fact the union organization, by means of its presence, makes it possible to link the piecemeal struggle to the overall battle; it is indispensable for giving the action its mass character.[20]

The conception of 'action' held by the French unions was very much wider than the strike. The strike tended to be regarded as the culminating phase of a 'period of action' in which there would be a steady acceleration of the mobilization of the base. This process would usually begin with the calling of general assemblies, and the formulation of a programme of relatively immediate demands. This might be followed by a petition that was circulated around the units for individual signatures and then handed in formally to management. When feeling was rising, the unions would begin to organize demonstrations, often delaying the starting hour of work. And then, finally, the strike would be launched. The French unions' conception of action involved a process of increasing by stages the level of active participation by the workers in the pursuit of a given programme. The underlying theory was that as people became actively involved they would become increasingly committed to the issues at stake. This long drawn-out procedure, found its rationale in the sequence of opportunities it gave the militants to put across their views in the context of steadily heightening emotional fervour. Periods of action were essentially periods of education in which the workers were to be brought to experience their collective strength, and to realize the fundamental nature of their opposition to a management that would only yield when the ultimate sanction had been applied. They provided a context that heightened the claim to relevance of the unions' ideological critique, and produced an emotional situation that facilitated the assimilation by the workers of the unions' basic conceptions.

The essence, then, of French union strategy was to develop a campaign of ideological warfare within the context of a carefully structured situation of a steadily rising level of active participation by the work force in the pursuit of a programme of relatively immediate demands.

The strategy of the T&GWU in Britain was to win concessions through negotiation backed up by a powerful organization. What is insisted on is the construction of an organizational strength that will be so potentially effective in its capacity to bring down sanctions on management that it will rarely have to be used. In its handbook for stewards the T&GWU puts forward its views in the following terms:

Toughness must never be confused with noisiness. The workers' strength does not lie in lung power, it lies in a good case, skilfully presented, backed by solid organization. With these things, the workers can be confident that they can get what they want by normal negotiation. Without them all the hullabaloo in the world will not help. It may well only irritate the management and make them stand on their dignity.[21]

The emphasis on developing organizational strength is a persistent theme throughout the T&GWU's advice to its stewards:

You carry in trust a responsibility for an organization which has taken generations of struggle and service to build up. Pledge yourself that your spell of office will keep up its high traditions. Remember that in the last resort the influence of trade unionism depends upon workers acting in unity.

If you do your work well as a shop steward the workers will see daily evidence of the value of their trade union membership. You need nevertheless to seize every opportunity of taking action to build up the strength of the Union — by recruiting new members, by keeping existing members up to scratch, and by turning 'cardholders' into trade unionists.[22]

The principal method of developing organizational strength is seen to lie in the effort that the stewards put into handling the day-to-day problems in the workplace: 'You will be judged finally by your members on your results. The loyalty of the members towards the Union in the big issues will be very largely built up on what they have seen of you in dealing previously with the small ones' (p. 12).

The capacity to provide such services, however, is clearly related to the preservation of spheres over which the stewards can exercise an effective influence over issues that are important to members. The greatest scope for steward initiative lies in their control of an incentive payments system. But the T&GWU recognizes that management is likely to try to buy these out in productivity deals, and stresses the need to ensure that the stewards obtain alternative areas of influence. 'Such changes need to be compensated not only by higher wages but by careful safeguards and the extension of the role of the trade union representatives in the workplace (particularly the right to negotiate on manning and/or the speed of the job' (p. 22).

The provision of services not only reinforces the organizational solidarity of people who are already members, but it is the crucial lever for extending membership. The stewards must be ruthless in refusing to come to the help of non-members:

There will be many opportunities for you to plug the Union direct. But a good organizing job can be done without appearing to go out of your way to recruit members.

First, by refusing to handle problems for non-members, and joining up on the spot any 'nons' who want help. You will need therefore to have a supply of application forms always handy. (pp. 77–8)

The other major technique that the T&GWU proposes for developing organizational strength is to encourage the active involvement of members. The stewards are recommended to make sure that members are well informed about whatever they are doing, but they are also advised to bring the members into the process of decision making. This has the advantage that the stewards will be able to make use of the ideas and experience that members may have, and it also makes it more likely that members will feel personally committed to the decisions that have been taken:

No one taken singly adds up to much. The whole history of the Labour movement underlines the helplessness of the individual worker. Strength came through banding together. Combination applies to brains as well as to brawn. The strength of a trade union rests upon the intelligent participation of its members. . . . The experience of as many members as possible should be called upon. A widely canvassed opinion is less likely to be formed in ignorance of some matter which affects perhaps only a minority of the workers. Moreover, workers who feel that they are in some measure responsible for the shaping of a decision will be more inclined to stand by it afterwards. (p. 14)

The broad principles of this strategy of developing organizational strength had been followed faithfully at the level of the refinery. The main departure from the guidance in the handbook was that, in addition to the techniques recommended, the stewards had enlisted the help of management in their work of maintaining the strength and power of the union.

The British representatives were locked in a form of exchange relationship with management. Management helped them to maintain their organization by assisting them in enforcing a closed shop. For instance, when a batch of new recruits were due to arrive, management would warn the stewards in advance so that they could be at the gate to meet them, check their cards, and, if they were not already members, hand them over a form for joining. If someone refused, management would 'interview' him, and inform him that it was management's preference that all its employees should be union members. It would be made clear to him that, unless he joined, it would be exceedingly difficult for management to guarantee that he would be able to remain long in his job. Another way in which management facilitated union organization for the T&GWU was by agreeing to the introduction of the check-off system by which union dues were directly deducted from the person's pay slip, and were handed over by management to the union officials.

Management, therefore, in the British refineries was instrumental in helping the unions overcome two of the deepest and most persistent problems faced by the French unions — the problem of preventing an increase in the category of non-members, and the problem of actually collecting the money from those who had been persuaded to take a union card.

The unions, on the other hand, offered management a certain amount of help in controlling the aspirations of the work force. Not only were negotiations invariably concluded by signed agreements which helped to legitimate management's actions, but these agreements had a substantial moral power in that both the full-time union officials and the shop floor representatives accepted that they had a responsibility for ensuring that their terms were carried out. The agreement was recognized by the representatives as bringing the curtain down on the existing issues of dispute, and as implying the willingness of the workers to accept practices and conditions to which they objected, if these had not been specifically resolved within the terms of the agreement. The full-time officials could be, and were, called on by management to come to the refinery to convince their members that certain actions were in breach of the agreement and had to be stopped. Even if it proved at times difficult to get the workers to accept the constraining character of the agreement, it did mean that the union officials and the shop floor representatives tended to use their influence to calm things down rather than to fan the flames. This contrasted sharply with the situation in France where, even if an agreement was signed by the unions, it was merely regarded as a temporary embodiment of the existing balance of power, and as a basis from which a new and more ambitious set of demands could immediately be unleashed.[23] There was, clearly a sense in which the negotiated agreement turned the representatives in Britain into agents for helping management to secure the acquiescence of the work force.

Within this broader context of an exchange relationship in which management helped the union maintain its organization while the union aided management in getting the work force to abide by the rules, there took place a fairly continuous face-to-face dialogue between representatives and management, during which they would often get to know each other well. It was said to us more than once that some of the most difficult issues in negotations at Kent refinery tended to be decided in the mid-1960s not in the formal negotiating room, but over lunch when the General Manager entertained the District Secretary. Whatever the truth of this, the very practice of successful negotiation built up an expectation of eventually agreeing, and indeed a sense that one should be able to come to an agreement through discussion and discussion alone. Both sides had developed a certain pride in their ability to maintain good relations, and both sides were anxious to retain their reputation for reasonableness. We get some idea of the attitude underlying negotiations in the report of the final meeting attended by one T&GWU full-time official before his retirement.

The full-time official 'spent a good deal of time in extolling the virtues of the T&GWU and its membership at the Refinery in contrast to the attitude sometimes adopted by other trade unions. He pointed out that labour relations at Kent Refinery had always been extremely good, and that his members had scrupulously honoured agreements reached on their behalf with no hint of overtime bans, go slows, or other "cowboy" tactics'. (July 1968)

There seems to have developed, then, a negotiating system in which, to a certain degree, 'harmonistic negotiation' became a value in itself. Possibly one of the important factors about productivity bargaining is that it brought the shop stewards much more fully into the orbit of this system, and thereby increased their level of integration. As we have seen, productivity bargaining not only led the stewards to focus their attention to a much greater degree than before on the crucial managerial problem of efficiency, but it brought them into much more frequent contact with higher levels of management. We can get some idea of how the senior representatives responded by the praise that management lavished on them.

When a new shift branch secretary was elected in 1965, the minutes read: 'Mr. M. (the Works Manager) welcomed Mr. R. as the newly elected Shift Branch Secretary, and paid tribute to the statesman-like way in which Mr. N. had filled the post for many years.' (12 Oct. 1965) Or later, at a tricky moment in the productivity negotiations: 'At this point Mr. P. (the Works Manager) said that before allowing Mr. B. (the full-time official) to proceed he would like to place on record the Management's appreciation of the responsible manner in which Mr. B., Mr. R. and Mr. L. (the branch officials) had accepted to put forward the Company's proposals.' (16 Nov. 1966)

Management's recognition of the statesmanlike qualities of the shop floor representatives could take a more tangible form in its willingness to promote into the ranks of management the men who had shown themselves to be successful negotiators. Of the four key shop floor negotiators in the two refineries at the beginning of the period of productivity negotiations, three had achieved positions in management within three years of the opening of negotiations. Given the generally low level of mobility from the shop floor into management that was discussed in chapter 9, such promotion was clearly visible to workers and may possibly have exercised influence on the type of person who came to put himself forward to be a steward. It showed that one clear way for the ambitious man to make his qualities evident, in a work situation in which they might be lost sight of, was to show his powers of leadership on the shop floor.

The nature of the negotiating system, with its powerful incentives towards the integration of the representatives and their adoption of a managerial perspective, may well then have helped to restrain the level of demand on management. But there was a limit to the extent

to which management could rely on this. If, at Kent, the branch
secretary and chairman who negotiated the 1967 productivity deal
do seem to have been so fully drawn into the orbit of management
that, when the crunch came, they failed in their task of representing
shop floor opinion, they soon paid the penalty, and at the next
branch elections were thrown out of office. Grangemouth management experienced these limits in a much more drastic way when the
process operators finally went out on strike over the shift allowance.
The threat of repudiation by the membership set an ultimate limit on
the extent to which the representatives could be integrated.

The essence of the T&GWU's strategy, then, lay in negotiation
backed by organizational power. An exchange system had developed
by which management aided the union to maintain its organization,
while the union helped management secure the workers' acquiescence
to the rules. Given its aims, this strategy had been highly successful,
and for a period of some twenty years the membership in both
refineries had been able to achieve what they regarded as satisfactory
outcomes to negotiations without ever having to make use of their
organizational power. Indeed the strategy had been so successful
that it had created a negotiating ethos in which the peaceful resolution of problems had to some extent become a value in itself. This
probably had considerable advantages for management in that it
helped to restrain the level of demand. It was, however, a negotiating
ethos that remained essentially fragile: management ignored deeper
dissatisfaction at its peril.

The flow of influence within the union

The two distinct conceptions of unionism in France and Britain were
linked with differences in the direction of the flow of influence
within the union structure. In both countries the factory union
organization was conceived as an agent linking the workers on the
shop floor on the one hand, and the national union organization on
the other. But whereas in France the main influence over its activities
came from the external central union apparatus, in the British refineries it very largely responded to influence coming from the shop
floor.

This difference was inherent in the contrasting conceptions of the
purpose of the union. The French militants saw themselves as involved in a fundamental struggle for the minds of the workers, and
they were concerned to instil a coherent and systematic counter

culture that involved a critique of the overall structure of society. But the task of developing the ideology itself would have imposed a formidable burden on the shop floor militants: they already not only had their normal work as employees, but they had to carry out their day-to-day functions as representatives — checking work conditions, listening to complaints, and attending committees with management. They were, then, heavily dependant on the central union apparatus for the elaboration of their ideological material, for the application of the general critique to the particular state of French society at that given moment in time, and for the formulation of broadly applicable shorter-term objectives that were consistent with the ultimate aims. The very conception that the militants possessed of a process of social change that could only occur through the development of collective consciousness in an ever-growing proportion of the working class placed a premium on the co-ordination of the ideological offensive, and necesssitated a constant reference to a stable source of ideological authority.

This dependence on the central union apparatus was most striking in the case of the largest of the French unions — the CGT. The secretary of the union section in the refinery would receive a constant flow of information giving him guidance as to the position the refinery union should adopt in relation to the problems of the moment. Sometimes the Federation would send directly a great mass of tracts to be distributed to the workers; at other times it would send a model tract and instruct the secretary to incorporate parts of it in the factory union's own productions. We can get an idea of the procedure from the instructions sent to the secretaries of the union sections concerning the attitude to be adopted to the referendum organized by the French President in 1972 on the question of British entry into the Common Market.

Dear Comrades,

You have received the declaration adopted on April 10th by the Federal Executive Committee.

You will find, attached, the text resulting from the discussions of the Confederal Executive Committee which met on the 12th April.

These two texts which were unanimously adopted, which express the same view and conclude that it should be NO, complete each other:

— the federal text, which was drawn up to give the essential ideas is necessarily shorter, more concise: we ask you *to reproduce it in the form of a tract and to circulate it widely.*

— the confederal text has not been specifically designed to be reproduced as a tract: the explanations are more detailed and will be useful to you in putting forward your case in the meetings which the Federal Executive Committee ask you to organize in its declaration.

(Memorandum from *Fédération Nationale des Industries Chimiques. Avril 1972*)

The CGT had developed a simple but effective system of control of ideological deviance. Each union section had to send to the Federation a copy of each of the tracts that it produced. The secretariat of the Federation could then immediately see if its views had been misunderstood or simply ignored, and could bring pressure to bear on the union section to modify its line. In cases of difficulty one of the secretaries would visit the refinery in question; and, if moral pressure failed, the union section would be excluded at the next Congress.

But the tracts also provided the Federation with detailed information about incidents in the individual refineries, and thereby gave it an overall picture of the new types of problems that were emerging as overt sources of tension. This gave it the possibility of co-ordinating ideas and action. It could try to generalize grievances that had arisen in one refinery to others, and it could get a crude indication of the level of social tension, and hence of the viability of trying to organize industry-wide strike action.

For it was the Federation that was the crucial initiator of strike action. It would usually select a week or a specific day during which the factory unions were instructed to mobilize the work force. The imperativeness of these instructions varied according to the criticalness of the issue and the Federation's assessment of the level of combativity in the industry. Sometimes the unions would be firmly instructed to bring the workers out on strike; at other times they would simply be asked to carry out the most intense form of action that was feasible in the light of the specific conditions of the enterprise. As an example of the stronger form of instruction, we can take the Federation's memorandum to the secretaries of the union sections on the 24 May 1965:

Dear Comrades,

ALL TOGETHER IN THE ACTION!

This is the title of the call for action decided upon by the Federal Executive Bureau in its meeting on Saturday 22nd May.

The text is at present in the press and it will be despatched to you in sufficient quantity to ensure a *massive distribution*. . . .

Take then, straight away, all the necessary measures:

— to collect your parcel at the post office
— to organize the *distribution of the tract the moment it arrives*
— to respond positively to the call of the Executive Bureau which asks *with insistence* that

STRIKES FOR LIMITED PERIODS OF TIME

be *carried out everywhere in the coming days.*
— immediately the union leadership should meet to examine the precise rallying call that will make it possible to draw the support of the majority of the workers.
— then, they will get into contact with the comrades of the other unions in order to make them precise propositions about the action to take. These propositions for action should have as their objective the achievement of *the demands of the inter-federal programme (as well as the local demands).* . . .

These actions should be active: no striking by staying at home, but interruptions of work with meetings and demonstrations. . . .

Inform us without delay of the arrangements that you have made, of *the first strike decided upon,* of those which are due to follow, and of *the way the strikes themselves develop.* . . . With this information in its possession, the federal direction will be in a position to take other initiatives to widen the action, co-ordinate it. . . .

With brotherly greetings,

Le Secrétariat fédéral

The importance of the central union apparatus in stimulating action is clear if we look at the pattern of strikes. Of the thirteen strikes at Dunkirk between 1964 and 1971, nine fell within a period of action called for by either the Federation or the Confederation of the CGT. Of the eleven strikes at Lavera between 1963 and 1972, ten were called by the Federation or the Confederation.[24] (See Table 38.)

The fact that the main ideological impetus and the main directives for industrial action came from the centre by no means meant that the factory unions were reduced to mere ciphers. Their task was a critical one: it was to reformulate the general positions of the union in a way which would integrate them closely with the everyday texture of life in the factory, and thereby make the higher-order issues

Table 38   *The source of initiative of strike action*

Level of the union organization	Dunkirk	Lavera
Confederation	5	5
Federation	4	5
Refinery	4	1

Note: The strike of May 1968 I have included in both cases under the category 'refinery'. This is debatable because the strike occurred on the 20th — three days after the strike call by the CGT Confederation. But given the climate in the country at the time we can assume that the refineries would have closed anyhow if the initiative had not been taken by the militants.

more easily accessible to the specific group of workers. The factory
unions were asked to develop their own programmes, giving expression to the higher union policy in terms of the concrete issues of the
workplace. The importance of the need to 'translate' the union's
ideology into terms directly applicable to the particular place of
work is constantly re-emphasized in the union's training documents
for militants. For instance, insisting on the importance of establishing
a regular union journal within each firm, the CGT states: 'Its role is
essentially to denounce the reality of the workers' exploitation in all
its forms: basing itself on precise facts that the workers know about,
at the place of work where the exploitation of the working class is
directly carried out.'[25]

The CFDT central union apparatus exercised a much less overt
ideological control over its grass roots militants. Indeed, in keeping
with its broader objectives of 'autogestion' or self-management, the
CFDT had an explicit policy of decentralizing initiatives as much as
possible, and maximizing the democratic nature of procedures within
the Confederation. There was certainly some evidence that there was
in reality a lesser degree of ideological centralization than existed in
the CGT. Although the Federation provided its militants with tracts,
journals, and booklets on specific issues, we found that in the collection of the CFDT tracts in the refinery of Dunkirk, a large number from the mid 1960s came not from the Federation itself, but
from the Federation's Paris regional organization. The multiplication
and strengthening of these regional organizations was official CFDT
policy; and the model of the precociously influential Paris region
was soon to be followed by the creation of regional organizations at
Lyon, Berre, Nantes, and the Nord.

Nonetheless, as we have suggested, it is in the logic of a union of
mobilization that the decentralization of ideological initiative cannot
be carried very far. Although the CFDT encouraged internal ideological dissent, the source of ideological initiative remained decidedly
elitist in character. This emerges clearly even in the period before the
CFDT had finally committed itself to the objective of mobilization.
The astounding transformation of the moderate Catholic union of
the 1940s into the radical lay organization of the 1970s certainly
demonstrated that the Confederation's leadership could not monopolize ideological innovation. But the dynamic of change was still
the work of elites. The more radical 'minority' section of the CFTC
in the 1950s quite explicitly looked to the group of militants that

had gathered from the journal *Reconstruction* for ideological guidance. As Maire (the CFDT's Secretary General) and Julliard quite explicitly state:

One can say that *Reconstruction* introduced the CFDT to socialism.[26]

Or again:

For a Federation like that of the chemical industry, *Reconstruction* above all spared its militants the need to go over once again the whole journey made by the French and international labour movement. The analyses of Reconstruction, confirmed by the 'minority group' enabled us to avoid a certain number of errors, the groping in the dark and the dead-ends in which socialism had gone astray in the course of its history. Many militants were thus able to discover the nature of the totalitarian socialism of Stalin, as well as that of the bastard socialism of social democracy, without, in the process, falling into the sterility of an extreme left critique disconnected from reality. On the contrary, without *a priori* prejudices, they walked straight into a new conception of socialism, guided by the research of an open-minded group that saved them from disappointments and useless revolt (p. 74–5)

The elitist character of the CFDT's evolution to radicalism is confirmed in a study carried out by Marc Maurice on the union's chemical federation. Maurice analysed the attitudes in 1962 of militants, members, and sympathisers to the fundamental question of whether or not the union should shed its remaining formal ties with Christian doctrine. Significantly, he found that the militants were far and away the most favourable to a change in the character of the union. Whereas 60% of the militants were in favour of dropping the formal connection with Christianity, this was true of only 37% of the members of the union, and only 28% of supporters. This makes it perfectly clear that the pressure for change was not coming from the shop floor supporters of the union; rather it gives a picture of a set of ideas formulated from above and filtering down through the various strata of the union organization, becoming progressively weaker as they reach the base.[27]

But, if the formulation of the union's ideology necessarily remained elitist in character and insured that the main influence on the attitudes of the militants in the factory unions came from the higher echelons of the external union apparatus, it does nonetheless seem to be the case that the factory unions were given a fairly high degree of autonomy in deciding on the type of action to adopt at any given moment within the factory. As with the CGT, the CFDT Confederation and the Federation specified periods for the mobilization of the base, but this seemed to be legitimately regarded by the militants as suggestion rather than instruction. Similarly, the militants seemed to be free to decide how far they wanted to co-ordinate their action with the CGT. At Dunkirk the CFDT made little effort to carry out the type of united action with the CGT advocated by the Confederation and the Federation, whereas at Lavera the practice of unity in action was fairly systematic.[28]

For the CFDT, then, the main influence of the central union apparatus lay in the formulation of the ideology. As far as action is concerned, it restricted itself to providing a broad framework within which the factory unions were allowed a considerable autonomy of decision.

In the British refineries — where the T&GWU representatives largely conceived of themselves as spokesmen of the shop floor — the main source of influence over the representatives' behaviour came from the workers themselves. The representatives' principal concern was to make sure that each demand had adequate shop floor backing.

The central union organization provided very little guidance in the formulation of demands. The usual process was for an issue to be raised by the stewards at the factory branch meeting, and the branch officials would then forward the demands of the members to the District Secretary. If the negotiation was purely concerned with a straightforward pay rise, the district official might be able to help by supplying details of deals in neighbouring firms. But his knowledge of the area was not always a firm asset to the stewards. The full-time official had to spend a good deal of his time negotiating for relatively low paid workers in the area, and it was understandable that he might at times feel somewhat impatient with the reluctance of the refinery workers to agree to a deal which seemed to him already immensely beneficial in comparison with many of the other agreements which he had negotiated in the area.

Moreover, as we have seen, the development of productivity bargaining, in which the negotiators needed a detailed knowledge of workplace conditions and of the values that workers attached to specific practices, led to a further erosion of the value of the interventions of the external union officials.

The central organization of the T&GWU had come to see this growing decentralization of initiative in the handling of negotiations not only as inevitable, but as something that was intrinsically desirable. In the *Shop Stewards Handbook*, the T&GWU explains its conception of the type of relationship that should exist between the shop floor representatives and the external union officials:

Our policy is to encourage as far as possible local devolution in negotiation. We want the workers in each firm and, better still, in each plant to have their own agreement. That means that the shop stewards must be able to carry out their own negotiations. The full-time officials will be there to advise, and help, if necessary. They must, indeed, be called in if there is any chance that a decision inside the workshop will have repercussions on agreements or Union interests elsewhere. But where the matter is one that affects only your own workers, you must be prepared to act on your own responsibility. (p. 16/17)

Given this decreasing role of the full-time officials in the formulation of demands and the process of negotiation, it followed that, far from being the stimulus of industrial conflict as they were in France, they tended at moments of crisis to maximize the ambivalence of their position. For instance, when Grangemouth went on strike, the full-time official took care not to commit himself overtly to support of the strike, but nonetheless to express understanding. *The Scotsman*, in its account of one of the very rare interviews given by a full-time official on the subject of the strike, reported: 'Although the strike is unofficial, there is some support from officials of the T&GWU, whose secretary Mr M. said "I will be meeting the shop stewards tomorrow and will discuss the provision of supplies for bus services, but these men are in dispute and to be effective there has to be some disruption." '[29]

The formulation of demands

The demands that the British representatives made on management were characterized by the relatively simple way in which they were formulated. In the typical negotiating round, the only demand that would be forwarded would be for a salary increase. The exact formula for the salary increase could vary. Sometimes it might be simply for a cost of living increase based on movements in the official retail price index; more often it would be for an unspecified 'substantial' increase that would implicitly imply the demand for an improvement in purchasing power. Most usually the demand was for a percentage increase, but this was not always the case. For instance, in January 1968, we find the Grangemouth representatives stressing to management that the branch wanted a flat rate increase, whereas in April 1971 they are insisting that it should be on a percentage basis.

The main new type of salary demand in the early 1960s was for increases in line with the growth of productivity. The unions at Kent (which is the only refinery for which our records are complete for this period) made quite explicit reference to the financial advantages gained by their colleagues at Fawley, and asked management to look into the possibility of securing comparable advantages for their own workers. In the 1970s the main development was a new insistence on proper compensation for shift work.

Very occasionally management would find itself confronted with other types of demand. In 1962, for instance, the unions asked for a reduction to a 40 hour week and got it in the same year. Similarly they would occasionally ask for additional holidays. What is noticeable is that the unions' usual procedure was only to forward one of these additional demands at a time. The overriding consideration seemed to be the belief that one should only put forward demands that management could be reasonably expected to meet in the near future.

Outside the main negotiating arena, there was, of course, an important undercurrent of demand being fairly continuously processed by the shop stewards, and focusing on detailed improvements of work conditions. But this was almost exclusively handled by middle management, it was kept highly informal, it was never formulated into any form of programme. It consisted of isolated, *ad hoc* demands that — with the exception of the issue of smoking facilities — never became major issues of principle.

Another notable characteristic of demands in the British refineries is that they were almost entirely about substantive issues, and procedural questions had at the most only marginal importance. This was despite a major effective extension of union powers of control. In the 1950s this extension of control had taken place in a purely *ad hoc* way, and in the 1960s it took place largely at the initiative of management. The only issue which appears to have involved any procedural disagreement was whether or not the unions had powers to negotiate the sickness scheme and pension arrangements, and this was by all accounts regarded as a secondary issue.

In Britain, then, the demands were simply formulated, they were advanced on a narrow front, and they were almost exclusively substantive in content. The contrast with France could not have been greater.

For the French unions the formulation of demands had to fulfil a triple function: it had to be designed to protect the work force against increased managerial exploitation; it had to implicitly or explicitly forward the unions' key ideological ideas; and it had to provide a rallying point around which the workers could be brought into active involvement in pursuit of a programme of action.

The first characteristic of the French scene is the complexity of the process by which demands are formulated at the level of the factory union. As we have seen, the main influence over policy positions came from the external union apparatus, but the factory unions were also expected to develop their own local programmes in a way that would make the basic union conceptions more immediately relevant to the specific work force, and thus enable the unions to bring the workers into active participation in pursuit of more general union demands.

In practice, the factory unions had to juggle with three distinct programmes: the programme of the Confederation, the programme of the Federation, and their own local programme. Although there was usually a great deal of overlap, the order of priorities at each level would frequently be different. The tricky part of drawing up a specific programme of demands behind which the workers would be asked to rally was the relative weight to give to each of these three elements. To place the emphasis on the Confederal programme was to underline the links between the refinery work force and the wider working class, thus enhancing the aim of creating a sense of collective class consciousness. This involved the risk, however, of failing to look into the preoccupations of the refinery workers, thus making it difficult to bring them into active participation. On the other hand, if the priority was given to the refinery union's local programme there was the risk of the development of a categorial consciousness. The usual solution was a judicious mix of programmes in which the central point of focus would often shift with alarming speed from one element to another. The most dominant element was usually the Federal programme, but this was frequently swept into second place by Confederal demands, and more rarely by issues specific to the refinery

A rough indication of the relative frequency with which the different elements dominated can be obtained by looking at the leading demands in strikes. We can see from Table 39 that, of the twenty-four strikes in the two refineries, Federal demands were placed at the head of the programme in 12, Confederal in 8, and refinery demands in 4.

There appeared to be no clear trend over time. If at Dunkirk the local refinery programme seemed to be becoming more important in the 1970s, it is notable that the last two strikes of our series at Lavera, in the summer of 1972, were both based on Confederal demands — demands which, as it happened, had no great relevance

Table 39[30]   *The source of the leading demands in strike programmes*

Level of the union organization	Dunkirk	Lavera	Total
Confederal	3	5	8
Federal	7	5	12
Refinery	3	1	4

for the specific situation of the refinery workers, since they had already obtained several years earlier the advantages in question.

A second characteristic of the French unions' demands is that they were advanced on a very broad front. There were usually five major categories of demand put forward simultaneously, and these categories were often capable of multiple subdivision. The Dunkirk inter-union programme of January 1971, for instance, consisted of seven major categories of demand, and altogether twenty-two specific demands. The basic union principle seems to have been to avoid allowing the list to run down. If a given issue was resolved, it provided space for a new one.

Given the kaleidoscopic character of French union programmes, it would be difficult to present one that could be claimed as altogether typical, but we can at least look at those categories of demand that regularly featured.

Salaries

The formulation of salary demands was in all cases the work of the Federations, and this was by far the commonest type of demand to head the list. The demand usually contained three separate components.

First, both the CGT and the CFDT aimed to reduce the margin of discretion exercised by employers over individual salaries, by demanding a faster increase in minimum salary rates than in the effective basic salaries practised in the enterprises. By 'jacking up' the category minima, the unions believed that they would be able to reduce the dispersion within categories since employers would be reluctant to get involved in the cost of regranting individual increases that would restore the previous pattern of differentials.

Second, the unions were concerned to cover for increases in the cost of living. Although this demand bore a superficial resemblance to its equivalent in Britain, it was in reality a good deal more complex. Both the CGT and the CFDT rejected the official prices index, and each union had developed its own index which it claimed reflected more faithfully the true impact of price increases on the working-class budget. The two unions put forward different cost of living demands based on fluctuations in their own particular index. The employers, of course, refused to accept the precision of anything but the official index.

The third demand was for an increase in real wages — based again on the unions' own estimates. Both unions had adopted a formula whereby the increases should be given at a differential rate varying according to the person's hierarchical position. The low paid were to benefit relatively to the high paid.

However, a major problem in the French negotiating scene was that there was a fundamental difference between the salary programmes of the two unions, and both sides attached a great deal of importance to the principles involved. The CFDT aimed not only to prevent an increase in differentials, which would have been achieved by the common union provisions for real wage increases, but actually to *reduce* them. This involved also giving the lower paid a disproportionate share of any cost of living increase — which was usually the largest sum involved. The CFDT's objective was to reduce the differential in minimum rates between departmental management and the unskilled labourer from its present ratio of 1 to 8.8 to a ratio of 1 to 5.8. The theory behind this was that salary differentials perverted authority relations, and were partly responsible for the sharp social status distinctions between management and the work force. Salary policy was, therefore, directly tied to the long term policy of democratizing the enterprise. The CGT, on the other hand, believed that this would only generate discontent among the better paid, lead to infighting within the working class, and shatter the possibility of achieving real unity of action.

Both French management and the French workers, then, found themselves in the middle of an intensely waged debate about what should be the underlying philosophy in the formulation of salary demands.

Classifications

The union concern over the classification system was twofold. First, they wanted it updated so that the job descriptions corresponded to the effective types of task carried out on the shop floor. The more that technological change made the descriptions anachronistic, the greater was management's latitude in interpreting the application of the classification system. Second, they wanted to reduce the number of grades, both to give a salary boost to intermediate categories and to increase the homogeneity of the work force. Once more the CGT and the CFDT differed sharply in their precise demands — which again were mainly formulated by the Federations. The CGT wanted a fairly even simplification across the hierarchical scale that would maintain overall differentials between the top and the bottom. The CFDT wanted to emphasize the suppression of grades at the bottom of the scale so that the lower graded workers would be catapulted up in relation to the higher. The immediate demand was again determined by the union's long-term objective of reducing status differences between leaders and led.

Employment/reorganizations

From 1967 the problem of employment in its broadest form was one of the sheet-anchors of the joint CGT–CFDT Confederal programme. At the national level the concern was with unemployment. Here there was a clear need to translate the demand into terms that would be meaningful to refinery workers whose security of employment was exceptionally high. The refinery unions forged the crucial link by means of the question of reorganizations. The immediate demand was for the maintenance and improvement of manning levels, but in putting it forward they stressed both the dangers that reductions posed for safety in the refinery, and also its implications for the number of jobs available in the region at a time when unemployment was growing. This could be driven home in a very personal way by focusing on the future job possibilities that would be available for the workers' children when they came to school-leaving age. It was a classic use of an internal problem to make people think about a wider issue.

Shift work conditions

One of the refinery unions' principal aims in the 1960s was to find a way of destroying the 'myth' that workers in continuous-process plants were less exploited than other categories of workers simply because they were paid very much more. The breakthrough came with the issue of shift work, and this formed the essence of the refinery unions' own local programme for mobilizing the workers.

We have already described the build up of the action over shift work in chapter 4. Here we can simply recall that the CFDT Federation drew up a complex programme of shift worker grievances in 1966, and that at about the same time the CGT began systematic agitation in the units on the issue. Although none of the refinery unions explicitly referred to the CFDT programme, there was a remarkable degree of correspondence between the issues they took up apparently piecemeal, and the issues the original programme had stressed; and this correspondence became increasingly noticeable in the late 1960s and the early 1970s as the unions increased their offensive on a steadily broadening front.

Union rights

When the CGT and CFDT created their inter-Confederal programme of 1966 the second most important demand was for the extension of union rights. Despite the reforms of the law of 27 December 1968, this has remained a major, if unclearly formulated, element in the Confederal programme. At the level of the refineries it was usually given relatively little salience, coming fourth or fifth in the list of demands. Nonetheless, it was a theme that frequently appeared in the commentary in tracts and in the minutes of management–union meetings. It took three main forms: (1) a demand for the extension of facilities within the plant (e.g. the right to hold meetings with members during work hours); (2) a demand for negotiatory rights over salaries at the level of the enterprise; and (3), at the refinery at of Dunkirk, a demand for negotiatory rights at plant level over aspects of work organization such as manning and training.

A study of French union militants by Claude Durand suggests that militants in the advanced sector prefer a strategy of negotiation over one of contestation in their relations with management.[31] The differences he found were not very great, and the study is methodologically weak. It is therefore difficult to know what value to attach to the results. We have left a more detailed consideration of the study for the appendix. If, however, we confine ourselves to the explicit demands made by the unions in our refineries, they appear to be entirely typical of demands in large French firms. The critical study for comparison is that by J. P. Bachy *et al. Représentation et Négociation dans l'Entreprise* which investigates industrial relations in the four sectors of banking, chemicals (including refining), commerce and metallurgy.[32]

If we take first the question of negotiation at the level of the enterprise, the authors make it clear that since 1955 the French unions have been cautious towards, but generally favourable to, *partial enterprise negotiations* — that is to say negotiations limited to specific topics. This strategy has proved particularly useful if the unions have failed to develop an industry level collective agreement, or if negotiations at industry level have become blocked, or in enabling the unions to play off one enterprise against another, by generalizing throughout an industry concessions gained in negotiations with one particular management. Enterprise level bargaining is invariably seen as an addition to, not as a substitute for, industry level negotiation; and there was a decided preference for partial bargaining since this left the unions free to contest on other issues.[33] At the time of their study, the unions in the advanced chemical–oil sector had been the least successful of the unions in the four branches in securing the opening of enterprise negotiation.[34] It is notable that in our refineries the demand first became marked in the period 1967/68 when industry level negotiations were proving exceptionally fruitless; and, in the period we were studying, the demand was put forward under explicit instructions from the CGT Federation.[35]

Second, there is the question of the claim for negotiatory powers over work organization for the union section at factory level. It is clear from a study by Reynaud that this was fundamental to the CFDT's conception of the union section as early as 1968. The union tried, but failed, to get negotiating rights over salaries, work conditions, and discipline, incorporated in the law of 27 December 1968.[36] Edmond Maire declared in June 1968:

The power of the workers organized in their union section is the power to check the arbitrary, to control the whole of the conditions of work — both in so far as they concern the individual: recruitment, transfer, promotion, dismissal, discipline, and in so far as they concern the collectivity: salaries, employment, future of the enterprise. . . . The great conquest of May 1968, the introduction in strength of the union into the place of work in order to extend the rights of the workers, marks an irreversible stage in a process of democratization of the enterprise where the workers have to conquer liberty and responsibility.[37]

Bachy *et al.* argue that, on the basis of their study, it is clear that this insistence on the right of the union section to negotiate over issues traditionally in the sphere of the Works Committees and the Personnel Delegates is common to both the CGT and the CFDT in metallurgy, chemicals, and banking.[38] This may well be the case, but the coding categories in which they present their data are so collapsed that it is difficult to interpret them with any precision. In our refinery of Dunkirk, the demand was clearly propelled primarily by the CFDT, and the CGT is notably unforthcoming on the issue in the minutes of the meetings with management. The chronology is perhaps revealing. In May 1970 the CFDT made its official conversion to an ideology of class conflict and adopted the demand for 'autogestion' as the cornerstone of its programme for socialism. In the same year the first tracts on autogestion began to appear in the refineries, and it was in November of that year that the CFDT union section at Dunkirk made its first formal demand for negotiating rights over issues within the competence of the Works Committee. The time-table suggests that it is a case of formal ideological radicalization at the centre filtering down somewhat slowly into concrete action at the base some six months later.

Political demands

There was a sense in which the political demands of the CGT perva-ded virtually its entire output of propaganda. Its hostility to, and rejection of the legitimacy of, the existing government was embedded in the set of core concepts that it used in describing and formulating most situations affecting the work force. For instance, attacks on the exploitative character of big business are invariably simultaneous attacks on the state, and there is a tendency to produce a constant word association between 'Patronat' and 'Pouvoir' so that the two ideas appear to fuse into an indissoluble whole.[39]

For instance, in announcing the agreement between the CGT and CFDT Confederation in 1966:

For some time, and particularly since the application of the 'stabilisation plan', the unions' desire to negotiate has been confronted by a wall of combined resistance by the State and the employers of the major enterprises. Authoritarian measures, unilateral decisions, arrogance towards the union militants have been the common practice of the public powers and the employers in the domain of social relations.

Or, at Dunkirk, at the time of the elections of the Works Committee in 1971:

Because the CGT considers the Works Committees as an instrument at the service of the union to carry through its action and improve the conditions of life of the employees, the Committees are, at the present time, the object of repeated attacks on the part of the State and the employers.

Or, at Lavera, mobilizing the workers for the strike of June 1972:

In reality, it's a matter of breaking open the lock of the coalition of the government and the employers, as much to bring about the achievement of the demands common to the whole of the working class, as to satisfy the specific demands of our enterprise and our industry.

The format of the CGT's factory journals equally ensured that political issues never lay long under the surface. Each issue devoted a regular section to some specifically political set of events — ranging from the war in Vietnam, to the government's anti-social and class-biased economic policy. At election time, of course, the CGT focused the full weight of its propaganda on the denunciation of the candidates of the right, and the government's past record.[40]

But besides the regular flow of more or less overt political commentary, the unions periodically marked out specific issues on which to arouse the work force into a confrontation with the government. These moves were usually the ones in which the Confederations played the leading role. When these demands were made, they tended to supersede both the Federal and the local refinery programmes, and emerge — usually for a relatively brief period of time — as the leading issues.

Usually once or twice during the year, the CGT, frequently supported by the CFDT, would explicitly organize a day of action that would rally the largest possible proportion of the total work force of the country into confrontation with the government. The issues would usually be chosen to highlight the interdependence of governmental power and the interests of big business. The moral was that major changes in the situation of the work force could only be obtained through the medium of state power.

There was, then, a quite striking degree of difference between the formulation of demands in the French and British refineries. In Britain, where the unions were unions of representation, the demands tended to be simply formulated and advanced on a narrow front. In France, where the unions were unions of ideological mobilization, the demands linked in a complex way societal and local issues; they were advanced on a much broader front; they were formulated as part of a coherent long term strategy; and they included major categories of demand — for control over managerial decisions and for action against the government — that were almost entirely absent from the British scene.

I I

Union strength and coercive power

Faithfully contradictory to the end, Blauner believed that automation would weaken the power of the trade unions, while Mallet believed that it would strengthen them. Blauner writes: 'The extraordinary organizational identification of oil refinery workers makes it extremely difficult for a CIO union to gain their allegiance.'[1] And, again: 'Generally lukewarm to unions and loyal to his employer, the blue-collar employee in the continuous-process industries may be a worker "organization-man" in the making.'[2] Mallet, on the other hand, confidently tells us that in the advanced sector we are seeing a rebirth of union strength. 'Enterprise unionism rediscovers, at the organizational level, certain of the characteristics of craft unionism: a high level of participation in trade union activity, debureaucratization through a reassertion of the importance of the enterprise union sections . . .'[3] He further tells us that unionism in the advanced sector is distinctive in that traditional union rivalries and competition are overcome, and are replaced by the creation of permanent inter-union committees that ensure the co-ordination and effectiveness of union action.[4]

Membership

In terms of sheer numerical strength there can be little doubt that Mallet gets the better of the argument. In the British refineries membership was 100%, and the unions effectively operated a closed shop. But even in the French refineries, where the unions did not have the benefit of management's assistance in maintaining their membership, we found that 77% of the Lavera operators and maintenance workers claimed to be union members, and 88% of those at Dunkirk. By French standards this is truly remarkable. In a national sample, in 1969, Adam *et al.* found that only 32% of French workers claimed that they were union members.[5]

But membership figures alone are only one indicator of strength

274

and, before arriving at any overall conclusion, we need to look at how effective the unions were in practice. In particular we need to look at the cohesiveness of union organization, the quality of relations with the base, and the effective power of the unions to coerce management.

The pattern of union division

In both countries there were major union divisions that separated members of the work force, and that constituted important obstacles to unity of action. In the British refineries there was a fundamental divide between the T&GWU that organized the operators and some of the less skilled maintenance workers, and the craft unions which organized the greater part of the maintenance force.

As we have seen, negotiations with management were carried out entirely separately in the two cases. Indeed, the separate pattern of negotiations was accompanied by a certain amount of status rivalry which revealed itself in a fairly permanent tension between the two groups about what should be the proper differential between craft and operator salaries. Indeed, at times, the concern not to lose ground to the crafts seemed to be the overriding element in the T&GWU's representatives' thinking.

At Kent, for instance we find:

Mr. B. (the T&GWU full-time official) referred to the recent wage increase negotiated with the Craft Unions, and said that this had placed the T&GW union in an impossible position. (12 Oct. 1961)

Mr. B. said that he and his members were embarrassed by the recent agreement concluded between the Company and other Trade Unions represented at the Refinery. He referred to an urgent exchange of views with the Industrial Relations Officer on the 10th of November which he had considered necessary in order to gain some appreciation of the situation. Having studied the document (summary sheet) which outlined the basis of the settlement with the Craft Trade Unions, Mr. B. believed that the Company was paying for increased productivity resulting from the use of Job Cards, a common overtime rota and natural wastage in the labour force. He claimed that the T&GWU members had made a far greater contribution to productivity over the year . . . (12 Nov. 1964)

It appeared to be exactly the same story at Grangemouth. Indeed, there, an increase in the craft/operator differential brought the first serious threat of strike from the operators. The T&GWU Branch Resolution of 9 December 1969 reads:

In view of the unrest created by Management as a result of the proposed increase in differential between the tradesmen and the T&GWU personnel, that unless Management finds something to redress the balance within 7 days of the tradesmen finalizing agreement, we the Branch are prepared to invoke a work to rule plus any other action deemed necessary by the Branch.

The Branch Secretary wishes to record his personal dissatisfaction with Management that in 21 years in the Refinery this is the first time that the Branch has had to resort to this action. This must reflect on the Management personally.

Only two years later we find a new Branch Secretary explaining why the Branch has suddenly reversed its apparently favourable attitude to a management offer in the following terms:

Mr. P. (the Branch Secretary) suggested that the attitude of Branch had changed when the basis of the Craft settlement was known. They considered that it was unfair to propose an increase which represented a lower percentage on salary than had been granted to the Craftsmen. (3 Sep. 1971)

In everyday relations within the refinery, there appeared to be a minimal degree of co-operation or even of formal contact between the two sets of shop floor representatives. It was true that once in the 1950s the craft stewards at Kent had suggested forming a joint stewards' committee, but, as a former T&GWU secretary explained, the suggestion was regarded with the utmost suspicion by the T&GWU:

Around 1958 the craft unions asked the T&G to join their Joint Committee with an elected chairman and secretary. But the T&G didn't want to join the Committee because it would only have had one vote although it was much larger than the other unions. So the committee would have been dominated by the crafts for craft purposes.

Reflecting on relations in the 1970s, the Branch Secretary of one of the refineries told us: 'For the last four years I've tried to get meetings between the T&GWU and the Crafts, but I've only once succeeded. There's no real explanation from the crafts why they can't — they just tell us it's not possible.'

The divide between the operator and craft union organizations was, then, a quite fundamental one. The work force at no time produced a united front in its relations with management, and there was no question of common action.

The French union movement was equally divided, but the division was ideological and not occupational. In contrast to the British situation where competition between unions for the same set of workers was relatively rare, in the French situation it was a fundamental of inter-union relations. At Dunkirk, there were three unions competing for the support of the work force; at Lavera two.

The CGT was easily the dominant union in both refineries. If we

Table 40   *The membership strength of the French unions among unionized workers* (% of unionized workers)

Union	Dunkirk	Lavera	National[6]
CGT	65	91	63
CFDT	22	9	16
FO	13	0	8
Other	—	—	12
	(N = 173)	(N = 155)	

look first at union membership, 70% of the workers interviewed at Lavera, and 57% at Dunkirk were members of the CGT. Its nearest rival was the CFDT which had a substantial base of 20% at Dunkirk, but a relatively weak membership of 7% of the work force at Lavera. Force Ouvrière had been eliminated at Lavera, but still had a firm foothold at Dunkirk where 11% of the workers claimed to belong to it. This rank order of union strength was identical to the pattern in the nation at large revealed by a national sample. To make the comparison easier, in Table 40 we have compared the strength of the unions among *unionized* workers.

The basic pattern of support for the unions in our refineries, and its consistency over time, is confirmed if we look at the voting in elections to the Works Committees between 1958 and 1973. (Table 41.) The main difference is that the CFDT appears substantially stronger at Lavera in terms of 'electoral influence' than in terms of membership, probably reflecting a failure of the CFDT militants in the 1960s to 'colonize' their potential base.

These figures show the remarkable stability of the pattern of union support within the work force across the 1960s and the early 1970s, with the CGT fluctuating within the 60% range at Dunkirk, and within the 70% range at Lavera. The rank order is the same as the wider pattern revealed in a study of large industrial firms in both the private and public sector of French industry.[7] Finally, we can compare our data with the Ministry of Works' analysis of the national pattern for 1972. On the basis of data from elections to 11,124 committees, it was found that the CGT received 51.4% of the vote, the CFDT 19.4%, and FO 7.6%.[8] The distribution of union influence in our refineries, was strikingly close to the wider national pattern.

If the British unions had been largely unsympathetic to each other, reluctant to co-operate, and involved in a marked status rivalry, this was still relatively innocuous compared to the very rough treatment

Table 41   *Percentage of the vote secured by each union in the elections to the Works Committees, 1958–1973: 1st college: Workers/Employees* (% support for each union)

Date of election	Dunkirk Votant	CGT	CFDT	FO	Lavera Votant	CGT	CFDT	FO
1958	79.9	60.0	21.7	15.5	81.3	65.9		34.1
1960	88.1	61.8	19.8	16.0	84.4	78.2	14.8	7.0
1962	88.8	63.5	19.5	15.2	80.0	75.4	15.7	8.8
1964	87.9	64.9	18.0	15.0	88.7	79.4	20.6	
1966	87.4	60.9	20.2	17.8	83.1	77.5	22.5	
1969	86.3	61.9	22.7	13.9	85.2	77.5	22.5	
1971	86.8	61.0	23.3	14.3	86.5	79.8	20.2	
1973	86.2	50.4	16.7	15.8	79.2	80.3	19.7	

Note:
1. There were changes in the definition of the Dunkirk electoral college in 1960 and subsequently in 1969, which may help to explain variations between the blocs 1960–1966 and 1969–1973.
2. The Dunkirk 1966 election was held in 1967.
3. In the 1973 election in Dunkirk the difference between the numbers voting and the numbers voting for the unions presenting candidates is explained by an abnormally high number of spoilt ballot sheets — 13.5%. The reason for this will be evident later.

that the French unions were capable of giving each other. The relationship between the militants of the different French unions was marked by a deep distrust which at times broke out into overt hostility. In planning their actions, the French unions operated simultaneously on two separate fronts. First, they were engaged in a contestation with management that was very much more fundamental in character than that of the British unions. But second, in almost every move they made, they had to bear in mind the need to win an advantage over their main union rival.

It was above all if the unions failed to agree on whether or not to risk a strike that the public polemic became particularly ferocious, as each side tried to justify to the work force the position that it had taken. Perhaps even Mallet would have had doubts about the future unity if he had been in the refinery of Dunkirk in the aftermath of the strike of 6 June 1972. According to the CGT:

There has been — the word is not too strong — an act of treason by the CFDT. That this organization, despite our efforts, did not wish to be associated with the movement, we can only regret, but that it adopted an attitude of opposition and gave support to management is something not worthy of trade unionists.

For if there is a defeat, and greater difficulties develop, it is the whole body of employees that will suffer. Also, a union that is worthy of the name does not place its self-satisfaction and its prestige above the interests of the personnel, and this is precisely what it has done. It has intervened with the Director, along with others, to put pressure on him not to close down the units; thereby running the danger of making him take thoughtless risks for the personnel, in order to defeat our call for action. . . . When the production units had been brought to a halt, certain representatives of this organization agitated to have them put back into operation, and acted as strike-breakers.

To which the CFDT replied:

All these statements are nothing but a pack of lies.

In consequence, in the light of such accusations which attack the honour of our organization, and by this, the workers who share our philosophy, we have made contact with our comrades of the CGT this very Friday morning in order to let them know that as a gesture of protest we will not be able to attend the private session of the Works Committee.

Indeed, how could we today have a fruitful dialogue with people who resort to such methods.

If the main polemic in the period 1971/1972 lay between the CGT and the CFDT, the decision by Force Ouvrière to sign salary agreements in industry-level negotiations rapidly changed the central focus of attack. By November 1973 we find the CGT in full-swing against Force Ouvrière:

FORCE OUVRIERE — Who do you think you are serving?

When you talk disparagingly of a unitary CGT/CFDT petition circulated within the refinery just as our employers would, and draw the conclusion that 475 signatures, gathered in 24 hours, shows that a majority of the personnel are in disagreement with the demands . . .

For our part, we think that this deep-rooted anti-cégétisme of some of your leaders, whom we do not confuse with all the employees who are members of, or support, FO, has the effect of undermining unity, serves the employers, and we regret it. (21.11.73)

By November 1974 relations between the CGT and FO had clearly degenerated to the point of outright conflict. FO was claiming that the CGT Secretary of the Works Committee — Miss Censor — was simply cutting out of the minutes most of what the FO representatives had said.

The present situation forces us to break our silence. Indeed, not being heard in the Works Committee, we are obliged to address ourselves directly to the workers of the refinery by means of a tract, since Miss Censor has just found herself a new hobby in cutting out a great part of our interventions from the minutes of the Works Committee.

If anyone wishes to criticize us for being polemical, we reply in advance that this tract is nothing beside the lamentable spectacle offered by the CGT's union representative to the Works Committee at the last meeting when we were subjected to the worst insults, and this in the presence of the Director. (November 1974)

In considering the source of these tensions, we must remember that the unions had profoundly different conceptions of the way in which socialism could be achieved, and, what was more, each believed that the strategy adopted by the other would not only be ineffective, but positively harmful to the possibility of making real progress. The undermining of the power of the other unions was not, then, merely the expression of power imperialism for its own sake, but was a crucial step in the logic of each union's programme for achieving its objective of a more perfect society.

Years of inter-union competition had inevitably rigidified the lines of irreconcilability — by giving rise to personal bitterness between certain militants in the different unions and by leading the militants to some degree of personal identification with the organizations that they had spent so long constructing and maintaining. In the altogether improbable situation that the fundamental ideological differences between the unions could be resolved, the chances are that the militants would still be deeply reluctant to merge their organizations in any fundamental way, and that were they to do so, the human problems of co-operation would be formidable.

Another major factor ensuring the permanence of a high level of inter-union rivalry was the nature of French law. It was extremely difficult for any one French union to monopolize the representation of a given work force, or to impose a closed shop along the lines that we encountered in Britain. The law enshrined the right of any union that had been recognized as representative at national level to set up a union section and put forward candidates for plant elections in any establishment in which it chose to do so. Given the high level of ideological commitment of the leading militants of each union, and the unwillingness of management to help the most powerful union — the CGT — by informal means, it only required one or two militants in a minority union to keep the flame burning, and to exploit the misfortunes of its more powerful brethren to make a come-back from the threshold of extinction.

Similarly, French law ensured that inter-union competition would remain immediate and explicit through the system of yearly elections to the personnel delegates and two-yearly elections to the Works Committees. These elections brought the unions into a situation of direct electoral competition and they were quite central to the militants' preoccupations. They were the visible and public sign of their organizational skill, and of the extent to which they had made progress towards their objectives or lost ground to their rivals. The system of intra-plant elections ensured that the confrontation at the theoretical level took concrete form in a daily struggle for tactical advantage.

Relations with the base

The French union representatives seemed to have much greater difficulty in their relations with the workers themselves than their British equivalents. One sign of this was that they found it much more difficult to get the workers to come to meetings. Even the CGT would often count itself lucky to get as many as 40 workers along even for a meeting on an important issue. In the British refineries, routine meetings would similarly get low attendance (45–80), but on major issues the branch officials claimed that between 300 and 500 workers could be counted on to attend.

We find in the French tracts repeated tirades against the lack of involvement and participation of union members. The documentation, which is reasonably full from the mid 1960s, suggests that the problem has been a fairly constant one across the years.

In 1966 we find the CGT at Dunkirk complaining:

The council of the union met almost regularly once a month, but it has only really brought together the elected representatives. . . . We are obliged to note that too many comrades thoughtlessly overestimate the role of their elected representatives and underestimate that of the union member, that is to say their own. To continue along this path is to run the risk of discouraging the militants, and making it more difficult to recruit new militants. (October 1966)

The CFDT was not apparently having an easier time:

Normally, the members of the *council of the union* should be elected by the members of the union section of the enterprise in a meeting of the *general assembly* . . . Alas, the general assembly of the 16th December 1966 brought together only some 20 members, and *the Bureau found itself obliged to appoint the members of the council*, the election being ridiculous in the circumstances. THIS IS ABSOLUTELY ABNORMAL. If it is to be democratic, the union policy of the CFDT must be elaborated by everyone, and respond to the aspirations of all its members. (8 February 1967)

By the 1970s the situation had, if anything, deteriorated. In the autumn of 1972 we find the CGT at Lavera castigating the tendency of members to complain about the union, while failing to attend meetings, with the following call to participation:

— I did not agree with the strike of the 23 June:
  I am going to say it at the *Assembly*.
— I do not agree with the present policy of the union:
  I am going to say it at the *Assembly* on the 19th

— I'm fed up with such and such a delegate and such and such a union officer
   I am going to say it at the *Assembly*
— I've nothing to say at the moment, but I'm going to get informed, and listen
   to my comrades:

I AM GOING TO PARTICIPATE AT THE ASSEMBLY

One can criticize because everything can be made more perfect, but first
of all one must criticize oneself. When a union goes well it is thanks to the
spirit of its members, when it goes badly it is because the members take no
interest. (12 October 1972)

In the autumn of 1973 the CFDT at Dunkirk tried to organize a
demonstration of solidarity *in support of the experiment in workers'
control* at Lip. It had this to say on the refinery workers' response.

SOLIDARITY AND ACTION, TWO WORDS THAT NO LONGER HAVE ANY MEANING AT THE REFINERY?

We don't think that this is so, but as a union we ask ourselves the question!
Indeed, the solidarity shown for LIP both in terms of action and in terms of
financial solidarity, was very feeble. The action — 50% of the morning shift
workers followed the half hour delay in starting work — only a dozen comrades
on day work followed the strike movement in the morning, and we shall not
speak of the pathetic representation of the refinery at the meeting and the
procession.
   Let us pose two questions:
   — Did the personnel feel concerned?
   — Are we still capable of efforts that will allow us to combat a certain egoism?
To the first question, must we reply that we are only interested in social improvements that affect our own enterprise? To the second question, must we reply
that the workers of the refinery will, more and more, think only of themselves?
   So let us be logical, do not leave the work of resolving all our problems to a
few enthusiasts of trade unionism without doing our share.
   Let us change this mentality: 'each person in his own little hole, each person
in his home, each person out only for himself'. (September 1973)

By June 1975 the CGT at Dunkirk was clearly even having difficulty getting support out of its militants:

To the comrade militants,
   On the 7th of February I sent to all the militants of the CGT a letter asking
each person to devote a little of his time to union tasks. However, not only did
this letter not have any response among the militants, but on the contrary, the
situation has since deteriorated even further . . .
   The problem that we have to recognize in all honesty is that many of our
militants, whose names I won't mention here, are just spectators. They are there
to make up the numbers, and to find out what is going on, but the last thing
they want is to have an influence on events. (27 June 1975)

Nor was this lack of involvement with union activity altogether
passive. At Lavera, in the autumn of 1972, a petition was circulated
throughout the work force containing a personal attack on the existing leadership of the CGT, and it was said to have secured some eighty

signatures. At Dunkirk, an ex-militant of the CGT established in
September 1972 a new union — the *Syndicat National des Travailleurs
Postés de l'Industrie du Pétrole* — that constituted a direct challenge
to all three existing national unions. Estimates of its membership
varied between 8% and 17% of the shift work force, although it is
certain that some of its adherents took care to simultaneously maintain their membership of their former union until they could see
whether the new union would really establish itself. In fact it seems
to have survived the propaganda onslaught of the other unions well,
and an unofficial ballot of the support it would have obtained in
elections to the Works Committee gave it some 150 voters or 19.4%
of the electoral college. It would, then, almost certainly have become
the second largest union in the refinery. Where it first ran into trouble,
however, was that it was unable to satisfy the rather complex set of
criteria of 'representativity' that alone would have legally allowed it
to put forward candidates in the plant elections. Nonetheless, as can
be seen in Table 41, the Works Committee elections for 1973 saw an
unusually high number of spoilt ballot sheets — 13.5%, and most of
these were almost certainly supporters of the new union. In both of
the surrounding years — 1969 and 1975 — the figure was less than
3%. The union would appear to have drawn support away from both
the CGT and the CFDT.

Management unquestionably regarded the establishment of the
new union as a major threat. In a letter of November 1972 the
Refinery Manager commented, 'Je tiens tout particulièrement à
minimiser l'impact de la création de ce nouveau syndicat'.[9] In effect,
in July 1973, he shattered it by dismissing the leader of the union for
a disciplinary fault. The person was a security guard, and had been
seen allowing somebody to smoke a cigarette at the guard post. The
evidence of many witnesses at a later court hearing strongly suggested
that smoking at this place was customary, and had been common
knowledge for many years. Nonetheless, the action of French management very possibly saved the traditional unions from their bitterest
ever inter-union war.

There can be no doubt then that the French unions had considerable difficulty winning the active allegiance of their base. Why was
this the case?

First we must take into account the nature of managerial power in
French factories. Management had developed a much more repressive
control system, and one whose sanctions were aimed at the individual.
There can be little doubt that people paid a high price for known

union involvement both in terms of their salaries and of their career possibilities. We find repeated complaints in the minutes of the Works Committees about the way in which union militants are professionally penalized, and it is perhaps symptomatic of the risks involved that the dismissed leader of the new union took six months to find a new job since all of the other major firms in the area had apparently received advanced notice. But the disincentive did not simply operate at the level of the militants. Management kept detailed records of strikes, and knew for each individual whether he had participated or stayed at work. It was understandable that the workers should suspect that management would take the worker's attitude over strikes as one indicator when it came to assess the worker's degree of 'co-operativeness' for the annual individual merit bonus.

But the difficulty clearly ran deeper than this because, if solidarity had been sufficiently great, it would have been substantially more difficult for management to single people out. One way of tracing the source of the difficulty is to look at the attacks which the unions explicitly replied to in their tracts. There is one theme which stands out quite clearly as their central preoccupation, and that is the attacks on the unions' involvement of politics in union action.

For instance, assessing the failure of the strike at Dunkirk in June 1972, the CGT singles out as the first factor:

The pressure brought to bear by the Press and the State, far from being neutral, went to the point of throwing the Prime Minister into the ring to prevent the success of the CGT's call to action. In these conditions, the political aspect appeared as the key point of the movement. Now, everybody knows that, even though they are wrong, a large number of workers still see no relationship between the difficulties they experience in getting their demands met and politics.
(June 1972)

In September 1973, the Dunkirk CFDT tackled the issue directly:

The union, what is it for?
The union serves no purpose, it concerns itself with politics, it costs a lot, etc., etc. . . .

It's political
And so! . . . Everybody is concerned with politics, and those who say they are not are perhaps those who are the most political.
Being political is not simply putting a ballot paper into the urn. Accepting to buy petrol that is going up in price, asking for a swimming pool for your local district, asking that the schoolclasses should not be overcrowded, these are political acts.
Politics isn't just what the opposition does. The opposition is only demanding a different type of politics from that being carried out by the majority. To

say nothing, then, is also to be political, it is to accept the politics of those who govern us.

To not join a union because it is concerned with politics, is then to be political. Can one really think that the CFT is an apolitical union? It's enough to make you laugh . . .

Some comrades have complained that we are concerning ourselves 'more and more' with politics! To these comrades we reply that:

1. In choosing, and staying in, our union — the CFDT — in order to be defended they are making a political choice, so let them be conscious of it.

2. We have always been concerned with politics, and we will become more and more so. We have always been very clear on this subject. We will recall what was agreed at our 36th Congress concerning the objectives for a transformation of society towards self-governing socialism: 'A whole series of objectives for social change leading towards socialism; for example: the pattern of economic development, the structure of management, socialization, decentralization, and planning.' These objectives are the objectives of anticapitalist and not only antimonopoly struggle, allowing a global offensive against capitalism. (July 1974)

The unions were perfectly correct in sensing a substantial antipathy to the overt political content of much of their shop floor action. We asked the workers in the sample: 'Do you think that a union should try to influence the opinions people have about politics?'. The answer in both French refineries was overwhelmingly — No. This was the case with 88% of the Lavera workers and 80% of those at Dunkirk. As appears from Table 42, this insistence on the separation of the economic and the political was a cultural norm common to both countries, but given the different conceptions of the role of unionism on the shop floor it clearly had radically different implications for the nature of worker–union relations.[10]

A second source of difficulty in union–worker relations can probably be attributed to the very success of part of union strategy. As we have seen, the unions aimed to make the workers aware of problems in their immediate work situation so that they would be able to understand in concrete terms the inherently exploitative and repressive nature of a capitalist economic system. In the refineries, their main line of attack lay through the problems of shift work and re-organization. Their success in mobilizing the workers on these issues

Table 42   *Should a union try to influence political opinions?* *

	Kent	Grangemouth	Lavera	Dunkirk
Yes	5	9	12	20 %
No	95	91	88	80
	(N = 209)	(N = 205)	(N = 202)	(N = 183)[11]

was unquestionable, and the passive refinery work forces of the 1950s became a powerful adjunct of national union strikes in the second half of the 1960s. But the very logic behind the drive to mobilize the workers over the concrete problems of the work place made it an inherently dangerous weapon for the unions themselves. They appear to have been perfectly correct in assuming that it was this that could most effectively heighten the workers' antagonism to management, and motivate them to action, but the success of the strategy depended entirely on the unions' ability to transform these concrete resentments into a wider consciousness of society. And it is precisely here that they appear to have run into trouble. If we look at the highly significant example of the revolt against the traditional unions in the refinery of Dunkirk, it is notable not for being less contestatory — the new union's language was in fact more militant and uncompromising than either that of the CFDT or FO — but for being uniquely concerned with the problems of the immediate work situation. It represented a highly categorial shift worker consciousness that believed in the virtue of direct action. It was led by one of the CGT's most successful agitators of the 1960s.

What appears to have happened is that the CGT successfully brought the shift workers into action through their classic strategy of the exploitation of immediate problems, but then found it difficult to control the resentments that it had created. The workers wanted to concentrate contestation on what were for them their most burning preoccupations, and were impatient of the efforts of both the CGT and the CFDT to weld the refinery action into action on wider national issues. Indeed, both the crisis in the CGT at Lavera and the creation of the new union at Dunkirk, followed the double strike in June 1972 when the unions tried — with different degrees of success in the two refineries — to bring out the refinery workers on the issues of a 1000 francs a month minimum wage, and retirement at 60. Both of these issues were of great importance nationally, but were totally irrelevant to the refinery workers who had already secured both advantages many years before. The unions seem, then, to a certain degree to have been caught by their own strategy, and we would suggest that this is an inherent risk in a unionism of mobilization. The well chronicled *débordement* of the French unions may well be due to the very success of much of their activity.

Finally, although both unions appeared to have sincerely wished for greater democracy in the running of the unions, it is perhaps not altogether surprising if the workers were less drawn by calls for democratic participation than the unions appear to have expected.

For the union conception of democracy was clearly somewhat para-
doxical. The unions' task was to develop in the work force a certain
state of consciousness, but at the same time they stressed the importance of bringing the workers into decision making within the
union. We have already seen the way the CGT formulated the relationship between these two ideas:

It has to be kept constantly in mind that the struggle helps raise the consciousness of the workers all the more if:

1. It is proposed by us, but decided by them.
2. It is preceded by good information, a discussion (the referendum is only an
appearance of democracy).[12]

A local tract elaborated the CGT's conception of democracy in
explaining to the workers why it was refusing to be bound by the
result of a referendum of the personnel on whether or not to strike:

Our union has carefully studied the meaning of the vote by the personnel. Our
union thinks that, above all, the vote for a strike must be only taken as an indication of intention, and it is for the unions to decide what action is to be taken.
The union organization must have the leading role.

For us, if it hands over its responsibilities to the personnel, the union is either
obliged to remain inactive, or to go against the interests of the workers. Our
method of organization is based on union democracy. The systematic vote is
based on worker democracy, and as a result weakens the union and the mandate
its members have given it.

Almost anything may be called Democracy. We are for true democracy, which
relies on workers who are responsible, on workers who are capable of choosing
with full knowledge of the facts, on workers who are free to make a real choice.
And this is not the case at present.

Our union is reinforced in its conviction by the fact that, after the Paris
meeting on salaries, management itself was in favour of a vote before a strike, for
tactically this is the surest way for it to manoeuvre and divide at its leisure. The
interests of the workers lie in their unity in opposition to the employers and
not on the chance result of a vote, and above all when one knows how a vote can
be influenced by the way the question is asked. (CGT, Naphtachimie. Tract: *Une
Organisation Syndicale Responsable*, 23 Fev. 1976)

For the CFDT, although the development of institutions that
would allow the maximum possible degree of self-determination was
much more central to its long term strategy, and although unlike the
CGT it saw positive advantages in referenda before strikes, its underlying conception of union democracy for the present was not all that
different. As Maire and Julliard explain: 'Of course, collective
maturity cannot be acquired instantaneously; it is a matter of permanent practice. To achieve an authentic system of self-government by
the base, it is the responsibility of the union to provide information,
training and organization.'[13]

The ideal was that the work force should democratically choose the perspective on society and the modes of action that the unions believed to be correct. If this could be achieved, then the requirements of mobilization and the requirements of democracy were indeed compatible. But what the unions did not seriously tackle at the theoretical level was how mobilization and democracy were to be harmonized when the views of the militants and the views of the workers conflicted. Yet this was precisely the problem that existed. As we have seen, the workers did not believe that the unions should adopt an overt political position when organizing shop floor action, and they were primarily preoccupied with the immediate problems of the work place. The unions, on the other hand, were primarily concerned to create class solidarity and unity of action, and to bring the work force to a higher consciousness of the exploitative character of the wider social system including the role of the state in preserving and serving the interests of business power.

In practice, the militants brought the workers into action mainly by the formulation of programmes that combined their own objectives with those of the workers themselves. But this constant interweaving of fundamentally different perspectives was a process that was highly visible to the workers, and that made it perfectly apparent that union democracy was something that was very relative. The demands that the workers actually put forward in general assemblies would frequently undergo a process of transmutation in which they would certainly not be lost, but in which they would reappear inserted in a much wider programme that the workers had not in fact legitimated. This was altogether consistent with the objectives of mobilization, but it necessarily undermined a good deal of the content of democracy. It was a procedure that clearly ran the risk of leading to a certain suspicion of union intentions, a low level of involvement in union activity, and a form of allegiance that always remained hesitant and unreliable. It is a problem that is inherent in a unionism of mobilization. To stand a chance of being successful, unionism of mobilization must adopt a semblance of democracy, but it is in structural conflict with democracy in the everyday sense of the word.[14]

Coercive power

The high level of inter-union rivalry and the hesitant allegiance of the base necessarily undermined the ability of the French union organizations to coerce management. French strikes had to be preceded by a complex process of inter-union negotiation during which the unions frequently addressed to each other formal public letters discussing the differences between them and suggesting possible bases of common action. Often until very close to the date of a proposed strike, it was unclear whether the unions would be able to co-operate or not. Part of the difficulty was clearly one of finding an acceptable common programme. But the tentativeness was also due to the problems involved in assessing the likely reaction of the base. The usual procedure was to call a general assembly but, since very few people attended, these offered little certainty as to whether the bulk of the work force would participate or not. We can get an indication of the difficulties the unions faced in a tract circulated by the Dunkirk CFDT in May 1974. In a moment of co-operation — largely due to their mutual antagonism to the contractual policies being pursued by Force Ouvrière — the CGT and CFDT had decided to hold two joint general assemblies in order to decide whether or not to launch a strike. The CFDT has the following comments on the result of the meeting:

> To begin with, given the fact that at the assemblies there were 66 participants including the representatives of the day and shift personnel (although that is not entirely negative), it seems to us impossible to commit ourselves at present to actions which have not been more widely commented upon by the workers of the refinery.
> In the course of these assemblies, the workers present decided on repeated actions in the two weeks to follow, and mandated the unions to make contact again with the personnel during the tours of the sectors. But there again the problem is posed whether the unions should on their own, supported by a minority of the personnel, carry the whole weight of decisions that involve the entire body of employees of the enterprise.
> The general assemblies are deserted although they are organized so that people can make their views known, and decisions can be taken collectively.
> (2 May 1974)

The last thing that a union wanted was to be landed with the blame for leading a failed strike. The tendency, then, was to minimize the possible risk by making the strikes very short. A union could just survive a poor turnout for a twenty-four hour strike, but if the base refused to follow when it had formally committed itself to a major and long lasting confrontation with management, then the union leadership would be totally discredited. Out of the 24 strikes in our two refineries between 1963 and 1971, only two lasted longer than twenty-four hours. One was a forty-eight hour strike, the other — the strike of 20 May 1968 — was a strike that the unions had not planned. This commitment to relatively short strikes was therefore a fairly inescapable concomitant of a high level of inter-union rivalry, and an unreliable allegiance of the base.[15] It was moreover a typical phenomenon in French industrial relations.[16] But although the twenty-four hour strike could be an embarrassment to management — especially if it occurred in isolation and therefore suggested less managerial skill in handling the work force — it could hardly put management in serious economic peril, nor so threaten the community that it brought in major pressure from outside organizations. The coercive power of the French unions was, then, exceptionally weak, and this was clearly a factor enabling management to maintain a highly paternalistic institutional structure.

If we turn, in contrast, to the British situation where the operators were organized by a single union, and where there was a higher degree of similarity between the objectives of the representatives and of the work force, the threat of a strike was something management had good reason to take very seriously indeed. At Grangemouth there was only one strike in the post-war period, but that strike had an efficacy that made the usual French strike look a very minor affair. Within a week, bus services throughout Scotland were grinding to a halt, schools were being paralysed by the lack of transport for schoolchildren, 1700 workers in the glass industry were being laid off, the steel industry was closing down major plants, and the principal cities were on the verge of being forced to abandon their refuse services. The severity of the effects of the strike was reflected in the bitterness of the region's leading newspaper:

... they seek to hold a pistol to management's head in a carefully calculated manner, striking against the economy, the people, their fellow trade unionists, and all those whose livelihood depends in some degree upon the output of the refinery (and in modern society that means just about everybody). Their action is nasty, unscrupulous, and brutal; a society which regarded the commonweal as paramount would regard it as criminal.[17]

A year after the strike, both management and the union representatives were convinced that it was likely to remain a very exceptional feature in the industrial relations scene. The sheer efficacy of the strike made it improbable that it would be frequent. It had faced management with major losses of production, but, perhaps even more important, it had brought both management and the unions under a very high level of public pressure. The shop floor leaders had gained most of what they had demanded, but on both sides the strike reinforced the feeling that settlement through negotiation was infinitely preferable.

In a situation, then, in which the work force was considerably less radical than in France, it was nonetheless possible for the British unions to threaten management in a much more decisive way than it was for the French unions. To a large extent this was due to the fact that the operators — who had the power to close the plant — were in a unified union organization, while the stewards could rely on the adhesion of the work force as a whole in the event of a prolonged conflict. British management's willingness to negotiate must then be seen in the context of the fact that it was fully aware that the price of a less amicable method of resolving differences could be very high. This connection between the perception of union power and the concern to develop good labour relations was made quite explicit by the man who was the chief negotiator of the Grangemouth Productivity Agreements, and who was later to become Refinery Manager. In 1967 he wrote:

Companies operate by permission of the Trade Unions or to be more accurate, by permission of their Shop Stewards. This is an unpalatable statement to make and Directors and Managers of Companies are sometimes loath to admit the truth of it. Yet they know that any shop steward at any time can bring their whole industry to a standstill. In this context, then, staff/labour relationships are vital if an enterprise is to run smoothly or is to run at all.

(Notes on Industrial Relations and Productivity Agreements, 1 Sep. 1967)

In summary, we have suggested that the refinery unions in the two countries had radically different conceptions of unionism. The French unions saw their role as one of mobilizing the work force for a far reaching structural transformation of society. To achieve this, their strategy was one of sustained ideological warfare in the context of a steadily rising level of participation of the work force in the pursuit of a programme of relatively immediate demands. The chief influence on the policies of the unions came from external union apparatus, and the demands that were advanced linked in a complex way societal and local issues, and involved a systematic effort to bring the work force into periodic confrontation with the government. This form of unionism, however, was associated with sharp inter-union rivalry, and uncertain relations with the base — two factors which, combined, sharply undermined the unions' power to coerce management and alter the prevailing institutional structure.

The British unions, in contrast, largely conceived of their role as one of representing the work force — that is to say pushing for demands that were consciously desired by the workers themselves. Their strategy was to win concessions through negotiation backed by powerful organizational strength. The main influence on the policies of the union came from the shop floor, and the demands the unions made were simply formulated and advanced on a narrow front. The allegiance of the work force could be relied on, and the unions possessed a high level of potential power to coerce management. This was a significant factor in ensuring the persistence and extension of a system of negotiated settlement of issues affecting the work force.

Part five

Conclusion

12

Managerial strategies, the unions and the social integration of the work force

The objectives of this study were to examine the implications of advanced automation for the social integration of the work force within the capitalist enterprise, for the structure of managerial power, and for the nature of trade unionism. The principal conclusion of the research is that the nature of the technology *per se* has, at most, very little importance for these specific areas of enquiry. Advanced automation proved perfectly compatible with radically dissimilar levels of social integration, and fundamentally different institutions of power and patterns of trade unionism. Instead, our evidence indicates the critical importance of the wider cultural and social structural patterns of specific societies for determining the nature of social interaction within the advanced sector.

The transformation of worker attitudes and aspirations?

Our first aim was to investigate empirically the implications of automation for worker attitudes. We can compare our findings with the theses that have been put forward by Robert Blauner and Serge Mallet. Broadly speaking, both of these authors shared the view that the main traditional sources of grievance in industry — salaries, and problems deriving from the nature of the work task and of work organization — were no longer of any salience. On the other hand, they differed sharply in their views about the implications of automation for attitudes to management. Blauner believed that it leads to a high degree of consensus and harmony between management and the work force, whereas Mallet has argued that it produces a new revolutionary consciousness aiming at a radical restructuring of the institutions of power within the enterprise.

The disappearance of traditional sources of grievance?

From the outset, we found that both Mallet and Blauner were clearly mistaken in their belief that salaries would necessarily lose their importance as a focus of grievance in continuous-process industry.

295

The most striking point to emerge from our data was the sharp contrast between the French and British workers in their degree of satisfaction with their incomes and their standard of living. The British were broadly speaking content; the French dissatisfied. This was not simply a marginal grievance for the French workers: it was the dominant source of their resentment about their situation as manual workers in French society. It led directly to strikes for salary increases despite the possibility that the workers were taking substantial long term risks with their own physical safety by closing down the units rapidly.

Further, there was a sharp difference between the French and British workers in their degree of satisfaction with the salary structure. The French were deeply convinced that the principles determining salary allocation within the industry were unfair; the British, on the other hand, were overwhelmingly satisfied with them.

Turning to the experience of the work situation, we found that although there was a fair measure of truth in the argument that many of the traditional hardships of the work task, and many of the worst features of the work environments of traditional mass production industry, had been eliminated, Blauner's description of the typical work task was a generalization of what was, in reality, the work of only a very small section of the work force. The work of most of the operators was substantially less advantageous than Blauner suggested, and the most common attitude towards work in our refineries was one of indifference. It is extremely doubtful whether automation leads to the overcoming of alienation in work in any profound sense of the term.

Moreover, and here our findings confirm the view of Pierre Naville, it is clear that the highly-automated work setting generates its own set of problems, and these can become an important source of worker grievance.

In the first place, continuous-process production requires shift work, and this imposes powerful constraints over the operators' total pattern of life. Shift work was considered intrinsically undesirable by the majority of operators in each of our samples in both France and Britain. It was seen as a major source of ill-health, and as a disruptor of family and social life. However, although the issue was an important one to workers in both countries, a salient point that emerged from our study was that the French workers had developed a much higher and more sustained level of militancy. From the mid 1960s the French unions were fighting for an extensive programme of reform of shift work conditions, and the question of shift work became one of the most central issues of dispute between management and the work force in the late 1960s and the early 1970s.

A second important area of potential conflict related to the level of manning. One of the distinctive features about continuous-process technology is that it is extremely difficult to define what constitutes a satisfactory level of manning, even from the sole viewpoint of technical efficiency. This ambivalence provided a fertile source of friction since management and workers had substantially different interests as to the way in which the problem should be resolved. Management in both countries was primarily concerned to reduce labour costs by reducing manning levels. The work force, on the other hand, had a strong interest in retaining existing levels or even increasing them, since the level of manning influenced the intensity with which they were required to work, the quality of team life, the degree of inconvenience caused by shift work, and their security in their existing posts and statuses within the organization.

In both countries the issue of manning was central to industrial relations in the second half of the 1960s, and in the early 1970s. Significantly, however, the areas of dispute were resolved peacefully in the British refineries, but led to a substantially higher level of tension in France. Thus, although the problem of manning was inherent in the technology, the extent to which it became a source of discontent with management clearly depended on other variables.

Problems deriving from the work setting had not been eliminated in the highly automated setting, but transformed. The existence of such problems posed an ever-present threat to the stability of management/worker relations, and in both countries they were central to industrial relations. The extent to which the problems were resolved peacefully, or became a source of overt conflict between management and the work force, differed sharply between the two countries, with the French refineries revealing a much higher level of social tension.

Attitudes to management

None of the existing studies provide us with any direct evidence on the way workers in highly automated plant perceive management or feel about the prevailing structure of authority. Given the crucial importance of these themes to their arguments, one of the major tasks of our study clearly had to be that of providing data directly focused on this problem.

Our first approach was to look at the types of criticism of management that workers mentioned spontaneously, on the grounds that this was the most reliable method of finding out what was most important to them. What emerged was that the type of criticism differed sharply between the French and British refineries. The British workers' criticism was principally 'technical' criticism, or criticism of the efficiency with which management carried out its duties. It is notable that these criticisms were not accompanied by a demand for greater control by the work force. The predominant feeling seems to have been that it was management's job to manage, but that management needed to put its house in order. What these criticisms appeared to reveal was a high level of identification with the underlying objectives of management — a commitment to increased rationalization and efficiency.

In France, in contrast, criticism mainly took the form of 'relational' criticism. It was concerned with the way the exercise of authority affected the worker's identity, with the worker's subjective experience of authority. The most central criticism concerned the high degree of social distance that was felt to exist between management and the work force. Management was seen as aloof and cold, fundamentally uninterested in the workers as human beings.

The existence of more strained relations between management and the work force in the French refineries was confirmed by two closed questions we asked. The first, focusing directly on the perception of social distance between management and the work force, revealed that the French workers were twice as likely as the British to feel that relations were distant. The second, examined the workers' perception of management's motives. Just as we would expect from the nature of their spontaneous criticisms, the British workers revealed a 'cooperative' image of the firm in which management was seen as working in the interests of everybody, whereas the French workers had an 'exploitative' image of the firm in which management was seen as primarily concerned with furthering the interests of shareholders.

This data provided support for neither Mallet nor Blauner. In the first place, it was clear that the problem of control of management decision making was not a salient grievance in any of the refineries. Concern for the issue of control was confined to a very small minority of workers, primarily concentrated in the French factories, and for the most part active in the French trade union movement, As it stands, then, Mallet's thesis has to be rejected. On the other hand, the data are not a great deal more encouraging for Blauner. Blauner had led us to expect that management/worker relations in the highly automated sector would be characterized by a very high level of harmony and by the existence of a sense of belonging to a common community. Certainly the British data seemed to fit this model. There was no explicit dissatisfaction with the structure of power, and the types of criticism that were made of management did indeed suggest an underlying consensus about organizational goals. But against this, we have to place the fact that the French data, far from revealing the existence of harmonious relations, indicate that the enterprise was seen by the workers as socially dichotomous, and exploitative. In short, Blauner's thesis of harmonious relations proves, under the light of cross-cultural analysis, to be culturally specific and cannot be taken as a general concomitant of advanced technology.

The second approach we adopted was to create a direct measure of the legitimacy of the formal structure of power, on the grounds that this would reveal the latent attitudes that existed.

The most striking characteristic of the data was again the sharp divergence between the responses of the French and British workers. The French felt that the existing structure of power was illegitimate, and a clear majority would have been prepared to see an extension of worker control over management's powers of decision into the very heart of the traditional areas of managerial prerogative, including the most fundamental strategic decisions about financial budgeting and new investment. In contrast, the British workers showed a high level of contentment with the existing procedures of decision making, and it was notable that even in those areas in which they recognized that they were excluded from any influence (such as high level economic decisions) on the whole they regarded this as perfectly legitimate. They appear to have believed in the value of a division of labour in which it was perfectly proper that management should be allowed to take certain crucial decisions in a relatively unfettered way.

Once more, then, considering attitudes to power at this more latent level, it is apparent that neither Mallet nor Blauner provide us with a satisfactory account. Neither author anticipated, or can explain, the fact that in almost identical technological situations workers should have radically divergent attitudes to the structure of power in different countries.

The most important characteristic of our data is the quite fundamental divergence between the attitudes of the French and British workers. In particular, we can note five major differences:

1. The French workers were dissatisfied with their salaries and standard of living, whereas the British workers were relatively satisfied.

2. The French workers were considerably more militant over common problems emerging from the work process — namely shift work and manning.

3. The French workers were considerably more critical of the state of social relations between management and the work force. They saw relations as dichotomous and socially distant, whereas the British workers saw them as relatively friendly.

4. The French workers had an 'exploitative' image of the firm, whereas the British workers had a co-operative image.

5. The French workers regarded the formal structure of power in the firm as illegitimate, whereas the British workers regarded it as legitimate.

In short, if social integration is defined in terms of a high level of commitment to the key substantive and procedural norms of the enterprise, the British workers showed a relatively high level of social integration and the French workers a relatively low level.

It is important to be clear that we cannot conclude on the basis of our data that advanced technology has no effect whatsoever on the degree of social integration into the firm. Although the critical determinants of worker attitudes clearly lie elsewhere, it may nonetheless be the case that technology has some influence within a specific national context. An examination of whether this is in fact the case would require a different research design. But what our evidence does suggest is that theories that automation *necessarily* leads to a high degree of social integration, and theories that it *necessarily* leads to new forms of class conflict are both mistaken. Further, we would argue that, given the high degree of polarization that we have found between the attitudes of the French and British workers, it is improbable that the characteristics of advanced technology are of any substantial importance in explaining the degree of social integration of workers within the enterprise.

The formal structure of power, the unions, and the social integration of the work force

A satisfactory explanation of the differences we have found between the attitudes of the French and British workers to the firm would be complex, and require analysis of the historical development of French and British social structure. We can, however, try to break into the chain of causality at a specific point, and ask what are the more immediate factors that generate, and reinforce, these specific patterns of attitude. Our suggestions here are tentative, and there is no claim that the data are sufficient to confirm them. They are put forward as an interpretation that we believe makes greater sense of the data than theories taking technology as their starting point.

In Part one, we pointed out that existing theories of the implications of automation had failed to give an adequate account either of the institutions of managerial power within the factory or of the nature and role of the trade unions in the advanced sector. In Parts two, three and four we have explored these questions in greater depth, and we now suggest that the empirical inadequacy of existing theories derives, in part, precisely from their neglect of these factors. The French and British refineries had very different managerial systems and very different patterns of trade unionism and these contributed in important ways to creating quite distinctive patterns of social interaction in the refineries in the two countries.

Starting at the most immediate level, we would suggest that the differences between the attitudes of the French and British workers could be best understood as the result of the interaction of the workers' specific patterns of aspiration and normative expectation with fundamentally different institutional systems of power.

The formal structure of power

The first point to note is that the institutions of power in the refineries in the two countries were radically different. The existence of important differences between managerial styles in French and British industry has frequently been recognized in the literature, although these comparisons tend to be highly impressionistic and their implications left unanalysed. However, the greater authoritarianism attributed to French management is commonly seen as a result of the relatively late development of French industrialization, and hence the prevalence of small family firms in which the employer felt that he had the right to exclusive control of a factory which was legally his own property. Consequently, it has been suggested that, as economic development progressed, French firms would adopt a 'constitutional' system of authority, and would accept the institutional integration of the trade unions.[1] A process of convergence would occur, and power would come to be wielded in a broadly similar way in the different advanced industrial societies.

However, our evidence suggests that this view is basically incorrect. France and Britain have now reached similar levels of overall economic development, and it emerges from our study that *even in the most technologically advanced sector of industry* in the two countries no such process of convergence is under way. Instead, the institutional systems of the newly emerged highly automated sectors appear to have been assimilated by, and firmly locked into, quite distinctive wider national patterns. In Britain, our highly automated factories were just a little earlier than others in making a further extension of the principles of 'constitutionalism', but in the light of the whole decade they remained unexceptional. In France, there had been a shift away from the more authoritarian forms of management that characterize many firms in the traditional sector; however, it was not a move towards 'constitutionalism', but a shift in the direction of an advanced form of paternalism. There was no sign of the two systems becoming increasingly similar over time; rather, during the 1960s they moved further apart.

Our French and British factories, then, were characterized by markedly different structures of power. In the French refineries, managerial power within the factory remained formally absolute, and the representatives had no rights of effective control over decision making. Although management was unquestionably relatively generous in fostering the social activities of the Works Committees, it excluded them from an effective influence over questions of work organization. Similarly, although management had accepted the presence of the unions before it was legally obliged to, it had at no point recognized their right of control over any aspect of refinery organization.

Where the French employers did agree to negotiate with the unions was in the industry-level Parity Commissions. In particular, it was at this level that salary negotiations were formally supposed to take place, although negotiations were restricted to only part of the workers' overall salary, and the rest remained discretionary. In practice the centralization, the very limited terms of reference, and the formal brevity of the meetings prevented any meaningful process of bargaining from taking place. Meetings invariably ended with a unilateral decision by management.

The institutional system in the British refineries was very different. The shop floor representatives had achieved effective control (in the sense of possessing veto power) over a wide range of aspects of work organization, including work conditions, grading, manning levels, deployment of personnel, and use of contractors. Formal negotiations with the unions, which took place at the highly decentralized level of the individual plant, were concerned with the overall salary that the worker received, and there was not a single instance in which negotiations had not been concluded by a signed agreement. In the course of the 1960s, with the introduction of productivity bargaining, there was an evolution in the pattern of negotiation, in which the stewards became steadily more central in the system of formal negotiation.

Broadly speaking, French management remained sovereign within the enterprise, whereas British management had conceded substantial rights of negotiation to the trade unions. Automation appeared perfectly compatible with two fundamentally different institutional systems. But it seems likely that these two systems had very different implications for the quality of relations between management and the work force.

Worker expectations

It is no more probable that particular systems of power *directly* determine attitudes to the firm than specific forms of technology. In both cases, the response of workers to these objective factors will be mediated by their expectations. We would suggest that, given the salience of egalitarian values in the working-class sub-cultures of most Western societies, there will be a general tendency for low participatory systems to generate significantly higher levels of discontent with the firm than institutional systems that allow a significant share in decision making to the people employed. But, in the particular cases we were studying, the situation was unquestionably made more complex by the fact that the French had higher expectations than their British equivalents. It is significant, for instance, that although they earned more than their British colleagues in real terms, and although they were better off in terms of both the national and regional manual worker averages, the French workers were substantially less satisfied with their standard of living. Equally, we have seen that although aspirations for control were not at the forefront of their minds, when they replied to direct questions about the ideal level of control that workers should exercise over the decision-making process, the French felt that workers should have substantially more extensive control than was desired by their British equivalents.

On both substantive and procedural issues, then, the French

workers had higher expectations. Moreover, in chapter 6, we saw that in their procedural expectations our French samples were in no way peculiar in their radicalism, but shared a wider cultural characteristic of the French working class. If anything, the French refinery workers appeared to be a little more conservative than the average French worker in the extent of control they wanted to exercise over the enterprise. The restricted reference groups and the relatively high level of income satisfaction of higher paid manual workers in the wider British working class have been documented by W. G. Runciman in *Relative Deprivation and Social Justice*.[2] It seems quite possible that the differences between our French and British samples reflected more general differences between the working classes of the two societies.

The problem of why the French workers should have had higher aspirations is unquestionably a complex one, and there can be no serious attempt to come to grips with it here. Other data that we have collected, and that we will be presenting in a separate publication, indicate that these differences in level of aspiration are rooted in different reference groups, in different images of society and in different conceptions of social justice. These cultural factors are themselves probably related to the broader social structural characteristics of each society, and may well have their origins in distinctive historical experiences.

However, at the relatively immediate level with which we are concerned here, we would stress that these cultural factors were reinforced and given relevance to the work situation by the continuous and systematic agitation of the French unions. The influence of the unions appears to have been substantial, although the French workers by no means simply assimilated union ideology. For instance, both the major French unions incessantly advocated abolition of the private enterprise system, but a majority of the French workers remained unconvinced. Similarly, the French workers rejected the legitimacy of the unions' constant attempt to associate 'industrial' and 'political' issues in shop floor agitation. But where the unions do appear to have been influential is in mobilizing resentments against specific aspects of the work situation, and in providing the leadership necessary to contest management in a situation of a very high level of managerial power. For it must be remembered that, given the cost of opposition under more authoritarian systems, there is not necessarily a direct link between the level of resentment and militancy and, indeed, there will probably be important pressures to submit, and to lower aspirations, rather than take the risks of contestation. Union leadership, then, becomes a crucial intervening variable for the effective organization of collective action, and involvement in such action is likely to be important in reinforcing, and possibly intensifying expectations. We saw, in chapter 4, that the most convincing explanation for the mobilization of the refinery workers into regular participation in industrial action in the 1960s is the success of the intense union agitation over shift work and manning levels. This appears to have broken down any sense of oil refinery workers forming a distinctive group within the working class, with privileged conditions of work, by emphasizing the social costs that automation involved. This, in turn, set in motion the dynamics of a system in which a high level of aspiration encountered autocratic institutions of decision making.

The interaction of expectations and the structure of power

A critical difference, then, between our French and our British cases was that the French workers, with higher substantive and procedural expectations encountered an institutional system that allowed a very much lower degree of participation in the decision-making process. This made it far more likely that they would reject the basic procedures of decision making as illegitimate, that they would be dissatisfied with the substantive rules of the organization, and that they would have an image of management as essentially exploitative. We have set out the reasons why this is likely to be the case in chapter 8. In summary, we suggested that:

First, in societies in which the value of equality is salient, low participative systems are likely to create normative conflict and hence the institutions of power are likely to be regarded as illegitimate by the work force.

In both countries workers had expectations for a certain degree of control but the evidence suggests that the French workers had higher expectations than their British equivalents, although they too accepted the fundamental tenets of a private enterprise system. In France workers had higher expectations for control but were confronted by an institutional system that offered a substantially lower degree of control. This created a higher degree of normative conflict, and a lower degree of legitimacy for the procedures of decision making.

It is important to note, however, that procedural aspirations were not of great salience to workers in either country. The degree of normative conflict over procedural rules was primarily important in contributing to a lower degree of acceptability of those substantive decisions that were important to workers, and for the implications of this for the attitude to the firm.

Second, a low participative system tends to reduce the likelihood of agreement over the substantive rules of the organization. This is because it deprives management's decisions of procedural legitimacy, it makes them more likely to appear as coercive, it reduces the probability of preliminary attitude change, and it discourages a process of exchange. At any given level of relative deprivation over substantive issues the more likely are the workers to accept organizational norms the higher the level of participation.

This, we would suggest, helps to explain the much higher level of dissatisfaction of French workers over organizational decisions. For instance, although problems of shift work and manning presented equally crucial issues to both the French and British workers, the French, faced with a substantially more autocratic system, were considerably less satisfied with the decisions that were taken and reacted with much greater militancy.

On the central issue of salaries, our evidence suggests that the French both had higher aspirations than their British equivalents, and were confronted with a system which was less likely to win their loyalty to compromise solutions. These two factors reinforced each other in generating a higher level of resentment.

Third, a low participative system, by creating normative conflict, by increasing resentment over specific decisions, by creating a pattern of work organization less satisfactory to the work force, by generalizing insecurity, and by channelling effective attempts to influence decisions exclusively into overt displays of power, tends to create an exploitive image of the firm. It seems likely that the more egalitarian the values of the work force, the more intensely this effect will be produced. Moreover, the pattern will presumably be reinforced over generations as one generation socializes another into its own definitions of reality. Although we can expect the attitudes of new recruits to the organization, coming into the work force for the first time, to be of low intensity and relatively plastic, they will already be predisposed towards an alienative interpretation of events in the factory, and thus will be particularly susceptible to the dynamics of a low participative system.

As we have seen, the French and British workers had sharply divergent images of management and the firm. The French workers regarded the firm as exploitive, whereas the British workers had a co-operative image of the firm. We should suggest that this can be accounted for by the fact that the French workers were somewhat more committed to egalitarian values than their British equivalents, but were confronted by a substantially less participative institutional system.

The control system and social distance

The differences between the institutions of decision making in the French and British refineries were paralleled by substantial differences in the methods by which French and British management sought to control the work performance of their personnel. This, we would suggest, was not accidental and it had important implications for the quality of social relations in the factory.

We investigated the nature of the control process in the highly automated setting in chapter 9. We found that, although Blauner was correct in emphasizing that a highly automated technology encouraged a certain degree of decentralization of control over the immediate work process to the operator teams, this decentralization had been pushed substantially further in the British refineries than in the French, it affected only one of several possible sources of managerial control, and it was largely irrelevant for the maintenance workers who made up a substantial proportion of the work force of each refinery.

Broadly speaking, British management had decentralized the control of the everyday work process to the work team among the operators, and had adopted a low power personal control system for the maintenance workers. French management, on the other hand, exercised a much tighter grip over the control process through higher ratios of supervisors to workers, through the implementation of a salary system that enabled it to penalize the work performance of individual workers, and through the adoption of a more severe system of disciplinary sanctions for more important failures in work performance or breaches of the rules.

It seems very possible that these different systems of control were to a considerable degree influenced by the nature of the institutions for decision making. British management had adopted a strategy involving a higher degree of participation of the work force, and this gave a greater degree of legitimacy to the authority structure and the decisions that emanated from it. At the same time it was probably an important factor in reducing the sense of opposition between management and worker objectives, and creating a certain degree of identification of the work force with management's own goals. Management then could count on a relatively high degree of motivation on the part of the workers, and could therefore more safely risk adopting a control system which relied little on direct managerial intervention but rather emphasized the control of the individual by his colleagues in the work team.

French management, by insisting on the preservation of an institutional system that gave the work force little or no control over the pattern of work organization and the conditions of life in the factory, succeeded in maximizing its autonomy in decision making, but at the same time confronted itself with considerable problems at the level of work motivation and the control of work performance. Since there was no assurance that the consent of the work force had been obtained when decisions on sensitive issues were made, French management had to anticipate a substantial degree of latent resentment which could well have important consequences for work performance. Since such discontent was likely to be a generalized phenomenon, it was doubtful whether the work team could be relied upon to provide as effective a system of control of individual deviance as in the British case. French management's adoption of a much tighter control system, in which management intervened much more directly, could be seen as a fairly logical response to an awareness of the risks of low involvement inherent in a system of low participation.

But we would argue that the choice of control system had, in turn, important implications for the quality of everyday relationships between management and the work force. It was central to the argument put forward by both Blauner and Woodward that the reduction of management's role in the control system was of major importance in making possible a closer, more consultative, relationship between management and the work force. The logic of this argument seems perfectly sensible, and our main criticism of these theorists is that they adopted too restrictive a conception of the control system, and that this led them to overemphasize the extent to which technology influenced it.

Where, as in the British refineries, the reduction of management's intervention in the control system in fact occurred, it was indeed associated with substantially closer relationships between managers and workers. On the other hand, where, as in France, management intervention remained prominent, this was associated with considerably colder and more distant relations. The French middle managers were deeply involved in the administration of the control system and this placed a considerable strain on their relationships with a work force that felt not only that it was being permanently judged, but that it was being judged arbitrarily. The importance of this can be seen in the fact that the most salient criticism by the French workers of the organizational structure of the refineries was precisely the degree of social distance between management and the work force, and that the French workers were twice as likely as the British to feel that relations were distant.

Managerial strategies and the trade unions

We have argued that one important factor contributing to the lower degree of social integration of the French workers was the formal structure of power in the French factories. This immediately raises the question of why the institutions of power should have been so different in the two countries? A full explanation would again be a very complex one, but we can, at least, consider some of the more immediate factors involved.

In the first instance, we would suggest that the two institutional systems reflected quite distinctive managerial strategies for ensuring effective work performance. In France management's strategy was paternalistic, and involved creating a sense of the individual's direct dependence on the firm for his well-being. The success of this strategy required that management should preserve the highest possible level of discretion over the reward system, and should defend a set of institutions that barred the representatives from any real say in the decisions that determined the substantive rules of the organization. British management, on the other hand, adopted a semi-constitutional strategy, and sought to ensure effective performance by obtaining the explicit consent of the work force to rules governing work organization and terms of employment. This required reducing the more obviously coercive aspects of power, and encouraging an institutional system that emphasized the joint character of decision making, and symbolized this in the form of the agreement.

But if the institutional system can be seen as relatively consciously designed to achieve managerial objectives, this raises the question of why French management should have wanted to, or was able to, maintain a system which had the disadvantage of generating substantial ill-will, and therefore involved substantial risks of undermining the motivation and commitment of the work force.

In the first place, it seems probable that French managers were socialized into a rather different managerial culture from that of their British equivalents with different normative assumptions about the importance of preserving managerial prerogative. This was certainly the view of one of our British Refinery Managers who had got to know one of his French equivalents at an international conference. He quite acutely summed up the differences in their approach:

I coax things along. I don't believe in insisting all the time on managerial prerogative. I don't think one should allow oneself to get het up by problems. I think, R. (the French Director) allows himself to get anxious about things too quickly. He lives by emergencies. He thinks he's defending capitalism and all that. He's looking for fights with the unions. Of course, the French managers come from the elite engineering schools whereas we're drawn from the gutter. R. believes in imposing things while I believe in getting people to agree to them.[3]

And, later in the interview:

The Industrial Relations Officer probably thinks I'm a bit starry-eyed. But I try to put myself in the position of a spectator watching management and the unions, and not to feel completely identified with the Company. The moment you get identified you start worrying too much and get too excited. R. (the French Director) completely identifies himself, and that's why he sees it as a sort of war. And he starts worrying about the effects on the economy of what he's doing, and not just what's going on in the refinery.

However, it would be a mistake to account for French management's commitment to its strategy simply in terms of some hangover of irrational and archaic attitudes deriving from the long predominance of small family firms in French industry. French management could, and did, justify its methods on highly pragmatic grounds — namely that they led to substantially higher levels of industrial efficiency. Quite how far this was true is difficult to say with precision. Given the complexity of pricing in the oil industry, refinery profits or losses are apparently largely fictional, and there is no easily available indicator of overall relative efficiency. But there certainly appeared to be a clear consensus that maintenance work was substantially faster and better organized in the French than in the British refineries and, given the enormous costs involved in a capital intensive industry with each additional day that a unit is out of action for maintenance, the financial implications of this must have been very significant. We saw in chapter 5 that British management was severely criticized by the workers themselves about the poor organization of maintenance work, and one of the British Refinery Managers, while warning us that comparisons of relative efficiency were extremely difficult to make with precision, told us:

If you take the completion time for overhaul, the French certainly seem to get them done more quickly. A crude unit seems to take about two weeks there compared to six weeks here. London is often putting pressure on us about maintenance. In fact maintenance is a big subject of discussion now in the Company. They're getting worried about just how big a cost maintenance is. Recently D.R. went across to Dunkirk to compare maintenance procedures and was pretty impressed. But he found them very secretive about information.[4]

It was later confirmed to us at the Company's Head Office that this estimate of the difference in time that it took to carry out maintenance overhauls in the refineries in the two countries was a fair one. Moreover, given the structure of power in the French refineries, French claims for greater efficiency are not altogether implausible. Management could draw up a blueprint for the organizational structure that would maximize efficiency, and then quite simply impose it by fiat. British management, in contrast, by adopting a semi-constitutional strategy, necessarily accepted powerful constraints on its freedom of action. Negotiation could only be made attractive if there was a genuine belief among the representatives that, by accepting responsibility for agreements, they would be able to achieve substantially better terms than if they refused to participate. British management, then, particularly on the craft side, was forced into making concessions that would have made French management shudder. In a semi-constitutional system, there is a risk that the process of organizational change may become much slower, and very much more time consuming for management. If the paternalist strategy risks creating deep resentment, the semi-constitutional strategy may impose significant constraints on management's efforts to maximize efficiency.

We have seen that our French and British refineries had been to a considerable extent assimilated into the institutional patterns characteristic of larger firms in the wider society. One must clearly be very cautious in generalizing from case studies, but this at least raises the question of whether one important factor in the strikingly different performance of French and British industry in the 1960s and early 1970s might not lie in the very substantial differences in the structure of power within firms in the two countries, and in particular in the differential ability of management to introduce rapidly radical technical and organizational change. This is congruent with the view that Britain's industrial weakness stemmed less from a lack of technological innovation than from a failure to *implement* new techniques.

This might be seen as an argument in favour of the reassertion of unlimited managerial power. But, equally, it could be suggested that the disadvantages of the British semi-constitutional system for industrial efficiency are attributable to the fact that it represents a half-way house, giving the representatives primarily a strong veto power with which to defend the interests of their members, and that a more fully participative system might lead to more ready consent on the part of the work force to radical changes since it would be in a position of still greater security, while commitment to the organization's overall goals would be substantially higher. In that case the efficiency of the French system might be achieved without the disadvantages of its very high social costs. Certainly, it would be premature to conclude from a comparison of semi-constitutional and paternalist systems that there is a *necessary* contradiction between efficiency and participation.

Finally, in considering why French management placed a very high price on its freedom of action despite the consequences for the attitudes of the work force, it must be remembered that it believed that it was confronted with a substantially more radical union movement than British management. Indeed, both French Refinery Managers gave this as the principal reason why they thought it would be quite impossible to introduce the type of system that existed in Britain into the French factories. The French managers believed — not altogether without reason — that the French unions would have been extremely difficult to integrate and would have driven very hard bargains before being prepared to legitimate decisions. The cost of ill-will was considered less important than the economic costs that would have been involved in establishing a system allowing a higher level of participation. The institutional system, which had such important consequences for the attitudes of the work force, was in good measure designed to provide a bulwark against the ideologically radical French unions.

We should be careful, then, not to oversimplify the factors involved in the French managers' preference for their own strategy. This was not merely the reflection of commitment to some free-floating cultural belief in the value of undivided power, but it was founded in a complex interpretation of the situation in which they were working, and in their beliefs about the probable outcomes of alternative strategies. But, given that French management had perfectly coherent grounds, in terms of its own value commitments, for wanting to maintain its institutional strategy despite the resentment it generated, we must still ask the fundamental question of how, in the face of such hostility, it was actually able to maintain that strategy.

Here, we would argue that the nature of the trade union movement was crucial. In Part four of this study we have focused on the character of unionism in the advanced sector in the two countries. Our overall conclusion was that, as with the institutions of power in the enterprise, automation had had little significant impact on the pattern of unionism. Rather, powerful trade unions in the wider society, with long-established traditions and well-set modes of ideology and organization, had succeeded in penetrating into the advanced sector, and had assimilated it into the wider patterns of the society.

The major unions in the two countries had fundamentally different conceptions of the role of the trade union in the factory. The French unions saw their task as one of heightening the consciousness of the work force so that it would understand the extent of its alienation within capitalist society and seek a major transformation of the basic institutional structures of society. Their strategy for achieving this was essentially one of sustained ideological warfare in the context of steadily escalating action over concrete disputes with management. The main influence over union ideas and action came from the central union apparatus, the Federation and the Confederation, and the specific demands that the French unions made on management were heavily coloured by their long-term social objectives.

The British unions, on the other hand, conceived of their role in the factory as primarily one of representation. They saw their job as one of forwarding objectives that were consciously and explicitly desired by the work force. Their strategy was to achieve their ends through negotiation backed up by a powerful, well-disciplined, and cohesive organization that would represent such a potential threat in the event of conflict that management was unlikely to risk being unduly unreasonable in negotiation. To achieve this, they were prepared to see the development of a system of exchange with management whereby management helped the union officials in building up the strength of the organization, while the unions gave management a certain degree of help in controlling the work force.

These two types of unionism appeared to have quite different implications for the coercive power that the unions could bring to bear on management. The French unions appear to have achieved a significant degree of success in their primary objective — to enhance the workers' awareness of the exploitative and alienating character of the society in which they lived. However, one consequence of the high level of ideological explicitness and systematization through which they sought to insulate the work force from the dominant cultural beliefs of its society was that the unions were themselves torn apart by ideological conflict, and by a fierce rivalry for the ideological allegiance of the workers. This inter-union conflict was reinforced by a legal system which made it extremely difficult for any one union to establish a stable monopoly of representation, and by the system of regular elections to Works Councils which constantly brought the unions into direct confrontation and provided a permanent measure of their ideological efficacity. Further, the commitment to ideological mobilization contributed to a rather problematic relationship between the union activists and their own base. Their consistent effort to forge explicit links between the issues of the work place and the wider political arena clashed fundamentally with the workers' own belief that political and industrial issues should be kept sharply separated. Their concern to heighten the class awareness of the workers by inserting local conflicts into a wider class struggle led to a constant transmutation of explicit worker demands into a wider programme that had not been legitimated and that made the workers somewhat doubtful about the authenticity of union democracy, reluctant to participate in union decision making, and fickle in their support of union initiatives.

The British unions, lacking any aspiration to mould the consciousness of the workers, or to challenge fundamentally the existing structure of society, concentrated their efforts on the process of organization, and on building up significant countervailing resources of power. Through careful avoidance of divisive issues, close attention to maintaining communications with the membership, and the development of a powerful system of sanctions through the closed shop, the British unions had secured a highly dependable base, and could effectively threaten management with severe economic losses if it failed to take into account their views, or to win their consent on issues which were felt to be of major importance by the work force. Our evidence indicates that British management's strategy was to a large degree determined by its awareness of the power of the unions and of shop floor organization. In Britain the costs of bargaining were outweighed by the costs of conflict. In France, in contrast, management quite correctly believed that the unions were unable to impose major economic losses on the firm, and the cost of conflict was considered negligible compared to the probable cost of bargaining.

It must be remembered, however, that French trade unionists would not consider the success of the British unions in controlling managerial power, and thereby ensuring a more agreeable work environment and a greater sense of security for the personnel, as evidence of the greater *long-term* efficacy of British trade union policies. Rather, they would argue that, in their bid to acquire power over immediate issues, the British unions had, in fact, paid the price of abandoning altogether the drive for really significant structural change. By confining themselves to a unionism of representation, and by deliberately evading controversial issues, the British unions were allowing, and even contributing towards, a progressive integration of workers within the existing structure of capitalist society. For French trade unionists this would be clearly illustrated by the fact that the workers in the British refineries had a 'co-operative' image of management, and legitimated the existing structure of decision making in the enterprise, despite the persistence of immense disparities of power and major inequalities in the distribution of material rewards. Although the French unions had failed to acquire power within the Company in the short term, they would argue that, by emphasizing ideological mobilization, they had made it much more likely that a radical left-wing government would be able to assume state power and, by so doing, had provided the conditions for a much more far-reaching structural transformation of society than would be conceivable in Britain. In support of their position, they could point to the fact that in 1974 the Communist–Socialist alliance failed to win the Presidency by only one per cent of the vote.

This debate about the longer-term efficacy of the two forms of unionism is, for the present at least, well outside the scope of viable sociological analysis, and we raise it here simply to make the point that the same data can be interpreted in two fundamentally different ways.

In broad outline, we have suggested that the advanced sector tends to become to a considerable degree assimilated into the broader social-structural patterns of the particular society in which it emerges. In the factories in the advanced sector that we studied, managerial policies represented relatively progressive versions of two quite distinct national patterns and, in both countries, the most powerful of the unions in the society as a whole had also become the dominant representative of the work force within the refineries. We suspect that some of the differences we found between the dynamics of social interaction in our French and British refineries reflect wider differences between the patterns characteristic of larger firms in the two countries.

In the first instance, it seems to us that the markedly lower degree of social integration within the capitalist firm of the French workers, in comparison to the British workers, resulted from the interaction of higher substantive and procedural expectations on the part of the workers with a much less participative institutional system within the factory. This led to a rejection of the legitimacy of the procedures of decision-making; it produced substantially greater discontent over specific decisions about salaries, shift work, and reorganization; and it reinforced an image of management as exploitative rather than as concerned with the welfare of all. The resentments thus generated, we suggest, posed a major risk of low motivation in work, and this helps explain why French management imposed a tighter system of control over work performance than existed in the British refineries. Although this seemed a perfectly viable way in which management could achieve its objectives, it had the further consequence of increasing friction between middle management and the work force, and heightening social distance within the factory.

The institutional structure, itself, reflected French management's commitment to a paternalist strategy for securing the allegiance of the work force, in contrast to the semi-constitutional strategy that had been adopted in Britain. Although the choice of this strategy may be partly attributable to socialization into distinctive French conceptions of authority that have a long historical tradition, we would emphasize that — at least in the shorter term — it was a perfectly rational strategy for maximizing profit and preserving capitalist relations of production in the context of an ideologically radical trade union movement that would have been very much more difficult to integrate than in the British case.

Most critically, however, the differences between formal institutions of power in the French and British factories resulted from marked differences in the coercive power of the unions in the two countries. The French unions clearly played a major role in sustaining, and reinforcing, the higher aspirations and expectations of the French workers, and in giving these relevance to the immediate work context. However, their commitment to ideological mobilization contributed in important ways to the weakening of their coercive power, and they were unable to bring sufficient pressure to bear on management to enforce any major changes in an institutional system that had substantial costs in terms of the workers' experience of employment. In contrast, in Britain, the unions made little attempt to raise worker aspirations or to influence their wider conception of society but, by concentrating on the development of organizational strength, they placed themselves in a position where it would simply have been too costly for management not to negotiate on those issues that the work force regarded as of major importance.

In the light of the factors which we suggest are important in determining the social integration of the work force, it is clear that we would not make rigid predictions about the *long-term* future pattern of worker attitudes and objectives in the advanced sector of industry. Issues of control might become of central importance for workers in the highly automated setting in either country and, similarly, it is conceivable that the work force could in both countries become socially integrated within the existing capitalist system. But what is essential to our argument is that if either of these developments do occur, *it will not be for the reasons suggested by authors such as Blauner and Mallet.* Rather, it will depend on changing cultural expectations within the wider working class, on changes in management attitudes, and on changes in trade union objectives. Similarly, it would follow from our argument that if these developments do occur, the automated sector will not be particularly distinctive. Rather, it will be participating in a very much broader movement occurring within industry in the particular society.

The interpretation of the data we have given is necessarily provisional. Its detailed assumptions need rigorous testing, and it is quite explicitly focused on certain links of a much more elaborate causal chain. The further explanatory problems it raises — for instance, about the sources of variation in worker expectations and the origins of managerial ideologies — involve complex issues that it would be foolhardy to try to analyse in a few pages. But what we have tried to do is to direct attention to the types of variables which we feel need very much more systematic research. On the whole, empirically orientated researchers in the 1960s directed us to abandon 'metaphysical' conceptions of the working class as a homogeneous social entity, and instead to seek to understand its critical lines of internal differentiation. The major determinants of worker attitudes were seen to lie in the particular type of local industrial or community setting in which specific sets of workers were located. While such local factors may be of some significance, we would suggest that rather more important are certain broader cultural and social structural factors, which can vary between societies and which can create quite distinctive social situations for their respective working classes. For, while the Western nations share a common capitalist mode of production that generates similar conflicts of interest between employers and employed, this underlying system contradiction can have very different consequences at the level of social integration. The crucial mediating variables, we would suggest, are factors like the managerial ideology, the typical structure of power in social institutions, and the ideology and mode of action of the trade union movement characteristic of the specific society. Moreover, if we are to understand the differences between the working classes of the various Western societies, we will need to look much more closely at their pattern of historical development, and examine the way in which different historical experiences have generated distinctive cultural and social structural patterns.

Appendix 1

Claude Durand, *Conscience ouvrière et l'action syndicale* [1]

Durand's work represents a substantial study in the field we have been considering and one that we have touched on only briefly in the text. Durand's analysis of a survey of over 1000 union militants suggests that there is a tendency for French unionism in the advanced sector to be somewhat different in character from unionism in other sectors. Our own theoretical interpretation is not intended to exclude the possibility of such differences, although we would argue that they would be kept within fairly tight limits by the centrifugal tendencies of French unionism. However, the local unions are required to 'translate' union objectives into locally relevant programmes, and the choice of particular modes of action is frequently left to the local unions even by the CGT, so the possibility of a certain degree of variation clearly exists. Nonetheless, we feel that Durand's argument — even if it is correct — has yet to be adequately demonstrated.

Durand's approach was to compare the attitudes of individual militants. His interviews were designed to enable him to classify militants into six distinct types differing in their self conceptions, the way they perceived their opponent, and the type of wider legitimating values to which they appealed to justify their actions.[2] In their simplest definitions these types are:

1. A1 Craft unionism
2. B1 Unionism of economic defence
3. B2 Class conflict unionism
4. C1 Unionism of occupational defence
5. C2 Bargaining unionism
6. C3 Unionism of planning and control[3]

They represent, he believes, an evolution from older to more novel forms of unionism, and two of them (C2 and C3) are orientated towards control. C2 is concerned with developing a form of contractual negotiation of the type to be found in the United States. It does not focus on the economic objectives of the enterprise, but is concerned rather with negotiating over its administrative system and its procedures of personnel management.[4] The second (C3) represents the most evolved form of union consciousness in which the militant demands participation both in the running of the enterprise, and in economic decision making at national level.[5] This is the type of unionism that Durand appears to identify with theories of the new working class.[6]

Durand selected the militants on which the study was based from three different types of work situation which, following Alain Touraine's scheme of technical evolution, he broadly classified as craft, mass production, and technical work situations.[7] When he examined the relationship between these types of work situation and the various forms of union consciousness, he concluded that those forms of unionism most orientated to control were to be found most frequently in the advanced technical sector.[8] Table A gives the critical figures which indicate this relationship.

Table A   *Types of union action*

Phases in the evolution of work	A1	B1	B2	C1	C2	C3	Base de calcul des %
Craft	5	18	38	10	10	20	N = 344
Mass production	3	21	31	14	12	19	N = 366
Technical	1	8	30	8	19	35	N = 367[5]

There is clearly a distinct, but not highly marked, difference between the forms of unionism in the three sectors. Of the militants in the advanced sector 35% are classified under control unionism, compared with 20% in the technologically most traditional sector. Class conflict unionism seems largely unaffected by the technological setting.[9] The main type that seems to be on its way out in the advanced sector is unionism concentrating narrowly on the defence of the worker's economic position.

The precise weight to attach to Durand's findings is difficult to assess because of the complexity of the method he adopts. The more transformations through which the data pass between the original conception of indicators and the final construction of indexes, the less easy is it to see the precise significance of what has in fact been shown. Certainly, in evaluating his results we need to take into account the following points:

1. His original theoretical construction of types of unionism involves the production of three-dimensional models. It is technically very difficult to devise single questions or single phrases that can adequately assess the existence or non-existence of models of this degree of complexity. It means finding a phrase that will give clear evidence on three separate questions: the self image of the actor, the image of the opponent, and the overall conception of society. If we look at most of Durand's questions they manifestly fail to cope with this degree of complexity and the options he offers for each model tend to emphasize one aspect or another. This is understandable but it reduces the significance of each item as an indicator of the original model.

2. Durand's strategy was to deploy an indicator for each model over 15 substantive issues.[10] The indicators were conceived as theoretically deductible attitudes on each issue, given the particular model of unionism. However, when he came to examine the internal consistency with which people chose the options attributed to each model, the results were disappointing. As we can see from Table B, in only three of the six options were more than half the items closely related to each other.

It is clear that it is only in models B2 and C3 that the author was reasonably successful in predicting the type of attitude that a holder of the model would adopt across a reasonable number of substantive issues. This is no doubt partly

Table B   *Model*

	A1	B1	B2	C1	C2	C3
No. of items significantly inter-related	9	3	12	6	6	11
Percentage of all items	60%	20%	80%	40%	40%	73%

Figures calculated by author from data presented in C. Durand, *Conscience Ouvrière et L'Action Syndicale*, 58–63. The later introduction by Durand of the coded answers to open questions weakened the index still further: 48% (A1); 29% (B1); 76% (B2); 33% (C1); 52% (C3). See, Durand, *Conscience Ouvrière et L'Action Syndicale*, 13.

explicable by our first point about the difficulty of this type of question construction, but where the success rate is less than 50% it is difficult not to believe that it reflects on the adequacy of the original theoretical model.

3. Confronted with the problem of the non-interrelation of many of his indicators, Durand's policy is to use only those that interrelate well within each model as the basis on which to classify people into one model or another. Since the indicators of some models were more successful in one group of questions, and the indicators of other models were more successful in different groups, this means that in many cases people are being classified into different models on the basis of answers to non-comparable issues. This is not necessarily a fatal procedure but it is evidently a dangerous one.

4. If we look at the items that were retained as the basis of classification it is not always evident that even taken cumulatively they evoke the conception of unionism intended in the original theoretical model. To take the crucial case of C3 (control unionism), which Durand appears to believe reflects the type of unionism envisaged by Mallet, we are told: 'La participation est revendiquée comme accès aux décisions non seulement dans l'entreprise mais au niveau national.'[11] If we examine closely the indicators retained for C3 it is difficult to believe that Mallet would have been altogether happy. Seven of the eleven items are not concerned with the problem of the enterprise which was Mallet's main concern. Of the remaining four items two are highly unspecific about the type of influence required — consultation or control. A third, on nationalization, involves a double-barrelled phrasing which makes it difficult to know which of the two rather different ideas — planning or enterprise control — in fact attracted approval.[12]

Given the fact that people are classified into a model on the basis of the majority tendency of their answers, it seems possible that a certain proportion of those classified in C3, given the balance of the indicators, may have expressed no interest whatsoever in the control of the enterprise.

Even if we examine their interest in 'planning', we should note that of the seven planning items, six merely indicate that planning is a good thing, and give little indication of the views of the person about the objectives to which planning should be directed. The C3 model could then embrace a variety of different ideological options.

5. One crude way of looking at the likely validity of the final indexes is to examine the way in which the militants in different unions responded.[13] B2 (class conflict unionism) seems to be rather good. It obtains a high level of adherence from the CGT, and very little from the CFDT and Force Ouvrière.

C2 would appear less successful. Force Ouvrière has tirelessly presented a public image of a union that wishes to negotiate on an Anglo-Saxon model but only 16% of its militants respond to the indicators that are supposed to represent the model.

C3 is a disturbing mixture. It does well in picking up the CFDT, which has publicly committed itself for a decade to a form of 'democratic planning', and which was increasingly showing an interest in control within the firm. On the other hand the union that does best of all in terms of C3 is the CGC, a moderate categorial union of middle managers that was most decidedly not committed to any very radical change of the existing social system. The CGC's response to the planning options probably reflects little more than French management's traditional interest in economic planning. The impression is confirmed that C3 can combine two rather different systems of thought, one fundamentally moderate and one considerably more radical. The balance between these in the statistics Durand presents is impossible to assess.

It is notable that the variations between unions appear to be very much more marked than the variations between forms of technology. This raises two problems. First, Durand, for entirely understandable technical reasons, has not tried to make a representative sample of the different sectors. This means that the variations in C3 between the technical and the other sectors may mainly reflect the weight of the different unions in his sample. Second, it poses the problem of the impact of ideological change in the unions. The CFDT of the 1970s, with its simultaneous emphasis on class conflict and control, would, I believe, be impossible to classify within any of Durand's six models. The study dates from the period before 1968.

6. Finally, we should note that his conception of the technical sector is a broad one — far broader than Touraine's original conception in La Conscience Ouvrière. It includes not only industries as diverse as atomic energy, space research, research centres, the chemical and pharmaceutical industries, the aeronautical, electro-chemical, electrical construction, and oil industries, but also, somewhat more curiously, photography, cinema, advertising, hospital services, the press, and the radio.[14] This is clearly a vast amalgam of different types of work situation, and it would be interesting to know what the results would have been like if the technical sector had been more strictly defined.

The effect of these different factors on Durand's results are difficult to assess. They represent possible distortions in his measuring instruments, and not evidence that they altogether lacked validity. The main worry is that, given the fairly small differences that he found between different technical sectors, the risk for the overall conclusion of any distortion due to the use of impure indicators is maximized.

Appendix 2

The questionnaire

These questions form part of a more general questionnaire about workers' attitudes to society. The data from the other questions — focusing on perceptions of inequality, class and politics — will be presented in a separate publication.

(1)   Do you think that your standard of living is:

      1. Very good
      2. Pretty good
      3. Not very good
      4. Very bad

(6) (a) Do you think that a worker has disadvantages in his life because he is a worker?

      1. A lot of disadvantages
      2. Quite a few disadvantages
      3. Few disadvantages
      4. No disadvantages

   (b) Probe if answer 1–3. What disadvantages are you thinking of?

(20)   Generally speaking, when you come to work, do you feel:

      1. Rather happy at the idea of an interesting day (or night) in the refinery
      2. Nothing in particular; not particularly happy or unhappy.
      3. A bit fed up at the idea of having to pass the day (night) in the refinery

(21) (a) What do you think about the way the refinery is organized? Do you think that:

      1. It is the best possible and should be preserved at all costs
      2. It is rather good and should be preserved
      3. It is quite good and might as well be preserved
      4. It could be better and certain changes could be made
      5. There are many things that need changing
      6. The whole system needs changing

   (b) Probe if answers 4–6. What types of changes would you like to see?

(22)   Do you think that for you personally it's better for the company to be run:

      1. By the State
      2. By the unions
      3. By the whole personnel
      4. As it is at the moment

(23) (a) Do you think that the salary system here is:
   1. Just
   2. Not very just
   3. Rather unjust
   4. Very unjust

   (b) Probe if answer 2–4. And why?

(24) (a) If you could have the same salary and the same type of job as you have now, would you prefer to work shift hours or a normal working day?
   1. Shift hours
   2. Normal working day

   (b) Probe. And why?

(25)   Do you think that, on the whole, management is most concerned with:
   1. The interests of the workers
   2. The interests of the shareholders
   3. The interests of everybody

(27)   Would you say that in their relations with the workers in the refinery, middle-level staff, that is members of staff between your immediate supervisors and the top management are:
   1. Very distant
   2. Quite distant
   3. Quite friendly
   4. Very friendly

(28a)   When a decision has to be taken about the arrangements for *shift work* (*or overtime*) in this refinery, how is it taken? Is it:
   1. Taken by management alone
   2. Taken by management alone, but after asking the opinion of the representatives of the workers
   3. Taken with the agreement of both the management and the representatives of the workers

   If it was up to you to choose the ideal way of taking this type of decision, which of these three possibilities would you choose?
   1. By the management alone
   2. By management alone, but after asking the opinion of the representatives of the workers
   3. With the agreement of both the management and the representatives of the workers

(28b)   When a decision has to be taken about *an increase or reduction of the work force*, how is it taken? Is it:
   1. Taken by management alone
   2. Taken by management alone, but after asking the opinion of the representatives of the workers
   3. Taken with the agreement of both the management and the representatives of the workers

   If it was up to you to choose the ideal way of taking this type of decision, which of these three possibilities would you choose?
   1. By management alone

2. By management alone, but after asking the opinion of the representatives of the workers
3. With the agreement of both the management and the representatives of the workers

(28c)   When a decision is taken about *salaries*, how is it taken? Is it:

1. Taken by management alone
2. Taken by management alone, but after asking the opinion of the representatives of the workers.
3. Taken with the agreement of both the management and the representatives of the workers.

If it was up to you to choose the ideal way of taking this type of decision, which of these three possibilities would you choose?

1. By management alone
2. By management alone, but after asking the opinion of the representatives of the workers
3. With the agreement of both the management and the representatives of the workers

(28d)   When a decision has to be taken about *how much of the company's profits should be put into* additional wages and share dividends, and how much into investment, how is it taken? Is it:

1. Taken by management alone
2. Taken by management alone, but after asking the opinion of the representatives of the workers
3. Taken with the agreement of both the management and the representatives of the workers

If it was up to you to choose the ideal way of taking this type of decision, which of these three possibilities would you choose?

1. By management alone
2. By management alone, but after asking the opinion of the representatives of the workers
3. With the agreement of both the management and the representatives of the workers

(28e)   When a decision has to be taken about *investment in new units*, how is it taken? Is it:

1. Taken by management alone
2. Taken by management alone, but after asking the opinion of the representatives of the workers.
3. Taken with the agreement of both the management and the representatives of the workers

If it was up to you to choose the ideal way of taking this type of decision, which of these three possibilities would you choose?

1. By management alone
2. By management alone, but after asking the opinion of the representatives of the workers
3. With the agreement of both the management and the representatives of the workers

(29) (a) In a decision such as whether or not to reduce the number of workers in the units, how great is the influence of:

	very great	*quite great*	*fairly small*	*very small*
1. The general manager				
2. The assistant works manager				
3. The section heads (day supervisors)				
4. The shop stewards meetings with the departmental heads, and with the works manager				
5. The union				
6. The workers				

(b) And now, if it was up to you to choose the ideal way of taking this sort of decision, how much influence would you give each category on the list?

	very great	*quite great*	*fairly small*	*very small*
1. The general manager				
2. The assistant works manager				
3. The section heads (day supervisors)				
4. The shop stewards meetings with the departmental heads, and with the works manager				
5. The union				
6. The workers				

(44) (a) Which union do you prefer?
(b) Are you a union member?

(45) Do you think that a union should try to influence the opinions people have about politics?

1. Yes
2. No

(47) (a) In what year were you born?
(b) In what year did you join this company?

(49) (a) Where were you born?
(b) Where do you live now?

Notes

Part one. Theories in conflict

1. Automation and social integration within the capitalist enterprise

1   J. H. Goldthorpe *et al.*, *The Affluent Worker: Industrial Attitudes and Behaviour* (Cambridge, 1968); *The Affluent Worker: Political Attitudes and Behaviour* (Cambridge, 1968); *The Affluent Worker in the Class Structure* (Cambridge, 1969).

2   R. Blauner, *Alienation and Freedom* (Chicago, 1964); S. Mallet, *La Nouvelle Classe Ouvrière* (Paris, 1963 and 1969).

3   Especially important in the United States were C. R. Walker & R. Guest, *Man on the Assembly Line* (Cambridge, Mass., 1952) and E. Chinoy, *Automobile Workers and the American Dream* (New York, 1955). In France, A. Touraine's work: *L'évolution du travail ouvrier aux usines Renault* (Paris, 1955) was widely influential, and a major synthesis of the early literature was provided by G. Friedmann's *Problèmes humains du machinisme industriel* (Paris, 1947).

4   Particularly important for this discussion are: G. Friedmann, *Problèmes humains du machinisme industriel*; A. Touraine, *La conscience ouvrière* (Paris, 1966); M. Collinet, *L'Esprit du syndicalisme* (Paris, 1952); M. Crozier, 'Sociologie du syndicalisme' in G. Friedmann & P. Naville eds., *Traité de Sociologie du Travail* (Paris, 1962); Blauner, *Alienation*; Mallet, *La Nouvelle Classe Ouvrière*; A. Andrieux & J. Lignon, *L'ouvrier d'aujourd'hui* (Paris, 1960).

5   See especially Blauner's descriptions of the assembly-line workers' attitudes, *Alienation*, 119–23, 178.

6   Ibid. 21.

7   Ibid. 134, 139.

8   Ibid. 144.

9   Ibid. 172/3.

10   Ibid. 24.

11   Compare Blauner, *Alienation*, sections 146 to 154, and 178 to 182.

12   Ibid. 146.

13   Ibid. 146.

14   Ibid. 178.

15   Ibid. 148.

16   Ibid. 25. See E. Mayo, *The Social Problems of an Industrial Civilization* (London, 1949).

17   Blauner: *Alienation*, 148.

18   Ibid. 180, 153.

19   Ibid. 128–30, 152, 180.

20   Ibid. 154.

21   Ibid. 150.

22   Ibid. 181.
23   J. Woodward, *Industrial Organization: Theory and Practice* (London, 1965) 199.
24   Ibid. 233.
25   Ibid. 185.
26   Ibid. 155.
27   Ibid. 123.
28   Ibid. 201.
29   Ibid. 202.
30   Ibid. 162.
31   J. Woodward ed., *Industrial Organization: Behaviour and Control* (Oxford, 1970) 38.
32   P. M. Blau, *The Dynamics of Bureaucracy* (Chicago, 1955); and P. M. Blau & W. R. Scott, *Formal Organizations* (London, 1963) ch. 7.
33   Woodward: *Industrial Organization: Behaviour and Control*, 55.
34   See for instance: M. Bouvier-Ajam et G. Mury, *Les Classes Sociales en France* (Paris, 1964).
35   Mallet, *La Nouvelle Classe Ouvrière*, 35.
36   Ibid. 36.
37   Ibid. 21.
38   Ibid. 80, 81.
39   See Mallet's discussion of the operator's role, *La Nouvelle Classe Ouvrière*, 110–11.
40   Ibid. 82.
41   Ibid. 82–3.
42   Ibid. 22, 43.
43   Ibid. 22.
44   Ibid. 137, 41, 43.
45   Ibid. 86, 92.
46   Ibid. 92.
47   Ibid. 90.
48   Ibid. 87.
49   Ibid. 92, 93.
50   Ibid. 93.
51   Naville and Mallet were presumably not altogether strangers to each other. Both held important posts in the extreme left socialist party — the *Parti Socialiste Unifié*; in 1964, Mallet was a member of the *Comité Politique National*, and Naville of the *Bureau National*. Equally, both were very active in an 'independent' study group — the *Centre d'études socialistes* — that was founded in 1959 to reinvigorate French socialist thinking and to influence the policies of the French working-class organizations.
52   P. Naville *et al.*, *L'Automation et le travail humain* (Paris, 1961).
53   P. Naville, *Vers l'automatisme social?* (Paris, 1963).
54   Naville, *Vers l'automatisme social?*, 203–4.
55   Ibid. 85.
56   Ibid. 28.
57   Ibid. 75, 205.
58   Ibid. 75, 117.
59   Ibid. 187.
60   Ibid. 185, 119.
61   Ibid. 119. For Naville's general commitment to a Marxist perspective in sociology, and for a fierce attack on the theoretical timidity, the

unwillingness to extrapolate, and the lack of concern for the 'general motor forces of society' of 'university' sociology, see: P. Naville, 'Marxisme et Sociologie' in *Les cahiers du centre d'études socialistes*, No. 34–5, 1963.

62   Many of these texts are gathered in P. Naville, *La classe ouvrière et le régime gaulliste* (Paris, 1964). The most systematic statement of Naville's theoretical position can be found in 'Lois sociologiques et action de masse' in *Les cahiers du centre d'études socialistes*, No. 13–14, Jan. 1962.

63   See: P. Naville, 'Planification et gestion démocratique' in *Les cahiers du centre d'études socialistes*, No. 23–4, 1963.

64   Although he felt automation favoured the contestation of existing social relations of production, Naville remained fundamentally pessimistic about the possibility of work becoming again a major source of life satisfaction. Control would certainly help in enhancing the meaningfulness of work, and was in any case a prerequisite for any fundamental change in the workers' overall life situation. However, in Naville's view, the main positive sources of satisfaction now lie primarily outside the work setting, and can only be increased by reducing to a minimum the amount of time actually spent at work. *Inter alia*, see: P. Naville, *Temps et travail* (Genève, 1972).

65   F. Furstenberg, 'Structural Changes in the Working Class' in J. A. Jackson ed., *Social Stratification* (Cambridge, 1968).

66   His own fieldwork in the California Bay area was clearly far too limited to provide an adequate corrective to the straitjacket imposed by his main sources of data. He managed to interview only twenty workers dispersed across three very different departments — operations, maintenance and distribution. If the departments had equal numbers he may have interviewed some seven operators, hardly enough to provide a solid grounding for the argument.

67   D. Wedderburn & R. Crompton, *Workers' Attitudes and Technology* (Cambridge, 1972).

68   An important difference, however, between Mallet and Naville lies in their approach to evidence. Mallet had nothing but contempt for the methods of empirical sociology, and this went together with a quite astonishing naivety in his actual handling of data — a naivety best illustrated by the meaningless jumble of 'facts' collected in the chapter 'L'après-mai 1968: grèves pour le contrôle ouvrier' in S. Mallet, *Le pouvoir ouvrier* (Paris, 1971). Naville, on the other hand, believed that it was crucial for Marxist theory to integrate and use methodological advances in the social sciences, see: P. Naville, 'Marxisme et Sociologie', *Cahiers du centre d'études socialistes*, 1963.

69   C. Durand, 'Ouvriers et Techniciens en mai 1968' in P. Dubois *et al.*, *Grèves revendicatives ou grèves politiques?* (Paris, 1971).

70   Ibid. 61.

71   For a worrying sign of ambiguity, see the curious formulation on p. 157, 'lutte politique classique pour l'ancienne classe ouvrière, lutte révolutionnaire pour les militants des entreprises techniques.'

72   Ibid. 19–20. Note that the CFDT which was explicitly committed to the issue of control by its executive in the opening days of the strike was more powerful in the technical sector.

73   Durand, 'Ouvriers et Techniciens en mai 1968' 51, 65, 83.

74   C. Durand, *Conscience Ouvrière et l'Action Syndicale* (Paris, 1971).

75   F. Harbison & C. Myers, *Management in the Industrial World* (New York, 1959).
76   D. Granick, *The European Executive* (London, 1962) 184, 188.
77   A. Tannenbaum, B. Kavčič, M. Rosner, M. Vianello & G. Wieser, *Hierarchy in Organizations* (San Francisco and London, 1974).
78   C. Kerr, J. T. Dunlop, F. Harbison & C. A. Myers, *Industrialism and Industrial Man* (2nd ed., London 1973) esp. chs. 4 and 7.
79   See for instance, J. H. Goldthorpe. 'Social Stratification in Industrial Society', *Sociological Review Monograph*, No. 8, 1964.
80   Tannenbaum *et al.*, *Hierarchy in Organizations*.
81   See for instance, P. Blumberg, *Industrial Democracy: The Sociology of Participation* (London, 1968); or A. Fox, *Man Mismanagement* (London, 1974).
82   Overviews can be found in W. Galenson, *Comparative Labor Movements* (New York, 1952); or W. Kendall, *The Labour Movement in Europe* (London, 1975).
83   See especially Goldthorpe & Lockwood, *The Affluent Worker: Industrial Attitudes and Behaviour*.
84   See, for instance, R. Hamilton, *Affluence and the French Worker in the Fourth Republic* (Princeton, 1967).

2. The research strategy

1   It is clear too that Mallet regarded his oil refinery case study as his 'purest' case, best revealing the pattern of the future. See S. Mallet, *La Nouvelle Classe Ouvrière*, 233–4.
2   For an interesting study showing that these differences existed even before the First World War in the form of different brands of socialism within the united socialist party, see Claude Willard, *Le Mouvement socialiste en France 1893–1905* (Paris, 1965).
3   Throughout this study the basic unit of analysis is the individual refinery, and the data are broken down by refinery. To avoid repetition, unless otherwise stated, the term 'by refinery' can be assumed in the titles to tables.
4   Data based on the sample. Question 49 in the interview schedule reproduced in Appendix 2.

Part two. The attitudes and aspirations of the work force

3. Salaries

1   The refinery workers had been moved onto a monthly salary system in the 1960s in France and at Grangemouth, while at Kent they had moved onto a system in which a stable salary was paid weekly.
2   S. Mallet, *La Nouvelle Classe Ouvrière* (Paris, 1969) 23:16.
3   Ibid. 96, 98; R. Blauner, *Alienation and Freedom* (Chicago, 1964) 154.
4   Ibid. 130; Mallet, *La Nouvelle Classe Ouvrière*, 38.
5   Blauner, *Alienation*, 154 (my italics).
6   Mallet, *La Nouvelle Classe Ouvrière*, 22.
7   See for instance, H. Lydall, *The Structure of Earnings* (Oxford, 1968).
8   A comparison with national manual worker averages reveals again a very substantial advantage in favour of the French refinery workers. They earned some 85% more than the national average male manual

worker salary. The British, in contrast, earned only 14% more (the most recent French figures are for 1968).

9 The precise question on which a table is based is from now on indicated by (Q. .). The questionnaire is given in Appendix 2. Tables in which the differences between the French and British workers are significant at the 0.01 level are marked with an asterisk.

10 The central importance of salary demands for French workers in the 'advanced' sector has equally emerged from a study by Christine Barrier of workers in the electricity industry. See C. Barrier, *Le combat ouvrier dans une entreprise de pointe* (Paris, 1975).

4. Work and work organization

1 S. Mallet, *La Nouvelle Classe Ouvrière* (Paris, 1969) 125/6.
2 Ibid. 129.
3 Ibid. 85.
4 P. Blauner, *Alienation and Freedom* (Chicago, 1964).
5 Or more accurately of a responsible operator in a British or American refinery. As we shall see in chapter 9, in the French refineries, the most senior operators had substantially less scope for the use of their initiative.
6 A more decisive objection to Blauner's argument on this issue emerges from Chadwick Jones' study of automation in a tinning plant in the steel industry. It is clear that Blauner's belief that automation *necessarily* leads to socially cohesive work teams offering a sense of community is incorrect. Chadwick Jones found that operators were spread out along a long production line, and that both interview and observational methods showed that the level of informal interaction was relatively low. See J. Chadwick Jones, *Automation and Behaviour* (London, 1969), chs. 6 and 11.
7 When they were initially allocated to jobs, people were, of course, selected to a certain degree on the basis of 'suitability'.
8 For further evidence, see C. Vamplew 'Automated Process Operators: Work Attitudes and Behaviour', *British Journal of Industrial Relations* (Nov. 1973). Vamplew found that the most frequent response to a question on job interest was: 'Interesting most of the time but with dull periods' (53 i) 418. For a more impressionistic account based on the same study see W. W. Daniel, *Beyond the wage-work bargain* (London, 1970) 44.
9 S. Wyatt, & R. Marriot, 'Night Work and Shift Changes', *British Journal of Industrial Medicine*, 1953, 10:164–72.
10 F. C. Mann & L. R. Hoffman *Automation and the Worker* (New York, 1960) 106.
11 Ibid. 134.
12 Company Memorandum. *Etude du travail en poste continu*, 'Rapport de Synthèse de la Commission Médicale', mars 1971, 5.
13 Mann & Hoffman, *Automation*, 114.
14 Cited by P. E. Mott, F. C. Mann, Q. McLoughlin & D. P. Warwick, *Shift Work* (Michigan, 1965) 235–6.
15 Ibid.
16 Ibid. 238.
17 Ibid. 301/2.
18 P. J. Taylor, 'Shift work and Day work: A Comparison of Sickness Absence, Lateness and other Absence at an Oil Refinery from 1962 to 1965', *British Journal of Industrial Medicine*, 1967, 24:93.

19 *Etude du travail en poste continu*; 'Rapport de Synthèse de la Com-
    mision Médicale', 15 mars 1971, 3.
20 Mann & Hoffman, *Automation*, 114; and Mott *et al.*, *Shift Work*,
    235–6, 240 and 280.
21 Mann & Hoffman, *Automation*, 124.
22 Mott *et al.*, *Shift Work*, 299.
23 *Etude du travail en service continu*: 'Groupe des Secrétaires généraux',
    18 mars 1971, 1.
24 *Le Posté*, Avril 1968.
25 For instance, Blauner, *Alienation*, 130; Mallet, *La Nouvelle Classe
    Ouvrière*, 82.
26 It is evident however from G. Caire's study of a Shell oil refinery in
    Southern France that higher aspirations had already crystallized by the
    early 1950s. See G. Caire, *Le Syndicalisme et l'Automation* (Aix-en-
    Provence, 1960), 331. Having underlined the unusually high level of
    security of employment of his refinery workers, Caire nonetheless goes
    on to tell us that security remained one of their most fundamental
    preoccupations.
27 It has since been confirmed to me that this prediction proved correct,
    and by January 1976 overall numbers at Lavera appear to have fallen
    by some 18% from the figure at the time of our study.
28 Blauner, *Alienation*, 139.

5. *The perception of management*

1   'Co-operative' is, I think, preferable in this context to 'Harmonistic'
    in that the latter tends to suggest an absence of criticism — which was
    clearly not the case here.

6. *The legitimacy of managerial power*

1   At the time of our research, the main attempt to measure empirically
    attitudes to power along these lines was that of Arnold Tannenbaum
    and his associates. See A. Tannenbaum, ed., *Control in Organizations*
    (New York, 1968). Our initial plan was in fact to use the Tannenbaum
    'control graph' for our own study. During the pilot survey, however,
    we came across several problems with this method which led us to
    change strategy. The most commonly used version of the control
    graph involved dividing the organization into a set of strata, and asking
    people how much influence each strata had over the way things were
    decided within the organization. In the pilot, we found that many
    people resisted such an attempt to give a global judgement about the
    power structure of the enterprise. It appeared that they had a complex
    and differentiated perception of power in the firm, and regarded the
    question as far too crude. Rather than compel people to produce an
    image that had no meaning for them, it was clearly essential to break
    down the decision-making process into several key decision-making
    areas. In effect, this meant that we had to abandon the Tannenbaum
    graph as our major device, and replace it with a simpler technique. For,
    although the control graph had been used in a more sophisticated way,
    differentiating between different issues, it was technically rather diffi-
    cult to use in this form as part of a wider-ranging questionnaire. Each

control graph was rather cumbersome to use, people took a lot of time to get used to it, and it took up a very large amount of interview time — indeed, if we had wished to use it to cover different issues it would have taken from a third to half of the overall interview time. We restricted our use of it, then, to one issue area; and, for the others, replaced it with our own simpler and rather quicker method of measurement.

2   Only respondents who replied to all ten items constituting the index have been included.

3   G. Adam, F. Bon, J. Capdevielle & R. Mauriaux, *L'Ouvrier Français en 1970* (Paris, 1970) 171.

4   See question 22.

5   Non-response has been distributed proportionately for comparability.

Part three. The structure of managerial power

7. The machinery of participation

1   The Law on the 'Comité d'Entreprise', 22 February 1945.

2   Rapport Sudreau, *La Réforme de l'entreprise* (Paris, 1975) 82.

3   The President of the Committee is the Director of the refinery.

4   SCIP Tract 4 May 1973.

5   FO Tract 23 April 1975.

6   CGT Tract 'Développer l'Action pour les Salaires' April 1972.

7   For an account of the political context of the ordinance see: P. M. Williams & M. Harrison, *Politics and Society in de Gaulle's Republic* (London, 1971) 302–8.

8   For a fuller account of the context of this agreement see chapter 4.

9   The Report of the Royal Commission on Trade Unions and Employers' Associations (HMSO, 1968).

10   H. A. Clegg, *The System of Industrial Relations in Great Britain* (Oxford, 1970) 244.

11   Carter L. Goodrich, *The Frontier of Control: A Study in British Workshop Politics* (London, 1920) 265.

12   I am using the term here to cover both the craft mass meeting and its functional equivalent — the Transport and General Workers' Union branch meeting.

13   A. Flanders, 'Collective Bargaining: Prescription for Change' in *Management and Unions* (London, 1970) 172. For the original study of the Fawley negotiations see: A. Flanders, *The Fawley Productivity Agreements* (London, 1964).

14   T. Cliffe, *The Employers' Offensive* (Pluto Press, 1970) 3.

15   This was also the case in the productivity bargain studied by S. Cotgrove. See S. Cotgrove, J. Dunham & C. Vamplew, *The Nylon Spinners* (London, 1971).

16   This effect seems to have been quite common with productivity bargaining. Flanders found that the stewards' role had been enhanced at Fawley, and the same general tendency is remarked on by several of the contributors to B. Towers, T. G. Whittingham & A. W. Gottschalk, *Bargaining for Change* (London, 1972).

17   Rapport Sudreau, *La Réforme de l'Entreprise* (Paris, 1975) 82.

18   For instance, see: Val R. Lorwin, *The French Labor Movement* (Massachusetts, 1954); F. Harbison & C. Myers, *Management in the*

Industrial World (New York, 1959); G. Caire, *Le Syndicalisme et l'Automation* (Aix-en-Provence, 1960), 169–70; M. Montuclard, *La Dynamique des comités d'entreprise* (C.N.R.S., 1963); M. Combe; *L'Alibi, Vingt ans d'un comité central d'entreprise* (Paris, 1969); J.-D. Reynaud, *Les Syndicats en France* (Paris, 1975).

19   The classic example of a major company is Citroën.

20   See Reynaud, *Les Syndicats en France,* 195/6.

21   Reynaud, *Les Syndicats en France,* 189; G. Caire, *Les Syndicats Ouvriers* (Paris, 1971), 568; G. Adam, J.-D. Reynaud & J.-M. Verdier, *La Négociation Collective en France* (Paris, 1972) 21–4.

22   For the general picture see: H. A. Clegg, *The System of Industrial Relations in Great Britain* (Oxford, 1970) chs. 1 and 7; W. E. J. McCarthy, 'The Role of Shop Stewards in British Industrial Relations' *The Royal Commission on Trade Unions and Employers' Associations Research Papers 1* (HMSO, 1966); and J. F. B. Goodman & T. G. Whittingham, *Shop Stewards in British Industry* (London, 1969).

23   See: W. E. J. McCarthy & S. R. Parker, 'Shop Stewards and Workshop Relations' *Royal Commission Research Paper No. 10, 1968*; and 'Government Social Survey' *Workplace Industrial Relations, 1968.*

24   The Report of the Royal Commission on Trade Unions and Employers' Associations (HMSO, 1968).

25   Clegg, *The System of Industrial Relations in Great Britain,* 301.

26   There are discussions of this problem in Flanders, *The Fawley Productivity Agreements*; B. Towers *et al.*, *Bargaining for Change* (London, 1972); and R. B. McKersie & L. C. Hunter, *Pay, Productivity and Collective Bargaining* (London, 1973).

27   The argument can be found in many different forms in Flanders, *Management and Unions.*

28   McKersie and Hunter, *Pay, Productivity and Collective Bargaining,* 47/8.

8. Participation and the image of management: interpretation

1   The distinction between unitary and pluralist managerial ideologies has been elaborated by A. Fox in *Industrial Sociology and Industrial Relations,* Research Paper 3 'Royal Commission on Trade Unions and Employers' Association) (London, 1966); 'Industrial Relations: a Social Critique of Pluralist Ideology', in J. Child ed., *Man and Organization* (London, 1973); and *Beyond Contract: Work, Trust and Power Relations* (London, 1974) chs. 6 and 7.

2   It must be remembered that in France such unitary conceptions are not necessarily felt to be antithetical to democracy, and indeed have their intellectual roots in both the authoritarian and the democratic traditions. Rousseau's conception of democracy as the spontaneous expression of the collective will, and his denigration of divisive intermediary bodies, has provided an ideological alternative largely absent in Britain.

3   We are concerned here with the ideological conception of relationships, and not with the question of the extent to which relations were authentically pluralistic or oligarchical.

4   For the specific case of continuous-process industry see: C. Vamplew, 'Automated Process Workers: work attitudes and behaviour' *British Journal of Industrial Relations,* 10 (November 1973) for Britain and

C. Barrier, *Le combat ouvrier dans une entreprise de pointe* (Paris, 1975) for France.

5   CFDT-PETROLE (*Syndicat des travailleurs des industries chimiques de la Région Parisienne*) No. 46, Février 1968.

6   For a survey of some of the literature of the problems of organizational change see: A. Touraine, C. Durand, D. Pécaut & A. Willener, *Workers' Attitudes to Technical Change* (OECD, 1965).

7   'Procès-Verbal de la réunion du 16 Décembre 1965 du Comité Central d'Entreprise' 5.

8   Minutes of the Dunkirk Works Committee, 12 Jan. 1967.

9   Minutes of the Dunkirk Works Committee, 17 Oct. 1966.

10 Article 3 of the Law on Company Committees, *Code du Travail*, 1968, 345/6.

11 Minutes of the Dunkirk Works Committee, 12 Jan. 1967.

12 Ibid. 16 June 1967.

13 Ibid. 9 Dec. 1968.

14 Ibid. 26 Oct. 1970.

15 Ibid. 12 Jan. 1967.

16 Memorandum of the Secretary General of Dunkirk: 'Préoccupation Dominante des Organisations Syndicales Ouvrières: Le Problème des Effectifs.' 22 Sep. 1966.

17 Internal Management Memorandum: 'Réflexions sur le mouvement revendicatif de Novembre 1970', 1.

18 Notes of Meetings with the Craft Unions (Kent), 14 Sep. 1961 and 4 Oct. 1961.

19 The day-to-day running of the refinery had been delegated to a Works Manager.

20 Management Memorandum, 'Note on possible terms of new agreement to be negotiated with the craft unions.'

21 'Meeting with the T&GW Union', Wed. 27 Jan. 1965. Management Notes.

22 Ibid.

23 Ibid. 7 July 1966.

24 Ibid. 22 Sep. and 18 Oct. 1966.

25 Ibid. 4 Dec. 1967.

26 Joint Working Party's Report: *Proposals for Increased Productivity on Work Undertaken by T&GW Union Members* (24 April 1969) 2.

27 Even the effect of this type of reward was reduced by management's unwillingness to commit itself to any definite scale of gradings at the moment that change was implemented. (Minutes of the Works Committee 16 June 1967).

28 For some experimental support for this part of the general thesis see, N. C. Morse & E. Reimer, 'The Experimental Change of a Major Organizational Variable' *Journal of Abnormal and Social Psychology*, 1956, 52:120–9.

29 For a discussion of the symbolic significance of institutional systems, see A. Fox, *Beyond Contract: Work, Trust and Power Relations* (London, 1974), ch. 2, esp. p. 93.

30 For some experimental support, see B. H. Raven & J. R. P. French, 'An experimental investigation of legitimate and coercive power' *American Psychologist*, 1957, 12:393.

31 See, for instance, L. Coch & J. R. P. French, 'Overcoming Resistance

to Change' *Human Relations*, 1948, 11:512–32. Flanders also emphasized the importance of procedure for preliminary attitude change. See
A. Flanders, *The Fawley Productivity Agreements* (London, 1964) 140,
203, 248.

32   This, as I understand it, is the principal explanation given by Coch &
French of their experimental results.

33   See W. W. Daniel, *Beyond the Wage-work bargain* (London, 1970),
and S. Cotgrove, J. Dunham & C. Vamplew, *The Nylon Spinners*
(London, 1971), for the implications of productivity bargaining for
longer-term satisfaction with the work environment.

34   For case study evidence, see P. Blau & W. Scott, *Formal Organizations*
(London, 1963), 128–34, on the effects of hierarchical differentiation
on communication.

35   Note that R. K. White & R. Lippitt, *Autocracy and Democracy* (New
York, 1960) 26/7, include short time perspective as one of the
defining characteristics of their 'autocratic' style of leadership. R. B.
McKersie & L. C. Hunter, *Pay, Productivity and Collective Bargaining*
(London, 1973) 322–32 argue that an important effect of productivity
bargaining has been to encourage longer term manpower planning by
management.

9. The control of work performance

1   The account here is based on T. K. Reeves & J. Woodward, 'The Study
of Managerial Control' in J. Woodward, (ed.), *Industrial Organization:
Behaviour and Control* (Oxford, 1970).

2   Ibid. 38/9.

3   Ibid. 39, 46.

4   See P. Blau, & W. Scott, *Formal Organizations* (London, 1963),
176ff. The Reeves and Woodward argument is in many ways simply a
systematization of Blau and Scott's discussion.

5   In Woodward *Industrial Organization: Behaviour and Control*, 203–33.
The essential parts of the argument are reproduced in their later book:
D. Wedderburn & R. Crompton, *Workers' Attitudes and Technology*,
(Cambridge, 1972), chapter 7.

6   Wedderburn and Crompton, 'Technological Constraints and Workers'
Attitudes', 224.

7   Ibid. 225. Curiously enough in the section on *quantity* control the
authors tell us that there was a bonus system that 'was based upon
calculations of inputs of measured work together with allowances for
other factors such as quality of output', 221. Without more information
it is difficult to evaluate this, but at first glance it does make one wonder
whether the system of quality control was not more complex than is
suggested in the section they devote to it.

8   R. Blauner, *Alienation and Freedom* (Chicago, 1964), 148 *see also* 178.

9   This effect of automation on the character of lower management
emerges sharply from Chadwick-Jones' study of the transformation of
a tinning plant in the steel industry from batch production to continuous-process production. He underlines the change that occurred
between a system in which supervisors were recruited from the more
senior members of the work force, to one in which they were chosen
from outsiders on the basis of their formal technical qualifications.

See: J. Chadwick-Jones, *Automation and Behaviour* (London, 1969) especially chapter 12.
10   See Blauner, *Alienation*, 149.
11   Our Dunkirk data were insufficiently differentiated to enable us to reconstruct the post structure at the level of the individual unit.
12   *Guidance Manual to Refinery Managements*: Ch. 4 'Les Sanctions', 46.
13   *Extrait Compte-Rendu Direction – Comité de Grève du Samedi 1 er Juin 1968.*
14   See Blauner, *Alienation*, 147/8. Although focusing on a different technology the argument is perhaps most coherently developed by Blau and Scott in *Formal Organizations*, 176ff.
15   Wedderburn and Crompton say of their craftsmen: 'The control systems affecting the tradesmen were thus largely experienced as "personal controls" ' *Workers' Attitudes and Technology*, 131/2.

Part four. The unions

10. The theory and strategy of the trade unions

1   CGT, *Les Classes Sociales et l'Exploitation Capitaliste*, 'Brochures Educatives du Centre Confédéral d'Education Ouvrière, Série A (Cours de Base)'. This is a small summary booklet of 'basic ideas' handed to me by the secretary of the CGT union section at Lavera as representing the type of elementary material presented to militants.
2   CGT, *Les Classes Sociales et l'Exploitation Capitaliste*. The very practical intentions behind this analysis are made clear in the booklet's introduction: 'This course gives . . . ideas that are indispensable for union militants and which they will be able to make use of in their actions in the service of the workers.'
3   The preparatory years for this change are well analysed in G. Adam, *La CFTC 1940-1958, histoire politique et idéologique* (Paris, 1964). The account of one of the major participants can be found in E. Maire & J. Julliard, *La CFDT d'aujourd'hui* (Paris, 1975). See also G. Lefranc, *Le Mouvement Syndical de la Libération aux Evénements de Mai-Juin 1968* (Paris, 1969).
4   See the *Document d'orientation adoptée à l'issue de la discussion du rapport 'Perspective et Stratégie' présenté par André Jeanson, président de la CFDT, au 35ème Congrès Confédéral (6–10 mai 1970).*
5   The formal equivalent of this for the CGT is Article 1 of the *Statuts*: 'S'inspirant dans son orientation et son action des principes du syndicalisme démocratique de masse et de classe qui dominent l'histoire du mouvement syndical français, la CGT s'assigne pour but la suppression de l'exploitation capitaliste, notamment par la socialisation des moyens de production et d'échange.'
6   The Transport and General Workers' Union, *Shop Stewards' Handbook* (1974), 4.
7   We shall be arguing later in the chapter that this somewhat tautological formulation is no mere accident. .
8   See E. Maire & J. Julliard, *La CFDT d'aujourd'hui*, 74.
9   The figures refer to the elections of 1971 – the nearest to the time of our study.
10   It is perhaps worth noting the difference in terminology. The French union representatives invariably refer to themselves as 'militants'. When,

returning to England from one of the French refineries, I inadvertently started talking about 'militants' to a shop steward who was regarded by management as somewhat 'radical', he stopped me in mid-phrase. He pointed out that they were stewards and not militants, and emphasized that the difference was an important one.

11   CGT, *Les Classes Sociales et l'Exploitation Capitaliste*, 13.

12   CGT, *Bulletin de l'U.L.*, après le Congrès des *14 et 15 décembre 1973* — 'Destiné aux Militants de tous les Syndicats et Sections Syndicales de l'Union Locale des Syndicats de Dunkerque et Environs'.

13   CFDT, *Document d'Orientation*, clauses 10–12.

14   T&GWU, *Shop Stewards Handbook*, 11

15   CFDT, *Document d'Orientation*, clause 50, section entitled 'La Stratégie'.

16   The time periods simply reflect the fact that these were the periods for which the documents were available at the time of our analysis.

17   CGT, *Les Classes Sociales et l'Exploitation Capitaliste*, 16.

18   CFDT, *Document d'Orientation*, clauses 59 and 60.

19   CGT, *Stage Moyen (Fédéral): L'Action et la Tactique des Luttes.*

20   Maire & Julliard, *La CFDT d'aujourd'hui*, 97.

21   T&GWU, *Shop Stewards Handbook*, 11.

22   Ibid. 5; see also 77.

23   See for instance the definition in the book co-authored by the Secretary General of the CFDT — Maire & Julliard, *La CFDT d'aujourd'hui*: 'Written statements of concessions that have been won, the agreement is never considered by the union as a signature of peace, but at the very most as an armistice which is always open to being revoked.' 104.

24   Subsequently to our research, an increase in refinery initiated action at Lavera in 1974/75 has apparently brought it much more closely into line with the pattern for Dunkirk.

25   CGT, *Formation Syndicale Générale de Base (2ème degré)*, section 14.

26   Maire & Julliard, *La CFDT d'aujourd'hui*, 52.

27   Marc Maurice, 'L'évolution de la CFTC', *Sociologie du Travail*, Vol. VII (1965), 83–93.

28   This contrasts with the situation in the early 1960s when it was the CFTC/CFDT that appeared to exercise the closest control over the actions undertaken by its militants; see: J. D. Reynaud, P. Bernoux & L. Lavorel, 'Organisation syndicale, idéologie, et politique des salaires', *Sociologie du Travail*, VIII, 368–88.

29   *The Scotsman*, 30 May 1974.

30   This Table does not, of course, indicate which echelon of the union *organized* these strikes (compare Table 38). The Confederations could orchestrate strikes based on Federal programmes.

Similarly, the formulation of Federal demands were usually only a specification of more abstractly formulated demands that could be found in the Confederal programme. When we indicate a Confederal demand it means, then, that a fresh issue has been thrust to the forefront which is not a standard part of the Federal programme.

31   C. Durand, *Conscience ouvrière et l'Action syndicale* (Paris, 1971).

32   J. P. Bachy, F. Dupuy & D. Martin, *Représentation et Négociation dans l'Entreprise* (Paris, 1974) Part 2.

33   Ibid. 170–4, 224, 327.

34   Ibid. 189/190, 357. We must remember that we have no indication of the representativity of their sample.

35   CGT Federation Memorandum: 'Développer l'Action pour les Salaires'
      avril 1972.
36   J. D. Reynaud, S. Dassa, J. Dassa & P. Maclous, *Mai-Juin et le système
      français de relations professionnelles* (Paris, 1970 Ronéo), Ch. 'Les
      Droits Syndicaux', 8:48.
37   Quoted in J. D. Reynaud *et al.*, *Mai-Juin et le système français de
      relations professionnelles*, 50.
38   Bachy *et al.*, *Representation et Negociation dans l'Entreprise*, 89-96.
39   I am grateful to Alfred Willener for first pointing out to me how pre-
      valent this practice is in the French union literature.
40   One difference between the CGT and the CFDT is that the CFDT has so
      far refused to officially endorse the Common Programme of the Com-
      munist and Socialist Parties. Its principal concern appears to be to
      keep its freedom of manoeuvre in the event of a left-wing government
      and to retain its own autonomous power of political intervention
      rather than delegating it to the parties.

11. Union strength and coercive power

1   R. Blauner, *Alienation and Freedom* (Chicago, 1964) 162.
2   Ibid. 181.
3   S. Mallet, *La Nouvelle Classe Ouvrière* (Paris, 1969), 93.
4   Ibid. 90.
5   G. Adam, F. Bon, J. Capdevielle & R. Mauriaux, *L'Ouvrier français en
      1970* (Paris, 1970) 135. Although the operators and maintenance
      workers were by far the largest groups of workers they were also pre-
      sumably easier to unionize than workers dispersed in the offices and
      laboratories, or involved in security or internal transport duties. The
      figures here are, then, probably somewhat higher than they would be
      for *all* workers in the refinery, although the overall membership level
      would remain very high by French standards. Also, it should be remem-
      bered that only about 70% of French union members get around to
      actually paying their union dues, so claimed membership may overstate
      real membership. (See *Le Monde*, 25 May 1976).
6   Adam *et al.*, *L'ouvrier français en 1970*, 135. Survey conducted in
      1969.
7   G. Adam, 'La représentativité des organisations syndicales', *Revue
      française de science politique*, avril 1968, 278.
8   Figures taken from *Syndicalisme*, 11 Nov. 1976. We should note that
      the figures exclude the mines, railways, and public administration.
9   Letter to the author.
10   Further evidence from automobile factories in the USA, Italy, Argen-
      tina, and India suggests the possibility that this may be a norm with a
      very high level of cross-cultural generality. See, W. H. Form, *Blue-Collar
      Stratification* (Princeton, 1976), 160-3.
11   Non-response rates were 0 Kent and Grangemouth; 0.5% Lavera; 6.6%
      Dunkirk.
12   CGT, *Stage Moyen (Fédéral)*: 'L'Action et la Tactique des Luttes'.
13   E. Maire & J. Julliard, *La CFDT d'aujourd'hui* (Paris, 1975), 799.
14   After reading this, the CFDT Secretary at Lavera made the following
      comment:
          It depends on whether one is talking about individual or collective

democracy. Moreover democracy is dependent on the socio-political system in which it is practised. In a self governing system — which supposes a prior change in mentality — that is to say in the educational system and in the relationship of one individual and another — democracy will appear in a very different form from the way it is at present. In the system in which we are living, democracy works through individualism and tries to bring about a convergence between group interests of individuals. In a self-governing system individual interests should fuse with the collective interests.

15 The CFDT was *in principle* favourable to longer strikes, but given its minority position, this had little weight in face of the CGT's firm adherence to the 'symbolic' strike. The CGT's caution in the use of the strike may also have been reinforced by its political strategy. Longer strikes might risk alienating useful non-worker sectors of the electorate, and enable the Government to resurrect the 'red' scare. Certainly the CGT federation 'advised' the Lavera refinery to keep its strikes short.

16 See E. Shorter and C. Tilly, *Strikes in France 1830–1968* (London, 1974).

17 *The Scotsman*, 6 June 1974.

Part five. Conclusion

12. *Managerial strategies, the unions and the social integration of the work force*

1 See, for instance: S. M. Lipset, 'The Changing Class Structure and Contemporary European Politics', *Daedalus*, 1964, 93:1; F. Harbison & C. A. Myers, *Management in the Industrial World* (New York, 1959) and C. Kerr, J. T. Dunlop, F. Harbison & C. A. Myers, *Industrialism and Industrial Man* (2nd ed., London, 1973).

2 W. G. Runciman, *Relative Deprivation and Social Justice* (London, 1966) especially chapter 10.

3 Personal initials have been altered for the sake of anonymity in this and the following quotation.

4 Personal initials have been altered for the sake of anonymity.

Appendix 1. Claude Durand, 'Conscience Ouvrière et l'Action Syndicale'

1 C. Durand, *Conscience Ouvrière et l'Action Syndicale* (Paris, 1971).
2 Ibid. 4.
3 Ibid. 13.
4 Ibid. 37–8.
5 Ibid. 9.
6 Ibid. 48–51. The sample was selected on the basis of several other variables as well.
7 Ibid. 109–11
8 Ibid. 100.
9 Ibid. 92.
10 I leave aside the six open questions that were also used in the construction of the final index as we have little information on their coding. Given the high failure rate on the structured items one can only assume the coding was a difficult procedure.
11 Durand, *Conscience Ouvrière et l'Action Syndicale*, 38.

12   It is also disappointing to see that Durand was unable to find coherent
      replies for C2 and C3 on his open question about the degree of danger
      in increasing the powers of the Comité d'entreprise — the only one of
      his open questions directly related to control within the enterprise.
      See p. 000.
13   Durand, *Conscience Ouvrière et l'Action Syndicale*, 238; for a more
      detailed table see Durand's article, 'La signification professionnelle et
      économique de l'action syndicale' in *Sociologie du Travail*, 1968, 121.
14   Durand, *Conscience Ouvrière et l'Action Syndicale*, 50.

Bibliography

Adam, G., *La CFTC 1940–1958, Histoire politique et idéologique* (Paris, 1964)
  'La représentativité des organisations syndicales, *Revue francaise de science politique, avril 1968,* 278
Adam, G., Bon, F., Capdevielle, J. & Mouriaux, R., *L'ouvrier français en 1970* (Paris, 1970)
Adam, G., Reynaud, J.-D. & Verdier, J.-M., *La Négociation Collective en France* (Paris, 1972)
Andrieux, A. & Lignon, J., *L'ouvrier d'aujourd'hui* (Paris, 1960)
Bachy, J. P., Dupuy, F. & Martin, D., *Représentation et Négociation dans l'entreprise* (Paris, 1974)
Barrier, C., *Le combat ouvrier dans une entreprise de pointe* (Paris, 1975)
Blau, P. M., *The Dynamics of Bureaucracy* (Chicago, 1955)
Blau, P. M. & Scott, W. R., *Formal Organizations* (London, 1963)
Blauner, R., *Alienation and Freedom* (Chicago, 1964)
Blumberg, P., *Industrial Democracy: the Sociology and Participation* (London, 1968)
Bouvier-Ajam, M. & Mury, G., *Les Classes sociales en France* (Paris, 1964)
Caire, G., *Le syndicalisme et l'automation* (Aix-en-Provence, 1960)
  Les syndicats ouvriers (Paris, 1971)
Chadwick-Jones, J., *Automation and Behaviour* (London, 1969)
Chinoy, E., *Automobile Workers and the American Dream* (New York, 1955)
Clegg, H. A., *The system of industrial relations in Great Britain* (Oxford, 1970)
Cliffe, T., *The Employers' Offensive* (Pluto Press, 1970)
Coch, L. & French, J. R. P., 'Overcoming Resistance to Change', *Human Relations,* 1948, 11:512
Collinet, M., *L'Esprit du syndicalisme* (Paris, 1952)
Combe, M., *L'alibi, Vingt ans d'un Comité central d'entreprise* (Paris, 1969)
Cotgrove, S., Dunham, J. & Vamplew, C., *The Nylon Spinners* (London, 1971)
Crozier, M., 'Sociologie du Syndicalisme' in G. Friedmann & P. Naville (eds.) *Traité de Sociologie du Travail* (Paris, 1962)
Daniel, W. W., *Beyond the Wage-work Bargain* (London, 1970)
Durand, C., 'La signification professionnelle et économique de l'action syndicale', *Sociologie du travail,* 1968, X:113
  'Ouvriers et techniciens en mai 1968' in Dubois, P., Dulong, R., Durand, C., Erbes-Sequin, S. & Videl, D., *Grèves revendicatives ou grèves politiques?* (Paris, 1971)
  Conscience Ouvrière et l'Action Syndicale (Paris, 1971)
Flanders, A., *The Fawley Productivity Agreements* (London, 1964)
  Management and Unions (London, 1970)
Form, W. H., *Blue-Collar Stratification* (Princeton, 1976)
Fox, A., Industrial Sociology and Industrial Relations, *The Royal Commission*

on *Trade Unions and Employers Associations Research Paper 3* (London, 1966)

'Industrial Relations: "A social critique of Pluralist Ideology"', in Child, J., (ed.), *Man and Organization* (London 1973)

Man Mismanagement (London, 1974)

Beyond Contract: Work, Trust and Power Relations (London, 1974)

French, J. R. P., Israel, J. & As, D., 'An Experiment on Participation in a Norwegian Factory', *Human Relations*, 1960, 13:3

Friedmann, G., *Problèmes humains du machinisme industriel* (Paris, 1947)

Furstenberg, F., 'Structural Changes in the Working Class', in Jackson, J. A. (ed.), *Social Stratification* (Cambridge, 1968)

Galenson, W., *Comparative Labor Movements* (New York, 1952)

Goldthorpe, J. H., 'Social Stratification in Industrial Society', *Sociological Review Monograph* No. 8 (Keele, 1964)

Goldthorpe, J. H., Lockwood, D., Bechhofer, F. & Platt, J., *The Affluent Worker: Industrial Attitudes and Behaviour* (Cambridge, 1968)

The Affluent Worker: Political Attitudes and Behaviur (Cambridge, 1968)

The Affluent Worker in the Class Structure (Cambridge, 1969)

Goodman, J. F. B. & Whittingham, T. G., *Shop Stewards in British Industry* (London, 1969)

Goodrich, C. L., *The Frontier of Control: A Study in British Workshop Politics* (London, 1968)

Granick, D., *The European Executive* (London, 1962)

Hamilton, R., *Affluence and the French Worker in the Fourth Republic* (Princeton, 1967)

Harbison, F. & Myers, C., *Management in the Industrial World* (New York, 1959)

Kendall, W., *The Labour Movement in Europe* (London, 1975)

Kerr, C., Dunlop, J. T., Harbison, F. & Myers, C. A., *Industrialism and Industrial Man* (2nd ed., London, 1973)

Lefranc, G., *Le Mouvement syndical de la Libération aux événéments de mai-juin 1968* (Paris, 1969)

Lipset, S. M., 'The Changing Class Structure and Contemporary European Politics' *Daedalus*, 1964, 93:1

Lorwin, Val R., *The French Labor Movement* (Massachusetts, 1954)

Lydall, H., *The Structure of Earnings* (Oxford, 1968)

Maire, E. & Julliard, J., *La CFDT d'aujourd'hui* (Paris, 1975)

Mallet, S., *La Nouvelle Classe Ouvrière* (Paris, 1969)

Le pouvoir ouvrier (Paris, 1971)

Mann, F. C. & Hoffman, L. R., *Automation and the Worker* (New York, 1960)

Maurice, M., 'L'evolution de la CFTC', *Sociologie du Travail*, 1965, VII:83

Mayo, E., *The Social Problems of an Industrial Civilization* (London, 1949)

McCarthy, W. E. J., 'The Role of Shop Stewards in British Industrial Relations', *The Royal Commission on Trade Unions and Employers' Associations Research Papers 1* (HMSO, 1966)

McCarthy, W. E. J. & Parker, S. R., 'Shop Stewards and Workshop Relations', *The Royal Commission on Trade Unions and Employers Associations Research Papers 10* (HMSO, 1968)

McKersie, R. B. & Hunter, L. C., *Pay, Productivity and Collective Bargaining* (London, 1973)

Montuclard, M., *La Dynamique des Comités d'entreprise* (Paris, 1963)

Morse, N. C. & Reimer, E. 'The Experimental Change of a Major Organizational Variable', *Journal of Abnormal and Social Psychology*, 1956, 52:120

Mott, P. E., Mann, F. C., McLoughlin, Q. & Warwick, D. P., *Shift Work* (Michigan, 1965)

Naville, P., 'Lois Sociologiques et action de masse', *Les cahiers du centre d'études socialistes*, no. 13–14, jan. 1962
   'Planification et gestion démocratique', *Les cahiers du centre d'études socialistes*, no. 23–4, 1963
   'Marxisme et Sociologies, *Les cahiers d'études socialistes*, no. 34–5, 1963
   Vers l'automatisme social? (Paris, 1963)
   La classe ouvrière et le régime gaulliste (Paris, 1964)
   Temps et travail (Geneve, 1972)
Naville, P. avec la collaboration de: Barrier, C., Grossin, W., Lahalle, D., Legotien, H., Moisy, B., Palierene, J. & Wackerman, G., *L'automation et le travail humain* (Paris, 1961)
Raven, B. H. & French, J. R. P., 'An Experimental Investigation of Legitimate and Coercive Power', *American Psychologist*, 1957, 12:393
Reeves, T. K. & Woodward, J., 'The Study of Managerial Control', in Woodward, J. (ed.), *Industrial Organization: Behaviour and Control* (Oxford, 1970)
Reynaud, J.-D., *Les Syndicats en France* (Paris, 1975)
Reynaud, J.-D., Bernaux, P. & Lavorel, L., 'Organisation syndicale, idéologie et politique des salaires', *Sociologie du travail*, 1966, VIII:368
Reynaud, J.-D., Dassa, S., Dassa, J. & Maclouf, P., *Mai-juin et le système francais de relations professionnelles* (Paris, 1970, Roneo)
Royal Commission on Trade Unions and Employers' Associations, *Report* (HMSO, 1968)
Runciman, W. G., *Relative Deprivation and Social Justice* (London, 1966)
Shorter, E. & Tilly, C., *Strikes in France 1830–1968* (London, 1974)
Sudreau, Pierre, *La Réforme de l'Entreprise*, 'Rapport du comité présidé par Pierre Sudreau' (Paris, 1975)
Tannenbaum, A. (ed.), *Control in Organizations* (New York, 1968)
Tannenbaum, A., Kavcic, B., Rosner, M., Vianello, M. & Wieser, G., *Hierarchy in Organizations* (San Francisco and London, 1974)
Taylor, P. J., 'Shift Work and Day Work: A Comparison of Sickness Absence, Lateness and other Absence at an Oil Refinery from 1962 to 1962', *British Journal of Industrial Medicine*, 1967, 24:93
Touraine, A., *L'évolution du travail ouvrier aux usines Renault* (Paris, 1955)
   La conscience ouvrière (Paris, 1966)
Touraine, A., Durand, C., Pécaut, D. & Willener, A., *Workers' Attitudes to Technical change* (OECD, 1965)
Towers, B., Whittingham, T. G. & Gottschalk, A. W., *Bargaining for Change* (London, 1972)
Vamplew, C., 'Automated Process Operators: Work Attitudes and Behaviour', *British Journal of Industrial Relations* 10 (November 1973)
Walker, C. R. & Guest, R., *Man on the Assembly Line* (Cambridge, Mass., 1952)
Wedderburn, D. & Crompton, R., *Workers' Attitudes and Technology* (Cambridge, 1972)
   'Technological Constraints and Workers' Attitudes' in Woodward, J. (ed.), *Industrial Organization: Behaviour and Control* (Oxford, 1970)
White, R. K. & Lippitt, R., *Autocracy and Democracy* (New York, 1960)
Willard, C., *Le Mouvement socialiste en France 1893–1905* (Paris, 1965)
Williams, P. M. & Harrison, M., *Politics and Society in de Gaulle's Republic* (London, 1971)
Woodward, J., *Management and Technology* (London, 1958)
   Industrial Organization: Theory and Practice (London, 1965)
   (ed.), *Industrial Organization: Behaviour and Control* (Oxford, 1970)
Wyatt, S. & Marriot, R., 'Night Work and Shift Changes', *British Journal of Industrial Medicine*, 1953, 10:164–72

Index

Adam, G., 147, 274, 333 n.3, 334 n.21, 337 n.3, 339 nn.5–7
Affluent Worker Studies, 4, 35
Alienation, 8, 19, 23–4, 56, 85–7, 248, 249
Anarcho-syndicalism, 17
Andrieux, A., 327 n.4
Authority relations, experience of, 107, 115–18, 221–2, 228–35, 298, 308–9

Bachy, J. P., 270, 271, 338 n.32, 339 n. 38
Barrier, C., 331 n.10, 334 n.4
Bernoux, P., 338 n.25
Blau, P., 15, 328 n.32, 336 nn.34, 4, 337 n.14
Blauner, R.
  overview, 9–13, 55, 295–9
  methodology, 26–7, 329 n.66
  on grading, 11, 216–20
  on meaningfulness of work, 9, 70, 79–81
  on salaries, 12, 51–7, 61–3
  on social integration, 10–13
  on trade unions, 12, 13, 33, 274
  on the work task, 9, 77, 79, 81, 82–4, 100
  on work teams, 11, 220–4
Blumberg, P., 330 n.81
Bon, F., 333 n.3, 339 n.5
Bouvier-Ajam, M., 328 n.34

Caire, G., 332 n.26, 334 n.18
Capdeville, J., 333 n.3, 339 n.5
Careers, 11, 99, 115–16, 217–20, 336 n.9
Chadwick Jones, J., 331 n.6, 336 n.9
Child, J., 334 n.1
Chinoy, E., 327 n.3
Clegg, H. A., 333 n.10, 334 nn.22, 25
Cliffe, T., 171–2, 333 n.14
Closed shop 172, 254, 274, 280
Coch, L., 335 n.31, 336 n.32
Collinet, M., 327 n.4
Combe, M., 334 n.18
Comité central d'entreprise, 161–2
Comité d'établissement, see Works Committees
Commissions paritaires, see Parity Commissions

Community setting, 40–1, 44–5, 90
Confédération française démocratique du travail (CFDT)
  conception of unionism, 240–1, 337 n.23, 339 n.14
  evolution of, 240, 261–2
  salary demands, 267–8, 160
  strategy, 247–52
  strength, 274, 277–8
Confédération française des travailleurs chrétiens (CFTC), 157
Confédération générale du travail (CGT), conception of unionism, 249–41
  salary demands, 267–8, 160
  strategy, 247–52
  strength, 274, 276–8
Confédération générale du travail-Force ouvrière (CGT-FO), 157, 160, 279, 289
Contractors, 84
Control, aspirations for, 19, 114–15, 120ff., 298
Convention collective national, 157
Convergence theory, 31, 301–2
Cotgrove, S., 333 n.15, 336 n.33
Crompton, R., 27, 215–16, 329 n.67, 336 nn.5–7, 337 n.15
Crozier, M., 327 n.4

Daniel, W. W., 331 n.8, 336 n.33
Dassa, J., 339 n.36
Dassa, S., 339 n.36
Decision-making procedures, perception of
  for company financial budgeting, 128–31
  for investment decisions, 128–31
  for manning levels, 124–6, 191–204
  for salaries, 126–8, 158–61, 185–91
  for work time schedules, 123–4
Délégués du personnel, 152–3
Discipline, 82, 224–9
Documentation, 50–2
Dubois, P., 329 n.69
Dunham, J., 333 n.15, 336 n.33
Dunlop, J. T., 330 n.78, 340 n.1
Dupuy, F., 338 n.32
Durand, C., 28–9, 270, 319–22, 335 n.6

345